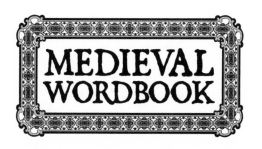

MEDIEVAL WORDBOOK

MEDIEVAL WORDBOOK

More than 4,000 Terms and Expressions from Medieval Culture

BY MADELEINE PELNER COSMAN

FALL RIVER PRESS

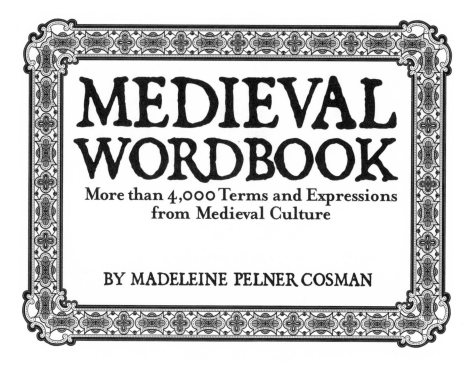

This 2007 edition published by Fall River Press,
by arrangement with Facts on File, Inc.

Fall River Press
122 Fifth Avenue
New York, NY 10011

ISBN-13: 978-0-7607-8725-0
ISBN-10: 0-7607-8725-5

Printed and bound in the United States of America

3 5 7 9 10 8 6 4 2

CONTENTS

ACKNOWLEDGMENTS

I celebrate intellectual debts to medieval and Renaissance scholars worldwide and especially to my lawyer and professorial colleagues, my medical students, and personal friends who contributed to this dictionary.

Medical law is a correlative profession requiring nimble boundary-crossings. At the turn of the millennium while working on the paperback version of this book and another volume for Facts On File, *Women at Work in Medieval Europe*, I suddenly was obligated to devote time and spirit to the Cather Court Project at the medical center of the University of California at San Diego. Therefore I acknowledge the professional talents and personal benevolence of my colleagues in that adventure: Michael Bouvet, Bard Clifford Cosman, Pamela Caren Cosman, Marin Cosman, Vicky Jones, D. Blickenstaff, Carla Nugent, Mary and Dennis Nugent, Maureen Harris, Paul and Kathleen Bremner, Katherine Nguyen and Young Yang, Betty and Donald Meader, Cecilia Gutierrez, Caroline and Bill McCullagh, George Fee and Susan Dersnah Fee, Du Luu, Bingh Luu, Hilary Spero, Phil and Pam Reed, Maureen and Bob Parsons, David Perez, Bernard Baruch, and Luz Aurora Mariscal. With Jinendra Jain, Linda Zraik, Jim Martinez, Richard Cieri, Christine Jobin, and Steve Rubino, I share a presumption of excellence. Ann Wille, colleagues in Rotary International, and a contingent of San Diego friends civilized the success of the Cather Court Project: Marie-Jo Dulade-Coclet, Roz Chasen, Carl Sedlak, Hylton Murphy, Catherine Edingfield-Murphy, Keith Richter, Susan and Ellsworth Joe Burwell, Emmet Jones, David McCollom, Ann Peay, Erwin Willis, and Dennis Neville.

At the City University of New York I enjoyed intellectual gifts of my medical students, Lipkin Fellows Ami Shah and Karen Kuo, my faculty and students of the medical law program, and the Institute for Medieval and Renaissance Studies, which for 28 years I directed. Scholar, editor, attorney, and linguist Daniel Furman in Jerusalem and New York made valuable contributions, as have my office associates at Medical Equity, Inc, especially Gladys Seitel, Bobbie Riback, and June Anne Greeley.

At the Benjamin M. Cardozo School of Law, I am particularly grateful to Frank Macchiarola, Joel Dobris, John Stephen Beckerman, Laura Cunningham, Elbert Gates, S. Robert Allcorn, Melanie Meyers, and Arthur Jacobson.

Among friends and colleagues with whom I built the Medieval Festival at Fort Tryon Park, I especially acknowledge Bob Isaac, Sidy Rosenfeld, Carole Weinstein, and Assemblyman Stanley Michaels. At the Cloisters of the Metropolitan Museum of Art I am grateful to Timothy Husband, Jane Heyward, and, when he was Director of the Lehman Collection at the Met, Dr. George Szabo.

We benefited from checking our definitions against those in the unabridged *Oxford English Dictionary; The Oxford Dictionary of the Christian Church* (2nd edition, edited by F. L. Cross and E. A. Livingstone, Oxford University Press, 1977); *Dictionary of the Decorative Arts* (John Fleming and Hugh Honour, Harper and Row, 1977); *Hobson-Jobson A Glossary of Colloquial Anglo-Indian Words and Phrases* (Henry Yule and A. C. Burnell, edited by William Crooke, Humanities Press, 1968); and *Black's Law Dictionary* (6th edition, West Publishing, 1990).

Susan Urstadt, Ltd. introduced me to the wonderful staff at Facts On File. Caroline Sutton welcomed this book. Randy Ladenheim-Gil saw it to press, assisted by Owen Eliot. Anne Savarese and Regina Sampogna guided the paperback though production.

This book is dedicated to all who appreciate the magnificence of medieval culture through their delight in its words.

WELCOME TO *MEDIEVAL WORDBOOK*

The glories of the Middle Ages are not for scholars alone. None of us today can visit a museum, travel in Europe, read a daily newspaper, get married or divorced, politely drink white wine, or sign a contract for buying a house without encountering three or four concepts directly traceable to medieval culture. Graduation caps and gowns, real estate contracts, marriage ceremonies, and table manners preserve medieval customs faithfully. *Medieval Wordbook* therefore is an adventure for those who love words, their origins, and the long histories of ceremonies of daily life.

Medieval Wordbook is a word treasury for people passionate about the Middle Ages: its art and architecture, science and medicine, literature and law, liturgy and ceremony, sex, costumes, cookery, magic, religion, astrology, warfare, jousting, and celebration. The book's more than 4,000 entries include basic ideas of feudalism, chivalry, courtesy, Christian saints and symbols, architecture, heraldry, and arms and armor. Equally important but less expected words derive from the whimsical, vigorous, intriguing vocabularies of alchemy, Judaism, sensuality, working women, birth's entrances, and death's exits.

This comprehensive collection of words and definitions resembles the encyclopedic medieval dictionaries, which did not adhere to the strict disciplinary boundaries that modern lexicography demands. Modern mathematical dictionaries would include a definition of the Fibonacci Series, as *Medieval Wordbook* does, but certainly would not include explanations of chemistry's alembics and athenors or art history's gadroons and entablatures, because these would be considered irrelevant to mathematics. *Medieval Wordbook* includes all of these subjects—first because the medieval educational ideal celebrated deep knowledge of many interrelated subjects, requiring a student to be expert in several specialties, and second because to justly appreciate the vestiges of medieval culture in painting, sculpture, architecture, and literature we must recognize inexorable interrelationships among medieval disciplines. In my three decades of professional work with medieval words and my concurrent half century of delight in them I have found it necessary to move swiftly and skillfully from the words and concepts of law to those of medicine, from art to mathematics, philosophy to farming, poetry to property. Fortunately, like others who have been tested by war, I had professional and personal experiences demanding linguistic facility and multiple vocabularies. Adversities and opportunities have forced me to write dictionaries of one sort or another since childhood.

As a Jewish child growing up during the Second World War, I was keenly aware of the power of word. A word carelessly spoken could not only reveal a hidden person but could cause that person to be apprehended, imprisoned, and condemned to death. Common words mispronounced, shibboleths, or a foreign accent might immediately pierce the disguise of a traitor or a savior. The word identifies the thing. If you can name it, you can see it clearly. If you can name it, you can control it. What the prepared eye looks for, it finds. Moreover, meticulous precision, accuracy, and decorum can be good anodyne for pain. As a child I became fluent in multiple languages, and by the time I completed my doctorate at Columbia University in 1964 I worked with confidence in French, Old French, German, Middle High German, Italian, Latin, Hebrew, Anglo-Saxon, Icelandic, and several Middle English dialects.

Languages were benevolently united with music during my college years at Barnard in New York. After working in biochemistry laboratories by day I took the subway at night to Carnegie Hall where I exchanged my lab coat, faintly fragrant with formaldehyde, for my costume to sing mezzo-soprano roles with an opera company optimistically named for the next year: Opera '56, Opera '57, and Opera '58. Translating emotion accurately through words—not simply through melody and gesture—was important to my performance training.

Medical law is my field. This specialty and my practice have required my creating glossaries for academic-political purposes. As an attorney and professional medievalist, I have worked for nearly 30 years at the conjunction of medicine and law, teaching medical students, college undergraduates, graduate students, surgery residents, fellows, physicians, and lawyers. Now Professor Emerita, I have been Full Professor at City College of City University of New York teaching most of the medical law courses for City University of New York medical students, and Director from 1969–1993 of the Institute for Medieval and Renaissance Studies, whose 15 departments, 153 undergraduate courses, and 101 graduate courses united a diverse faculty of historians, linguists, physicians, attorneys, engineers, chemists, architects, and one astrophysicist. Peace and productivity among practitioners whose disciplines have exclusive jargon required dictionaries. If in a forensic pathology study the dramatic law court document expressed in technical language of specialists a jealous husband's murder of his wife and lover, "a bachelor who before grabbing his hauberk angrily tossed wine from the dinanderie hanap upon the lozengier's pourpoint and poulaines," the collaborating scholars as well as the intelligent audience merit translation. *Medieval Wordbook* translates such scholarly words to welcome those intrigued by the subjects but excluded by the language.

There is no end to the fascination of medieval words. The scope and size of *Medieval Wordbook* are unusual in at least six ways. First, its intellectual boundaries are greedy. I do not know a truly satisfactory definition of "Middle Ages." The worldview customarily called "medieval" dates from approximately the year 500 to approximately the year 1500. Nevertheless, in certain countries and in certain subjects, things medieval began early and ended late. Therefore in *Medieval Wordbook* I include words which might truly derive from an earlier or later century if the medieval idea they represent is best expressed by them. Anyone working deeply in the field knows that there was a demonstrable, authentic "Renaissance" in the twelfth century. But I am unwilling to relinquish the glories of Chaucer and Gothic architecture solely to Renaissance scholars. Furthermore, in music, dance, costumery, medicine, surgery, and law certain quintessentially medieval concepts are best known to the world by their later titles. Therefore, I hope Renaissance scholars will not be offended if I claim a particular galliard dance step or real property law as medieval. I can provide the appropriate "early" documentary evidence. Out of my respect for you, the reader, who might welcome a word's presence, and out of certitude that were I the reader and not the writer I would cherish the definition, I have included it.

Second, since some words in definitions will be friendly and familiar, yet others unknown, rather than asking you to compare and seek out cross-references, I have integrated them into the definition marked by small capital letters. For example, if you already know the subject is BOETHIAN, you will be pleased for the reminder in the definition; if you want to know the meaning, you have the option to look it up.

Third, some entries are short phrases while others are longer and somewhat encyclopedic. People confronting a sumptuous portrait of the Angelic Doctor will be glad for the reminder of the importance of that man who was neither angel nor physician. Likewise, people trained to assume that women were "liberated" in the twentieth century will be pleasantly startled to encounter words associated with women in the professions such as the matronymics baxter and webster, and therefore will appreciate a brief entry on women physicians and surgeons and women writers and poets.

Fourth, this book could have been titled "Medieval Wordbook of the Western European World," excessively long but accurate, because its scope is Western Europe. I know that between the years 500 and 1500 vigorous cultures thrived in China, Japan, India, Russia, Africa, America, Australia, and elsewhere. Except for those words pertaining to commercial trade routes and intercultural exchanges with Western Europe, however, I restricted this book's words to countries whose languages I know.

Fifth, *Medieval Wordbook* is not an etymological dictionary. However, I have provided origins of words when I thought them particularly interesting and I have translated commonly appearing Latin phrases and inscriptions where I thought them helpful. Where a word's linguistic roots are disputed, I have not provided indicators of controversy. If the medieval word was derived from Latin, even if comparative linguists argue that the word is a Latin corruption of a Persian original translated from a Syriac version of an Arabic antecedent, I state as conclusory: "from Latin *paternoster*, meaning 'our father'."

Sixth, this reference book necessarily is selective. I am well enough trained in law, science, and life to know that nothing ever is done as well as it might if there had been more time, more hands, and more minds for the task. If you would prefer more entries on certain subjects and greater emphases upon others, certainly suggest them to me and to the editors. Meanwhile, here is a conveniently portable single volume providing enough at hand for pleasurable, knowledgeable, reassuring, and exhilarating glimpses into the main ideas of one thousand years in the West.

Medieval Wordbook is meant to be your friendly medieval companion while you are visiting museums, trekking through castles in Europe, congenially arguing over words at dinner, reading in academic halls or libraries, and playing College Bowl, Scrabble, or breezing through crossword puzzles. For lovers of the medieval world, here are 4,000 *squints* into its magnificence.

A

abada

The rhinoceros, sometimes thought to be the female UNICORN, the horn of which, in powdered form, was renowned as an APHRODISIAC and antidote to poison. Like the NARWHAL, the abada was avidly hunted during the fifteenth century and later.

abandon hope

"Abandon hope all you who enter here!"—the inscription on the gates to Dante's Other World in the *Divine Comedy.* In DREAM VISIONS, after the hero or heroine has passed a water barrier, voyagers to celestial or nether realms enter through a gate of pearl (as in heavenly gates) or through a GATE OF IVORY or horn, signaling the rite of passage and the impossibility of returning to earth.

abased

Said of an HERALDIC FESS or CHARGE placed lower than its usual position in a COAT OF ARMS.

abbess

A superior of a MONASTERY for women, or of a COEDUCATIONAL MONASTERY, usually BENEDICTINE. She was a significant LADY BOSS possessing essentially EPISCOPAL powers, such as hearing confessions of subordinates (but forbidden from doing so in the thirteenth century). Her insignia are a ring and staff, similar to those of a BISHOP.

abbey

A large or venerable MONASTERY for monks or nuns, or a COEDUCATIONAL MONASTERY, directed by an ABBOT or ABBESS.

abbot

The male head of a MONASTERY or COEDUCATIONAL MONASTIC house, of BENEDICTINE or related order, whose insignia are the ring, staff, and, often, the MITRE.

abgesang

The concluding section of the MINNESINGER's tripartite courtly song called the BARFORM, the equivalent of a CAUDA.

absolute truth

Complete and total understanding, best obtained by faith and revelation. Difficult to acquire, it was frequently sought in science, requiring predictable, acceptable, natural explanations for observable events and effects, even though human knowledge of the physical world was deemed provisional, probable, and approximate. Such fourteenth-century natural philosophers as Jean Buridan and Nicole Oresme opposed temporal sufficient truth versus tentative useful truth, both mere vergings toward absolute truth. Buridan's empirical observation plus natural reason could provide truth sufficient for human purposes; for Oresme, natural knowledge being uncertain, several equally plausible alternatives could tentatively apply to data. Absolute truth was a major controversy between AUGUSTINIAN and THOMIST followers of the ANGELIC DOCTOR.

absolution

A PRIEST's or BISHOP's conferring of formal forgiveness of sins by Christ's GRACE to the penitent; or a service of prayers for a dead person's soul.

abutment

Masonry or brickwork on a PIER or wall that supports an arch.

acanthus
(Greek, thorn) The spiny-leaved yet graceful plant decorating CORINTHIAN capitals, GOTHIC SPANDRELS and CORBELS, MANUSCRIPT ILLUMINATIONS, jewelry, ENAMELRY, and goldsmithery; it was one of the most popular botanical portraits.

accentuation
MIDDLE ENGLISH, like other Germanic languages of the INDO-EUROPEAN family, fixes accents on a particular syllable (as in friend'ly, friend'less, friend'ship, friend'liness) rather than shifting them, as in Greek and Latin (tel'egraph, teleg'raphy, telegra'phic).

accidie
(Latin *acidia,* "lethargy, laziness") Sloth, spiritual and physical torpor or indifference, one of the SEVEN DEADLY SINS. An allegorical figure in MORALITY PLAYS and art; in medicine and morality, it was a dangerous precursor to MELANCHOLY.

accosted
In HERALDRY and ornament, two figures placed side by side, rather than ADDORSED or ASPECTANT.

achievement
In HERALDRY, the arms on a shield with a tilting helmet and a crest (CRESTING) with mantling (MANTLE), LAMBREQUIN, and motto; at funerals, called a HATCHMENT.

acolyte
A member of the second highest of the church's MINOR ORDERS, ranking below a sub-DEACON until 1207, when the sub-deaconate became one of the MAJOR ORDERS; an assistant in administering the EUCHARIST and a carrier of lighted tapers in ecclesiastical processions.

acrostic
A poem or prose work in which the initial letters of each line, when read down or up, form a name, word, phrase, or sentence.

adder
A serpent or snake, prominently described in bestiaries (BESTIARY), its name changing by METANALYSIS from nadder.

addorsed
In HERALDRY and decorative arts, two figures placed back to back, rather than ACCOSTED or ASPECTANT.

Adonai
(Hebrew, Lord) A substitute in speech and prayer for the unutterable TETRAGRAMMATON.

Adoptionism
An eighth-century (essentially Spanish) heretical doctrine denying the equality of all three members of the TRINITY, insisting that Jesus Christ was simultaneously Son of God and Son of man, adoptive in humanity but not adoptive in divinity. Partially derived from ARIANISM, Adoptionism was associated with Nestorianism (NESTORIANS).

adoration
After the ANNUNCIATION TO THE SHEPHERDS by the ANGEL of the Lord, their praising the infant Christ at Bethlehem; similarly, the Three Kings coming with gifts to celebrate Christ's birth, commonly called the adoration of the THREE MAGI.

ad te levavi
(Latin, To you I have raised up) From the INTROIT of the MASS, originally from PSALM 24, and celebrated on the first Sunday in ADVENT.

Advent
(Latin *adventus,* coming) The Christian ecclesiastical season beginning on the Sunday nearest SAINT ANDREW'S DAY, and the four successive Sundays preceding CHRISTMAS. Characterized by liturgical solemnity, penitential observance, purple VESTMENTS, silent organ, the season marks the symbolic representation of the soul's preparation for Christ's arrival, the coming of Christmas, and Christ's SECOND COMING.

adverse possession
Transfer of legal title to a possessor of land who has acted with open hostility, continuously, and within a statutory STATUTE OF LIMITATIONS; a legal assault upon the true landowner for LACHES.

advocatus
An attorney or one who pleads, intercedes, and defends; as INTERCESSOR for sinners in a heavenly tribunal, Jesus Christ or the Virgin Mary.

aedicule
(Latin *aedes,* a dwelling) A niche for a statue; a small room or house for a holy object; or St. Peter's tomb.

Aeolian
In PLAINSONG, one of the AUTHENTIC MODES of the musical CHURCH MODES.

aetheling
An ANGLO-SAXON nobleman, prince, hero, or, simply, man.

affeering
Withholding produce from market in order to increase demand and raise prices.

afforcing
(Or afarsing) A cooking process for thickening the texture or increasing the quantity, as in stuffing or "stretching" a dish to serve more feasters than the recipe intends, while adding nutritive value; its opposite is ALLAYING.

agate
A hard semiprecious stone with striped or variegated patterns caused by infiltration of minerals; commonly used in jewelry, cutlery handles, CHALICES, and garment decorations. Medically, the twelfth-century physician Hildegard of Bingen suggested the agate as an effective sucking-stone tucked between cheek and gum to aid in dieting.

Agatha's veil
Saint Agatha's headgear, thought a miraculous protector against fire and volcanic lava because she stilled an eruption of Mt. Etna a year after her martyrdom.

agere et pati
(Latin, to do and to suffer) A definition of the human condition as acting and suffering, a formulaic theme or TOPOS nearly as frequent as the GREAT CHAIN OF BEING. The phrase reflects the medieval concept that real or literary experience either is initiated and acted or received and endured; people are either actors or patients.

Agnus Dei
(Latin, Lamb of God) A section of the ORDINARY of the MASS, usually sung three times after the consecration and before COMMUNION and derived from John 1:29. It was also a graphic representation of the eschatological triumph of Christ as the LAMB OF GOD according to the vision of the APOCALYPSE in REVELATION 5:6.

agraffe
An ornamental fastener for closing a garment's neck or belt, in the form of a hook, clasp, or buckle, or a pierced or open-work metal clasp of two interlocking pieces; originally devised for securing ARMOR pieces. In building construction, a cramp or hook joining girders.

Agricolan
Pertaining to Agricola's *De Re Metalica,* an important metallurgical and mining text.

aids
Financial services that a TENANT holding land TENURE owes to an overlord.

aiere
A dancer's bodily swaying upward and down (*elevato movimento* and *dolcie et unanissimo relevamento*), one of the Jewish DANCE MASTER Guglielmo Ebreo's SIX REQUISITES FOR A GOOD DANCER.

aiglet
(Or *aglet*) A metal point attached to a ribbon, cord, or lace for tying fifteenth-century clothing accessories, as fastening a CODPIECE to BREECHES or sleeves to armholes. The device was later replaced by buttons or hooks.

ailette
A small square shield worn on the shoulders of a KNIGHT'S ARMOR, origin of the modern epaulet.

air
(Or *ayre*; French *air de cour,* court song), a sixteenth-century solo song, usually to LUTE accompaniment.

air twists
Spiral turning on furniture legs or on glass footings of CHALICES.

aisle
(Latin *ala,* wing), the passage on either side of a CHURCH NAVE, usually separated from it by a row of columns; or the pathway between rows of pews, or, in GARDENS, trees.

akedah
Abraham's binding of his beloved son Isaac to sacrifice him at God's command. Taken from Genesis, this VIRTUE DEFINED BY TRIAL, pervading Jewish LITURGY and art as the central TORAH reading of the HIGH HOLY DAYS, is a popular, poignant Christian TYPOLOGY or PREFIGURATION of God the Father's sacrifice of Christ.

alabaster
Either calcite (calcium carbonate) or gypsum (calcium sulphate) stone used for sculpture, useful objects, and architectural embellishments. Grayish-white in color, polished to a glossy translucence, it was used in small windows in Italian churches, and in England for small religious sculptures, such as the notable Nottingham Alabasters.

alb
An ankle-length white linen, sometimes embroidered, TUNIC. Originally a secular garment, it later became exclusively liturgical, decorated with a front and back ORPHREY, often woven with precious metal thread and ornamented with jewels, and worn by a priest or deacon beneath a CHASUBLE.

alba
(Provençal, dawn), a TROUBADOUR or TROBARITZ morning- or dawn-song signaling the coming of daylight (or of a jealous husband), ending illicit lovers' amorous night. Sung by either partner, it laments dawn's arrival and passion's loss; sung by a faithful lookout, it warns of danger. Usually it contains a refrain: *et ades sera l'alba,* soon Dawn comes!

albarello
(Arabic *elbarani,* bamboo) A cylindrical drug jar, concave-waisted, with a sloped shoulder and narrow-lipped mouth. Used for a compound medication, ELIXIR, or herbal medicament, it was covered with parchment tied with string or sealed with wax, and a label was affixed to the parchment or baked under the jar's GLAZE.

Albigensian Crusade
A CRUSADE against the ALBIGENSES, 1208–09 through 1218. Ordered by Pope Innocent III and conducted with great cruelty by Simon of Montfort, it destroyed much of southern France, including major Provençal courts, and the culture of COURTLY LOVE, TROUBADOURS, and TROBARITZ poetry.

Albigenses
A twelfth-century southern French branch of the CATHARI sect, named after the town of Albi. Strongly dualist (MANICHEAN), Albigenses rejected the flesh and the material world as evil. Believing the New Testament an ALLEGORY, they spurned the SACRAMENTS, belief in the RESURRECTION of Christ's body, MARRIAGE, and the authority of the CHURCH, insisting the CROSS a SYMBOL of victory of Satan over Christ. The PERFECTI elected death by ENDURA. The movement was crushed by the ALBIGENSIAN CRUSADE.

albion
An astronomical instrument invented by the fourteenth-century ABBOT of St. Albans, Richard of Wallingford. A mechanical device, an EQUATORIUM, for finding positions of planets, it was an influential astronomical computing device along with his RECTANGULUS and HOROLOGIUM.

alchemist
A chemist or an adept at ALCHEMY seeking the ARCANUM or the transmutation of base metals to gold: AUREFACTION.

alchemy
Chemical, scientific, and philosophical inquiries into the ARCANUM and the secrets of life, particularly the attempt to transmute base metals into gold, AUREFACTION, plus the search for ALKAHEST. Paracelsus, echoing earlier writers, called it the science of the FOUR ELEMENTS and their conversion one into another.

alcochoden
In ASTROLOGY, the planet in a configuration of the ZODIAC determining length of life.

aleberry
A fragrant, nutritious, brew made from ale boiled with spices, such as cinnamon, nutmeg, cardamom, basil, and sugar, topped with toasted brown-bread SOPS or croutons, similar to WASSAIL.

alecost
A composite plant similar to TANSY, added to ale for aroma and pungent flavor.

alembic
A medical, alchemical, and metallurgical distilling apparatus of glass, pottery, or metal. It consisted of a CUCURBIT containing the distillable substance, surmounted by the head or cap of the still, which transferred vaporous products to a receiver for cleaning.

ale passion
A severe headache after excessive ale-drinking; a hangover.

ale wife
A woman seller of ale or a female tavern keeper, sometimes called a TAPPSTER.

ale-stake
IVY on a pole, signifying a tavern selling beer and ale.

Alfonsine Tables
Established by King Alfonso of Castile (Alfonso the Wise) and 50 astronomers, these thirteenth-century ASTRONOMICAL TABLEs forecast human and political events: wars, PLAGUES, and disease prognoses. Based on a PTOLEMAIC UNIVERSE design and computed on meridians for Marseilles, Paris, Pisa, Palermo, and London, they competed in popularity with TOLEDAN TABLES.

Algamiado
Arabic literature in Spain, using the Arabic alphabet for a Spanish dialect sprinkled with Arabic words, comparable to the blending of Hebrew with Spanish in LADINO.

alidade
A pivoting bar on an ASTROLABE or other instrument for siting heavenly bodies, and showing degrees of the *arc* for measuring their height above the horizon.

aliper
A pungent garlic-and-pepper sauce for meats, fowl, fish, or cheese.

alkahest
The universal solvent in ALCHEMY, thought capable of dissolving all stones, metals, and substances; probably named by Paracelsus.

alkali
In early chemistry and ALCHEMY, a specific substance thought to be "fixed" in soda and potash, and volatile in ammonia.

allaying
The process by which food was diluted in pungency or, conversely, increased in piquancy by adding to a sweet mixture a liquid such as vinegar or another to provide a sharp, sour "sting" or "bite"; its opposite is AFFORCING.

allegory
Personification of abstract ideas, METAPHOR's ultimate development; a vivifying, intensifying, artistic device in which comparison becomes substitution, then animation: "She is graceful as a gazelle!"

An allegory of the human being adrift on life's waters of temptation, lured by the Devil and beckoned to by God. (From *Le grant kalendrier et compost des Bergiers*, Nicolas Le Rouge, Troyes, 1496)

SIMILE); "Truly she is a gazelle!" (metaphor); "Fleet-footed, imperially slim Gazella speaks!" (allegorization). A significant habit of thought, for example, visualizing Wrath as a fiery, frazzle-haired, knife-wielding woman, or Arithmetic as an imperious, scholarly lady, facile with figures. Modern speakers verge on allegory or PSYCHOMACHIA (mind war) when stating "I nearly succumbed to desire but discretion controlled me." A battle rages within the mind between conflicting strong ideas to control human action. Allegorically: on the mind-battleground, Desire, tempestuous, red-garbed warrior-maiden riding her red CAPARISONed war-horse, vigorously attacks restrained, powerful, blue-clad Discretion, who, beautifully balanced, thrusts the decisive counter-stroke, winning the fray. In allegory, VICEs, VIRTUEs, SEVEN DEADLY SINS, moral qualities such as Perseverance in *morality plays,* such natural objects as a pearl or a rose, have multiple, concurrent levels of meaning, as in FOUR-FOLD INTERPRETATION of art and reality.

Alleluia
An exultant section of the PROPER of the MASS containing such MELISMAs as the JUBILUS.

Alleluia clausum
The last time ALLELUIA is sung before EASTER on the Sunday of SEPTUAGESIMA.

allemain
An enormous pudding in which jugglers or acrobats are hidden to leap out at a dramatic moment to amaze banqueting guests and pique their admiration.

Allemande
A dance known as "German," popular in the 1550s, performed in moderate double-time, appearing in the works of Tielmann Susato, Pierre Attaignant, and in the Fitzwilliam Virginal Book; also called *Alman* and *Almayne.*

alley
In GARDENs, a broad path between rows of trees either cut through a forest or, more usually, specially planted and formally tended, to allow a grand vista, a protected walk, and a display of outdoor ornamental sculpture. Overarching tree boughs when interlaced form a "pleached" alley.

All Hallows
Another phrase for ALL SAINTS.

alliteration
Repetition of initial consonants in sequential words (as in fierce, foul, ferocious, fire-fuming dragons), important in Germanic and ANGLO-SAXON literature: EPIC, elegy, and works of the ALLITERATIVE REVIVAL.

alliterative revival
The re-establishment in fourteenth-century England in the northwest Midlands dialect of the ANGLO-SAXON poetic technique of ALLITERATION (as a fine, fashionable, functional form) in ROMANCEs and other literature, as in *Sir Gawain and the Green Knight, Pearl, Piers Plowman,* and the *Alliterative Morte Arthur.*

allodial
In early Germanic law, an ESTATE IN LAND called an allodium held in absolute ownership without service to a superior or overlord, as opposed to a feudum or FEUD, a property of FEUDALISM in which TENURE imposed strict duties.

All Saints
A Christian FEAST celebrated on November 1 for all Christian SAINTS canonized, uncanonized, known, and unknown. Also called ALL HALLOWS, it may have been instituted by Pope Gregory III in the eighth century.

All Souls
A Christian FEAST on November 2, following ALL SAINTS, dedicated to prayer for souls suffering in Purgatory and influenced by tenth-century Odilo of Cluny who commanded its celebration in BENEDICTINE monasteries. Three MASSes are celebrated.

almacantar
In an ASTROLABE, parallels of altitude, the horizon, and circles of the sphere parallel to it, crossing the meridian.

Almagest
The title of Ptolemy's popular astrological treatise.

almanac
A MANUSCRIPT and early printed calendar describing phases of the moon, weather prognostications, crop

planting rotations, seasonal agricultural activities, HOUSEHOLD medications, BLOODLETTING or PHLEBOTOMY schedules, astrological lore, and HOROSCOPES.

al marco
The process for weighing together a large number of smaller coins of equal face value to determine whether the average coin is still within the legal weight. For larger, more valuable coins, weighing is performed AL PEZZO.

Alma Redemptoris Mater
(Latin, O Gracious Mother of the Redeemer) The first line of an ADVENT ANTIPHON to the Virgin Mary, dedicated to her as the Blessed INTERCESSOR. It was sung by Chaucer's poignant 7–year-old martyred boy in the *Prioress's Tale* and was the subject for polyphonic settings by such composers as Dunstable, Dufay, Ockegham, and Josquin.

Almogavares
A fourteenth-century company of mercenaries, directed by Roger de Flor, that fought in Spain, Sicily, and Byzantium, conquered a part of Greece, and, beginning in 1311, occupied the duchy of Athens for about 70 years.

almond milk
Ground nuts boiled in milk or water yielding a drink, a stock for soups and sauces, and a mixer for medicines.

almoner
A castle's servitor or religious HOUSEHOLD official charged with dispensing alms (monies, food, or small useful objects) to the poor via an ALMS DISH from the ALMONRY.

almonry
The place from which charity or alms was distributed by the ALMONER, usually a special room, building, or place at a castle or religious HOUSEHOLD gate.

alms
Charity; giving alms was a moral and religious duty to provide food, money, and practical relief for the poor; an individual doled gifts by hand from a personal ALMS BAG, gave through an ALMONER, and paid through the church an ALMS FEE.

alms bag
A small pouch or purse worn by men and women for distributing gifts of coin or food to the poor, later developing into a more secular, practical AUMONIERE.

alms dish
A vessel for collecting and distributing small gifts of coins, food, or household objects to the poor.

alms fee
(Anglo-Saxon, *aelmes feoh,* charity money), a payment made to the Pope, it was also called PETER'S PENCE, CHURCH SCOT, and ROME-SCOT, similar to the secular SCOT-ALE.

almuce
A cloth or fur hood worn by secular men and women. The clerical version often had pendant bands draped over the wearer's chest. It was also known as AMICT, AMISS, and AMESS.

almutem
The prevailing or ruling planet in a HOROSCOPE.

al pezzo
The procedure for weighing large valuable coins piece by piece, rather than AL MARCO.

Alpha and Omega
The first and last letters of the Greek alphabet, commonly symbolizing God as life's beginning and end, and a sacred MONOGRAM similar to the CHI-RHO MONOGRAM and I H S.

alta danza
(Spanish, old dance) A fifteenth century Spanish equivalent of the Italian SALTARELLO and French PAS DE BRABANT, according to Italian DANCE MASTER theorist Antonio Cornazano.

altar
The raised structure or consecrated table upon which sacrificial offerings are placed, and, in Christian tradition, the EUCHARIST is celebrated.

altar book
A MANUSCRIPT for group liturgical reading and sumptuous display, usually written in MAJUSCULE, such as large INSULAR books, antiphonaries, and hymnals, as distinct from POCKET-BOOKS.

alteration
A variety of musical MENSURAL NOTATION, raising or lowering a note by means of a sharp or flat.

Althing
The Icelandic assembly of all free men. Established in 930, and convened yearly at Reykjavik under the island's 144 chiefs, or GODOR, the assembly judged crimes, resolved vendettas, adjudicated claims, and promulgated laws.

ambitus
In music, the interval of PLAINSONG and GREGORIAN CHANT melodies, from a fourth (as in simple ANTIPHONs) to an octave or more (as in GRADUALs and ALLELUIAs).

ambo
A pulpit in the center AISLE of a CHURCH, from which the GOSPEL lesson is read.

Ambrosian chant
Elegantly florid liturgical CHANT, thought to have been established in the fourth century by Saint Ambrose, bishop of Milan (then the imperial capital of the West). Like MOZARABIC chant, its Eastern liturgical tradition omits PLAGAL MODEs of the GREGORIAN CHANT. It is one of the FOUR MUSICAL DIALECTS of Christian chant.

ambulant
In HERALDRY, a walking animal or human figure, as opposed to SEJANT or COUCHANT.

ambulatory
(Latin *ambulare,* to walk), a processional AISLE behind and around the high ALTAR of a CATHEDRAL, allowing pilgrims to see and touch saints' RELICs.

amelioration
The semantic change in a word's meaning from an earlier and more serious import to a tamer one. Anglo-Saxon *drenchan,* to die by drowning, became Middle English *drench,* to get very wet. *Luxuria,* one of the SEVEN DEADLY SINS—Lechery—as *luxury* now means expensive indulgence; the FABLIAUX's *QUEYNT*—vagina—now means quaint and charming. *PEJORATION* is the linguistic opposite.

amict
Another word for ALMUCE.

amidah
(Hebrew, standing) The central prayer in Jewish liturgy, recited standing, consisting of 18 benedictions.

amigaut
A short slit in the center or side of the neck of the twelfth through fourteenth-century SURCOAT making it easy to pull over the head; or a small fabric panel decoratively reenforcing the slit.

amor de con
(Provençal, love of sexual intercourse) The explanation of William IX of Poitiers, a noble TROUBADOUR, of his and other men's inexorable amorous proclivities.

Amor Dei
(Latin, love of God) Sixteenth-century Spanish mystic Saint Theresa of Avila's vision of an angel plunging a long-pointed spear with a flaming tip into her, piercing her heart and impregnating her with God's love.

amor de lonh
(Provençal, love from afar) A TROUBADOUR and TROBARITZ poetic conceit of COURTLY LOVE from a distance. Suffering that ennobles affection, deprivation that increases desire, and obstacles that separate lovers protected this fragile ideal which physical closeness might shatter. Geographical distance, war, CRUSADE, or inviolable social barriers also might distance lovers.

amoretto
A winged naked chubby child, Cupid, or sprite of love. In a secular context, it is a PUTTO; in ecclesiastical, a CHERUB.

amor vincit omnia
(Latin, Love conquers all, from Virgil, *Eclogues* 10:68) A commonplace phrase frequently inscribed on jewelry and tapestries, but misplaced on the elegant, ostentatious brooch worn by the Prioress in Chaucer's *Canterbury Tales.*

amphora
A two-handled wine or oil vessel, usually ovoid, broad lipped, and narrow-mouthed. Some large storage or

measuring jars ranged between the Greek equivalent of the modern nine-gallon capacity and the Roman six gallons seven pints.

amyndoun
Reminiscent of the "peas porridge hot" in the nursery rhyme, this midsummer wheat thickener of food texture (but thinner of taste and stretcher of ingredients) takes nine days and nine nights to prepare; it is used in AFFORCING.

anaesthesia
Analgesic, soporific, and anaesthetic effects were achieved by FUMIGATION, inhaling vapors from burned, dried preparations of (or sponges soaked in) opium poppy, hyoscyamus, hemlock, or MANDRAKE, or by imbibing these substances in DECOCTIONs, ELIXIRs, TINCTUREs, or PILLs, sometimes provided alone, in compound drugs with one another, or with other ingredients, as celandine and melissa.

anamorphosis
An art game or experiment in perspective, perception, and illusion by fifteenth-century (particularly Florentine) artists and architects concerned with optics, the science of light and vision. Leon Batista Alberti's, Leonardo da Vinci's, and Holbein's anamorphic distortions appear grotesque or incomprehensible from one point of view, yet from another, are perfect both in perspective and proportion. The viewer's position above, below, obliquely left or right, or via special viewing devices such as cones, cylinders, or PERSPECTIVE CABINETs determined his or her appreciation of the painting, MINIATURE, MURAL, WOODCUT, or INTARSIA wood panel. Some creations were designed for recreation, surprise, and delight, while others were primarily for symbolism (one perspective's bauble is another's death's head) and for decorum (sexual scenes are hidden in bland contexts).

anapest
One of the FIVE METRICAL FEET: two short beats followed by one long.

anareta
In astrology, the killing planet that destroys form; in a HOROSCOPE, when the APHETA reaches the place of anareta, the NATIVE dies.

anathema
(Greek, suspended; similar to Hebrew, cursed or cut off) A curse, ban, or excommunication from the community of believers; anathema maranatha (I Corinthians 16:22) is the severest form.

anchorites and anchoresses
Male and female religious hermits attempting a life *imitatio Christi* (in imitation of Christ) by withdrawing from the world. Some described their spiritual visions and devotions in moral, didactic literature, as Walter Hilton's fourteenth-century anti-heretical *Ladder of Perfection,* Dame Julian of Norwich's ebullient visions, and the late twelfth-century INSTRUCTION BOOK for female hermits called *Ancrene Wisse,* the Anchoress's Rule.

"and his or her heirs"
In COMMON LAW, the classic conveyance in a will for creating a FEE SIMPLE absolute transfer of an ESTATE IN LAND, a form of TENURE.

"and the heirs of his or her body"
The legal words in a will under COMMON LAW for creating a FEE TAIL, a tenurial ESTATE IN LAND.

anelace
An ornamented decorative dagger.

anemone
A usually scarlet flower symbolizing Christ's blood and the martyrdom of CRUCIFIXION.

angel
(Greek, messenger; Hebrew, *malak Jehovah,* messenger of Jehovah) A divine messenger and ethereal spirit, a close companion of God in the GREAT CHAIN OF BEING, a high-ranking minister in the ORDO MUNDI whose winged radiance is light-bearing and an illumination of human understanding (as the fallen angel LUCIFER ought to have been), a minion of God announcing his gospel, as in the ARCHANGEL Gabriel's ANNUNCIATION to the Virgin. Important in Jewish, particularly KABALLAH, tradition and in Muslim as well as Christian theology, angels were included in the hierarchic and hieratic ordering of spirits, the NINE ORDERS OF ANGELS.

angel beam
The wood-carved ANGEL, or sometimes human head or body, terminating a HAMMER BEAM.

Angelic Doctor
Saint Thomas Aquinas, the thirteenth-century DOMINICAN philosopher and theologian, synthesizer of ARISTOTELIAN philosophy and Christian revelation, writer of the *Summa contra Gentiles* and the *Summa Theologica*. His writings systematically investigate harmonies between reason (distinguished from truth by the philosophers Averroes and Siger of Brabant) and faith (believed identical to truth by the AUGUSTINIANs), act and potence, matter and form, essence and accident, and celebrate the QUINQUE VIAE. He codifies in church doctrine Aristotle's antifeminism by celebrating clerical celibacy, prohibiting abortion, and forbidding ordination of women.

Angelic Hymn
The Greater DOXOLOGY, which is *GLORIA IN EXCELSIS.*

angel touch
The representation of celestial ministers and minions with wings, or of human beings having ascended to such superior spirituality, wearing halos and feathered wings.

angelus
Probably the most frequently practiced liturgical devotion, named after the first word of the initial VERSICLE: *Angelus domini nuntiavit mariae* (The angel of the Lord has announced to Mary). This commemorates the INCARNATION of Christ and praises the Virgin Mary for accepting Gabriel's ANNUNCIATION. The devotion consists of three Hail Mary's with VERSICLES and a COLLECT.

Anglo-Norman literature
Works written in Norman French dialect in England between the NORMAN CONQUEST (1066) and the fifteenth-century that were refined, fashionable, courtly competitors of native ANGLO-SAXON attitudes and literature. Examples include the imaginative LAIS (poetic tales) of Marie de France; pseudo-historical, self-congratulatory chronicles such as Gaimar's *L'Estoire des Engleis* (*History of the English*), and Wace's *Roman de Brut* (*Story of Brutus*), an Arthurian legend; and ROMANCES such as Thomas of Britain's *Tristan*. Although CHAUCER'S ENGLISH was virtually standard in the fourteenth-century, his contemporary John Gower proudly wrote his *Mirour de l'omme* in Anglo-Norman.

Anglo-Saxon
Also called Old English, the earliest English language spoken and written in England from approximately 700 through 1100. There were four major dialects: Northumbrian (spoken North of the Humber River, an Anglian dialect); Mercian (between the Thames and the Humber, also Anglian); West Saxon (south of the Thames, a Saxon dialect); and Kentish (in Kent and part of Surrey, the dialect of the Jutes). *Beowulf* is the finest long poem in Anglo-Saxon, but exquisite elegies such as *The Wanderer* and *The Seafarer* demonstrate the linguistic vigor of this alliterative language which later develops into MIDDLE ENGLISH, whose major dialect is CHAUCER'S ENGLISH.

annulet
A small metal or stone ring or FILLET around a column's shaft, or in HERALDRY, a ring indicating a fifth son in CADENCY.

Annunciation
ARCHANGEL Gabriel's announcement to the Virgin Mary of Jesus's INCARNATION, as well as the ANNUNCIATION TO THE SHEPHERDS. The Christian Feast of the Annunciation is celebrated on March 25.

Annunciation to the Shepherds
The ANGEL Gabriel's appearance to two or more shepherds announcing the birth of Jesus and his miraculous INCARNATION (Luke 2).

anthem
An ANTIPHON, a musical composition sung responsively by two voices or choirs, usually a liturgical song of praise, derived from CHANT.

Antichrist
Jesus Christ's chief antagonist in theology, literature, and drama, appearing on earth preceding Christ's SECOND COMING and the world's end. A lawless, self-deified maker of mock miracles causing apostasy and mass defections from the true CHURCH, he ultimately will be destroyed by Christ.

The Annunciation of Gabriel to the Virgin Mary. (Woodcut from the *Geistliche . . . Lebens Jesu Christi*, Johann Zainer, Ulm, 1485)

antimony
In ALCHEMY and pharmacy, the blue, brittle metal antimony tri-sulfide or stibnite (with comparable uses to classical stibium and Arabic alcohol) employed to purify metals and cosmetically to stain eyelids. Anticlerical satirists maintain that the chemical repels monks: antimomy = anti-moine = monks' bane. So-called "philosophical antimony" cleanses and purifies "philosophical gold" just as common antimony "perfects" common gold.

antiphon
Short scriptural texts sung; during the eight CANONICAL HOURS, an alternating pair of choruses sings each word in simple syllabic style, presenting successive verses of a PSALM or CANTICLE.

antiphonal
(Or *antiphonary*) A book, often with ILLUMINATIONS, containing musical ANTIPHONs, verses, or passages sung by alternating choirs in Christian worship, especially the choir CHANTs for the OFFICE, exclusive of the MASS.

apanage
(French, *apaner*, to endow with means of subsistence) A lucrative estate, appointment, or income to provide for the younger children of a king, prince, or nobleman.

aperture
A gap, cleft, chasm, or open space between portions of solid material in jewelry, architecture, sculpture, or costumery.

apheta
In ASTROLOGY, the planet that delineates life's progress in a HOROSCOPE. When this planet carrying the NATIVE's life reaches the ANARETA, the person dies.

aphrodisiac
HEALTH MANUALS, dietaries, HERBALS, medical texts, and ecclesiastical treatises preserve recipes for erotically-stimulating foods and wine, such as beef wrapped in saffron pastry, figs stuffed with cinnamon and ricotta cheese, sparrow's eggs, clams boiled in ale, turnips and asparagus steamed with dill and basil, roasted chestnuts and cream, and red wine spiced with rosemary, sage, and rue. Erotic inhibitors include chicory and lettuce.

Apocalypse
The allegorical vision of Saint John the Evangelist in REVELATION foretelling Christ's SECOND COMING, his New Jerusalem on Earth, Satan's overthrow, and the final destruction of the wicked. Included also are the visions of the APOCALYPTIC BEASTS, LAMB OF GOD, SEVENTH SEAL, FOUR HORSEMEN OF THE APOCALYPSE, and GRAPES OF WRATH.

apocalyptic beasts
SYMBOLS of the FOUR EVANGELISTS: a winged man, Matthew; a lion, Mark; an ox, Luke; an eagle, John. In Saint John's vision in the APOCALYPSE (Revelation 4:7), they are the beasts with eyes all around them; in Ezekiel (1:10–11), they have faces only.

Apocrypha
The "hidden writings," not part of the Old or New Testament canon, declared spurious by the early Church Fathers but thought exciting by artists who utilized them in literature and graphic art; especially important are the Gospel of Nicodemus (Christ's

descent into Hell), the Gospel of Thomas (Christ's ENFANCES), the Book of James (nativity and childhood of the Virgin, and of Christ), and the so-called Letter to Adso.

apostil
A volume containing the New Testament EPISTLES.

Apostles
The twelve original disciples of Jesus: Andrew, Barnabas, Bartholomew, James the Less, James, Philip, John, Jude, Simon, Matthew, Peter, and Judas; Matthias replaces Judas in one account (Acts 1:26).

Apostles' Creed
A short statement of basic Christian beliefs, thought to have been originally formulated by the TWELVE APOSTLES. It is liturgically important in BAPTISM, and often said before MATINS and PRIME, after COMPLINE.

apostle spoon
Popular since the fifteenth century, the spoon's handle has a sculptured saint on the FINIAL, usually with an apostolic EMBLEM. Sets of TWELVE APOSTLE spoons are sometimes accompanied by a thirteenth, representing Christ.

applique
An embellished trimming sewn or pasted upon another material to decorate it or serve as a BADGE or EMBLEM.

apprentice
(Old French *aprendre,* to learn) A person legally bound to the instruction of a MASTER of a craft, trade, or profession; during a specific number of years, an apprentice learned enough to be classed a JOURNEYMAN; if skilled and capable of producing a MASTERPIECE, the practitioner might become a master.

apron
As architectural ornament, a raised panel below a window sill, oftentimes elaborately shaped and decorated; as costume, a cloth or leather, backless, craftsman's clothing protector usually tied around neck and waistline. (Originally *napron,* its "n" lost by METANALYSIS.)

apse
A semi-circular or polygonal extension from the east end of a CHURCH or CATHEDRAL, derived from BASILICA architecture, as at England's Norwich cathedral.

apsidal chapel
A small, polygonal chapel, usually one of an odd-numbered series, attached to a church's APSE and often dedicated to the Virgin Mary; in England called a LADY CHAPEL, as at Tewksbury, Westminster, Ely, and Gloucester.

aqua clarissima
(Latin, clearest water) A clear liquid medication, significant in the 14th century French medical malpractice cases brought by the University of Paris against a brilliant WOMAN PHYSICIAN, Dr. Jacqueline Felicia, in 1322; her compounding and dispensing of this medicine achieved dramatic cures for grateful patients, both women and men, testifying in court to her excellence.

aqua fortis
(Latin, strong water) Nitric acid, used in chemical separations of gold and silver and in alchemical distillations.

aquamanile
(Latin, handwasher) A water pitcher of bronze, gold, silver, or DINANDERIE for ceremonial handwashing, usually whimsically or ALLEGORICALLY shaped as a lion, griffin, horse and rider, or woman (Phyllis) riding the back of a man (Aristotle); it was also used as a Christian liturgical LAVER.

aqua metallorum
(Latin, water of metals) An alchemical name for mercury.

aqua permanens
(Latin, permanent water) Alchemical mercury, the "water" of the sun and moon, "permanent" because it does not evaporate.

aqua vitae
(Latin, water of life) In ALCHEMY, ardent spirits or unrectified alcohol.

arabesque
Graceful, flowing line decoration, thought to be inspired by Moorish, Muslim, or Arabic art forms, elaborately and fancifully entwining leaves, flowers, and geometric shapes, excluding human and animal figures in early works, but extravagantly using them later.

arain
A spider; a creature sometimes found in BESTIARIES and Bibles, its webs and crawling, insinuative movements were analogies for human follies, foibles, VICEs, and VIRTUEs.

arba kanfot
An undergarment with four fringes (TZITZIT) attached to the four corners of the cloak and worn by observant Jews following the biblical injunction in Numbers 15:38.

arbalest
A sturdy steel CROSSBOW with a wood shaft and mechanism for shooting arrows, bolts, and stones.

arbitress
A woman mediator and settler of disputes. Numerous LADY BOSSES performed in reality the role that Chaucer's patient Griselda and Melibee's wife played in literature.

arblaster
A cross-bowman; one who is skilled in the use of an ARBALEST.

arbor
A cool, treed shelter often embellished with herbs, flowers, and rose trellises; the popular HERBER of GARDENs.

arboretum
A tree or shrubbery collection, including TOPIARY, specially planted as landscape decoration or botanical curiosity.

arc
In astronomy and ASTROLOGY, the part of a circle through which a heavenly body appears to pass, above (diurnal arc) or below (nocturnal arc) the horizon.

arcade
Arches supporting a wall or roof, or a covered passageway between two rows of arches or between an arch-row and a wall.

arcanum
One of the great chemical secrets or mysteries of nature ALCHEMISTS worked to discover. Paracelsus called it an incorporeal, immortal substance beyond the understanding and experience of man and woman, its medical excellence, as a marvelous ELIXIR, exceeding that of any element entering the human body.

arcanum of human blood
In hermetic and alchemical writings, MERCURY, the base principle of metals, metaphorically was comparable to the blood of animals nourishing their total bodies and to human blood animating the corporeal frame.

archaeus
In ALCHEMY, a vital force, the immaterial principle Paracelsans believed presided over animal and vegetable economy. In human beings, the chief archaeus was believed to reside in the stomach and subordinate archaei to regulate peripheral organs.

archangel
A chief ANGEL, a messenger and intermediator closest to God, as Michael, Gabriel, and Raphael; Jewish tradition names four more: Uriel, Raquel, Saniel, and Ramiel; a member of the highest rank in the NINE ORDERS OF ANGELS.

archbishop
A metropolitan or primate, the head of an ecclesiastical province or a national ecclesiastical hierarchy, such as an archdiocese.

Archimedean
Pertaining to the third-century B.C. Syracusan philosopher Archimedes, celebrated for mathematical and mechanical devices such as his screw, a water-raising screw-and-cylinder, his POU-STO, and for his famous cry of delight, *EUREKA*, "I have found it!"

archimime
A chief buffoon or mimic imitating manners, gestures, and speech of people, living or dead.

Archipoeta
The principal poet of the GOLIARDS whose true name is unknown.

architrave
A horizontal beam surmounting columns; the lowest section of an ENTABLATURE.

archivolt
The inner curve of an arch as seen from below, often with ornamental moldings.

archlute
A long, large LUTE, its base strings lengthened, as in a *theorbo.*

arcuated
Pertaining to a building supported by arches, rather than by columns and beams, as in most GOTHIC CATHEDRALS; opposite of TRABEATED.

arenga
An introductory, non-legal preface to a legal document.

Areopagite
A member of the Athenian supreme court; or Dionysus the Areopagite, converted by St. Paul to Christianity (Acts 17:34), and often confused with a third-century bishop of Paris. He was the putative author of mystical neo-PLATONIC writings important for SCHOLASTICISM but truly written three centuries later by the sixth-century Pseudo-Areopagite or Pseudo-Dionysus.

argent
Silver in color, or white; often opposed in HERALDRY to *or,* gold, one of the two METALS.

argentum vivum
(Latin, living silver) Quicksilver, or a reduced or digested form of MERCURY, according to the CLAVICULA of Raymond Lull.

Arianism
The heresy of third-century priest Arius of Alexandria, maintaining that in the TRINITY, the Son and the Word are not equal to God the Father, being of inferior and different substance. Arianism was attacked by Saint Athanasius and probably influenced ADOPTIONISM.

arigot
A Provençal musical pipe played with a TABOR; a FLAGEOLET.

arisard
A MANTLE or PLAID or cloak worn by Scottish women, covering head to ankles, cinched or draped at the waist.

Aristotelian
Pertaining to the logical, empirical, deductive tradition (as opposed to the PLATONIC) of the fourth-century B.C. Greek philosopher, inspiring emulation or stimulating refutation, particularly during the renaissance of the twelfth century when his newly translated works were re-introduced to European scholars. His precepts on government, ABSOLUTE TRUTH, ethics, logic, epistemology, psychology, essence and existence, animals and humanity, and humankind's place in the GREAT CHAIN OF BEING were adapted by Christian thinkers. His *Historia Animalium* classifying animal life indirectly affected the content and caliber of medieval bestiaries. His anti-feminism was translated into Christian doctrine in the works of Albertus Magnus and especially Pseudo-Albertus Magnus's *De Secretis Mulierum* (Concerning WOMENS' SECRETS), perniciously perverting science to political ends.

ark
A refuge on land or water, as Noah's ship saving him from the Deluge; an enclosed book cabinet in libraries or houses of worship, as the Judaic holy ark, ARON HA-KODESH, housing the TORAH.

armed
In HERALDRY, depiction of animals displaying teeth, claws, or beak; a man or woman wearing ARMOR.

armiger
A knight's ARMOR-bearer or ESQUIRE.

armilause
A short silken cloak worn over ARMOR.

armillary sphere
A skeletal celestial globe consisting of metal rings or hoops representing the equator, ECLIPTIC, tropics,

Arctic and Antarctic circles, and revolving on an axis.

armoire
A cupboard, wardrobe, or enclosed storage space, usually constructed of wood and utilized in various rooms of the HOUSEHOLD: the AUMBRY in the banquet hall, GARDEVIN and GARDMANGER in the kitchen, and GARDEROBE in the sleeping quarters.

armor
A fighter's defensive body covering, usually made of metal, including the HAUBERK, CHAIN MAIL, ARNET, GAUNTLET, and miscellaneous anatomical protectors, usually embellished with HERALDIC BADGES, EMBLEMS, and a COAT OF ARMS. Horse armor customarily was covered by a CAPARISON. Armor also is the total offensive and defensive accoutrements of warfare.

armorial device
An INSIGNE, BADGE, or HERALDIC design painted on a knight's shield, carried as a pennant on a pole or LANCE, or embroidered on a TUNIC or coat, to distinguish a particular person, family, or HOUSEHOLD.

arms
A COAT OF ARMS or ACHIEVEMENT. In HERALDRY, the major types include: arms of alliance (gained by marriage); of community (belonging to a corporation or legal body as a city or university); of concession (granted or conceded by a ruler); of dominion or sovereignty (belonging to a ruler or nation); of family (adopted by a person and clan, shared by all, usually, male descendants); of patronage (indications of specific jurisdiction for lords of manors, governors of provinces, added to their own family arms); of pretention (the INSIGNE of an area claimed but not possessed, added to the bearer's own); and of succession (emblems of a family whose estate the possessor inherits).

armure
A decorative fabric woven with a small pattern resembling CHAIN-MAIL ARMOR.

arnet
A fifteenth-century helmet.

arondi
In HERALDRY, describing a circular surface.

Aron ha-kodesh
(Hebrew, ark of the Law) The holy ARK of the Jewish SYNAGOGUE's eastern wall, containing the TORAH scrolls of law read during religious services.

arquebus
A portable gun or small cannon supported on a tripod or rest.

arras
The rich tapestry fabric originating in the Artois town of Arras. Hanging arras screens afforded privacy, warmth, and hiding places, and made lavish political gifts, war booty, prisoner ransom, or significant export to the East in return for Oriental luxuries.

arrescu
A northern Spanish ceremonial dance executed with vigorous frenetic steps and gestures, describing older wooing ceremonies.

arrowslit
A narrow cross-shaped slit on a BATTLEMENT of a castle, MOTTE, CHURCH, or city wall, through which bowmen can shoot.

ars amatoria
(Latin, the art of love) An INSTRUCTION BOOK for the art of loving, often based on a classical prototype such as Ovid's *Ars Amatoria*. Andreas Capellanus' twelfth-century *Art of Courtly Love* includes disquisitions on amorous etiquette, sexual politics, and practical but psychological manipulative ploys; others include APHRODISIACs and pre-coital play techniques.

ars antiqua
(Latin, old art) Fourteenth-century musical theorists of the *Ars Nova* call their predecessors practitioners of the "ancient art," particularly thirteenth-century masters Leonin and Perotin of the NOTRE DAME SCHOOL, experimenters in rhythm and makers of MOTETs. The best sources for this music include the codices of Montpellier, Bamberg, and Huelgas.

arsenic
A poison used for murder and "divorce Italian style," but often rendered innocuous by the BEZOAR stone.

In cosmetics, it was used to whiten skin and in ALCHEMY, to whiten gold or lighten copper.

ars moriendi

(Latin, the art of dying) A type of devotional text and INSTRUCTION BOOK for preparing for a good death, and for perishing elegantly.

ars nova

(Latin, new art) The new musical art of the fourteenth century, a reaction against the ARS ANTIQUA and characterized by brilliant POLYPHONIC musical composition, performance, and notation, particularly in Italy and France. Centering around poet-composers and mathematical experimenters such as Philipe de Vitry (who in 1325 introduced the name for the movement), Guillaume Machaut, Giovanni da Cascia, and Jacobo da Bologna, the music incorporates harmonically-interesting bold dissonances and rhythmic complexities, audaciously using syncopation and beat displacement to make in BALLADs, RONDEAUx, and VIRELAIs intellectually adventurous, rhapsodic melodies.

An ars moriendi's impatient patient kicks his medical attendants. (From a Dutch block-book edition of *Ars Moriendi*, 1465)

Arthurian romance

A prose or poetic tale concerning an historical noble warrior (a *dux bellorum*), a sixth-century fighter named Arthur whose several minor exploits were first recorded in works by Gildus, Nennius, Geraldus Cambrensis, and Geoffrey of Monmouth. The tales were later embellished by twelfth-century poet Chrétien de Troyes whose *Cligès, Lancelot,* and *Perceval* were popular and imitated, possessing chivalric heroes, noble imperious DAMEs, and much magic, mystery, mysticism, and marvels derived from Celtic heritage. Wealthy, erudite patrons of art, such as Eleanor of Aquitaine and Marie of Champagne, assured art's mirroring of contemporary life's elegance and interests in SERVICE OF LOVE, AMOR DE LONH, illusion, human perfectibility, COURTLY LOVE, and VIRTUE DEFINED BY TRIAL. Courtly life also ceremonially imitated art. Knights of the Round Table, such as Sir Gawain, Tristan, Perceval and Lancelot, were subjects of separate romances in various languages, their adventures usually ranging from a marvelous ENFANCE through rescuing besieged damsels and towns, fighting fiery dragons, to dying magnificently.

artichoke glass

A handle-less transparent glass drinking vessel whose rows of knobby protuberances resemble those of the vegetable.

arudshield

"The velvet covered razor," an elegant, logical, rhetorical technique for cutting through cant to truth, celebrating the simplest explanation among a panoply of complexities or obfuscations, and resembling OCKHAM'S RAZOR.

ascendant

In ASTROLOGY, the ECLIPTIC point, or the rising of the planet ruling the sign of the ZODIAC above the Eastern horizon at a particular moment (birth, conception, injury, or illness onset); important in HOROSCOPES, GENETHLIALOGY, and CHRONOPHYSICA, the astrological times were calculated by an ASTROLABE, QUADRANT, or VOLVELLE. Chaucer's Physician always plotted his patients' ascendants.

Ascension
Christ's final triumphal appearance on earth before leaving his astonished APOSTLES at Bethany, outside Jerusalem, and ascending from Mount Olivet into Heaven (Luke 24); in LITURGY, celebrated on the sixth Sunday after EASTER. In astronomy, the rising of a celestial body or the increasing elevation of the sun in the heavens between the vernal equinox and summer solstice, studied with sophisticated instruments as the ASTRARIUM, JACOB STAFF, ALBION, and HOROLOGIUM.

ashlar
A smooth-faced wall whose precisely cut, regularly placed stones are finely jointed.

Ash Wednesday
First day of LENT, six-and-a-half weeks before EASTER, the Wednesday after QUINQUAGESIMA Sunday; celebrated by blessings and by placing of ashes on foreheads of penitents.

aspectant
Two heraldic forms facing each other, opposite of ADDORSED.

asperge
A brush-sprinkler for holy water, usually with a SITULA, a water jar; or the act of the celebrant's sprinkling the ALTAR, clergy, and people at the beginning of high MASS.

aspergill
A holy water sprinkler or ASPERGE brush used in BAPTISM or at MASS.

assart
Forest land cleared and leveled to make arable fields, usually requiring payment of a TALLAGE.

assassins
(Arabic, hashish eaters) A band of fanatical Muslims intoxicated by hashish, led by the OLD MAN OF THE MOUNTAINS to murder Christian leaders of the CRUSADES.

assation
A technique in early chemistry of placing a waxy substance in a glass vessel to dry it over hot ashes; or roasting or baking.

Asses' Feast
(Latin *festum asinorum,* feast of the asses) A Christian celebration either on CHRISTMAS or January 14, commemorating the prophecy of Balaam's ass (Numbers 22), or the Flight into Egypt (Matthew 2:13–15).

assimilation
A linguistic change caused by a word's "social environment" and not its inherent elements: for example, a ship's loading side or ladeboard becomes *larboard* in analogy to STARBOARD. Also, the change of a sound to one more similar to the following sound: *ad* +*frontare* ("to" plus "forehead") becomes *affrontare,* to insult, to slap in the face. Its opposite in linguistic technique is DISSIMILATION.

assize
In England, a court or legislative body or one of its decrees, as the Assize of Arms or Assize of Measures; also a legal ordinance regulating weights and measures of common commodities, or a court dedicated to trying its violations, as the Assize of Bread or the Assize of Ale.

Assumption
Following her dormition (DORMITION OF THE VIRGIN), the Virgin Mary's reception into heaven, her body uncorrupted, pure, and perfect (often depicted ascending on a MANDORLA pallet). The feast is celebrated on August 15. One of the SEVEN JOYS OF THE VIRGIN, Mary was "taken up," but Christ "went up" in the ASCENSION.

assurgent
A HERALDIC or decorative animal or figure ascending from the sea or earth.

astrarium
The astonishingly accurate and beautiful fourteenth-century *clockwork* OF GIOVANNI DA DONDI (superseding the ASTROLABE), consisting of seven dials displaying motions of sun, moon, and the then known five planets, a 24-hour dial, dates of fixed and moveable feasts, nodes or points of intersection of solar and lunar orbits, and sunrise and sunset times in Padua. All simultaneous motions were geared, driven by a verge and balance wheel escapement powered by a hanging weight. A facsimile runs today in the Smithsonian Museum in Washington, D.C.

astrolabe

A reckoner of time and calculator for observing positions of heavenly bodies, measuring heights, distances, and latitudes, and important for HOROSCOPY and medical ASTROLOGY, CHRONOPHYSICA. A veritable analog computer for problems dealing with time, star positions, and length of day or night, the astrolabe consists of concentric discs and a pierced metal RETE, a stylized star map, essentially a stereographic projection of the skies, rotated upon a series of plates or TYMPANs incised with images of celestial spheres projected onto a plane parallel to the equator, and drawn for specific latitudes, depicting horizon, zenith, altitude, meridian, Tropics of Cancer and Capricorn, and resting in a flattened disc, the *mater* or "mother." Atop all pivoted the ALIDADE, a pointer with a citing bar, flexibly anchored by a "horse," or "bird," a pin often whimsically shaped. A remarkable chronometer, precursor to the ASTRARIUM and the modern mechanical CLOCKWORK.

astrological man

A graphic medical depiction of the human body's association with divine heavenly harmonies, a ZODIAC MAN.

astrological professions

In GENETHLIALOGY, an individual's predilection by temperament and talent for particular professions is predictable by the ZODIAC SIGN read in the BIRTH TIME MIRROR or CONCEPTION TIME MIRROR. Physicians and clock-makers are born under the sign of Mercury; poets, painters, and cooks are under the jurisdiction of Venus.

astrology

The practical application of the art and science of astronomy to human uses. Natural astrology includes the calculation and prediction of phenomena such as tides and eclipses, calendar making, time measuring, and weather prediction. Judicial astrology encompasses prediction of the influence of stars and planets upon human affairs, and prognostications by HOROSCOPEs.

astronomical tables

Mathematical computations and lists based upon astronomical observations, used to predict specific celestial conjunctions (as the malevolent union of Jupiter and Saturn in Scorpio, by which Dürer and his contemporaries explain the 1484 syphilis pandemic), to forecast weather, and to elect auspicious times for human action. Some included tables for planetary longitudes and latitudes, often based on the ALFONSINE TABLES.

astrum

A perfect, essential spirit or quintessence of a substance or human being. The human astrum was a microcosmic "heaven" engraved in a being at the hour of birth, replicating the celestial heaven and constituting character. In ALCHEMY, it was a condensed, reduced oil exceeding the natural virtues of a substance, as SULPHUR.

atarah

A Jewish TORAH crown.

Athanasian Creed

Probably composed during the life of fourth-century Saint Athanasius, an official statement of Christian doctrine concerning the Holy TRINITY and INCARNATION. It is spoken on the Feast of the HOLY TRINITY and is often called QUICUMQUE VULT (Whosoever is willing), the opening words.

athanor

An ALCHEMIST's or metallurgist's furnace maintaining a high constant heat by a self-feeding charcoal supply tower. The furnace of the philosophers is an athanor animated by innate "sophic fire," constant, perfect, and perpetual.

Atonement Day

The annual Jewish fast day, YOM KIPPUR.

atour

A two horned hat; or the BIFURCATED, cylindrical, or parallel cone-shaped hairnet or hat worn by fifteenth-century women to cover or shape "horns" of hair; also, a cocked HENNIN worn over each ear.

atrium

An open entrance court before a CHURCH or house.

attribute

A material object recognizable as appropriate to, symbolic of, or representative for a person or political or holy office, as well as an iconographic identifier. SAINTS AND THEIR ATTRIBUTES include Saint Sebastian's arrows, Barbara's tower, Catherine's wheel, Saints Cosmos's and Damian's urine flasks; in secular life, BADGES or EMBLEMS.

aubade
A morning song, the Northern French TROUVERE equivalent of the Provençal ALBA.

Aubusson
A type of French TAPESTRY whose exquisite, expensive, figured weavings were utilized for wall hangings, furniture covers, carpets, table coverings such as SANAPs, and decorative garment borders; named after its town of origin.

auctores
Classical authors cited as real or supposed "authorities" to dignify or verify ideas or events. Even Chaucer's humorous hen Pertelote in the "Nun's Priest's Tale" from the *Canterbury Tales* used this rhetorical device from SCHOLASTICISM to buttress her own theories on dreams while blasting those of her rooster husband.

aufgesang
In MINNESINGERS' songs, the two STOLLEN of the major stanza followed by the ABGESANG; aufgesang plus abgesang equal Dante's FRONS (or two PEDES) plus CAUDA for the tripartite courtly songs of the DOLCE STIL NUOVO, TROUBADOURS, TROBARITZ, and TROUVERES.

augmentation and diminution
Musical presentation of a melody in doubled (augmentation) or halved (diminution) timing.

Augustinian
A member of one of the FOUR ORDERS OF FRIARS, following the rule of Saint Augustine, founded in 1256; one of two major Christian traditions, in opposition to THOMIST followers of the philosophy of St. Thomas Aquinas, the ANGELIC DOCTOR.

aumbry
A multi-tiered cabinet for ostentatious display of banquet service objects, as well as site for final preparation of elaborate foods before their service.

aumoniere
A small drawstring purse of fabric or leather, resembling an ALMS BAG, worn by women or men, hung from a belt or girdle.

auncer
A very small balance scale for weighing foodstuffs or precious minerals and gems, carefully calibrated according to town or national standards of weights and measures.

aureation
Gilding language's lambent gold; a rhetorical and literary device exaggeratedly celebrating ceremony and stately personages and events; favored by fifteenth-century Scottish poets, such as Dunbar, Douglas, and Henryson.

aurefaction
Gold-making; ALCHEMY's attempt to transmute base metals into gold, a metal strong, incorruptible, beautiful, and rare, therefore SYMBOLIC of immortality and perfection. To make gold was to create both wealth and the possibility of everlasting health, a cultural preoccupation exemplified in medicine's AURUM POTABILE and in AUREFICTION. Other than salvation, gold was early death's only anodyne.

aurefiction
Creating the effect of gold by applying to baser items minute quantities of the precious metal as in GILDING with GOLD LEAF in cookery, art, MANUSCRIPT ILLUMINATION, and architectural decoration; or by imitating gold with shining golden substances such as saffron and egg yolk. Also, imitating ALCHEMY's attempt at AUREFACTION.

aureole
The golden glory surrounding either the whole figure of a saint, Christ, or holy personage, or the nimbus, halo, or crown surrounding the head of a saint, MARTYR, virgin, doctor of the church, or venerated personage. Elliptical, it is a MANDORLA or VESICA PISCIS.

aurum potabile
(Latin, potable gold) A potion of drinkable gold, gold's quintessence, the highest of all ELIXIRS: rejuvenating, purifying, and preserving the human body. It

was prescribed in medical texts as a treatment for various diseases (particularly rheumatoid arthritis), and by Chaucer's physician in the *Canterbury Tales.*

authentic mode
In LITURGY, one of the two CHURCH MODES whose musical cadences fall within an octave of the final: the major triad on the dominant, then the triad on the tonic; to be distinguished from PLAGAL MODE.

auto-da-fé
(Portuguese, act of faith) A ceremony of the Spanish INQUISITION. After MASS and a sermon, a heretic, wearing a SAN BENITO, was transferred to secular authority for burning at the stake.

Auxilium Christianorum
(Latin, help of the Christians) A title of the Virgin Mary as blessed INTERCESSOR.

Ave Maris Stella
(Latin, Hail, Star of the Sea) A popular GREGORIAN CHANT HYMN celebrating the Virgin Mary, used in MOTETs.

average
Work done for the feudal lord by the serf and his oxen. In international trade, a maritime or customs tax on shipped goods.

Ave Regina Coelorum
(Latin, Hail, Queen of Heaven), one of four popular ANTIPHONs to the Virgin Mary sung after COMPLINE or as a VESPERS HYMN between the PURIFICATION FEAST and Wednesday of HOLY WEEK. Dufay composed a MASS around the CHANT melody.

avowtrye
Adultery or, simply, any sexual intercourse for "fleshly delight." Chaucer's Parson rages against this sin because sex is not performed for church-sanctified production of children. In Pseudo-Albertus Magnus' *De Secretis Mulierum* or WOMEN'S SECRETS, it is an act physically exhilarating but spiritually corrupting.

azoth
In ALCHEMY, the name for MERCURY, the essential first principle of all metals. It was also Paracelsus' universal medicine, counter-poison, and ELIXIR of life, which he carried in his sword-pommel.

azure
A vivid blue color or LAPIS LAZULI; in HERALDRY, one of the FIVE TINCTURES for a figure or background.

azurite
A beautiful dark-blue stone; powdered, it yields blue pigment. Though often confused with LAPIS LAZULI, heated azurite turns black, but lapis remains unchanged.

B

bachelor
(Latin, *baccalarius,* farm assistant) A junior knight or knight-in-training, unable to rally VASSALS under his banner, as could a BANNERET or BARONET. A knight-bachelor in the King of England's HOUSEHOLD, given maintenance but no land in return for service, was not financially able to marry. One who takes the first university degree.

badge
A heraldic INSIGNE or identifying device, sewn or otherwise applied to a garment or headdress to signify social class, such as the JEWISH BADGE or ROUELLE.

badger
An itinerant grain merchant, usually Jewish; an entrepreneurial middleman often accused of causing famines. Blaming badgers, pogroms were launched to destroy Jewish communities in Germany and Austria, and anti-Semitic coin money (as the KORN-JUDE) was minted depicting them as grotesque.

baggage
(Probably from the French *bague,* bundle) A loose-living, camp-following prostitute, or a flighty, scatter-brained, sexually exuberant young woman.

bagpipe
A musical instrument having one or more reed pipes called CHANTERs, with sound holes for making melodies, and other pipes producing a DRONE or continuous BURDON, attached to a windbag providing air power.

bailey
A fortified enclosure or space inside the outermost walls of a castle, often enclosing a MOTTE, an artificial mound, surmounted by a KEEP, the innermost tower or stronghold.

bailor
A true owner of property who voluntarily places it in the possession of another, the bailee, who has custody, not ownership, of the bailor's merchandise stored in a warehouse or jewelry or wagons left for repair.

balandras
A twelfth-century hooded rain cape, opening at the front or side.

baldacchino
A BALDAQUIN or baldachin.

baldaquin
A richly embroidered, tapestried or velvet fabric awning and backing to a HIGH TABLE, throne, bed, or EPISCOPAL seat, marking the place of honor; or a mobile canopy with four or more columns carried in religious processions above the BISHOP or the SACRAMENT.

bal des ardents
(French, incendiary masquerade ball) During MASQUEs, MASQUERADEs, banquets, and costume ball festivities, courtiers seeking entertainment disguised themselves as wild men or mad men in masked costumes of grasses, straw, and sisal fibers, risking immolation by torch sparks. Froissart's *Chronicles* depicts France's fourteenth-century King Charles VI surviving such disaster when an inquisitive guest accidentally ignited him and some of his courtiers; a quick-witted woman quenched his flames with her skirts.

baldric
A fabric or leather band worn diagonally across the chest and back, anchored at one shoulder, tied or buckled at the opposite hip. Foresters, such as Chaucer's YEOMAN in the *Canterbury Tales,* wore green ones, with a sheath of arrows affixed to the back; knights, monarchs, and ecclesiastics sported them for ceremonial occasions, encrusted with jewels, mottos, medals, EMBLEMS, and APPLIQUES.

ballad
An orally transmitted, anonymously produced dramatic narrative poem containing formulaic expressions and meters, and INCREMENTAL REPETITION. Usually sung to instrumental accompaniment, the melody is repeated for each successive VERSE, with the most common meter being a seven-beat line, broken into four and three.

ballade
A popular musical and poetic form developed in the fourteenth century by Guillaume Machaut and Eustache Deschamps, and in the fifteenth century by Christine de Pizan, Charles d'Orleans, and François Villon, influencing Chaucer and Gower. Generally consisting of three eight-line stanzas plus a quatrain ENVOY, it was favored by the TROUVERES; depicting love and joyous or unrequited emotion, it resembles the Provençal CANZO and German LIED or BARFORM.

ballata
A major fourteenth-century Italian poetic and musical form, derived from the French VIRELEI rather than the BALLADE. Most six-line stanzas are preceded and followed by a two-line refrain yielding a RONDEAU-like scheme.

Ballet Comique de la Reine
An early BALLET DE COUR, a five-hour spectacle in a two-week celebration of the marriage of a duke to Marguerite of Lorraine, it was one of the first ballets with extant music, constantly imitated in the early Renaissance.

ballet à entrée
A theatrical pastoral and mythological dance.

ballet de cour
An early sixteenth-century dance spectacular, often with political intent, melding elements of the MASQUERADE, INTERLUDE, and TRIUMPH with horse ballet (Italian, BALLETTO A CAVALLO and French, DANSES EQUESTRES) plus declamation, music, song, sets, and "machines" (in the manner of DEUS EX MACHINA).

balletto
A type of Italian CANTI CARNASCIALESCHI.

balletto a cavallo
(Italian, horse ballet or equestrian dance) Mounted, elegantly CAPARISONED horses perform intricate geometric, graceful designs, for spectacular and political purposes, often part of a BALLET DE COUR.

ballo
Fifteenth-century dramatic choreography utilizing dance steps, mimic gesture, and exaggerated facial expressions, described by DANCE MASTER Antonio Cornazano in his book *The Art of Dancing,* 1450.

balm
A comforting, soothing ointment or salve, medicinal or symbolic (as Jeremiah's balm of Gilead); an aromatic resinous medicinal gum, BALSAM, or antiseptic oleo-resin.

balsam
A healthful, restorative, oily medication, said by the alchemist Paracelsus to exist as a life-preserving principle in all living things. In medicine, a BALM: it was burned and its fumes inhaled as a soporific; rubbed on the skin of the dead, it preserved bodies from decay.

baluster
An upright column or post supporting a handrail, atop a wall or aside a stairway.

balustrade
Several BALUSTERS; a PARAPET.

bann(s)
A public proclamation of engagement and intended MARRIAGE, to allow time for the complaints of any who might object to the union; after the fifteenth century, the word was used in the plural, as in "posting the banns," reading, or publishing them.

With armorial banners pendant from their trumpets, heralds announce the emperor in procession with a royal retinue. (From Ulrich von Richtenthal, *Beschreibung des Constanzer Conziliums*, German, 1450–1470; courtesy of New York Public Library)

banner

A square or rectangular flag displaying the ARMS of a ruler, baron, knight, ecclesiastical dignitary, or a corporation as an identifying device, rallying point in battle, display of authority, or indicator of rank in processions.

banneret

A BARONET, or a baron's heir.

bannock

A flaky, gritty, unleavened barley, pease, or wheat bread often embellished with currants or glazed fruit, popular in northern England and Scotland, and differing from SCONEs.

baptism

One of the SEVEN SACRAMENTS, a religious initiation rite into the Christian CHURCH; realized either by immersion in water or by its sprinkling via an ASPERGILL, it signifies spiritual purification appropriate for ritual celebration of Christ in the EUCHARIST.

baptistery

The site for the rite of BAPTISM, either a section of a CHURCH or a particular building adjacent to it.

baptized

A person blessed by BAPTISM.

bar

A town wall's gateway; in music, it was the Minnesingers' BARFORM; in law, it was a pleading which stopped a claim or legal action. In HERALDRY, a bar is a horizontal strip across the shield, no more than one-fifth the shield's width, being horizontal and neither DEXTER nor SINISTER; heraldic sub-types include: bars GEMELLE, two bars; CLOSET, a half bar (one-tenth the shield); barrulet, half a closet (one-twentieth the shield).

barbed

The heraldic small leaves between petals, as in "rose GULES barbed proper."

barber pole

(Latin *barba,* beard) The red and white striped vertical pole was a barber-surgeon's visual announcement or sign for services of BLOODLETTING or PHLEBOTOMY; barbertonsory was performed by a less well-educated subgroup devoted only to shaving and cutting hair of the head, mustache, and beard.

barbette

A linen headband or veil passing over the chin or just under it, essentially hiding chin and neck, with a COVERCHIEF forming the WIMPLE worn by older women and widows.

barbican

A castle entrance-gate's fortified defensive outer tower, or a watchtower over a gate.

bard

A northern European poet, itinerant or court-bound, oral historian, entertainer, news-bringer, and national-honor celebrant, having in his WORD-HOARD formulaic verse structures and patterned epithets for persons and events, ennobling them by correlative imagination. In ARMOR, protective metal plates for a horse's neck, breast, or flank; in cookery, a bacon slice.

barform

The MINNESINGERs' conventional song structure, characterized by a major stanza, the AUFGESANG, consisting of two rhythmically similar STOLLEN, plus the ABGESANG.

barge board

An ornamental carved wood board attached to a pointed or gabled roof of a building.

bargello work

A variety of EMBROIDERY or needlework in which each element of a pattern is worked in graduated hues of a single color, creating a pointed or flame-like design; also called FLAME STITCH or HUNGARIAN STITCH.

barley twist

A furniture design of spiral twisting for leg stretchers and uprights on chairs, cabinets, beds, and other household objects, sometimes also appearing in jeweled tabernacles and CHASSEs, emulating the spirals and whorls of barley sugar stalks.

barm

The nutritious beer froth created by yeast's fermenting grain liquor; by analogy, beer hall pleasure; from this derives the epithet "barmy," meaning light-headed, undependable, insubstantial, and foolish.

barmcloth

(Also called *barmskin*) A worker's clothing fabric or leather APRON.

barnacle

A crustacean afflicting the hulls of seafaring ships.

barnacle goose

A species of wild goose thought born in the sea from shells with white "feathers" protruding. A popular, highly favored, well-flavored succulent flesh, it was forbidden during Lent if classified as a goose but permitted if ranked as a fish.

baronet

A BANNERET: a senior knight capable of rallying vassals beneath his BANNER, superior to a BACHELOR.

baroque

Flamboyant late-Renaissance art, architecture, and music style uniting intricate yet expansive ornamental flourishes, naturalistic detail, and exuberant decorations.

barrel vault

A continuous semi-circular arch VAULT in ROMANESQUE architecture, supported by two parallel vaults or ARCADEs.

barrette

A round felt or wool hat; also, a hair restraint often worn beneath a RETICULE.

barrow

An earth-built burial mound, as at SUTTON HOO; if constructed of stone rubble, called a CAIRN. Frequently encountered in English archaeology as: *long barrow,* a family tomb with interior chambers of stone, timber, or turf; *round barrow,* a convex, inverted bowl-shaped structure surrounded by a ditch; *bell barrow,* a flared bell shape with a surrounding ditch and "lip" mound; *disc barrow,* a small mound enclosed in a larger flat area surrounded by a ditch with an external lip mound; *saucer barrow,* like disc, a mound flattened into a shallow inverted saucer-like shape extending to a ditch; and *pond barrow,* technically without a mound, a hollow shallow shape, edged by a lip mound, whose bottom contains pits for human bones.

barrulets

In HERALDRY, a quarter BAR.

barruly

A heraldic shield charged with ten BARRULETS, alternating METAL and TINCTURE.

bartizan

A nineteenth-century term for a castle or church tower's small overhanging BATTLEMENTed TURRET.

Bartolism

The legal theories founded by fourteenth-century Italian lawyer Bartolus de Saxoferrato, doctor of laws, judge, professor at Perugia, ambassador, acquaintance of Emperor Charles IV. His explanation of ARMS was the first treatise on the science of HERALDRY. Founder of international law, he wrote about tyranny and reprisals, defined property and eminent domain, distinguished human from civil rights, elucidated sovereignty, and praised government of the people, by the people, and for the people.

bascinet
A BASSINET.

bas de page
A MANUSCRIPT painting at the base of a page, below the major MINIATURE; often satiric or a realistic genre scene.

basilica
Related to ancient Greek royal-judicial palaces or assembly halls, an early longitudinal CHURCH, particularly one of the seven churches in Rome founded by Constantine: St. John Lateran, St. Peter's, St. Paul's Outside the Walls, Santa Maria Maggiore, St. Lawrence Outside the Walls, Holy Cross-at-Jerusalem, and St. Sebastian's; or one of the eleven minor basilicas.

basilisk
A fabulous reptile hatched by a serpent from a cock's egg, thus half cock, half snake; its hissing frightens other serpents, and its breath and gaze are fatal to human beings. It is a SYMBOL of the Devil or ANTICHRIST, as in PSALM 91.

bas-relief
(French, low relief) Carving, EMBOSSING, or sculpture slightly raised from a flat or curved base, yielding three dimensions but not "in the round" as is HIGH RELIEF.

basse dance
(French, low dance) A popular fifteenth-century ceremonial French court dance, important in Burgundian culture, consisting of elegant "low" gliding and mannered walking movements contrasting with "high" leaps and jumps of the GALLIARD.

bassinet
A light, conically pointed steel helmet or CHAIN MAIL hood.

A knight wears a bassinet with camail. (From brass rubbing, Unknown Knight, Laughton, Lincolnshire, England, 1400)

bassoon
A slightly conical double-reeded musical instrument, the bass oboe, its tube bent back on itself, a crook containing the reed at right angles from its upper end. Its earlier forms include the CURTAL and DULCIAN.

bastard
A sweet Spanish wine not only drunk but used for cooking, as in the dessert dish MALMENS BASTARD, which consists of three pounds ground almonds, two quarts clarified honey, one pound pine seeds, one pound currant raisins to two gallons bastard wine, plus sandalwood, cinnamon, ginger, salt, and saffron.

bastarda
A hybrid handwriting combining the Gothic bookhands (*textura*) with the informal Gothic cursive hands (*notula*, secretarial hand) of the thirteenth through fifteenth centuries. Caxton's early printing fonts were based on local variants of this CALLIGRAPHY.

bastille
A fortified defensive military stronghold.

bastion
A projecting part of a fortification's wall, usually at corners and gates, built to reduce "dead angles" otherwise unreachable by defenders.

baston
A BATON.

batiste
A sheer, finely woven linen and wool fabric, lighter than challis or silk, named for the thirteenth-century French weaver Baptiste Chambrai.

baton
(Or baston) A HERALDIC ORDINARY band or BEND, a diminutive (one-quarter width) of the bend SINISTER, diagonally superimposed upon all other CHARGES. In France, it denotes consanguinity; in England, BATON SINISTER signifies bastardy. As a ceremonial stick held by secular or ecclesiastical dignitaries, it was used for pointing and as adjunct to gesticulating, sometimes concealing a sword or weapon.

battledore
The solid wood or stone clothing beater used by launderers (LAVERS or LAVENDERS).

battlement
A crenelated PARAPET at the top of a wall, with an alternating evenly spaced "tooth-and-gum" design; the "tooth" (MERLON) was the position from which to shoot, through ARROWSLITS, the "gum" (EMBRASURE), the point behind which to seek shelter.

bawd
A licentious, dissolute, "bawdy" person, or a procurer and PANDERER, male or female.

baxter
A professional woman baker.

bay
A rectangular or curvilinear architectural opening in a wall, enclosing a door, window, or space for artful ornament.

A baxter selling breads and pretzels obtains new supplies from her portable oven. (From Ulrich von Richtenthal, *Beschreibung des Constanzer Conziliums*, German, 1450–1470; courtesy of New York Public Library)

Bayeux tapestry
A long (231 feet by 20 inches high) linen and wool EMBROIDERY, made in the eleventh century by noblewomen probably upon the orders of Odo, Bishop of Bayeux and half-brother of William of Normandy, depicting William's conquest of England in 1066.

beading
A type of embellishment similar to GRANULATION in which small spheroid, bead-like protuberances cover or edge the surface, making it resemble a flat plane uniformly covered with bubbles.

beaker
A large cylindrical, usually straight-sided, large-mouthed, and sturdy drinking vessel, with thick walls

but without handles, and made of glass, ceramic, or metal ware.

beast epic

A popular satiric tale utilizing language, episodes, and actions suitable to classical epic but voiced and performed by animals, thus achieving double mockery of epic's high-flown subjects and style and of humankind's vices and foibles. Traceable to Aesop's *Fables,* collected in Latin in the first century by Phaedrus, the genre includes the twelfth-century *Roman de Renart,* Heinrich de Glichezare's *Reinhart Fuchs, Ysengrimus the Wolf* stories, and Chaucer's "Nun's Priest's Tale."

Beast of the Apocalypse

A beast from the sea, a panther with a bear's feet, lion's mouth, ten horns with diadems, and seven heads inscribed with blasphemous names, the heads representing seven hills on which the "great city" is built, and associated with the whore of Babylon and the sacred number 666 (Revelation 13 and 17); often confused with the APOCALYPTIC BEASTS.

beasts of prayer

Bird-headed or beast-faced human figures depicted in Jewish manuscripts from Germany about 1300, doubtlessly influenced by mystical ideas of KABALLAH and twelfth-century HASIDISM.

Beatitudes

Any of the EIGHT BEATITUDES (blessings) Christ promises in the SERMON ON THE MOUNT (Matthew 5:3–11).

beaver

A hinged metal attachment to a fifteenth- and sixteenth-century helmet, the ARNET, protecting the lower part of the face; later, it became the moveable face guard of the BASSINET, consisting of overlapping plates.

beefeater

A respected and respectable servant paid in food and room, or given board in addition to salary. After 1485, he was a YEOMAN of the guard in the English king's HOUSEHOLD, or a yeoman warden of the Tower of London.

Beghards

(Or Beguins) One of the male lay religious communities in the twelfth-century Low Countries inspired by Lambert Begue, founder of the women's BEGUINES, originally recruiting among Flemish cloth industry workers, later significant in the Rhine Valley. The community was dedicated to caring for the sick, burial of the dead, and abjuring private property (unlike the Beguines).

beguin

(Or biggon) A universal headcovering for men, women, and children from the twelfth century on, named after the BEGUINES. It consisted of a three-piece cap made of finest linen for the wealthy and coarser cloth for the common people.

Beguines

A powerful twelfth-century semi-monastic women's religious movement dedicated to chastity and perfect imitation of Christ's teachings, thought, and work. The movement, founded by Lambert Begue, the Stammerer priest of Liège (Belgium), required lenient vows and allowed marriage. Their lay sisterhood was protected by Pope John XXII despite his persecution of male BEGUINS or BEGHARDS, who were suspected of heresy because of their affinity with the FRANCISCANS and other thirteenth-century mystical evangelical groups. Their characteristic headdress was the BEGUIN.

Beguins

BEGHARDS.

beit hamidrash

The Jewish study-house or SYNAGOGUE.

bel chose

(French, lovely thing) A woman's PUDENDUM or QUEYNT.

belfry

(German *berfray,* to guard the peace) A siege tower for attacking walled castles or towns, like the CULVERIN and other mobile armored defensive or aggressive weapons. It acquired an alarm bell in its translation from military moveable use to civilian stationary use.

bellarmine
A large, glazed jug with a capacious belly and narrow neck, usually stippled brown or drab green, ornamented with a small BAS-RELIEF or incised face; it originated as a burlesque on Cardinal Bellarmine, an opponent of the Dutch Protestant party.

bell, book, and candle
The ceremony of excommunication. A fourteenth-century English proverb gives the liturgical object order as candle, book, and bell, though later ecclesiastical directions insist "do to the book, quench the candle, ring the bell," to deliver a cacophonous discord publicly announcing a person's expulsion from the community of saints.

bells
Small tinkling silver bells were jingled from belts, jeweled girdles, neck strings, cape edges, cloak closures, soft shoe and POULAINE points, bracelets and rings, jesters' garb, liturgical VESTMENTS, and horses' CAPARISONs, bridles, and SADDLES. Market bells tolled commercial hours; municipal bells and church bells rang the time, announced political events (a royal progress, declaration of war or peace) and rites of passage (marriage and death), and signaled alarm; tollings often were determined by CHANGE RINGING.

bellum intestinum
A mind's internal warfare among conflicting ideas that determine decision; an intellectual battle or PSYCHOMACHIA.

Belshazzar's Feast
Nebuchadnezzar's son, feasting in riotous orgy with courtiers, wives, and concubines, and using the exquisite jeweled objects stolen from the Jewish Second Temple in Jerusalem, was interrupted by a mysterious handwriting on the wall: *Mene, mene, tekel, upharsin* ("You have been weighed, measured, and found wanting"). He required the prophet Daniel to translate this prediction of Belshazzar's death and the fall of Babylon in 539 B.C. to Cyrus of Persia (Daniel 5).

beltane fire
A pagan summer solstice fire, a BONFIRE, allegorized by such Christian theologians as Saint Augustine (following Pope Gregory's dictum to emend the old to serve the new) as a ceremonial fire honoring Saint John the Baptist.

belvedere
A raised, covered terrace or pavilion allowing a beautiful view and prospect of surrounding country; alternatively, the Roman copy of a Greek sculpture of Apollo (now in the Vatican Museum), wearing an arrow quiver and cloak, originally created in the fourth century B.C., later imitated in courtly secular art.

bend
A HERALDIC ORDINARY, a diagonal band across a shield; a *bendlet* is a narrow bend, one-sixteenth of the shield; a COLISE is even narrower.

benedict
A person ultimately succumbing to the blandishments of marriage after long resistance, in a reference to Saint Benedict, patron saint of celibates and founder of the BENEDICTINES.

Benedictine
Though Saint Benedict of Nursia did not create a major order, numerous MONASTERIES, particularly after the CAROLINGIANs, lived according to the BENEDICTINE RULE, making an art of liturgical prayer, OPUS DEI, in an essentially cloistered, contemplative, yet active existence. Benedictine monks (BLACK MONKs) and Benedictine nuns, established by Benedict and his sister Saint Scholastica, share the identical rule.

Benedictine Rule
Regulations for the religious life created by Saint Benedict of Nursia in the sixth century. The rule, emphasizing both individual pious humanity and monastic administrative order, was followed variously by the CARTHUSIANS, by houses abiding by the CLUNIAC REFORM, and numerous other communities whose main purposes were celebration of the DIVINE OFFICE.

Benedictus
Either the thanksgiving HYMN of Zacharias celebrating his son Saint John the Baptist (Luke 1:68), or that part of the MASS after the SANCTUS: *Benedictus qui venit* ("Blessed is he who comes in the name of the Lord").

benefice
In CANON LAW, an ecclesiastical office or reward for clerical duties, "spiritualities," rendered to parishioners.

bergamasca
A popular poetic dance and musical entertainment from the district of Bergamo, Italy.

bergbarte
An axe used by German tin and silver miners for shaping timbers and shoring up mine tunnels, its long blade set asymmetrically, often imitated in ceremonial ARMOR and depicted in art.

Bernadines
The alternate popular name for the Italian branch of the Feuillants, the stricter, more disciplined MONASTIC order of BENEDICTINES, reformed CISTERCIANS patronized by the twelfth-century mystic, Saint Bernard, ABBOT of Clairvaux.

bestiary
An unnatural natural history, derived in part from the anonymous second-century *Physiologus,* a verse or prose didactic text describing characteristics of beasts plus moral or religious teachings: as the fox is fraudulent and ingenious, duping others to feed him, so the devil craftily deceives the unwary; as the bear LICKS INTO SHAPE its blind babies, so Christianity completes humankind. Wildly extravagant beasts conflated from travelers' tales (as *camelelephantoleopard*) complement the kneeling elephant (most pious of beasts), SALAMANDER, CALADRIUS, and YALE, providing imagery for HERALDRY, art, and information for medicine.

beyond the pale
An outlaw or social reject who must remain outside the paling fences or REVETMENTS reinforcing the EARTHWORKS of a castle, fort, or town, therefore existing unprotected by a community and vulnerable to attack from other outlaws.

bezant
A BYZANTINE gold coin; in HERALDRY, a gold roundel, signifying that the bearer had been to the Holy Land.

bezoar
(Persian, to protect against poison) A poison-testing stone, particularly a calcareous concretion from the alimentary canal of Persian goats and other ruminants. Dropped into suspect wine, ale, or liquid, it absorbed and revealed arsenic and other poison and was said to neutralize it; the stone also was important in the CREDENCE test in secular and ecclesiastical courts (and, in modern laboratories, proved chemically effective in revealing arsenic).

biblia pauperum
(Latin, poor peoples' books) Paintings, BAS-RELIEF sculptures, MOSAICs, FRESCOes, MURALs, and other pictorial representations of the life of Christ, lives of the saints from the LEGENDA AUREA, and popular homilies and PARABLEs which decorate walls of churches and cathedrals, edifying and pleasing those who can read and those who cannot.

bicinium
An exquisite two-part vocal song (also called DIPHONA) contrasting to the rich textured MOTET and MADRIGAL.

bifurcated
Divided into two branches or two divisions, as a road, stream, hallway, or the extravagant fifteenth-century two-horned headdress, the ATOUR.

biggon
The BEGUINES' headgear called BEGUIN.

bilious
An irascible, acerbic person characterized by a surfeit of one of the FOUR HUMORS, black bile.

billet molding
Ornamental carved wood or stone horizontal finishing to NORMAN architecture or buildings utilizing that style.

billiards
(French *billart,* a short stick or log) The popular ball and cue table game, which, along with checkers, CHESS, and backgammon, served as indoor sport for courtiers and townsmen.

bird told me, a
A formulaic excuse for not revealing a source of information, derived from Ecclesiastes 10:20, or the folk notion that privileged knowledge often is transmitted through the secret language of birds learned by the human elect, as Siegfried discovered in the *Nibelungenlied*.

biretta
Originally a soft skullcap, it developed into the fashionable headdress for churchmen, professors, and physicians, a fine fabric hat built over a rigid hat-framework consisting of three or four panels topped by a pom-pom.

birth stool
An obstetric chair allowing the woman in childbirth complete visual and tactile participation in her babe's birth, gravity aiding the child's descent down the birth canal.

birth time mirror
A shining circle or convex orb reflecting the nocturnal heavenly bodies, depicting the exact astronomical configuration at a birth. Studied in GENETHLIALOGY, it was used for predicting astrological inheritance: physical, temperamental, intellectual, emotional, and professional.

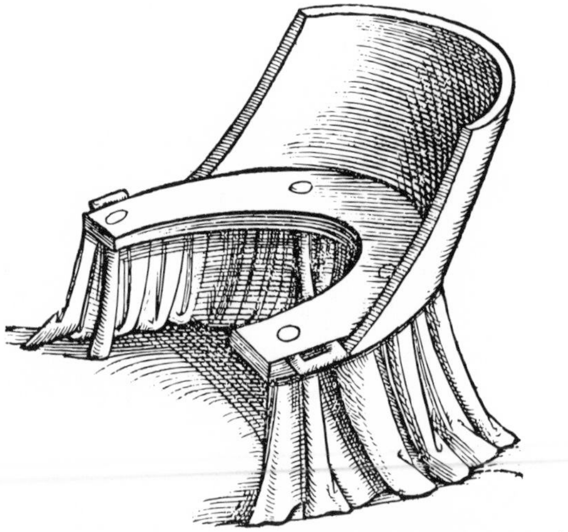

A birth stool. (From Jakob Rueff, *De Conceptu et Generatione Hominis* [1554]; courtesy of New York Academy of Medicine)

bishop
An ecclesiastical overseer or leader of a diocese consecrated by other bishops as successor to the TWELVE APOSTLES; his insignia are a MITRE and CROZIER.

black acre
Land growing peas and beans, unlike grain fields or WHITE ACREs. Black rent, *reditus nigri,* was payable in cattle, grain, and work.

black art
NECROMANY.

Black Death
A horrific outbreak in the fourteenth century of the BUBONIC PLAGUE that decimated parts of Europe, annihilated communities, caused one-quarter to one-third diminution of population in some states, and affected literature, art, economics, politics, technology, religious ideals, and human understanding of the spiritual condition. It was variously thought to be caused by God's wrath, by malign astrological conjunctions, or by Jews or other scapegoat pariahs. People attempting salvation of both body and soul indulged in extravagant self-searching and self-abuse, causing the flourishing of such rabid, mass hysterical movements as the FLAGELLANTS.

Black Friar
A member of one of the FOUR ORDERS OF FRIARS, the DOMINICANS, founded by Saint Dominic in the early thirteenth century, so named because of the black-hooded HABIT worn by regulation.

blackguard
A castle kitchen's menial helper, similar to the QUISTRON, charged with caring for (black) pots, pans, and utensils, and their removal from HOUSEHOLD to household; also, an army camp cook's itinerant helper.

Black Letter
A typeface in early fifteenth-century printing, also called GOTHIC or Old English, distinguished from (and later superseded by) Roman, the more popular type font.

black letter day
A Christian calendrical designation for a lesser saint's day, as opposed to a major festival, a RED LETTER DAY.

blackmail
Scottish for rent or tribute, paid in grain, meat, or chattel, as opposed to "white mail" required in silver coin.

black monk
A Benedictine MONK living according to the BENEDICTINE RULE, wearing the black HABIT as required dress from the thirteenth century on.

blanchet
In fashion, a woman's long outer garment, a type of DOUBLET, usually white, lined, and fur-trimmed; in textiles, a low grade, inferior wool fabric such as RUSSET, used for clothing by the poor.

blandreth
A pot or cauldron fitted to a tripod stand, or a three-footed pot raised above the coals of a kitchen fire or an alchemist's blaze.

blasphemy
Profane, irreverent, impious statements against God and holy things.

blazon
A heraldic device, ARMS painted on a knight's shield, appliqued or embroidered on his SURCOAT, painted or engraved on his helmet, or decorating his horse's CAPARISON.

Blessed Sacrament
Most holy of the SEVEN SACRAMENTS: the EUCHARIST.

bliaut
A long "unisex" overgown, often richly ornamented; the women's version was closely fitted at the bustline, with long wide sleeves, and slits at the sides to allow easy horsemounting; the male garment was worn beneath CHAIN MAIL.

blind gallery
An ornamental wall ARCADE blocked by walling or masonry.

A cook stirs a blandreth while another works nearby with peles on a shelf above her head. (From a German woodcut of 1507 by Froschauer; courtesy of Metropolitan Museum of Art)

blind story
A CHURCH's TRIFORIUM, dark and unwindowed, as opposed to the light-admitting CLERESTORY.

bloodletting
The popular technique for restoring balances among the FOUR HUMORS: PHLEBOTOMY.

bloodletting calendar
A PHLEBOTOMY calendar of seasons and particular days auspicious for bloodletting, indicating specific PHLEBOTOMY POINTS for FLEEMING, CUPPING, or LEECHING.

bloodletting woman
Describing the appropriate point for PHLEBOTOMY for specific diseases or injuries, a depiction of a nude female figure with indicated PHLEBOTOMY POINTS; similar medical-pedagogical female forms appeared as ZODIAC WOMAN and DISEASE WOMAN.

blue mantle
A HERALDIC name of the four PURSUIVANTS in the fifteenth-century COLLEGE OF ARMS in London.

bodkin
A long, sharp, dagger-like needle used by printers (an awl for removing long letters from set type), knitters, and threatened women (an ornamental pin for fastening hair and for self-defense).

Boethian
Pertaining to Boethius, the sixth-century pagan Roman counselor of Emperor Theodoric jailed on a false accusation of treachery and executed in 524. His influential *Consolation of Philosophy* (translated by King Alfred and by Chaucer) celebrated the unreliability, instability, and inscrutability of earthly FORTUNE, and the human fall from prosperity to misery in TRAGEDY. His famous treatise on music defined the THREE CLASSES OF MUSIC.

Bogomil
A Bulgarian Christian heretical sect doctrinally similar to the CATHARI and ALBIGENSES.

bole
A drab red pigment usually mixed with SIZE for attaching gold leaf to panels for painting, and to pages for ILLUMINATIONs and MINIATUREs.

bolt
The short, strong arrow of the CROSSBOW; later called a QUARREL. Also a sieve for flour and fine grains.

bombazeen
(Also bombazine) A twilled English fabric, a FUSTIAN, made of cotton or of cotton blended with wool or silk, dyed black for mourning.

bond
A fashion for arranging bricks, stone, or masonry in a wall, ensuring its strength or stability, with regional variations in design, as English or Flemish.

bonfire
From the pagan, particularly Celtic, bone fires and BELTANE FIREs built to celebrate MIDSUMMER EVE and other seasonal holidays, adopted into Christian festivals along with other sun-worship ceremonies such as the serpentine ROGATION PROCESSION.

bonnet
Like the BEGUIN, a three-piece head covering tied with strings under the chin; also, the fifteenth-century French sugarloaf bonnet: a particularly high-crowned man's cap worn over bobbed hair.

bonus socius
(Latin, good companion) A fourteenth-century manual of indoor games such as CHESS, dice, checkers, and backgammon.

Book of Hours
A popular prayer book containing specific prayers for the eight HORAE or CANONICAL HOURS: the psalms, prayers, hymns, and readings of the DIVINE OFFICE, usually accompanied by special groups of prayers honoring the Virgin (as the Little Office of the Virgin), Hours of the Cross, Hours of the Holy Ghost, penitential psalms, prayers to special saints, and the Office of the Dead. A lay person's BREVIARY, it was often ornamented with holy and secular ILLUMINATIONs, frequently the TWELVE LABORS OF THE MONTHS and astrological and astronomical decorations; for noble patrons, MANUSCRIPT illuminators provide personal compliments and political jokes in the MINIATUREs and BAS DE PAGEs.

boon-work
In feudal TENURE, the extra work upon a lord's DEMESNE, as at haymaking or harvest time, distinguished from WEEK-WORK. A wet-boon gave free ale and dinner; a NUNCHEON, a free noontime quench.

boost
A lift, push, or burst of energy, as to lever a heavy stone in architecture, to raise a collapsed wall, to hoist a knight in ARMOR onto his horse, or to metaphorically establish a POU-STO.

booze
(Dutch *buyze,* to tipple, or *buise,* a drinking mug; or Hindustani *bouza,* drink; fourteenth-century English *bouse,* to quaff) To drink deeply with aesthetic pleasure.

bordel
A brothel, as the STEWS and COCK'S LANE in London.

boss
A round, prominent projecting ornament in architecture, costumery, jewelry, or furniture.

botijos
A common kitchen jug for staples such as olive oil; used in pharmacies and markets for syrups, BALSAMs, and oils, usually crudely decorated.

Bougre
A heretic, a BOGOMIL from Bulgaria.

boujet
A water bucket, often represented in heraldic ARMS.

bourquinotte
A Burgundian BURGONET.

bourrée
A sixteenth-century French court dance consisting of skipping, crossing steps, and foot-stamping.

bowels of compassion
In PHYSIOGNOMIES, certain emotions, intellectual qualities, and incorporeal ideas were thought to reside in specific anatomical parts: in the brain or heart is the soul; in the liver, courage; in the bowels, mercy.

box stretcher
The set of braces or rails connecting and strengthening legs of tables, chairs, or beds. Other stretchers were flat, curved, recessed, hooped, scrolled, X-shaped, or BARLEY TWIST.

boxwood
A dense, finely grained wood resembling ivory in texture, excellent for minute carving and embellishments, important for decorative hair combs and extraordinary sculptured beads with secular and religious panoramic scenes.

boy bishop
A young boy elected on Saint Nicholas's Day, December 6, in English MONASTERIES, schools, and country parishes to perform church functions of a BISHOP, until December 28, HOLY INNOCENTS Day. Dramatically expressing the GOSPEL's reverence for children, this ritual similarly was celebrated in Europe, particularly Germany, on the feast of Saint Gregory the Great, March 12.

bozetto
A sculptor's small sketch in wax or clay, a preliminary model for the larger final work in durable material; a MACQUETTE.

bracket
An angled support, sometimes a small ornamental shelf or ledge, underpinning a sculpture or reinforcing a chair.

braes
Men's BREECHES.

Braggadocio
(Italian, braggart) A character used in ALLEGORY to represent the epitome of pomposity and vanity.

braguette
The CODPIECE of BREECHES.

braiel
A fabric or leather belt for holding up BREECHES, HOSE, or CHAUSSES.

branc
A woman's smock.

brandeum
A death SHROUD or winding sheet, the cloth of life's exit, parallel to the entrance fabric, SWADDLING BANDS.

bransle
(French *branler,* to sway) A popular fifteenth-century courtly dance either in double or triple meter of the "follow the leader" design, a type of BASSE DANSE. ORCHESOGRAPHY lists over two dozen bransles, including Burgundian, Cassandra, hay, official, Scottish, Maltese, Washer Woman's, hermit's, clog, candlestick, and horse.

brass
The bright golden or yellow alloy of copper and zinc in the proportion two-to-one; it is stronger, harder, and more malleable than copper and was the primary material for elaborate candlesticks, ceremonial objects, kitchenry, and banquet gear, often with jeweled adornments.

brassart
Art ARMOR.

brasses
Funereal memorial tablets set into the floor of a church or CATHEDRAL, engraved or EMBOSSED with effigies, inscriptions, and HERALDIC EMBLEMS.

bratchet
A lithe, graceful, swift hunting dog.

brawl
A raucous dancing party, developing from the elegant stately BRANSLE.

braye
A small fabric triangle covering the opening of men's BREECHES, removable and fastened with AIGLETS or eyelets, later developing into the CODPIECE or BRAGUETTE.

Brazil wood
A tree (*caesalpinia*), yielding a glowing, flaming red dye color, imported from Ceylon via Alexandria to Europe, important in the art and fabric trade for the production of red ink, purplish-pink Italian Humanist inks, rose colors for MANUSCRIPT and panel painting, and dark transparent reds for RUBRICS, later superseded by MADDER.

breacan-feile
A Scottish Highland costume of many yards of fabric folded, pleated, and fastened at the hips by a leather belt. The lower part formed the kilt, the upper was fastened over the shoulder by a BROOCH, the end hanging behind, and the PLAID was serviceable as a coat by day, a blanket by night.

breakfront
The front surface of a bookcase or cupboard interrupted, then continued on another plane, its surface raised or depressed more for ornament than for structure or function.

breast-plate
ARMOR protecting the breast; or any large decoration worn on the chest, as the bejeweled ATTRIBUTE of the Jewish priest Aaron.

breastsummer
A massive beam extending horizontally over a large opening, sustaining the superstructure of a wall or shop front.

breeches
Trousers of lengths ranging from ankle to short trunks, usually worn beneath a BLIAUT; also called PETIT-DRAPs or BRAES.

Breton literature
Referred to and imitated, but not extant, literature in a Celtic language related to Welsh and Cornish (spoken by fifth- and sixth-century immigrants to northern France fleeing from the ANGLO-SAXONs). It popularized the Celtic-British hero King Arthur, and influenced subsequent ARTHURIAN ROMANCE. The Breton LAI inspired Marie de France's LAIS and Chaucer's Franklin's and Wife of Bath's Tales.

breviary
A daily devotional book containing PSALMs, HYMNs, and prayers, often with ILLUMINATIONS and ornaments, essentially for clerical use; opposite of the BOOK OF HOURS for laypeople.

brewet
A hearty thick soup, similar to MORTREWS and stews, popular with townspeople and the nobility.

brewster
A professional woman brewer of ale or beer. It was also a MATRONYMIC: children of a male beer-maker take the family name *Brewer*; progeny of a female alemaker have the last name *Brewster*; similarly, BAXTER and WEBSTER.

brick-nogging
In architecture, a wood-and-brickwork partition, usually not weight-bearing, between vertical timbers.

bridal
A wedding celebration's communal ale party honoring the bride, the bride-ale. A married couple later attended a SCOT-ALE; if both were SANGUINE and pacific, they might BRING HOME THE BACON.

bride-man
(Anglo-Saxon *brydgume*) The bridegroom, whose female partner is the *brydwyf*, the bride-woman.

brigandine
An ingenious, triple-layered, lightweight ARMOR for foot soldiers, consisting of a sandwich of leather or cloth spread with metal leaves or scales. Brigands wore it in their companies, brigades.

bring home the bacon
A twelfth-century reward for marital felicity, a whole pig or side of bacon for the sworn testimony that the past year was spent without quarrel or regret at connubial bond.

brodequin
A light boot (derived from the closed Roman shoe, the *caliga*) worn inside heavier boots. Newly consecrated bishops, crowned monarchs, or the wealthy ostentatious wore them fashioned of richly ornamented stitched silk or velvet.

broderie
Musical embroideries interweaving voice ornaments and interlacing harmonic colors in complex fifteenth-century French POLYPHONY.

broigne
A rugged leather or linen jerkin strengthened by a metal or bone framework, popular with twelfth-century knights before the HAUBERK became principal dependable protection.

broken
Interrupted continuity or uniformity of line, usually altered in direction, the lines forming an angle, as in the neck of a LUTE, the handle of an APOSTLE SPOON, or an architectural BROKEN PEDIMENT.

broken pediment
An interruption or omission of part of the apex of a triangular space formed by the ends of a pitched roof. Later, a Renaissance architectural conceit embellishing facades of buildings, cabinets, coffers, cupboards, jewel caskets, and ornamental doors.

bronze
A metal alloy of copper and tin, stronger, harder, and more durable than BRASS and DINANDERIE; its colors ranging from silvery to rich orange-red, bronze is used for casting sculpture, and for liturgical and secular objects having heavy use.

brooch
In jewelry, an ornamental pin or clasp fastener for a cape or cloak. Chaucer's worldly Prioress wore one with a crowned "A" and the legend AMOR VINCIT OMNIA (love conquers all things). In archaeology, a thick-walled communal farmhouse with a tower-like stone building containing passages and chambers, common in Scotland.

brusttuch
A wide, fabric stole, falling loosely over the chest, usually bejeweled and decorated with pearls, cradling the hands as a muff.

buboes
Easily infected skin lesions resembling black blisters, characterizing the dreaded BUBONIC PLAGUE or BLACK DEATH.

bubonic plague
A dreadful infectious disease, differing in infection site from PNEUMONIC PLAGUE, characterized by raised dark pustules, BUBOES on the body, causing painful death to millions; its most virulent form was the BLACK DEATH, which reached its height of horror in 1348. Medical treatises, such as those by doctors Augustine of Trent, Geoffrey of Meaux, Gentile da Foligno, and William of Marra, suggested etiologies and therapies.

buccine
A straight trumpet or trombone, a wind instrument for accompanying dances.

buckled down to work
A metaphor for serious concentration derived from unbuckled ARMOR being unsafe at any equestrian speed.

bud decoration
A series of tiny projections resembling undeveloped flower buds or unfurled leaves, adorning architectural surfaces and MANUSCRIPT pages.

budge
A type of fur: either kidskin with the hair still attached or lambskin with the wool dressed outwards. Four-

teenth-century SUMPTUARY LAWS proscribed WHORES from wearing day- or nightgowns trimmed with minnever, squirrel, brown rabbit, hare, or any "noble budge."

buffon
A costumed, sophisticated sword dance, including such steps as the ESTOCADE and FEINTE, and related to the MORRIS DANCE.

bulldoze
To threaten or overwhelm, as with a bull pizzle as instrument of flagellation.

bun feet
The terminal ends of legs of a chair, bed, AUMBREY, or other furniture, resembling small, round, slightly flattened cakes.

burdon
A note of long duration sung or played on a musical instrument with a DRONE or pedal, as the low pitched bass course of a VIELLE and HURDY-GURDY which can be sounded continuously against a melody played on higher strings. Chaucer's scrofulous Summoner in *The Canterbury Tales* sang a stiff burdon to the effeminate Pardoner's high pitched melody.

burgonet
A bonnet-like metal helmet with nose and cheek protections, featuring an UMBRIL or brow piece as an eye protector, favored by fifteenth-century Burgundian knights; also called BOURQUINOTTE.

burin
A metal ENGRAVING instrument.

burr
In the INTAGLIO graphic arts process called DRYPOINT, the ridge cut by a needle or BURIN in the surface of a metal plate, creating in the print a soft, subtle line and varied tonality.

butler
The HOUSEHOLD servant charged with ordering, supervising, and serving from the butts or casks of wine, beer, and ale, as well as mixing the fragrant, healthful, spiced wines, such as HIPPOCRAS.

buttcap
The thickened end by which a CROSSBOW is held, usually inscribed or incised with a mark for shooting.

buttress
(French *bouter*, to thrust) A vertical masonry or brickwork mass projecting from a wall to stiffen it or resist an outward thrust of a VAULT or roof-truss; FLYING BUTTRESSes became more massive the higher the vertical skyward thrust of the GOTHIC CATHEDRAL.

buxom
Gracious, malleable, and willing; later, well-endowed in hips and bosom.

byrnie
A Northern European coat of body ARMOR made of metal links or CHAIN MAIL.

byrrus
A traditional, heavy, woollen cowled cloak.

byssine
A fine silk fabric.

Byzantine
The art, architecture, and cultural style of the city of Byzantium (rebuilt by Emperor Constantine I in A.D. 340 as Constantinople, capital of the Roman Empire), and its subsequent influence on the cultures of Venice and Ravenna, Italy, Syria, Greece, Russia, and other countries, until Constantinople's fall to the Turks in 1453. The style is notable for masterly MOSAICs on DOMEs and half-domes; exquisite ICONs painted via the encaustic method; ENAMELS, ivory carvings, luxurious silks; MANUSCRIPT ILLUMINATIONS such as the Homilies of Gregory Nazianzus, or the Joshua ROTULUS and the Paris PSALTER. Its decorative art emphasizes Christ as PANTOCRATOR, and graphically depicts Christianity's hierarchies. The BASILICA CHURCH, such as HAGIA SOPHIA, typifies Byzantine artistic control of monumental domed space.

C

cabal
From the Jewish mystical tradition, the KABALLAH, whose mysteries, symbols, and liturgies influenced various Christian thinkers and sects, a conspiratorial secret meeting.

caban
An early fitted coat with wide sleeves, probably derived from the Arabic *gaba,* and introduced from the East to Europe through Venice in the fourteenth century. Its sleeves were open under the armpit.

Cabballah
The Jewish mystical KABALLAH.

cabinet à deux corps
Two-part furniture, a chest or cupboard, the top section surmounting a stand or base with drawers and doors.

caboched
(Or cabossed) In HERALDRY, a full-face portrait of a horned beast, showing no neck.

cabochon
A convex or dome-shaped design element, as in the setting of a stone in jewelry, or a carved wood, stone, or metal ornament upon an architectural component.

cabriole
An exuberant dance or caper, the steps imitative of movements of the front legs of a rearing horse, probably introduced to court ceremony through horse ballets and CAROUSELS.

caccia
(Italian, hunt) A popular fourteenth-century Italian poetic and musical design, having both the subject of hunting and hunt qualities in the musical form, such as a two-part CANON in which "chasing voices" are followed by a CAUDA, itself often a canon. Melodies sometimes imitated HUNTING HORN MUSIC. Allegorical HUNTS OF LOVE provided elegant topics; the French CHACE and English CATCH are virtually identical.

Cacodemon
The astrological twelfth house, a malefic ZODIAC configuration.

cad
(French *cadet,* young) A prodigal, often mendacious young man, who via PRIMOGENITURE inherited little or nothing from his father's estate. Forced to seek money and career in the armed forces or the church, he had to make his fortune by his wit (as in the nursery tales of the Marquis of Carabas's *Puss 'n' Boots,* or Dick Whittington and his cat).

cadence
A GALLIARD dance step.

cadency
In English HERALDRY, a mark superimposed upon ARMS, flags, or BANNERS to demonstrate descent of various sons: first son merits a LABEL; second, a crescent; third, a MULLET; fourth, a MARTLET; fifth, an ANNULET; sixth, a FLEUR DE LIS; seventh, a rose; eighth, a CROSS moline; ninth, a double QUATREFOIL.

caduceus
An insignium consisting of two snakes twisted and entwined about a vertical rod capped by wings; the identifying sign of a physician, of the god Mercury, or of an ALLEGORY of Peace.

caesarian
A common obstetrical method for delivering a child from a mother with a narrow, injured, or deformed pelvis, via an abdominal incision at the midline or side. According to Pliny, Julius Caesar was so born.

caesura
A pause in a poetic line marking a phrase's end, or dramatic excitement or agitation; also, the regular mechanical division of stressed beats each half-line, as in ANGLO-SAXON verse.

caftan
A long-sleeved, unbelted outer garment made of wool, brocade, or velvet, usually longer than knee length.

cairn
A stone-rubble mound, either for burial, comparable to a BARROW, or for seeing afar.

caladrius
A white bird often depicted in medical MANUSCRIPTs, bestiaries, encyclopedias, and ROMANCEs of Alexander the Great, who found such birds at the court of Xerxes. Considered a prognosticator of death: if the bird turned its face away when brought to the hospital bed of a patient, it predicted death; if the bird gazed at the ill person, the patient would recover. Its gaze also cured jaundice. In the PHYSIOLOGUS, it typified Christ.

calata
A sixteenth-century Italian dance.

calcination
The metallurgical process of reducing a substance by fire to a calx, a powdered, friable substance. ALCHEMISTs purified metals by fire to separate them and to reduce them to "first principles" without destroying their essential virtues.

cale
A linen skullcap for men, fastened under the chin, worn under a hat. Without the chinstrap, it is a COIF.

caliga
A Roman leather shoe later developing into the BRODEQUIN.

calligraphy
Decorative, elegant handwriting with national and chronological styles.

calm
A thin, flat lead strip with grooves for close, secure fitting of pieces of STAINED GLASS in windows.

calotte
A thirteenth-century flat skullcap, of leather, velvet, wool, or cotton; by analogy, a cap-shaped sword-hilt or architectural VAULT.

caltrop
A viciously sharp-spiked, four-pronged iron ball, a military obstruction for horses.

Calvary
Crucifixion Hill, near Jerusalem, its name a Latin translation of the Aramaic word for skull (as in GOLGOTHA), upon which Jesus was executed on a central cross flanked by crucified thieves. In ICONOGRAPHY, the Calvary cross usually surmounts a triple-stepped platform symbolizing Christianity's THREE THEOLOGICAL VIRTUES: faith, hope, and charity.

camail
(French *coif de mailles,* mail hood) A CHAIN MAIL hood with buckled fastening worn over an iron skullcap in thirteenth-century England, covering head, neck, and shoulders.

came
A leaden strip of CALM.

Camerata
A group of distinguished musicians, poets, scholars, and artists who met in the palace of Count Bardi at Florence (around 1580) to establish a new monophonic style in imitation of ancient Greek drama.

camise
A long linen undergarment, a woman's CHEMISE.

camlet
A rich camelhair costume fabric, often woven with silk and gold, brought west from Asia Minor by twelfth-century Venetian and French travelers.

camoca
Figured-silk cloth, sometimes striped with gold and silver thread, its satin base with DIAPERING, like fine linen; it was so lustrous that a document in 1401 described the cloth as enamelled.

campagus
A popular BYZANTINE low boot worn until the CAROLINGIAN age: it was fitted above the ankles and laced over the instep.

campanile
A detached bell tower or BELFRY.

cana
A liquid-containing vessel, often used as a relic exhibited for the veneration of the faithful in celebration of Christ's miraculous conversion of water into wine at the Marriage at Cana (John 2:9).

canary
(Or canarie) A dance in 3/4 or 6/4 time, accompanied by CASTANETS, popular in England and France. Described by Arbeau in his ORCHESOGRAPHY, it was probably native to the Canary Islands or was a courtly imitation of "savage" or WILDMAN movement.

cancion
A fifteenth-century Spanish poetic and musical song style differing from the popular VILLANCICO by its regularity of verse structure, complementarity between metrics and melody, and courtly audience.

cancioneiro
A twelfth- through fourteenth-century collection of poems, often with musical scores, from Portugal and Gallicia, including the CANTIGA DE AMIGO, CANTIGA DE AMOR, lovers' laments, longings, and celebrations, and the satirical and bawdy CANTIGA DE ESCARNIO.

cancionero
A collection of Spanish court and folk songs.

candelabrum
An ornamental branched candle holder usually for multiple lights, such as the Judaic MENORAH and the hanging chandelier.

Candlemas
A Christian feast honoring the PURIFICATION of the Virgin Mary and PRESENTATION OF CHRIST IN THE TEMPLE, 40 days after birth, as required by Leviticus 12:1–4, celebrated on February 14 with an elaborate LITURGY and the blessing of multiple candles prior to the MASS.

cane
A walking stick, fashionable at various times in specific countries, made with or embellished by rare woods, ivories, or precious metals, and jewels. Eleventh-century France favored applewood bound by fillets of gold.

canel
Cinnamon, one of the most frequently used spices in cookery, literature, and medicine, required for confections of fruits, dredges for beefsteak, glazes for fish, and spicings of wine such as HIPPOCRAS.

canker
A pathological disease, such as syphilitic enlargement of the genitalia. Chaucer's Parson railed against men's fashionable short TUNICs because they exposed their genitals, revealing PRIVY members as if they were beset by canker or SAINT ANTHONY'S FIRE.

cannula
A surgical tube, usually made of silver or gold, for a TRACHEOTOMY or the draining of fluid from an abscess or organ.

canon
In LITURGY, it is the consecratory part of the ORDINARY of the MASS, beginning after the SANCTUS with the words "Te igitur" (You, therefore), and ending before the PATERNOSTER. In church hierarchy, a member of a CATHEDRAL's chapter or of a religious community, as an AUGUSTINIAN. In music, a round or ROTA, a polyphonic composition in which all parts have the same melody but each starts singing at prescribed different points, each interweaving and strictly imitating the preceding musical phrase: the fourteenth-century English CUCKOO song, *Sumer is icumen in,* is deceivingly simple, but others were as overtly obscure as RIDDLEs. Tinctoris in his *Diffinitorum* defined a canon as a display of the composer's intention—obscurely.

canones evangeliorum
CANON TABLES.

canonical hours
The eight times (at three-hour intervals) in the 24-hour day for required Christian prayer of the DIVINE OFFICE: MATINS, LAUDS, PRIME, TERCE, SEXT, NONES, VESPERS, and COMPLINE. Each hour's devotion consists of several PSALMs, CANTICLEs, readings, ANTIPHONs, and COLLECTs. CLEPSYDRAE, ASTROLABEs, and BELLS would tell the hours which mechanical clocks would strike and ring by mid-fourteenth century.

canonization
The Pope's declaration of the beatification and ordination of a new saint in the Church, conferring such honors as a listing in the catalog of saints, dedication of prayers, churches, and MASSes, artistic representations, and preservation of RELICs.

canon law
The rules and regulations concerning tenets of faith, ecclesiastical government, clerical discipline, administration of the SEVEN SACRAMENTS, laws on marriage, and holy orders. Compiled from early papal letters, DECRETALS, plus judgments of church councils and decrees of important BISHOPs, then it was collected, selected, and ordered in the twelfth century into GRATIAN'S DECREE. Later additions were made by Innocent III, Gregory IX (in his *Extravagantes*), Boniface VII, John XXII, and the COUNCIL OF TRENT (1545–63).

canon tables
Numerical tables of concordances among the FOUR GOSPELS, devised in the fourth century by Eusebius of Caesarea. The tables often appeared in biblical MANUSCRIPTS in HIBERNO-SAXON art set in arcaded arches, as in the GOSPELS of Lindisfarne and Saint Willibrord. Text harmony was symbolized in the TETRAMORPH.

Canterbury blue
An exquisite, vivid, bright blue STAINED GLASS color wrought by the twelfth-century glass makers of Canterbury Cathedral.

canti carnascialeschi
Fifteenth- and sixteenth-century Tuscan and Florentine CARNIVAL songs, similar to the FROTTOLA, VILLANELLA, CANZONETTA, and BALLETTO, designed for the elaborate court festivities of the Medicis and other nobility, full of contemporary caricature, ALLEGORY, allusion, and satire.

canticle
A HYMN sung in a CHURCH or SYNAGOGUE and derived from the Bible, specifically from the Song of Moses or the Song of Solomon; also in Christian LITURGY, the Canticle of Simeon.

cantiga
A thirteenth-century monophonic song in Gallician-Portuguese language, either secular or honoring the Virgin Mary. More than 400 *Cantigas de Santa Maria* reside in the Madrid Escoriale library MANUSCRIPTs. Collected for King Alphonso el Sabio, they are charming, pious, often irreverent, hyperbolic, and ingenuous, and accompanied by fine ILLUMINATIONs.

cantiga de amigo
A twelfth- through fourteenth-century Portuguese lover's poem celebrating and lamenting emotion; also called CANTIGA DE AMOR, and collected in a CANCIONEIRO.

cantiga de amor
A Portuguese lover's lament, also called CANTIGA DE AMIGO and comparable to the Provençal CANZONE.

cantiga de escarnio
A hilariously bawdy or realistically satiric Portuguese poem from a CANCIONEIRO, celebrating the body and sexuality.

cantilena
An element of GREGORIAN CHANT; also, a monophonic or polyphonic secular vocal work or dance song, such as a BALLADE or RONDEAU.

cantilever
A projecting beam, overhanging an interior or exterior space, often supporting a CORNICE or eave.

cantillation
Solo chanting; musical recitation intoned in SYNAGOGUEs for prayers and Bible readings, having such formulaic configurations as *moonath, sohf-pahsuk,* and *zakayf-gadol.* Christian solo PSALMODY is based on it.

canting arms
In HERALDRY, a device revealing the name of their bearer, real or pretended: the three medicine PILLS of the Medici Family later become an IMPRESA.

cantir
A pouring vessel, a pitcher or flagon for drinks such as wine, ale, or cider.

canto
A major division of a long epic poem such as Dante's DIVINE COMEDY or Ariosto's *Orlando Furioso.* The total number of cantos or lines often is numerologically or symbolically significant.

canton
A small territorial district.

cantor
In Christian church services, one of the song leaders singing solo portions of a CHANT sung by the chorus, the SCHOLA. In Jewish SYNAGOGUEs, the ordained singer of the liturgical songs and chants of the religious service.

cantoris
In an Anglican CATHEDRAL, the north or cantor's side of the CHOIR where the CANTOR sits.

cantus
A fifteenth- and sixteenth-century polyphonic melody, usually the upper or soprano line: the basic melody which the other voices vary and embellish. Of the three types—*cantus figuratus, fractus,* or *mensuratus*—each had exactly measured note values of different lengths resulting from the breaking-up of a long note into smaller parts.

cantus firmus
A fixed melody, the base of a polyphonic composition by adding voices in COUNTERPOINT.

canzo
The Provençal TROUBADOUR and TROBARITZ musical and poetic song usually concerned with love, consisting of many six-line or seven-line stanzas in a basically tripartite metrical scheme: two PEDES of the FRONS followed by the CAUDA. The French TROUVÈRE BALLADE and the German MINNESINGER BAR were essentially identical.

canzone
An Italian verse form of Provençal origin, usually made for singing, not reading, with elaborate metrical patterns, lengths, and precious subjects. Popular with thirteenth-century Sicilian poets and later Tuscan writers such as Cavalcanti, Guinizelli, Petrarch, and Dante, it was written through the seventeenth century. Serious lyrical disquisitions on love, such as Petrarch's, are predecessors of the MADRIGAL.

canzonetta
A short song, usually with three voices, light-hearted lyric, and jaunty melody, a type of CANTI CARNASCIALESCHI.

capa
A short, silk-lined, hooded cape worn by eleventh-through thirteenth-century women and men.

cap and bells
The jester's costume characterized by a cap with ass's ears that were tipped with silver BELLS, worn over a petal-scalloped shoulder cape. The fool's scepter-rattle was a self-mocking self-portrait: a miniature head, cape, cap and bells, the jester's ATTRIBUTE.

caparison
A horse's ornamental and ceremonial blanket or costume, worn with PEYTRAL, CRUPPER, and CHAMFRON, embellished with armorial DEVICES and ornamented with BELLS and fringes, for identifying its rider's HOUSEHOLD and rank, and ostentatiously affirming wealth.

caparisoned
A horse dressed in a CAPARISON for battle or ceremonial procession.

On a caparisoned horse, an armored knight rides to battle. (From a 15th-century woodcut; courtesy of Galeria Medievalia, Tenafly, New Jersey. Reprinted in *The Middle Ages*, ed. E. V. Gillon, Dover Publications, New York)

capeline
A small iron skullcap worn by military archers.

capital
A carved or molded head of a column important in all CLASSICAL ARCHITECTURAL ORDERS.

Capitoline antiques
Sculptures and other classical vestiges housed in the Museum of Roman Antiquities on the Capitoline Hill, Rome; one of the oldest municipal collections, it was begun by Pope Sixtus IV in 1471, and later ennobled by Michelangelo's design for the Capitoline Square.

Capriolz
(Or capriole) A young, ingenuous man desiring to learn dancing, he was a character in Arbeau's ORCHESOGRAPHY; also, a particular, rapid, scissors-like step in a GALLIARD leap.

capstone
A horizontal stone slab covering a stone chamber, or the crowning or top stone in an arch.

capuchon
A universal hooded cape, related to the CHAPE, worn long or short by secular men and churchmen. Its pointed hood later became the CHAPERONE turban with an extravagantly pendant tail, a LIRIPIPE.

caput mortuum
(Latin, dead head) The alchemical and metallurgical remains after the processes of DISTILLATION or SUBLIMATION, only for disposal.

carat
A measure of weight and fineness for diamonds, precious stones, and gold, from SAINT JOHN'S BREAD, a carob seed or a seed from a locust tree pod.

carbon-14 dating
A modern test for determining authenticity of medieval artworks. Because the radioactive component of organic carbon decays at a measurable rate from the death of the organism, its remnants in such organic substances as bone, wood, and charcoal permit archaeologists and art historians reliably to date artifacts and remains constructed of those substances.

carbuncle
A radiant red precious stone, perhaps sapphire or garnet (Pliny describes twelve separate types), possibly ruby, or a magical gem emitting rays of light in the dark. In HERALDRY, the stylized depiction of multiple rays from a center stone.

carcaille
The extravagantly flared collar of a POURPOINT or HOUPPELANDE, rising right up to the wearer's ears.

cardinal signs
In astronomy and ASTROLOGY, the two points of the equinox and the two points of the solstice on the

ECLIPTIC, matched with the corresponding signs of the ZODIAC: Aries, Cancer, Libra, and Capricorn, whose cusps coincide with the cardinal points of the compass: east, west, north, and south.

cardinal's red hat
A wide-brimmed, originally secular hat, tied by a cord beneath the chin, slung on the back when off the head. Apparently rarely worn but carried in ceremonial processions, after a cardinal's death his hat was hung above his tomb. Pope Innocent IV in 1245 asserted red as the color for cardinals, whose rank is defined by the number of tassels terminating the cords.

cards, in the
Expression referring to human fate predicted and the future divined by proper reading of TAROT cards. Propitious practical decisions, and felicitous actions were determined by celestial INFLUENCE, read, welcomed, or mitigated.

caricature
In literature and art, ridicule or satire by distortion and exaggeration.

Carmelites
A thirteenth-century male mendicant religious order, one of the FOUR ORDERS OF FRIARS, as the Brothers of Blessed Virgin Mary of Mount Carmel. They are also called WHITE FRIARS. Discalced or barefoot Carmelites, members of the women's religious order, were founded by the receiver of AMOR DEI, Saint Theresa of Avila, in 1562, reforming the fifteenth-century women's order of calced nuns.

Carmina Burana
The collection of songs of the GOLIARDS, the wandering itinerant scholars singing of life, love, chastity, drink, whores, sex, and obscenity. Texts and some musical notation were preserved in a remarkable twelfth- or thirteenth-century manuscript at Benedictburen in Bavaria.

carnival
(Latin *carnem levare,* to remove flesh or meat) Several days of dancing, feasting, and merrymaking preceding LENT. It was celebrated with SHROVETIDE plays, FASTNACHTSSPIELE, and MUMMINGS.

carol
An English song originally derived from a circle or round dance, with a BURDON or refrain. It might be either secular or sacred, as the famous *Deo gracias, Anglia* of King Henry V celebrating his victory at Agincourt, or a traditional Christmas song.

Carolingian
The eighth- through ninth-century art, architecture, and culture of the court of Charlemagne, crowned emperor ("of the Romans") in 800, characterized by a renaissance of classical learning inspired by Alcuin of York and Theodulf the Goth and pursued by Walafrid Strabo and Einhard. While churches were mostly BYZANTINE and ROMANESQUE in influence, new importance was lavished on the vast, multistoried WESTWORK, as the octagonal-domed Palatine chapel at Aachen, and churches at St. Denis, Corbie, and Reichenau. Monastic centers such as Tours, Metz, St. Denis, and Rheims created liturgical MANUSCRIPTS, such as the spectacular Gospel Book by eighth-century Godescalc, and others in Carolingian MINUSCULE, as well as the lively Utrecht PSALTER, the portable ALTAR of Arnulf, and magnificently carved ivory book covers.

carpe diem
(Latin, seize the day) To take advantage of the day's OPPORTUNITY, snatch life's pleasures, for the chance to eat, drink, and be merry is uncertain, but death is sure.

carpet page
A MANUSCRIPT page completely covered with intricate design, usually symmetrical, animal INTERLACE, and no text, significant in Irish, Persian, and HIBERNO-SAXON art.

carousel
Dance figures of fine intricacy and geometric originality performed on horseback, forerunner of dance choreography in BALLET DE COUR.

carry the banner
To identify the self or social class by a standard with a BLAZON, EMBLEM, pennon, or flag-identifying device. Fourteenth-century biblical translator Wycliffe described wandering rich beggars masquerading as poor, carrying banners, early signs for unemployment.

Carthusian
An important, purely contemplative, monastic order of hermit monks vowing silence. The order was founded by Saint Bruno in 1084 after Bishop Hugh of Grenoble had a portentous dream of SEVEN STARS, foretelling Bruno and his six companions. They built between Grenoble and Vienne the magnificent GRANDE CHARTREUSE, a typical CHARTERHOUSE with separate houses or cells for each monk, a common REFECTORY in which all abstained from meat and ate vegetarian, including the DONATES or lay brothers. The HABIT was a pure white COWL and gown.

cart of shame
A horse-drawn or person-pulled open cart for carrying malefactors through a town as demeaning punishment. Queen Guinevere imposed a severe test upon her lover Lancelot as an irrational SERVICE OF LOVE: to endure the ignominy of riding in such a cart as proof of his love.

cartoon
A full-sized drawing for transferring a design to a painting, TAPESTRY, FRESCO, or STAINED GLASS surface.

cartouche
An ornament in the form of a scroll, sometimes bearing an inscription or COAT OF ARMS; in HERALDRY, the oval ESCUTCHEON of the pope and churchmen of noble descent, or LOZENGE or scroll for a LADY.

carver
A banquet hall servant in charge of elaborate knife choreography requiring special cutlery and implements wielded in elegant prescribed fashion for dismembering particular animals at table: breaking a deer, winging a partridge, thighing a pigeon, and untaching a curlew.

caryatid
A female-figure-shaped column, supporting an ENTABLATURE.

cascardas
A sixteenth-century Italian dance in quick triple meter, similar to the GALLIARD.

casket
A small COFFER or box usually decorated by carving, painting, EMBOSSING, APPLIQUE, or ENAMEL, depicting COURTLY LOVE or HERALDIC themes, often celebrating a love affair. A casket was used to hold jewels, letters, and treasures, and to convey secret messages by ICONOGRAPHY if not by document.

casque
An armored defensive or ornamental helmet, with or without a VISOR.

casquetel
A light, open helmet without BEAVER or VISOR.

cassone
A large, rectangular, low storage chest for household goods, particularly linens and clothing. Preceding marriage, it was used as a "hope chest," the wood molded, bordered, decorated, gilded, painted, or ornamented with COURTLY LOVE scenes.

castanets
Small shell-shaped, hinged percussion instruments played with the thumb and first finger, to which they were secured by a thong.

castellated costume
A garment's decorative cuttings and slashings with square cut edges, resembling the CRENELATIONS and PARAPETS of castle towers. DAGGING made equally fantastical ornamentation.

castellation
Decorative BATTLEMENT or CRENELATION.

castle in Spain
(Or a castle in the air) An imaginary glory, a pompous lie. The phrase derived from a French expression for daydreams and airy promises, since a castle in Spain was not verifiable nor likely to come into possession when the Moors controlled the country.

catacomb
A subterranean burial chamber, often decorated with MURALS and inscriptions.

cataphract
An armored ship.

catapult
(Greek, to smash downward, penetrating a shield) A siege machine, a ballistic missile launcher for stones or arrows against enemy soldiers, city walls, BATTLEMENTs, or ships. It was also a mechanical contrivance utilizing a mathematical cube-root extractor, a brilliantly designed torsion spring and universal joint plus winch, as in the ONAGER and TREBUCHET.

catch
A popular English chase or hunt song, identical to the Italian CACCIA and French CHACE, the hunt melody and text in CANON form.

catechumen
A new convert to Christianity under instruction before BAPTISM, or one learning the rudiments of religion.

Cathari
(Greek, pure ones) A twelfth-century Christian heretical sect dedicated to spiritual purity, which, like the MANICHAEAN heresy, saw the world as in powerful antitheses: the kingdom of purity and light versus the kingdom of darkness and evil. The Cathari flourished in Germany, Italy, and particularly strongly in the South of France. Along with the ALBIGENSES, they were brutally persecuted by the INQUISITION and destroyed by the ALBIGENSIAN CRUSADE.

cathedra
The BISHOP's chair or throne of honor, authority, and office, housed in his CATHEDRAL.

cathedral
The significant church housing the BISHOP's CATHEDRA or throne; the major, usually architecturally magnificent, edifice, of a diocese.

cathedral wall
Usually structurally tripartite: a PIER ARCADE surmounted by a TRIFORIUM topped by a CLERESTORY.

cauda
A musical tail or cadenza to a song or instrumental composition. The TROUBADOUR and TOBARITZ CANZONE has a bipartite FRONS plus cauda, which Dante considered the ideal tripartite song configuration; in mensural musical notation, it was the vertical dash attached to certain notes or to LIGATUREs.

caudle
A fragrant, warm beer, ale, or wine mixed with spices and milk, served to the ill, to women after childbirth, and to patients' visitors.

caul
An elaborate headdress consisting of silken sheaths concealing strands or braids of hair, covered by a netting of reticulated gold or silver cord embellished with pearls, beads, jewels, spangles, sequins, or BELLS.

causewayed camp
A Neolithic hilltop encampment protected by a bank and ditch, the ditch several times crossed by causeways leading to openings in the bank.

cautery
The process of scorching skin or a blood vessel with intense heat applied by CAUTERY IRON. Particularly important for reestablishing equilibrium among the FOUR HUMORS, cauterization was recommended by Celsus, Avicenna, Albucasis, Caelius Aurelianus, and physicians of twelfth-century Salerno to eliminate "corrupt matter," prevent infection, stop hemorrhaging, and "comfort bodily members." Cautery figures, resembling VEIN MEN, ZODIAC MEN, or ASTROLOGICAL MEN, delineated CAUTERY POINTs for routine or medically required cauterization, according to regimes similar to PHLEBOTOMY or BLOODLETTING.

cautery iron
A long-handled iron heat applicator used for scorching, scarifying, and coagulating blood.

cautery man
A drawing, painting, or print of a nude human figure depicting the CAUTERY POINTs for medical administration of a CAUTERY IRON.

cautery point
A particular spot on the human body for application of a CAUTERY IRON for proper CAUTERY, graphically described in texts and charts containing a CAUTERY MAN. Points were associated not only with the diseased or injured part of the body but with the astro-

logical insignia influencing them and the procedure's propitious timing.

caveat emptor

(Latin, Buyer beware!) The legal doctrine that the buyer of merchandise or real property has responsibility to investigate it for imperfection and danger; also, the seller has no liability for negligent manufacture, transport, installation, or design, and there are no implied warranties of value, utility, freedom from defect, nor, for a house, habitability.

cavetto

A hollowed molding, in the shape of a concave quarter-round or quarter-ellipse, created from wood, stone, or metal in architecture, furniture, jewelry, and decoration. Each element in profile appeared as a circle's quadrant, and was often found in CORNICEs.

celestial kinematics

Solving intricate astro-mechanical problems by graphical representation of planetary motions. Part of the science of dynamics, it examined the laws and actions of motion in a system of material particles without reference to the forces acting on that system. It was practiced by astronomers such as England's Richard of Wallingford in the fourteenth century and John Killingworth in the fifteenth.

celestial sphere

The imaginary sphere on whose surface all heavenly bodies are projected. Earth is equidistant between it and the earth's center and the equator's projection onto the sphere, the celestial equator.

Celtic field

In archaeology, a small rectangular field dating from the late Bronze Age or early Iron Age, identifiable by a LYNCHET.

cendal

A silk fabric resembling taffeta, made in multiple grades of elegance from the shearest and most luxurious to the coarse and practical; used for the elegant gowns of noble courtiers and ecclesiastics as well as cheap cloak linings and painted armorial banners.

cendale

A Jewish woman's headdress required both by fashion and certain civil laws, such as in Modena, where women were forbidden access to town without the headdress, where it functioned as a JEWISH BADGE.

cenotaph

An empty sepulchre, a TOMB or memorial marker for a dead person buried elsewhere, or Christ's empty monument after His resurrection.

censer

A pierced vessel for dispensing the odors of burned incense, often swung from a hand-held chain. The aromatic gums and spices produce sweet or hypnotically pleasing odors for religious ceremony, medical FUMIGATION, and surgical ANAESTHESIA.

centaur

A mythological creature with head, trunk, and arms of a man joined to body and legs of a horse.

centum

(Latin, one hundred) The INDO-EUROPEAN languages: Hellenic, Italic, Teutonic, and Celtic, distinguished from the SATEM.

cephalophore

(Greek, head-carrying) A decapitated saint, such as Denis of Paris, depicted with his head tucked under his arm.

ceramics

Clay objects hardened by fire, including earthenware, stoneware, and porcelain, whose sturdiness and texture are dependent upon the degree of firing heat.

certosina

Bone or ivory INLAY on dark wood background, usually small geometric stars, triangles, CRESCENTs, and geometric patterns.

cestui que use

(Latin, he who has use) A right to use and obtain profits and benefits of land and buildings to which another person has legal title, possession, and responsibility to defend. This use without title essentially was abolished by Henry VIII's STATUTE OF USES.

chace

Like the Italian CACCIA and English CATCH, a French musical CANON concerning hunting and imitative of hunting horns, hunters, and dogs, each of two voices "chasing" one another in a ROUND.

chaffare
(Or chaffaire) In a market context, merchandise, goods, wares for sale; in a sexual, a woman's favors.

chaffer
A knife for cutting large bread loaves; in a PANTRY, it was generally wielded in association with a parer and TRENCHER knife for smoothing edges of edible bread platters.

chain mail
Flexible, mesh-like link-and-ring protective ARMOR.

chainse
A long TUNIC-like body garment, long-sleeved, tightly fitted at the wrist, and worn by men and women beneath the BLIAUT. Fabric, color, and decoration distinguished the social rank of the wearer. By the thirteenth century, this hemp, linen, delicate wool, or silk chainse shortened to the CHEMISE.

chainsil
A linen fabric for clothing, bed sheeting, and wall covering; a particularly fine variety was manufactured in Rennes in Brittany.

chalice
A footed drinking cup or goblet, with or without a lid, sometimes a double cup called a HANAP. In Christian LITURGY, the wine cup for celebrating the EUCHARIST used in association with the CIBORIUM.

chamarre
A long, wide, fur-lined, braided and decorated coat derived in the late fifteenth century from the sheepskin *samarra* of Spanish shepherds.

chamber
A euphemism for a woman's vagina, vulva, or Chamber of Venus. A "member of generation" that the Wife of Bath celebrated, as did the erotically ingenious FABLIAUX WOMEN, just as popular poetry spoke of the gentle COCK resting each night in his lady's chamber.

Sir Fitzralph wears chain mail from head to toe. (From a brass rubbing, Pedmarsh Church, Essex, England, 1320)

chamber candlestick
A popular European cylindrical candelabrum whose open sides to each candle socket facilitated the removal of candle ends for their recycling. The PRICKET was less practical for wax reuse.

chamberlain
The HOUSEHOLD officer managing the family's private chambers.

chamfer
A type of ornamental decoration utilizing channeling, FLUTING, furrowing, and grooving.

chamfron
A horse's head ARMOR.

champlevé
(French, elevated field) An ENAMELRY technique: a design hollowed out of the background metal, then filled with colored glass pastes, smoothed, fired, and polished, flush with the metal surface. Exquisite jewels and CHASSEs from the Maas region during the twelfth and thirteenth centuries used this technique or, alternatively, CLOISONNÉ.

chancel
The location of the main ALTAR in the eastern end of the APSE of a CHURCH, continuing the NAVE, after the CROSSING.

chancellor
A judge in a court of equity, the court of CHANCERY; called keeper of the kings's conscience.

chancery
A court established in England during the reign of King Henry V (1413–1422). A court of equity (granting injunctions and specific performance), as opposed to a court of law (granting money damages), it was presided over by a CHANCELLOR.

change ringing
Ringing of BELLS according to numerical, not musical, schemes by sounding all possible sequences of all bells (as for 6 bells, 720 strikes ring all possible changes). Such ringing announced CANONICAL HOURS, holidays, danger, celebration, birth, death, marriage, martial success, inauguration, investiture, and excommunication. Rhythm, pitch, timbre, and numbers of strikes were arranged by complicated sequential, sometimes symbolic numberings.

chanson
(French, song) A lyric poem for singing, the northern French TROUVÈRE musical equivalent of the Provençal TROUBADOUR and TROBARITZ *vers,* not the stanzaic CANZO. A rhapsodic song about love, and not in the style of a fixed-refrain (such as BALLADE, VIRELAI and RONDEAU); though seemingly simple it was mannered and often mathematically constructed.

chanson de gestes
(French, song of deeds) A French epic narrative of heroic deeds, usually having basis in fact but elaborated by legend and art, such as the *Song of Roland* or the *Song of William.*

chanson de toile
(French, song of cloth) A spinning song, the woman's answer to the CHANSON DE GESTES in which, generally, she lamented her ill-mating, unrequited love, and uneventful or perilous life.

chansonnier
A MANUSCRIPT collection of songs of the TROUBADOURs and TROUVÈREs, including biographies of some of the poet-composers.

chant
A short melody or phrase for singing PSALMs and CANTICLEs in public worship, having a long reciting-note to which an indefinite number of syllables are sung, followed by a rhythmical cadence. Musical intoning generally is either single CHANT sung to one verse of a psalm, consisting of two strains of three and four bars, each beginning with a reciting note, or double chant, which is twice the length of a single and sung to two verses. Both were derived from GREGORIAN CHANT and form one of the FOUR MUSICAL DIALECTS of the Christian church and its PSALMODY.

chantepleure
A jug-shaped watering pot perforated with holes to serve as a sprinkler.

chanter
A melody pipe, single or double reed, with finger holes, of a BAGPIPE, as opposed to the DRONE.

chant-fable
A composition part prose, part verse, part spoken, part sung. The charming *Aucassin et Nicolette* exemplifies this French dramatic genre as does Adam de la Halle's pastoral play *Le jeu de Robin et Marion,* incorporating the melody of a CHANSON DE GESTES. The German equivalent was the SINGSPIEL.

chantry
(French *chanter,* to sing) A BENEFICE for having MASSes said for specific purposes, or a small chapel containing an ALTAR in which a mass is sung either for the soul or another expressed intention of the benefactor endowing it.

chape
A variety of CAPUCHON worn to protect a person against the rain or a reveller against identification.

chapeau
Either an ordinary hat or a HERALDIC cap of dignity worn by rulers, made of crimson velvet and bordered with ERMINE.

chapel de fer
(French, iron hat) A helmet, resembling a COWL worn over a CAMAIL.

chaperone
A graceful headdress for a man, popular between the twelfth and sixteenth centuries, consisting of a turban wound upon a ROUNDLET and a long GARGET.

chaplet
A head wreath, usually a garland of leaves or flowers; or a circlet with gems; or a twisted cloth or padded roll holding a veil onto the head.

chapter house
An assembly house or meeting room in a MONASTERY or CATHEDRAL.

charge
In HERALDRY, a DEVICE on a COAT OF ARMS or ESCUTCHEON.

charger
A large serving platter fashioned of gold, silver, copper, PEWTER, DINANDERIE, or CERAMICS and ornamented with incising, EMBOSSING, painting, or jewels. It generally was displayed on an AUMBRY or HIGH TABLE.

charta bombycina
Early paper, made in Baghdad, Damascus, or southern Spain, manufactured from rags.

charterhouse
An Anglicization of French *maison chartreuse,* a CARTHUSIAN monastic building.

chasing
A decorating technique for metal by which designs were incised on the surface by PUNCHes, not by the removal of metal. Embossed chasing or REPOUSSÉE combined hammering part of the design from the back of the surface and punching the other part in from the front. In sculpture, the finishing after BRONZE casting: the chiseling, polishing, and removing of imperfections and seams left by the casting molds.

chasse
A box, case, or shrine, usually for saints' relics. Some of the most lovely are twelfth-century French ENAMELRY, either CLOISONNÉ or CHAMPLEVÉ.

chasuble
(Latin *casula,* little house) Worn by a priest, the outer-most liturgical vestment, the color of which depends on the church season or feast being celebrated. The chasuble was worn over an ALB during ecclesiastical processions and while elevating the EUCHARIST. Usually ornamented with a cross on the back and an embroidered ORPHREY, it is thought associated symbolically with Christ's CRUCIFIXION garment, or the all-encompassing VIRTUE of Christian charity.

chatelaine
An ornamental metal ring or chain from which personal and culinary necessaries were hung, as a sheathed knife, scissors, nail file, comb, tweezer, and keys; it was worn from a belt, GIRDLE, or chain slung around the waist or hip.

Wearing a chatelaine around her hips, a woman and her lover, wearing poulaines, sit on a curtained, linen-fold-backed bed. (From an engraving by Israel van Meckenem, German, 15th century)

chattels

Movable possessions and wealth, including cattle and capital, or anything negotiable owned; distinguished from real estate.

Chaucer's English

Among Geoffrey Chaucer's remarkable poetic and political achievements was the regularization of both pronunciation and spelling of English at the royal court and among the citizenry. Formidable regional dialects and speech variations made MIDDLE ENGLISH not one but many languages: the northwest Midlands dialect of *Sir Gawain and the Green Knight* and poems of the ALLITERATIVE REVIVAL; the Kentish speech of the *Ancrene Riwle*; the eastern Midlands or London dialect of Chaucer's *Canterbury Tales*; and the Scandinavian language variants from the DANELAW. Chaucer's contemporaries called him "the first finder of our fair language."

chausses

Lightweight colored or striped leggings worn by men and women. Knitted or woven of linen, cotton, silk, or wool, they originally covered only foot and leg, but later rose up along the trunk when short robes became fashionable; they are antecedents of modern tights.

cheap

(Anglo-Saxon *ceap,* to buy or sell; compare the German family name *Kaufman,* a merchant, with the English, Chapman) A market, ultimately naming its place, as in London's Eastcheap and Westcheap.

chemise

A body garment of soft wool or fine linen derived from an earlier long TUNIC, the CHAINSE, and ultimately shortened to become the shirt.

cherub

A chubby, nude infant or child ANGEL, often depicted in architectural decorations, FRESCO, painting, MANUSCRIPT ILLUMINATION from the fifteenth century through late Renaissance. Cupid, pagan god of love, was similarly represented as a cherub or PUTTO. The cherub is second in hierarchy of the NINE ORDERS OF ANGELS.

chess

The popular board game, as well as ALLEGORY for love and morality. Caxton translated and printed *The Game and Play of Chess* (Bruges, 1475), an instruction book on education, social etiquette, and the duties of nobility, a MIRROR OF PRINCES.

chester

(Latin *castra,* an encampment) A walled or fortified town.

chevaux de frise

Pointed wooden stakes or sharp stone obstacles for defense of a prehistoric encampment or fort.

chevet
A CHURCH's east end, including all aspects of the CHOIR, APSE, AMBULATORY, and radiating side chapels.

chevron
A *V*-shaped ornament, right-side-up or upside-down; or the rafters or couples of a roof, meeting at an angle. In HERALDRY, it is an ORDINARY in the form of an inverted *V*, one-third the width of the shield (an inverted chevron is an upright *V*).

chiaroscuro
In art, clear-bright elements are juxtaposed with dark-obscure elements, thus utilizing light and shade, white and black, or other opposing colors rather than multiple hues. In literature, clarity paired with obscurity, joining cheer with gloom, praise with blame, as in an OXYMORON.

chiasmus
(Greek, letter *chi, X*) Grammatical or poetic intercrossing. In chiasmus, the word order in one line or clause is exactly inverted in the next; or the first part of the first line must be read with the second part of the second line, the second of the first, read with the first of the second, thereby creating an "X" shape in their reading.

Chichevache
Having a scrawny or an ugly face. In Chaucer, it was the lean, ugly cow, a fabulous monster that fed on patient wives, and thus was always famished; the opposite was Bicorne, the fat contented cow, two horned and perhaps a CUCKOLD, that fed on patient husbands. Chaucer's "Clerk's Tale" sardonically reminds prudent wives never to let humility nail their tongues lest Chichevache swallow them in her entrails.

Childermas
December 28, the feast of HOLY INNOCENTS.

child marriage
For dynastic, political, and economic purposes, children were betrothed by their parents and wed early, often before puberty. In the twelfth century, a baby boy groom died and left his 10-year-old widow in the custody of her mother, who controlled her daughter's lands inherited in marriage as well as those of her 10-year-old married son and his wife, an heiress who owned a huge English manor by age five. Even unborn children could be promised in marriage. COURTLY LOVE might have interjected a true (or intellectual) amorous ardor into a love life otherwise determined by parental or civil politics.

children in domestic service
Noble families' children served in courts for education in domestic service as well as chivalric and courtly lore. A PAGE or SQUIRE in a significant household had opportunity for political and professional advancement: hearing politics at the table, meeting and serving the great, and learning the decorum of court. Sir Thomas Moore as a youth waited at table for Cardinal Morton, who predicted the boy would prove a marvelous man. Courtly food service was context for the education of many a ROMANCE hero.

chintz
A popular twelfth-century fabric imported from Persia or India, printed with a design and wax-glazed.

chi-rho monogram
The first two Greek letters, *chi* ("ch") and *rho* ("r"), of the name Christ (Christos). A common symbol on sarcophagi, liturgical vessels, and oil lamps, comparable to the ALPHA AND OMEGA and IHS ciphers. A sign or SIGIL similar to the chi-rho appeared in a dream of fourth-century Constantine before the battle at Saxa Rubra, the Milvian Bridge.

chiromancy
Magical divination by studying the lines of the hand, also known as palmistry.

chivalry
(Old French *chivalerie,* horseback warfare) The philosophy and practice of valorous service. Celebrating honor, TROTH, VIRTÙ, GENTILESSE, COURTESY, and COURTLY LOVE, a KNIGHT held land TENURE in exchange for his military service in ARMOR on horseback. Chivalric ceremony was expressed in the COLORS, COATS OF ARMS, and DEVICES of HERALDRY. Questions of honor and disputes of arms not subject

to the COMMON LAW were resolved by a COURT OF CHIVALRY, a *curia militaris.*

chivaree
(Latin, *charivari,* erotic music) Melodies and rhythms played as a wedding march to stimulate the consummate coupling of the bride and groom; also called SHIVAREE.

choir
The part of the church east of the NAVE in which the service is celebrated. Usually extending from the CROSSING to the APSE, it is also called the west CHANCEL. A pilgrimage choir contains an apse, AMBULATORY, and chapels, called the CHEVET.

choir book
An oversized music MANUSCRIPT or printed volume, with large notes and letters generally placed on a LECTERN or stand for a group of singers to read.

choir screen
A ROOD screen, or in BYZANTINE churches, an ICONOSTASIS, carved and ornamented, which separated the CHOIR from the NAVE.

cholent pot
A large, heavy, metal stewing pot, usually with a rim inscription and cover, for Friday's cooking of the Jewish Sabbath meals eaten on Saturday when kitchen work is forbidden. Cholent is a nutritious, savory, herbed stew with meats, vegetables, and fruits.

chorale
A sacred choral song. Luther's vernacular HYMNS, original or based on Latin hymns, Jewish melodies, or popular tunes and rhythms, typified worship in Germany's Reformed Church.

chouxfleurs
A TAPESTRY background of large rounded-leaved flowers, such as cauliflower or cabbage.

chrism
Olive oil mixed with BALSAM, consecrated by a BISHOP at the blessing of oils on MAUNDY THURSDAY, and signifying diffusion of divine grace. Chrism is used particularly for anointing at CONFIRMATION.

chrismatory
A sacramental vessel containing CHRISM and other kinds of consecrated oil utilized for BAPTISM, CONFIRMATION, anointing the sick, EXTREME UNCTION for the dying, or any other significant liturgical event requiring it. The UNGUENTARIUS or oil and ointment seller was an important figure in drama.

Christmas
The Christian feast honoring the birth of Christ, celebrated December 25 since the fourth-century Philocalian calendar. Three MASSes (night, day, and dawn) symbolize Christ's trinal birth: eternally from God the Father; humanly from the womb of Mary; and mystically in the faithful Christian soul. The holiday's merry-making festivities are derived from the Roman winter festival of Saturnalia.

Christophoria
(Greek, bearing Christ) A Christian feast-day celebrated January 7, the day after EPIPHANY, commemorating Christ's return from Egypt.

chronocrater
The ruler of time, usually the sun by day, the moon by night. Ptolemy separated human existence into the SEVEN STAGES OF LIFE, roughly comparable to the SEVEN AGES OF MAN, assigning the care of the first four years to the moon; years five to 14 to Mercury; from 14 to 21, to Venus.

chronophysica
Time medicine, the remarkable association among medicine, astrology, and chronometers, leading to the development of the mechanical clock from earlier measurers of time, such as the ASTROLABE, ASTRARIUM, PULSILOGIUM, and meters for pulse music. The propitious time for medicine or surgery was computed from figures derived from a patient's birth time, injury time, and the anatomical part injured or ill, accorded with the ZODIAC MAN and astrological configurations.

chronosynchronisity
TEMPORAL SIMULTANEITY.

chrysography
The art of writing in gold or silver ink on PARCHMENT, usually purple, a celebrated MANUSCRIPT tech-

nique for precious liturgical texts of the ninth through twelfth centuries.

church
(Greek *kyriakon,* house of God) The Lord's house, the building to house the EUCHARIST, the SACRAMENTS. The place where the LITURGY for the community and congregation is performed.

church modes
Formulaic configurations of musical tones in GREGORIAN CHANT, specifically octave segments of the C-major scale. The range is called AMBITUS, and the center tone is the FINALIS, of which there are six: D, E, F, G, A, C. The two sub-groups of six modes are the *authentic:* Dorian (finalis D), Phrygian (E), Lydian (F), Mixolydian (G), Aeolian (A), Ionian (C); and the PLAGAL, in which the prefix *hypo* is added to each of the six modes, as in hypo-Dorian.

church scot
An ecclesiastical tax also called the ALMS FEE or PETER'S PENCE.

ciborium
The usually elaborate and ornamented vessel for holding the consecrated wafer of the Christian EUCHARIST. It was often a lidded CHALICE surmounted by a cross FINIAL, but sometimes a box or PYX, or crenelated, battlemented tabernacle; also, the wall-tabernacle with a lockable door for housing the consecrated host.

cilice
A penitential hair shirt, the sack of sackcloth and ashes (Matthew 11:21), worn by public penitents from ASH WEDNESDAY until reconciled with the church on MAUNDY THURSDAY, or by monks, hermits, and pious lay folk during LENT, as intentional suffering in *imitatio christi* (in imitation of Christ) but worn by would-be saints as a daily garment.

cimier
A removable heraldic DEVICE or whimsical favor of COURTLY LOVE floating from or cresting a warrior's helmet; often a beloved's LAMBREQUIN scarf, an exotic bird's plumage, horsetails, sculptured animals, or miniature models of human figures.

cingulum
A priest's white GIRDLE or colored rope to belt his ALB when dressing for the MASS; also, a SYMBOL of abstinence.

cinnabar
A red crystalline form of mercuric sulfide, often associated with DRAGON'S BLOOD.

cinq pas
(French, five step) A basic dance configuration in the GALLIARD, five steps executed during six musical beats, also called the SINK-APACE.

cipher
A letter or group of letters such as the initials IHS, used as a literal or decorative device or monogram to identify a secular or sacred person or institution.

circlet
A headdress holding back the hair, consisting of a narrow band of precious metal, silken braid, flowers, or bejeweled fabric that a man or woman wore encircling the forehead between eyebrows and hairline.

circlette
A round, aromatic almond and cardamon finger cake with currants, topped by a dab of raspberry jam.

cire-perdue
(French, lost wax) The "lost wax" metal casting process: a wax sculpture is covered with clay to form a negative mold; molten metal such as BRONZE poured in melts away the wax, resulting in the final positive metal cast.

Cistercians
A monastic order based on strict interpretation of the BENEDICTINE RULE, founded in 1098 by Robert, Abbot of Molesme at Cistercium or Cîteaux. Saint Bernard, Abbot of Clairvaux, in 1200 founded the BERNADINES, a Cistercian branch; their devotion to sites marked by clear-flowing water appears in monasteries' names, as Clairvaux, Fountains, and Rievaulx. The HABIT is white or gray under a black SCAPULAR, thus their popular name, WHITE MONKS.

cistern
A water reservoir, such as at Cistercium or Cîteaux, the eleventh-century site for the founding of the CISTERCIAN monastic order.

cithera
A triangular musical instrument having seven to eleven strings. Derived from an ancient Greek instrument comparable to the LYRE or phorminx, it was often called ZITHER and sometimes played with a plectrum.

cittern
A pear-shaped musical instrument with a characteristic neck: the base side is thinner than the treble, allowing the player's thumb easily to reach around the nine strings in four groups or similar configuration.

civil law
A citizenry's laws and jurisprudence exclusive of questions ecclesiastical (under CANON LAW), martial (under a COURT OF CHIVALRY), and criminal.

civitas
(Or cantonal town) The administrative center of a Roman provincial local government. The civitas was identified by the dominant tribe's name, which was used in legal documents long after the tribes disappeared, as *civitas Andegavensium* or Anjou.

clandestine marriage
A hidden, but legal marriage. The simple pledge "I take you to be my spouse!" before one or two witnesses—or none at all—plus, if possible, an exchange of rings, was all the required ceremony for a civilly and clerically recognized conjugal union before the sixteenth-century COUNCIL OF TRENT required marriage performed by clerics in CHURCHes.

clarenceux
An English chief HERALD or king-of-arms who directed the funerals of knights south of the Trent River. Also the SURROY, his northern counterpart was the NORROY.

clarification
The liquefying of older, grainier, solid honey, heated to restore translucence and a syrupy consistency; conversely, solidifying honey that is too runny.

clarion
A stirring, thrilling, shrill trumpet call.

classical architectural orders
The three basic Greek styles, ranging from the simplest most restrained through the most embellished and exuberant: Doric, Ionic, and Corinthian. The Romans adapted and added Tuscan (a variation on the Doric) and Composite (Ionic plus Corinthian, extravagantly embellished). Standards regulated three essentials of public buildings: the stylobate, or the base; the column, or the structural pillar; and the ENTABLATURE, or the beams surmounting the pillars.

clausula
In the musical repertory of the thirteenth-century School of Notre Dame, a POLYPHONIC composition using as a CANTUS FIRMUS, a short MELISMA of a CHANT. It was a clearly defined, self-contained musical section; or a musical cadence.

clausura
(Latin, closure) Cloistered: said of nuns or monks restricted to their monastery or CONVENT and prohibited from communication with the outside world.

clavendier
(Latin *clavis,* key) A keyholder suspended from the belt, often a chain associated with a CHATELAINE or belt hook.

clavichord
A fifteenth-century stringed instrument consisting of a rectangular case with a keyboard whose hammers strike the strings to maintain pressure until they are released, producing an exquisitely soft muted tone.

clavicula
A small key; metaphorically, a short treatise, as on magic, such as the *Clavicle of Moses* or *Clavicula Solomonis.*

claw and ball
A decoration depicting the sharp-clawed foot of a bird or beast grasping a ball—a common footing to a CHASSE, COFFER, chair, AUMBRY, tub, or bed.

clepsydrae
Water clocks. Often combined with other devices, they were used as alarm clocks, table extravaganzas,

adult toys, and PULSE counters. Physicians, such as Hippocrates of Cos (fifth century B.C.) and Herophilus of Alexandria (ca. 300 B.C.) and others through the seventeenth-century, used these non-portable mechanisms that outdoors froze solid in Northern winters and evaporated in Southern summers. The guild of Cologne clockmakers created them in their special thirteenth-century market street *Urlogingasse,* and physicians practiced CHRONOPHYSICA with them. They were superseded by Giovanni da Dondi's CLOCKWORK.

clerestory
Windows near the ceiling in a room, hall, or CHURCH receiving light from above the roofs of neighboring buildings.

cleric
A member of the clergy who has received one of its EIGHT ORDERS. By the thirteenth-century, the term also described a graduate of a university, especially if teaching or holding an important position there, such as the official bookseller.

climax
The number 63. Numerological theory defined the product of seven and nine as important for events and human life: a person aged 63 was likely to endure yet longer; or a 63rd building stone was deemed the strongest and worthiest of embellishment.

clinophilia
Passion for beds. Some noblemen and women favored their bedstead, truckle, trundle, tester, balustrade, bed curtain, bed tapestry, trussing, or traveling beds. Favorite beds were transported from castle to town by servants called yeoman-hangers or bedgoers. England's King Richard III had bed manias. King Henry V bequeathed to the Duke of Exeter a bed of ARRAS, embroidered with scenes of hunting and hawking. The exquisite UNICORN tapestries, now at the Cloisters in New York City, may be such a bed hanging.

cloak
(French *cloche,* bell) A bell-shaped outer cape.

clockwork of Giovanni da Dondi
The physician, astrologer, and clock-maker Giovanni da Dondi in 1348 created a mechanical clock so gorgeous, complex, and dependable that it was known in its time as a wonder of the world. The device included hours, minutes, planets in their orbits, heavenly bodies in rotation, calendrical feast days, and dragon embellishments. An efficient ASTRARIUM, and more dependable than the manual ASTROLABE, the clock reproduced in a machine the regular, inexorable timing of the human PULSE. That rhythm itself was in microcosmic harmony with the heavenly spheres. The clock probably was medically required by the depredations of the BUBONIC PLAGUE, which necessitated that physicians use dependable timers for CHRONOPHYSICA. A facsimile runs in the Smithsonian Institution in Washington, D.C.

The astronomical clockwork of Giovanni da Dondi. (Reproduced in modern facsimile in the Smithsonian Institution, Washington, D.C.)

clockwork's second-hand

Timing seconds mechanically, the second hand though invented by John Fitter in 1665 had its first major application in Sir John Floyer's physician's PULSE watch, superseding Galileo's extraordinary PULSILOGIUM, and reaffirming the association between SPHYGMOLOGY and time technology.

cloisonné

An ENAMELRY technique in which thin wires are twisted and soldered to a metal surface to create small cells later filled with colored vitreous paste. The jewel was then fired, smoothed, and polished, yielding an exquisite, luminous work for either secular (as the love COFFER, CASKET, and jewel box) or liturgical (as the CHASSE, CIBORIUM, and PYX) purposes.

cloister

(Latin *claustrum,* an enclosed place) A covered walk for work, recreation, and conversation usually connecting a church with CHAPTER HOUSE, infirmary, REFECTORY, dormitory, and other monastic buildings; also, the part of a religious house forbidden to all but house members.

close

The precincts of a CATHEDRAL enclosing all its buildings, including the deanery, canon's house, REFECTORY, dormitory, and SYNOD house.

cloth of gold

A lustrous fabric woven with gold thread or wire with fine silk or wool. The Field of the Cloth of Gold near Calais was the extravagant meeting place for the courts of France's King Francis I and England's King Henry VIII in 1520. There, 5,804, people were opulently accommodated in hundreds of tents with feasts, musical and dramatic entertainments, and golden TAPESTRIES.

clout

A groin-cover, or a diapered fabric, either for an infant or for an agricultural worker.

clunch

Soft white limestone common for decorative interior carving.

Cluniac Reform

A powerful monastic movement founded in the tenth century by William of Aquitaine at Cluny in Burgundy, encompassing over 1,000 MONASTERIES by the twelfth century. The movement emphasized a strict interpretation of the BENEDICTINE RULE, personal spirituality, splendor of worship, celibacy of clergy, manual labor, repression of SIMONY, and efficient financial management of ecclesiastical holdings.

Clyde-Carlingford

Archaeologically important burial CAIRNs in southwest Scotland and northeast Ireland, with elaborate patterns of interior chambers and walls; a variation is the court cairn, often associated with medieval physical or architectural remains.

coagulation

A pharmacological process of solidifying a substance by evaporation or crystallization of solid matter from solution.

coals to Newcastle

To take salt to Salzburg or coals to Newcastle is to state the obvious or transport the superfluous, both cities being famous for their respective commodities.

coat of arms

Originally a vest or tunic with identifying insignia worn by knights over ARMOR or by HERALDs and by SQUIREs to identify their HOUSEHOLDs. It has become the heraldic DEVICE, BLAZON, ESCUTCHEON, or BADGE, the graphic depiction by SYMBOLS and COLORS of family, nation, or corporation.

cob

Wall material of unbaked clay and straw.

cobla

A short, single-stanza, thirteenth-century epigrammatic poem from Provence.

cock

The male chicken, an important BEAST EPIC and literary figure, such as Chaucer's magnificent Chaunticleer of the "Nun's Priest's Tale"; also, the familiar, rude title for a man's penis in FABLIAUX, ROMANCES,

Chaucer's Miller's and Reeve's tales, and popular poems, such as "I have a little cock," which spends its night perched in his lady's CHAMBER.

cockentrice
(Or cockatrice) A BESTIARY animal created by ingenious court cooks sewing the uppers of a baked chicken with the nethers of a roast pig. In HERALDRY, it is a hybrid monster with a COCK's head, wings, and feet on a serpent's body with barbed tail.

Cock's Lane
Name of the fourteenth-century London red-light district or whores' market, like the STEWS.

cock-sure
Perfectly, arrogantly dependable and safe. Possibly from the stop-cocks BUTLERS constantly checked to prevent pilferage and adulteration of wines or beers kept in barrels.

codex
A MANUSCRIPT volume or bound book, rather than a scroll or ROTULUS.

codpiece
A piece of fabric covering the opening of men's long hose or BREECHES, to permit urination, attached by buckles at the front. Sixteenth-century fashion made them large, stiff, and protuberant, useful for pocketing small cash and necessaries.

coeducational monastery
Directed by an ABBOT or ABBESS, a double monastic community uniting works and days of monks with nuns. Particularly important churchwomen such as Hilda of Whitby, Hersende of Fontevrault, and Eloise of Paraclete managed vast lands and finances, collected taxes and tithes, directed scholarly projects, organized SCRIPTORIA, arbitrated disputes on farms and lands, argued differences with rival ecclesiastics or with the Pope himself, established hospitals and clinics, and judged questions of LITURGY and miracles. Some abbesses were LADY BISHOPS.

coffer
(Or cofret) A small box or CASKET fabricated of wood, leather (usually CUIR BOUILLI), leather-covered wood, or metal, used for home storage of jewels, precious documents, and papers, or employed as a traveling case or security box for the business day's profits. Often elaborately decorated with painting, impressing, tooling, or APPLIQUE, secular boxes depicted scenes of COURTLY LOVE and literary ROMANCE; love-treasure boxes, called MINNEKASTCHEN, served to convey or preserve love tokens as well as to offer by iconographic decorations an invitation to seduction.

coffering
Decorative or structural recessed paneling in ceilings, domes, or VAULTS.

cog
A single-masted, square-sailed ship with a round, raised prow and raised stern, particularly popular in England and Scandinavia, along with the DROMOND and GALLEY.

cognizance
A DEVICE, BADGE, or token identifying retainers of a noble HOUSEHOLD.

coif
A close-fitting cap made of linen and worn beneath a helmet or hood. It was essentially a CALE without its chin strap.

coilles
A FABLIAUX term for testicles.

coillions
Testicles. Though Chaucer's eunuch Pardoner might be "a gelding or a mare," the furious Host of the *Canterbury Tales'* pilgrimage requested the clergyman's testicles in order to cut them off for enshrining in hog's turd.

cointise
A scarf or fabric favor, worn from the peak of a lady's headdress such as a HENNIN, or provided for her knight to display on his jousting helmet as a CIMIER. It was a COURTLY LOVE token as well as heraldic insigne, and sometimes called a LAMBREQUIN.

cokenay
An effeminate man, a homosexual. In Chaucer's "Reeve's Tale," the Cambridge University student, John, feared to be thought one, so while his companion lustily SWYVEs the miller's daughter, he leaps upon her willing mother.

colise
In HERALDRY, a particularly narrow BEND.

collar-beam
A wooden connecting beam joining the mid-points of sloping rafters of a pitched roof.

collect
A short prayer within the rite of the EUCHARIST and usually part of the DIVINE OFFICE recited during the CANONICAL HOURS. It consists of an invocation, petition to God, and a celebration of divine glory.

college of arms
Chartered by England's King Richard III in 1484, and headed by an Earl Marshal. There are three kings-of-arms (GARTER, CLARENCEUX, NORROY); six HERALDs (Lancaster, Somerset, Chester, Richmond, Windsor, York); and four PURSUIVANTs (Rouge Croix, Rouge Dragon, PORTCULLIS, BLUE MANTLE).

collyrium
A salve, ointment, liquid, or semi-liquid medicinal remedy, particularly for the eyes, often made with egg white.

colonnade
A row of columns.

colors
In HERALDRY, the accepted pigments and hues in emblems, DEVICEs, and flags. There were six TINCTURES: blue (AZURE), red (GULES), green (vert), purple (purpura), sable (black), orange (TENNE); two METALS: silver (ARGENT) and gold (or) and FURS: ERMINE and VAIR. LITURGICAL COLORS governed CHURCH decoration and SUMPTUARY LAWS affected color in costume.

colt's tooth
Youthful exuberant sexuality. Chaucer's Wife of Bath admires what she herself possesses: "I always have had a colt's tooth."

combust
In astronomy and ASTROLOGY, a planet is combust when closest to the sun. Its INFLUENCE is considered weakened, burnt up or destroyed, or, conversely, strengthened and enhanced, depending upon the planet's nature. Scorpio, for example, is a perilous ZODIAC sign because of the VIA COMBUSTA.

comet
A celestial body (bright star-like nucleus followed by a train-of-light tail) thought to INFLUENCE or presage great events in the earth, atmosphere, and affairs of human beings. Epidemics and PLAGUES, an individual's accidents and diseases, and natural cataclysms were associated directly with a comet's appearance.

comitatus
A band of warriors joined by mutual obligations and privileges to one another and to their leader. Described by Tacitus in his *Germania,* the comitatus is thought to have inspired the medieval feudal association between LORD and VASSAL.

commanding signs
Six ZODIAC SIGNS: Aries, Taurus, Gemini, Cancer, Leo, and Virgo; opposite of the OBEYING SIGNS.

commedia dell'arte
Itinerant sixteenth-century Italian theatrical troupes that performed improvisations on formulaic situations (the love triangle, intelligent fool's revenge, pompous physician's folly) with stock characters (SENEX AMANS—the old lover; MILES GLORIOSUS—the braggart soldier) and Harlequin, Columbine, and PANTALOON.

common law
In England, the body of customary law based on decisions of the common-law courts, especially the King's Bench, Exchequer, and Court of Common Pleas. Doctrine is determined by judicial decisions or precedents, rather than by the CIVIL LAW system. For certain matters it was opposed in jurisdiction to CANON LAW of the church.

common profit
(Or commonweal) The good of the realm: family, nation, or humankind. The self must be subservient to the larger communal benefit.

communion
The rite creating a spiritual union between a Christian and Christ by celebrating the EUCHARIST, commemorating Christ's LAST SUPPER, the eating of the spiritual food of souls: "He that eateth me, the same also shall live by me." It is one of the SEVEN SACRAMENTS.

comparisons are odious
John Lydgate said this around 1430, before Shakespeare's Dogberry misappropriated it in *Much Ado About Nothing* as "comparisons are odorous."

Compendium Salernitanum
A twelfth-century HERBAL listing culinary and medicinal plants, compiled by Johannes Platearius, and incorporating works from classical predecessors and his contemporaries at the medical school of Salerno in southern Italy.

complaint
A despondent lover's song of love's sorrow, or an injured being's poetic lament on the world's cruelty.

compline
(Latin *completorium,* completion) One of the eight CANONICAL HOURS, the last night prayer, concerning sleep and awakening, death and life, sin and grace.

comptoir
A counting house; a merchant settlement, or trading post for foreign merchants, often allowed privileges by local rulers, including jurisdiction of its officials over their compatriots.

computus
The calculation of the calends, new moons, and tables of lunar and solar cycles, in order to list fixed holy days as CHRISTMAS and to determine moveable feasts as EASTER, and other FEAST AND FAST days of the liturgical year.

con
Like QUEYNT, a FABLIAUX word for vagina; some TROUBADOURS suffer from AMOR DE CON.

Conceptio Christi
A Christian feast celebrating the actual moment of incarnation of God the Son, when ARCHANGEL Gabriel announced to Mary that Christ will be born; also known as the ANNUNCIATION, according to Luke.

conception time mirror
A glass mirror or polished metal orb reflecting the constellation of the moon and stars in the night sky, depicting the ideal astrological moment for sexual intercourse so as to produce a perfect heir with specific physical and spiritual characteristics. The child's birth would be reflected in a BIRTH TIME MIRROR, the computations guided by GENETHLIALOGY.

conductus
(Latin *conducere,* to lead or escort) A twelfth- or thirteenth-century metrical Latin song either monophonic or POLYPHONIC. A counterpart of TROUBADOUR and TROUVÈRE form, it could be religious, contemplative, lyrical, political, or satirical, perhaps derived from liturgical rhymed TROPEs accompanying the priest's entrance.

confession
A penitential acknowledgment of sin in private or in public worship; or a martyr's profession of faith; or a martyr's tomb or a relic-holding crypt, as the Vatican's *confessio* of Saint Peter.

confirmation
One of the SEVEN SACRAMENTS: a baptized believer is anointed with CHRISM and so receives the HOLY GHOST in affirmation of faithfulness to Jesus Christ.

conge
A dance movement involving a bow when taking leave of a lady partner.

conical
A geometric figure in the shape of a cone.

consecration
The solemn act of dedicating to the service of God a person, such as a PRIEST or BISHOP, or an otherwise secular object, such as a newly built altar or CHURCH; a central prayer of the EUCHARIST service celebrating TRANSUBSTANTIATION.

consideration
Money or valuable goods paid in return for a promise in a legal contract.

console
A curved bracket, often more ornamental than weight-bearing, generally surmounted by a CORNICE or full ENTABLATURE; or a martyr's tomb or relic chamber, beneath an ALTAR, with a grill so that pilgrims can touch the RELIQUARY.

constable
(Latin *comes stabili,* count of the cavalry stable) A military commander-in-chief, later a hereditary title.

Constantine's cure
Fourth-century Roman Emperor Constantine the Great, suffering from leprosy, which was supposedly curable only by innocent children's blood, was BAPTIZED by Pope Sylvester. Constantine's conversion ended persecution of Christians.

continenza
In fifteenth- and sixteenth-century dance, a simple, elegant side step, the heel of one foot placed against the instep or middle of the other.

contrafactum
(Latin, made instead) A song whose original text was replaced by another, a sacred by a secular, or a bawdy by a divine. TROUBADOURS, TROUVÈRES, and MINNESINGERS used contrafacta, usually liturgical melodies with a popular love text, or a panegyric praise of a virgin on a melody once dedicated to the Virgin.

contrapasso
An Italian dance step, performed in reverse; also, a dance containing such steps.

contraposto
The artistic ideal of harmonious balance in portraying a sculptured standing figure, usually poised with its weight on one leg (the engaged limb), the vertical axis of the body assuming a modified "S" curve.

convent
The building housing a religious community of at least 12, obeying some rule other than the monastic; MENDICANT FRIARS usually live in convents, not MONASTERIES.

conversion
A French dance term, referring to a change in the direction of the PAVAN.

cope
Originally a secular, hooded rain cape. In ecclesiastical VESTMENTS, a semi-circular, armless, hoodless cape or CLOAK worn over the ALB by priests and bishops. Designed from silk, brocade, or embroidered fabric, it fastened by a BROOCH or MORSE. The cape often was ornamented with an ORPHREY and imitation hood.

Copernican revolution
The heliocentric (sun-centered) scheme of the universe discovered by the Polish astronomer Copernicus. It overturned the dominant PTOLEMAIC geocentric system, thereby affecting science, theology, art, and ideas of humankind's place in the GREAT CHAIN OF BEING.

coping
Brick, stone, or masonry "capping" or finishing for a wall or architectural edge for protection against weathering, breakage, or accident, or simply for ornament.

Coptic
The culture of Egyptian Christians, from approximately the third through the twelfth centuries. The name derives from an Arabic variation of the Greek term for Egypt. One Egyptian CRUCIFORM hieroglyph is a T-shape surmounted by an oval loop, which inspired the Coptic CROSS.

copyhold
A TENURE right to use land and buildings granted by the will of the overlord; a customary ESTATE IN LAND visibly verifiable by copies of court rolls.

coranto
(Italian *correre,* to run) A popular dance in England, and later a favorite of France's Louis XIV. Originally an Italian step danced double time or to a rapid, gliding triple time: ". . . danced with pliant movement of the knees, recalling a fish plunging lightly through the water and returning suddenly to the surface."

corbel
A horizontal supporting projection from a wall, column, or chimney, often carved or shaped in geometric, animal, or human form.

cordovan
Soft, fine-grained goat skin leather from Cordova, Spain, used for clothing, shoes, wall covering, furniture, and jewel boxes. Supple yet strong, it was often painted, gilded, or embroidered.

corduroy
(French *cord du roi,* cloth of the King) A cotton or silk velvet with raised ridge wales, narrow or wide, yielding a ribbed, variegated surface.

Corinthian column
Of the CLASSICAL ARCHITECTURAL styles, the one with the most elaborate base, shaft, CAPITAL, and ENTABLATURE, the capital generally embellished by tendrils, fan-shaped palm-leaf ornaments, and VOLUTES emerging from ACANTHUS leaves.

corn
Any grain such as wheat, oats, or barley, but not New World maize (corn).

cornage
(Latin, *cornus,* horn) English land TENURE giving land in return for the holder's readiness to blow a horn of alarm to alert local people to danger, a form of grand sergeanty.

cornalia
For women, a pointed stiff veil or headdress resembling a horn; or a double-horned hat. The HENNIN evolved from the simpler ORALIA, in Germany called the FLIEDER or RIESE.

cornetto
A wooden, ivory, or leather musical wind instrument, a curved horn topped by a trumpet-like mouthpiece, fingered like a RECORDER; also called a ZINK.

cornice
A projecting upper section of an ENTABLATURE, more for decoration than structural integrity; or a convex molded projection at the joining of a roof and wall.

cornucopia
The legendary horn of plenty containing wondrous variety of the world's agricultural bounty which resulted from divine gift as well as humankind's careful husbandry.

coronach
Irish stylized funereal lamenting, moaning, and keening.

coronation of Our Lady
Christ's crowning of the Virgin Mary in heaven, one of the SEVEN JOYS OF THE VIRGIN.

coroner
Since the twelfth century, an officer administering the private property of the English crown, the *custos placitorum coronae* (guardian of the crown's pleas) or the inquest officer who investigated the bodies of those dead by accident or violence. After 1194, women and men "searchers" interviewed witnesses and suspects, examined the cadaver, and performed proto-autopsies.

corposant
SAINT ELMO'S FIRE, that dramatic display of static electricity adorning mastheads and yardarms of tall ships.

Corpus Christi
(Latin, the Body of Christ) Reference to the EUCHARIST as well as the feast celebrating the EUCHARIST. Observed on the Thursday after TRINITY SUNDAY, the festivities included ecclesiastical spectacles, processions, pageants, and plays.

corrody
The privilege of room and board in a MONASTERY allowed to benefactors or those who purchased goods from the monastery.

corset
A closely-fitting underbodice of canvas or CUIR BOUILLI worn by men and women, strutted by wood or bone stays, and laced to diminish waistline size; sometimes, a woman's gown, tightly laced and fur-lined.

Cosmic Mind
God, imagined as the universal sphere, a circle's perfect concentricities of spirit, mind, and matter, radiating from its exemplary center.

cosmological diagram
A circular design demonstrating the world's unities of FOUR ELEMENTS, TWELVE SIGNS OF THE ZODIAC,

FOUR AGES OF HUMANKIND, four seasons, and FOUR CONTRARIES (heat, cold, moisture, dryness).

costrel
A covered, fluid-holding vessel similar to a canteen, flat on one side to nestle nicely against the body, made of wood, leather, or earthenware, often painted and decorated.

cotehardie
A long, close-fitting overgarment for men and women, held by a hip GIRDLE or belt, usually tight-sleeved, embellished with buttons from elbow to pinkie finger. Its high neck was usually secured by a drawstring.

cotelette
In Germany, a popular sleeveless, open-sided overdress worn without a belt by young girls and unmarried women; also similar to a SUCKENIE or SARGENES.

cotteron
The short, standard, utilitarian peasant smock ranging in length according to climate and season from an astonishingly short mini-shift to a long commodious APRON.

cotyla
The physician Sanctorious's primitive timing device for measuring PULSE rate, a hand-held pendulum clock, modelled after Galileo's PULSILOGIUM.

couchant
In HERALDRY, an animal lying on its belly, its legs and paws extended forward and head lifted, as opposed to DORMANT.

couching for cataract
A medical technique utilizing chemical drops and surgical scalpels to depress the opaque lens of the eye, in order to avoid blindness from cataracts.

Council of Ephesus
The fifth-century ecclesiastical meeting of Greek and Roman bishops in Asia Minor. They condemned as heresy the NESTORIANS' claim of Christ's dual nature and their rejection of the Virgin Mary as Mother of God, THEOTOKAS. Confirmation of Mary's title led to extravagant portraiture of the Virgin as MATER MARIA DEI (Mary, mother of God) and SANCTA DEI GENETRIX (holy mother of God), which became an incentive to MARIOLATRY.

Council of Nicea
The church conclave in 787 (Second Council of Nicea), asserting ecclesiastical rules for artistic representation of religious themes and subjects.

Council of Trent
An ecumenical council of the Roman Catholic Church for solving problems of dogma, liturgy, ecclesiastical government and discipline, and matters of state raised by the Protestant Reformation. With interruptions and postponements caused by PLAGUE and politics, it met in 1545–47 under Paul III, in 1551–52 under Julius III, and in 1562–63 under Pius IV. The Council issued dogma and decrees pertaining to ORIGINAL SIN, the SEVEN SACRAMENTS, BAPTISM, TRANSUBSTANTIATION, veneration of relics and images, invocation of saints, INDULGENCES, MARIOLATRY, the index of forbidden books (INDEX LIBRORUM PROHIBITORUM), regulation of FEASTS AND FASTS, and other controversies of CANON LAW.

counter
In HERALDRY, the CHARGES or figures placed in opposing or reversed position or COLOR: counter-changed, a charge with COLORS reversed; counter-barry, the bars counter-changed; counter-bendy, the BENDs formed of two halves of different colors; counter-flory, or ordinary with paired flowers on opposite side; counter-passant, two animals passing in opposite direction; counter-salient, two animals leaping in opposite directions.

counterpoint
Instrumental and vocal POLYPHONY.

counterscarp
A narrow earth bank on the outer wall or slope of a defensive ditch.

counter tenor
A male alto singer, the name derived from the technical expression, *contratenor altus,* found in a fifteenth-century four-part song. The quality and pitch represent the highest male vocal range.

coup de pied
A GALLIARD dance step resembling a violent kick.

courante
An exuberant courtly French dance that Arbeau's ORCHESOGRAPHY described as jumping movements. Its evolutions and embellishments varied according to the dancer's ability and fancy; its shifting meters, rhythmically unstable, danced to 3/2 or 6/4 time.

Courteous Spaniard
Saint Lawrence, a deacon in Rome who was beheaded under Valerian. According to legend, he rolled over in his grave to make room for the bones of Saint Stephen, buried in 415.

courtesy
The obligation of courtiers to behave ethically and elegantly, protecting the poor, the helpless, and the disenfranchised, and to attempt to establish in the court or city of mankind the ideal Christian ethics of the city of God. In *specula principis* or MIROIRS DE PRINCES, the good courtiers' rights and privileges were balanced by responsibilities and obligations of courtliness. It is sometimes confused with CURTESY.

courtly love
Inherent suffering derived from the sight or contemplation of the dearly beloved, an affection inspiring intellectual vigor and martial prowess, or, conversely, causing confusion, forgetfulness, and life-threatening loss of appetite, sleep, and lust for living. In the realm of twelfth-century Queen Eleanor of Aquitaine, Andreas Capellanus analyzed this love in his *Art of Courtly Love*. As literary conceit or as life's MIMESIS of art, courtly lovers almost invariably were adulterers, the married dame or DOMNA of higher social rank than the lover, requiring from him self-sacrificing SERVICE OF LOVE, and necessitating the personnel and stratagems of secrecy: SENJAL, duenna, and DOG-COMPANION, so that the jealous husband, the JALOUX, would not learn from the court scandal-mongers, the LOZENGIERS, about the illicit affair, be it cerebral, sexual, or AMOR DE LONH.

court of chivalry
Called the *curia militaris*, or military court, this was a heraldic court, instituted in the late fourteenth century in England and France, under a CONSTABLE and earl marshal for adjudicating military matters and questions of ARMS. It followed CIVIL LAW, particularly Bartolist ideas (BARTOLISM), as in his treatise *De insigniis et armis*.

court of love
Juridical DEBATE on the propriety of COURTLY LOVE relationships and specific amorous actions. As intellectual exercise and amusement, noble courtiers, particularly women, argued fine points of sexual politics. Vestiges exist in Andreas Capellanus' *Art of Courtly Love* and Chaucer's "Wife of Bath's Tale" (in which a noble knight of King Arthur's court raped a maiden; the judge, Queen Guinevere, imposed upon him the punishment of answering the MASTERY QUESTION and discovering "what women most desire" or else suffer decapitation for sexual perfidy. His answer that women desire mastery over men satisfied the court and saved his head).

cove
A concave molding, as at the juncture between a wall and a ceiling.

coverchief
(French *couvre chef*, headcover) A fabric headdress piled or wound, sometimes fastened beneath the chin and crowned with a standing starched band. Chaucer's Wife of Bath's exuberant headgear weighed nearly 10 pounds.

coward
A heraldic beast with its tail beneath its legs. The name possibly was derived from the timorous, undependable rabbit, Coart, of the BEAST EPICS *Reynard the Fox* and *Ysengrimus*.

cowl
A monk's hooded garment.

cracelle
A cog rattle or ratchet noisemaker twirled on ceremonial occasions in CHURCHes in place of BELLS during HOLY WEEK. It was comparable to the GREGOR sounded by Jews celebrating PURIM, desiring to drown in cacophony the name of the hated Haman. Lepers also sounded their malady music, warning others of their approach.

cracowes
Polish shoes popular at the Cracow court, having outlandishly long-pointed toes that required anchoring by thongs or chains at the knee or waist. Fashionable in French and Burgundian courts, there they were called POULAINES.

craftswomen
Women working in fine and manual crafts, in farm fields, produce markets, and silver mines had special laws governing their actions, protecting their interests from intrusions by competitors, local or international, or their husbands. Called FEMMEs SOLEs (women alone), they often successfully combined home life with their professions (babies or children could be brought to work or remain at home with relatives). Craftswomen belonged to professional guilds, trained apprentices, and commanded high pay for excellent work. Some even dominated select professions, such as the fourteenth-century Parisian silk fabric trade.

credence
The ceremonial yet practical procedure of testing wine for poison. Either the cupbearer could take a trial taste, or mineral or gem pendants, such as the BEZOAR stone, which changed color or texture in the presence of particular poisons, were dipped in the suspect drink.

credenza
A side table or chest on a stand upon which food and wine were placed in banquet halls before their testing by tasting or CREDENCE. It was also a cabinet for ostentatious display of precious plate, comparable to the AUMBRY; or, in churches, a table holding the unconsecrated wafer and wine for COMMUNION.

credo
(Latin, I believe) A short, concise, formal statement of important Christian doctrine, such as the APOSTLES' CREED; a section of the PROPER of the MASS followed by the OFFERTORY.

crenelation
On a BATTLEMENT or a fortified PARAPET, the indentations or open spaces (crenets) for shooting or launching projectiles upon a beseiging enemy. Crenets alternated with the MERLONs.

crescent
In HERALDRY, a crescent-moon-shaped CHARGE, its horns pointing upward: if the points are DEXTER (to the right), the charge is increscent, or waxing; if towards the SINISTER (to the left), decrescent, or waning. It is an English CADENCY insigne for the second son.

crespinette
A CAUL headdress.

cresting
Ornamental ridging such as CRENELATION or DAGGING, in architecture, costumery, and kitchen sculpture.

crimson
A deep red dye from a pulverized insect, the Arabic dye-stuff KERMES.

crisis
In CHRONOPHYSICA, physicians following the classical example of Hippocrates insisted that diseases, fevers, and the courses of injuries have propitious moments, numerologically associated with threes and sevens, and crises at which prognosis is sure. The known and predictable CRITICAL DAY for every periodic fever or infection was observed as time for decision for medication or surgery.

critical day
The medical and astrological CRISIS or turning point in a disease, determining the ultimate prognosis for the patient.

crochet
A musical quarter note. It was also a handled hook used in lacemaking and other loomless fabric weaving. The surgical hook used for extracting a dead fetus or the unexpelled afterbirth from the womb also was an abortofacient.

crocket
A projecting ornament, usually gracefully FOLIATE, of a CAPITAL, canopy, BUTTRESS, or GOTHIC spire.

crocodile tears
Travel writer and natural historian John Mandeville in the fourteenth-century testified that crocodiles or

gravel worms enjoy human meat, though they will hypocritically cry at dinner.

cromorne
A KRUMMHORN.

cronicas
Spanish or Portuguese chronicles of wars, personalities, and events on the Iberian peninsula.

cross
The most characteristic symbol of Christianity, representing the cross upon which Jesus was crucified at CALVARY, though bearing upon it no figure, as does a CRUCIFIX, but occasionally, a sacred CIPHER or the monogram I H S. The STATIONS OF THE CROSS commemorate the specific events culminating in the CRUCIFIXION. The CROSS IN HERALDRY is one of the commonest of the ORDINARY insignia.

crossbar
A transverse bar placed or fixed across another to add strength or decoration, as for a chair, furniture chest, or architectural crossbeam.

crossbow
A hunting and fighting weapon, a bow with a crosspiece or stock through the center, to which a string was attached. When drawn, a trigger released the string, propelled an arrow, BOLT, QUARREL, with silent discharge, admirable accuracy, penetrating power, and hundreds of pounds of "pull." Usually it was constructed of steel or lamina of horn, whalebone, and flexible woods covered with birchbark, and often decorated with ARABESQUES, INTARSIA, or INLAYS of ivory or variegated woods.

crossing
In a CATHEDRAL or CRUCIFORM CHURCH, the square space at the intersection of NAVE and TRANSEPT, generally beneath the STEEPLE tower.

cross in heraldry
In HERALDRY, one of the simplest CHARGES, a vertical up-right band, the pale, taking approximately one-third the field, and a horizontal band crossing it perpendicularly, the FESS, also one-third wide. More complex variations have decorations at the ends of the cross's arms, such as smaller crosses and flowerettes: *cross botony* or *treffled* (with triple buds or TREFOILS); *cross-crosslet* (with small crosses at each end); *crossfitchy* (the lower end sharpened to a point); *crossflory* (with FLEURS-DE-LIS); *cross moline* (with MILLRIND-like terminals); *cross of chains* (four chains fixed to a central ANNULET); *cross of Jerusalem* (surrounded by four crosslets); *cross of Malta* or MALTESE CROSS (arms narrow at junction, expanding towards end, each arm indented at extremity); *cross of St. Andrew* or SALTIRE (X-shaped white on blue); *cross of St. Anthony* or *tau* (the Greek letter: *tau*-shaped); *cross of St. George* (red cross on white); *cross of St. Julian* (saltire with arms crossed); *cross of St. Patrick* (red SALTIRE on ARGENT); *cross patee* (narrow at juncture, widening towards ends forming nearly a square); *cross patriarchal* (upper arms shorter than lower); *cross potent* or of Jerusalem (four T's as terminals); *cross quadrate* (a square superimposed on conjunction of arms); *cross quarterpierced* (an empty square marking conjunction of arms); *Latin cross* (three upper limbs equal, lower longer).

cross knop
A small decorative knob surmounted by a CROSS, usually on the cover of a CIBORIUM or covered CHALICE, for lifting or grasping, or simply for decoration.

Crown of Thorns
An INSTRUMENT OF CHRIST'S PASSION on the VIA DOLOROSA. In the thirteenth century, Saint Louis built the Sainte-Chapelle in Paris to house the RELIC.

crow's feet
Fine, branching age wrinkles surrounding the eyes, resembling either impressions of the bird's feet on wet sand or in cement or the uneven, lined skin of avian legs. Chaucer in *Troilus and Criseyde* says "you may live long and proud till crow's feet grow under your eyes."

crozier
An ecclesiastical, crook-shaped staff, often with a curled top resembling fern, sometimes exquisitely carved, jeweled, enameled, and embellished, signifying the authority and jurisdiction of a BISHOP or mitered ABBOT or ABBESS. It is used to perform liturgical functions and to carry in religious processions.

crucible
An earthenware vessel capable of enduring great heat for fusing metals; a melting pot.

crucifix
A CROSS bearing upon it a representation of Christ crucified; also, the major element of the total CRUCIFIXION. Either a cross or crucifix was associated in TYPOLOGICAL SYMBOLISM with Eve's and Adam's eating from the Tree of Life in the Garden of Eden and the subsequent FELIX CULPA, the fall from grace that made redemption necessary and salvation possible.

crucifixion
The entire scene of Jesus Christ's execution on the CROSS at CALVARY, along with the figures of the crucified thieves, as well as Mary and John; often associated with symbols of the FELIX CULPA.

cruciform
Cross-shaped.

cruet
A small stoppered bottle or vial for oil, vinegar, or liquid in the kitchen or banquet hall; or for water or wine for celebrating the EUCHARIST in the MASS.

crupper
ARMOR for a horse's haunches.

crusade
A holy war, utilizing the CROSS as rallying symbol. From the eleventh through thirteenth centuries, each crusade was a military foray to recapture Jerusalem from the infidels; or to suppress local heresy such as the Albigensian; or to fight against Muslims in Spain or Prussian heathen in Eastern Europe. Individuals also went on a crusade to store good works toward salvation, as an elaborate PILGRIMAGE.

crypt
The underground burial chamber or room beneath a church, or under its CHANCEL, sometimes possessing an ALTAR and used as a chapel.

cubebs
A pungent spice, important in medicine, pharmacology, and cookery, probably the berry of the Javanese climbing plant *piper cubeba,* recommended in HERBALS and dietaries as wonderful for dyspepsia and for strengthening a "windy" stomach.

cucking stool
An obnoxious instrument of torture for slanderers and WITCHes, particularly women: a seat, attached to the end of a long pole, to which the victim was strapped for dunking, and, often, drowning in a pond, lake, or river. TRIAL BY ORDEAL often killed. If they were dunked and floated, that unnatural buoyancy justified their being burned as witches. If they sank and drowned, their innocence was proved.

cuckold
A husband whose wife is sleeping with another man or men; from the habits of the CUCKOO bird.

cuckoo
The sign of a CUCKOLD, from the European cuckoo bird's domestic habit of laying its eggs in another bird's nest, thereby avoiding the perils and responsibilities of nest-building and of rearing young. Only apparently ingenuous, the delightful ROTA "Sumer is icumen in, lhoude singe cuckoo," one of the earliest English ROUNDs, actually is an invitation to seduction.

cucurbit
A cucumber-shaped vessel used in chemistry and metallurgy.

cuenca
A Spanish pottery-tile decorative technique: impressed patterns form small cells or walls to prevent glaze colors from intermingling.

cuirass
An ARMOR breastplate.

cuir bouilli
(French, boiled leather) Leather softened in resin, then shaped while wet for use in ARMOR, corsetry, surgical instrument cases, jewel boxes, furniture, wall coverings, and carrying cases, often tooled, incised, painted, gilded, or embroidered.

culverin
A lightweight, portable, long-barreled cannon, designed in the fourteenth-century by armament engineer Konrad Keyser, also known for his floating folding bridges, moveable assault towers, cannon-equipped armored vehicles, multiple-tubed cannons with revolving barrels, underwater artillery, and diving suits.

cumelin
A bucket or wine cooler, generally footed.

cup-bearer
The banquet servitor required to test wine and ale by tasting, CREDENCE, before presenting the vintage to the host or most honored guest.

cupboard
A board, table, or cabinet with shelves for storage and display of cups, plates, CHARGERs, and kitchen or banquet gear.

cupola
A small rounded VAULT or DOME roofing a building, or, supported on columns, surmounting a tomb. It sometimes required horizontal arches. In ALCHEMY and metallurgy, a cupola furnace melts metals before their casting.

cupping
One of three PHLEBOTOMY techniques, along with LEECHING and FLEEMING: the application of vacuum cups or glasses to the nicked skin's surface to draw blood.

curate
In the Church of England, a clergyman charged with the "cure" of souls, having spiritual responsibility for laymen.

curfew
(French *couvre feu,* cover the fire) The ceremony either for protecting small relightable embers or entirely extinguishing cooking and lighting fires for the night. As a precaution against civil conflagration, town regulations required each HOUSEHOLD head to be sure no live flame existed after the curfew signal.

curry favor
(French *estriller fauvel,* to curry-comb a chestnut horse or donkey) As in the hilarious, satiric *Romance of Fauvel,* mocking human foibles and vices, to bow in subservience like a sycophant.

curtain wall
A castle's connecting wall or rampart between fortified projections or BASTIONs, usually with a sentry walk and CRENELATIONs.

curtal
An early form of the BASSOON, related to the DULCIAN.

curtana
The sword of the CHANSON DE GESTES' hero, Roland. Also, Edward the Confessor's "Sword of Mercy," a pointless sword, carried before the English kings at coronation, placed next to a sharp-pointed "Sword of Justice."

curtesy
Right of a widower to a life estate in all freehold lands of his late wife. The opposite of DOWER, it is often confused with COURTESY.

curvilinear
Compass-drawn ornamental curves, circles, and ovals; opposite of RECTILINEAR.

cushion
(French *cuisse,* thigh) The haunch of a large animal such as a cow or deer, roasted and served to specific classes of feasters; metaphorically, a prostitute.

cusp
In architecture, an apex or pointed projection; in ASTROLOGY, the beginning or entrance to a zodiacal HOUSE, an imaginary border between signs.

cusp and foil
Elements of ornamental carved TRACERY: the cusp is the projection on the underside of the arch separating foil from foil, the arcs which create a three-leafed (TREFOIL) or four-leafed (QUATREFOIL) shape, often in the stone or wood decorations above STAINED GLASS windows.

cutching

Gold beating, in which a gold sheet is placed between VELLUM, PARCHMENT, or paper, and beaten with a mallet to obtain GOLD LEAF.

cutlass

A short sword for cutting not thrusting, with a slightly curved, wide flat blade.

cyclas

A short cape-like cloak worn by men and women; also, a rich silk manufactured in the Cyclades. At the coronation of England's Henry III, the guests, citizens of London, wore the cyclas over VESTMENTS of silk.

D

dabiki
Produced and exported from Damietta in the fifteenth century, a delicate, gold-threaded, woven fabric so light that 50 yards could form a single COVERCHIEF or turban.

dactyl
One of the FIVE METRICAL FEET of poetic metre consisting of a long beat followed by two short beats.

dado
(Italian, dice or cubes) The lower section of a wall decorated with square glazed tiles or wood blocks crafted for the illusion of a continuous wall-to-wall pedestal; or WAINSCOTing, painting, papering, or paneling the lower part of an interior wall, differentiating the lower decoration from the upper.

dagger
A short, sharp, double-bladed knife generally worn in a sheath at the belt, brought to table for cutting and carving, and carried outdoors for utility and self-defense.

dagging
Ornamental cuff edgings of garments, with borders shaped as leaves, tongues, or scallops. As with CASTELLATED COSTUME, its whimsical excesses were forbidden by SUMPTUARY LAWS.

dainties
In hunting manuals and dietaries, choice culinary treats: testicles of deer, served with sweet and sour seasoning. They were emulated in the ILLUSION FOOD called HASLET.

daisy
The sun, or the day's eye. The flower was important in divination.

dalliance
Amorous conversation, coquettish flirting, precoital play, of which Chaucer's Wife of Bath and FABLIAUX women were masterful celebrants.

dalmatic
A formal, knee-length over-TUNIC worn by kings at coronations and by ecclesiastics, especially DEACONs, during MASS. The VESTMENT often was made of silk and designed with an embroidered, ornamental border that decorated wide flaring sleeves, neck, and openings. A jewel-studded belt encircled the wearer's waist.

damask
Treasures inspired by or brought from the city of Damascus, specifically, a rich silk fabric elaborately woven and decorated with designs and colors, often with gold and silver thread; a popular perfume and culinary additive, Damaskan rose water, distilled from European roses originally from Damascus. Damascened steel, important in ARMOR, weaponry, jewelry, and automata, was variegated iron and steel, richly embellished with acid-incised floriate designs.

dame
A woman, the DOMNA of ARTHURIAN ROMANCE; or the descendants of Eve and the Virgin Mary in the EVA-AVE ANTITHESIS.

damoiseau
The masculine correspondent of DAMSEL: a young gentleman not yet dubbed a knight.

In a danse macabre, Death's minions lead a physician with a urine flask and a nobleman. (From *La danse macabre des hommes*, Antoine Verard, Paris, 1486)

damp
A noxious vapor exhaling from industrial chimneys or TUWELS, as during the YEAR OF GREAT STINK, or from the nostrils of dragons.

damsel
(from French, *damoiselle*) A young, unmarried gentlewoman, whose male equivalent is a DAMOISEAU; or wife of a SQUIRE, not a LADY.

dance masters
Responsible not only for choreography but also the cultural ceremony of court, Antonio Cornezano, Domenico da Ferrara, Giovanni Martino, and Guglielmo Hebreo, the Jewish dance master, taught courtly dancing, as well as aesthetic, physical, and political exercises.

Dance of Death
A popular graphic depiction of life's uncertainties and death's inexorable arrival: a fearsome figure compels the unwilling to dance, as old man Death with SICKLE or SCYTHE cuts down the living; or Father Time's hourglass with the sands of life running out; or a skeleton drags printers from presses, physicians (carrying UROSCOPY flasks) from clinics, revelers from carousing, or lovers from the DANCE OF LOVE. The DANSE MACABRE democratized this MEMENTO MORI.

dance of love
That OLD DANCE, erotic, precoital, manipulative exercise, both psychological and physical, which sex manuals describe and lusty creatures as FABLIAUX women and Chaucer's Wife of Bath perform.

dancing mania
An epidemic mass hysteria, perhaps SAINT VITUS' DANCE, contemporary with the FLAGELLANTS, affecting thousands in Germany, Italy, and the Low Countries. Screaming and mouth-foaming, seemingly "possessed" people, often having gathered to celebrate a church festival such as MIDSUMMER EVE, danced in frenzy until overcome by exhaustion, injury, violence, or death.

Danelaw
The area of north, east, and central England settled or controlled by Danish invaders since the 9th century, where Danish custom or modified Saxon law was the law of the land. The Scandinavian heritage remains in over 1,400 place-names: those with the suffix *by* (farm), as Grimsby, Whitby, Rugby; *thorpe* (village), as Althorpe, Bishopsthorpe, and Linthorpe; and *toft* (ground or an earth-mound), as Brimtoft, Eastoft, and Langtoft.

danse macabre
A graphic depiction of social equality in death, in which people in strict political hierarchy, from the greatest to the least, each hold hand with each; a type of DANCE OF DEATH and remembrance of mortality, MEMENTO MORI.

danserye
A written collection of dances, as the sixteenth-century PAVANS, GALLIARDS, BASSE DANCES, and BRANSLES collected by Tielman Susato.

danses equestres
Equestrian dances, BALLETTI A CAVALLO.

Dark Ages
A condescending epithet for the thousand years between Rome's fall and the Renaissance. Spectacularly important intellectual events and achievements in literature, art, music, philosophy, religion, science, architecture, medicine, science, metallurgy, and technology demonstrate not the darkness of ignorance but the scintillating light of the creative human spirit characteristic of the time.

d'Arundel's case
An important will in England after the NORMAN CONQUEST in the eleventh century, in which the words "to Jonathan and his heirs" gave no land interest to the heirs but simply created the highest right of ownership, to hold, enjoy, or sell the land, technically a FEE SIMPLE absolute ESTATE IN LAND.

daye
A dairy woman, such as Chaucer's poor yet contented farm woman who owned the remarkable COCK Chaunticleer.

deacon
In Christian ecclesiastical hierarchy, the next minister below the ranks of PRESBYTER or PRIEST and BISHOP, originally charged with collection and distribution of alms, as an ALMONER.

dead as a doornail
Proverbial in the fourteenth century: door-carpenters used headless nails or brads which irretrievably sank into wood and were thus dead to further usage.

dean
(Latin *decem,* ten) Originally a minor ecclesiastical official responsible for 10 novices; in England, a CATHEDRAL's officer accountable for LITURGY, service, and property.

debate
The literary genre derived from classical oratory in which a pair of disputants argue opposing ideas according to established rules, presenting primary, secondary, and incidental propositions, rebuttals, and refutations on philosophical, political, practical, and spiritual subjects in styles serious or satiric. TROUBADOUR, TROBARITZ, TROUVÈRE, and MINNESINGER debate poems argued love's qualities. Some PSYCHOMACHIAs are debates. Popular in England were the witty *Owl and the Nightingale, Debate of the Body and the Soul, Wynner and Wastour,* and *Cuckoo and the Nightingale.*

debility
In ASTROLOGY, a planet in a sign opposite to the sign ruled by the planet or in which the planet is exalted; opposite of DIGNITY.

debt
In a sexual context, Saint Paul's First Epistle to the Corinthians (7:3): *Uxori debitum vir reddat: similiter autem et uxor viro*—a man has a sexual debt to his wife, she to him, in giving sexual pleasure.

decani
The south or DEAN's side of the choir in a CATHEDRAL, where the dean sits opposite the CANTOR in the CANTORIS.

decoction
(Latin, to boil down) A medicinal EXTRACT concentrated by long boiling in water, the fluid allowed to evaporate.

decretals
Papal letters containing answers to specific questions on points of church law received the force of law when included in collections of church decisions and regulations, as in 1234 by Gregory IX, and continued by Pope Clement V and Pope John XXII.

deesis
(Greek, supplication) A common BYZANTINE (and later) depiction of Christ enthroned between the Virgin Mary and Saint John the Baptist, as INTERCESSORs for mankind before God's judgment.

Dei Genitrix
Mother of God, MATER MARIA DEI, an ATTRIBUTE of the Virgin Mary.

Deipara
A title of the Virgin Mary, the bearer of God, MATER MARIA DEI.

Delft
In England and Holland, the name of the Netherlandish town famous for its CERAMICS, tin-GLAZED earthenware called MAJOLICA in Spain and Italy, and FAIENCE in France.

demesne
In England, land held in possession for one's own use, as belonging to oneself, *tenere in domineo:* lands possessed by free tenure, as opposed to lands held in service: *tenere in servitio.*

demi-ceint
A silver chain worn at the belt, carrying daily necessities as scissors, knife, file, keys, and BODKIN, accompanying or replacing a CHATELAINE; or a silver belt with ornamentation only in front.

demi-lune
Shaped like a crescent or half-moon.

dentil
Tooth-like square blocks in Ionic and Corinthian CORNICES and other building elements derived from CLASSICAL ARCHITECTURE and utilized in construction adornments, liturgical objects, and secular jewelry.

deploration
A stylized musical or poetic lament on a death, as for a musician and teacher by a pupil.

derrick
In building construction and the theater, the hoisting crane replacing or augmenting the block and tackle, celebrating the English hangman Derrick of Tyburn.

derring-do
"Desperate deeds of derring-do" is the fifteenth-century English writer John Lydgate's imitation of Chaucer's phrase "daring to do."

descant
(Or discant) In POLYPHONY, a composed or improvised musical part performed against the PLAINSONG.

Descent from the Cross
After the CRUCIFIXION, the removal of Christ by his disciples; in art, Joseph of Arimathea sometimes is portrayed with the disciples.

desco da parto
(Italian, birthing desk) For women during obstetrical labor, a decorated food tray. Usually adorned with scenes answering the MASTERY QUESTION by depicting women's mastery over men: Phyllis riding the back of Aristotle; Hercules (in women's clothes) using Omphale's spinning wheel; Virgil in a basket ascending to the tower-room of the Emperor's daughter; or Samson shorn in Delilah's lap.

deus ex machina
(Latin, god from the machine) A mechanical theatrical device for introducing divinities and ethereal creatures on stage by pulleys, ropes, and elaborate WINDLASS, DERRICK, and mechanical contrivances for an INTERLUDE, BALLET DE COUR, or TRIUMPH.

device
A heraldic EMBLEM or identification BADGE sewn, embroidered, APPLIQUEd, or otherwise applied to garments, hats, capes, blankets, CAPARISONs, furniture, swords, flags, furniture, and architecture, the figures including geometric shapes, plants, real or fantastic animals, often portrayed in flamboyant colors; also called an ACHIEVEMENT.

dexter
Right-handed; metaphorically, it can mean easy, handy, facile, propitious; opposite of SINISTER, left-handed (difficult and ill-boding).

diabolus in musica
The NICKNAME for the musical tritone, the devilish interval of three whole tones.

diadem
A crown or ornamental headband, symbolic of honor, royalty, or dignity; or a metal or fabric FILLET, simple or adorned with jewels, circling the head, worn low on the forehead.

diapason
In music theory, the octave, the interval including "all the tones."

diapering
A two-dimensional pattern on a wall or background of a work of art, consisting of square, rectangular, or LOZENGE shapes in a regular alternating pattern. In architecture, brick diapering creates geometric patterns via arrangements with two or three different colored bricks; in painting, backgrounds are diversified with a small uniform pattern of alternating diamond shapes; in fabrics, a weave of threads whose various reflections of light from the surface cause lines to cross diamond-wise, the spaces filled by leaves or dots.

diastema
A space between two front teeth, important in PHYSIOGNOMIES, also called GAT-TOOTHED. Like the NEVUS, it was a sign of lasciviousness and lechery.

Diatessaron
Tatian's second-century Greek, Syriac, or Latin continuous narrative of the GOSPELs, the important standard text before the fifth century, when the FOUR GOSPELS separated. Their unity was preserved in CANON TABLES and symbolized in the TETRAMORPH.

Dies Irae
(Latin, day of wrath) The SEQUENCE in the MASS for the dead, often appearing in poetry and art. Probably written by a thirteenth-century FRANCISCAN, it is an intensely personal REQUIEM.

dietary
A lay person's health manual or professional medical instruction book, a combination of cookery, HERBAL, and medical hygiene text, including recipes, advice on health, food, physiology, and temperaments, diet therapies for diseases such as asthma, palsy, gout, arthritis, and cancer, and instructions on healthful clothing, cosmetics, exercise, mood control, and sleeping habits. Examples include Platina's *On Honest Indulgence and Good Health,* Andrew Boorde's *Dietary of Health,* and Nares' *Haven of Health.*

dight
Slightly more refined than SWYVE, to have sexual intercourse; in a nonsexual context, to order, arrange, get dressed.

digitus infamus
The middle finger, astrologically ruled by Saturn, and rarely bearing a ring. Rigidly extending this finger was a magical sign against the evil eye; by PEJORATION, it is now a vulgar sign of contempt.

dignity
In ASTROLOGY, a planet acquired strength to do either good or evil, according to its nature, by entering a sign in which it is the Ruler or Exalted. Contrast DEBILITY.

dimidation
In HERALDRY, combining of ARMS: DEXTER (right) half of the male side with SINISTER (left) half of the female side.

diminuendo
Progressive diminution in size of letters in MANUSCRIPT pages, particularly in the INCARNATION initial in HIBERNO-SAXON art; in music, progressive softness of sound.

dinanderie
A metal alloy, sturdy BRONZE-colored metalwork from Dinant, Belgium, popular for kitchen and banquet utensils and ceremonial vessels.

diphona
A two part song, the BICINIUM.

diptych
(Greek, folded together) In two panels or parts, the ecclesiastical diptych was a pair of religious portraits, ranging in size from pocket to monumental, and hinged together, like a book, so that they could be closed and clasped. The diptych sundial allowed time-telling by the "new" equal hours of the early Renaissance as well as by traditional unequal hours, with astrological and astronomical computations listed. In liturgical practice, a diptych contained lists of names of Christians living and dead to be read during the two prayers for the quick and the dead.

direction
Astrological measuring of the space between any two parts of the heavens to determine at what period in life a promised event or effect will appear; a certain number of degrees to the right of the ASCENSION of the sun which, when it has passed over, completes its direction or its ARC.

disease woman
For teaching physicians and laymen, a depiction of a naked female figure suffering from a panoply of diseases and injuries associated with specific anatomical organs; comparable to a BLOODLETTING WOMAN and ZODIAC WOMAN.

A woman farmer carrying a distaff follows the herd into the field while a shepherd tends a flock and noblemen discuss rural occupations. (From a manuscript by Petrus Crecentius, 15th century; courtesy of the Pierpont Morgan Library, New York)

dissimilation

Linguistic exchange between *l*'s and *r*'s in words originally containing two or more of one or the other: two *r*'s become *r* and *l*, as Latin *purpura* becomes *purple*, or as the word *colonel* is pronounced "curnel."

dissolution of monasteries

Contemporaneous with the STATUTE OF USES, England's King Henry VIII terminated the rights and privileges of monasteries, taking for the crown their real estate, rents, wealth, and tangible possessions.

distaff

The vertical cleft stick holding the wool or flax from which a SPINSTER draws thread. The distaff became an EMBLEM of women's contributions to the fabric trades (as in MATRONYMICS); SYMBOL of the female branch of a family.

distillation

Chemical and metallurgical conversion of a substance into a vapor by heating it in an ALEMBIC, then condensing it by cooling to liquid form in a refrigeratory; or the extraction of an essential oil or "spirit" of a substance by evaporation and condensation of its liquid solution.

dit

A pedagogic poetic genre derived from the classical Latin *exemplum*, a poem of practical instruction in etiquette and morals as well as religious and courtly conduct.

Chemists at distillation chambers with athanor furnaces prepare a chemical. (From Philip Ulstadt, *De Secretis Naturae* [1544], courtesy of New York Academy of Medicine)

Divine Comedy
The expression is derived from the tripartite *Commedia* by Florentine poet Dante Alighieri (1265–1321), describing his voyages through Inferno, Purgatorio, and Paradiso (Hell, Purgatory, and Heaven), each of the three divisions consisting of 33 CANTOs, a literary epitome of the symmetrical, hierarchical, analogical, allegorical universe, and depicting the journey of the human soul from despair in Hell through purification in Purgatory to cosmic awareness in Paradise.

divine office
Daily prayers separate from the sacrifice of the MASS, an obligation of priests, clerics, and other religious; the OPUS DEI.

docere et delectare
(Latin, to teach and to please) Two seemingly antithetical desiderata ideally united in the best art: instructing and pleasing. In the *Canterbury Tales,* the host offers a free meal as prize for the tale of "best SENTENCE" and "most SOLACE" that both teaches and delights. Adhering to the PLATONIC idea of decorum (as Chaucer paraphrases Plato's *Timaeus,* words are perfect cousins to deeds), elegant EPIC characters speak refined language, while rude boors spout lascivious obscenity.

Docetism
In the early Christian church, the heretical interpretation of Christ's sufferings as only apparent, not real.

doctor, to
To adulterate with additives; physicians' pharmacological combinations and natural substances were added to wines and ales to create digestives, palliatives, and cures, including tasty aromatic drinks like HIPPOCRAS, CAUDLE, and METHEGLIN.

doctrine of worthier title
A legal doctrine to prevent avoidance of taxes, a living donor's attempt to convey an ESTATE IN LAND to a recipient who otherwise would receive it after the donor's death was deemed null and void. Beneficiaries obtained a reversion, not a remainder, requiring payment of death or inheritance taxes.

Dodecachordon
A significant book of musical theory by Glareanus that expanded the traditional eight CHURCH MODES to 12.

dogaline
An aristocratic Venetian fashion for men and women: a long brocade or velvet robe with wide, flaring sleeves that reached down to the knee. Lined and bordered with fur, the sleeves' lower edges fastened to the shoulder to reveal the undergown sleeve.

dog companion
Lovers' mediator or go-between, carrying messages, consoling grief. Its canine heritage derived from the mythic friendly beast-guide to the Other World. Examples include the dogs Petit-Cru and Husdan of the Tristan legend and the Chatelaine de Vergi's intelligent pup.

dolce stil nuovo
Dante called "the sweet new style" the Tuscan imitations of Provençal TROUBADOUR COURTLY LOVE poems that idealized women and noble conduct, emphasized SERVICE OF LOVE and VIRTUE DEFINED BY TRIAL, as in his own lyric cycle *Vita Nuova* and the poems of Guido Guinizelli and Guido Cavalcanti.

dolmen
A stone, timber, or turf chamber, or a CROMLECH.

dome
A hemispherical roof formed by a series of converging arches springing from a circular or polygonal base.

Dominican
One of the FOUR ORDERS OF FRIARS, a monastic and teaching brotherhood begun by Saint Dominic, also called the BLACK FRIARS or JACOBINS. Emphasizing ARISTOTELIAN philosophy and life of the intellect, they were great educators.

domna
(Or dame; Latin *domina,* lady, she who rules) A highborn, imperious, capricious woman, the inspiration for and beloved of TROUBADOUR poets' COURTLY LOVE lyrics, herself the recipient of the SERVICE OF LOVE.

donates

Lay brothers, or laymen living in a monastic community but taking no vows, particularly CARTHUSIANS; originally, children given ("donated") to a MONASTERY by their parents to be raised as monks; also called OBLATES.

Donation of Constantine

A powerful but fabricated eighth- or ninth-century document, a false DECRETAL to increase the power of the Church, especially the Roman See, by purporting Emperor Constantine's gift of dominion to the fourth-century Pope Sylvester I, over Antioch, Jerusalem, Constantinople, Alexandria, Rome and all Italy. Authenticity of the document was disproved by Nicholas of Cusa.

Donatism

A fourth-century, rigoristic Christian sect of North Africa claiming the SACRAMENTS invalid if given by a priest who is a sinner.

donet

A key to fundamental ideas, an introduction to an art or science, as in fifteenth-century Reginald Peacock's *The Donet of God's Law* or *Key of Christian Religion*. Students memorized grammatical definitions by donet ("What is a verb?" "A part of speech with tense and person, but without case, meaning to do or to suffer"). The donet was named after the great fourth-century Latin grammarian Donatus, so celebrated that Dante, in his DIVINE COMEDY, placed him in the radiant circle of the sun.

donjon

A massive stronghold tower of a castle; sometimes written "dungeon."

donor portrait

In a DIPTYCH or TRIPTYCH, the patron paying the artist was portrayed on one panel piously praying or enthusiastically adoring the religious personage(s) depicted on the other panel or panels; a VOTIVE PAINTING.

doppio

A fifteenth-century double-meter dance step.

Dorian mode

A CHURCH MODE.

dormant

In HERALDRY, an animal sleeping on its belly, head resting on paws, mouth and eyes closed.

dormer

A structure, usually with a window, projecting from the side of a pitched roof; over the window is a GABLE.

Dormition of the Virgin

(Latin *dormitio,* the falling asleep) In the Eastern Church, the celebration of the death of the Virgin, August 15. Having died after the CRUCIFIXION, she is portrayed with the APOSTLES Peter at the head of her death bed and John at its foot; corresponding in the Western Church to the ASSUMPTION.

dorsal

An embroidered fabric or TAPESTRY backing a seat or chair, a modified BALDAQUIN.

dorser

A basket worn on the back by a person or animal, used for carrying produce to market.

double

A dance step in the PAVAN or the BASSE DANCE.

double monastery

A COEDUCATIONAL MONASTERY or monastic community.

double procession

The dual origin of the HOLY GHOST from both God the Father and God the Son, FILIOQUE.

double queued

An animal in HERALDRY, usually a LION, with two tails; for example, ARMS granted to the author of BARTOLISM.

doublet

Originally a short, fitted, quilted undergarment worn under a BLIAUT or HAUBERK ARMOR. Later, it became a variety of the military GIPPON or GAMBESON, its rich fabrics popular for civilian men's costumes, embellished with trimmings and edgings, and usually worn with CHAUSSES or HOSE.

doucette
Commercially produced savory tarts baked in a sweet dough, filled with meat, fowl, fish, jelly, fruit, or combinations of these, sold in bakeries ready for tavern, home, or "take out."

douze pers
(French, twelve equals) The twelve peers, the great, noble warriors at the court of Charlemagne, celebrated in CHANSON DE GESTES.

dower
In Germanic customary law, the part of the husband's property assigned to the wife in the marriage agreement, as her insurance policy: if the husband died or divorced her, she took possession of the dower for the rest of her life, but it reverted to the husband's family on her death or remarriage; often confused with DOWRY. In England, it was the morning gift (MORGENGABE) publicly promised to the new wife in front of the church; or the legal right of a widow to a life estate in one third of all freehold properties of her late husband, opposite of CURTESY.

dower house
A widow's house, generally allowed her for life or until she remarried.

dowry
In Roman law, the wife's share of her family's fortune that she brings to her marriage; the husband administers it but the wife regains it on his death or their divorce.

doxology
The formulaic spoken or sung praise of God's glory dedicated to the HOLY TRINITY. The Greater Doxology is GLORIA IN EXCELSIS DEO (Glory to God in the highest), as in the ANGELIC HYMN; the lesser, is GLORIA PATRI (Glory to the Father).

dragon's blood
In ALCHEMY, TINCTURE of ANTIMONY; also an important vegetable pigment for red paint derived from the East Indian shrub *draconea draco,* whose sap dries to a deep brown-red gum resin.

dragon's head and tail
Imagery inherited from the East, an astral design of a great malefic dragon that continually attempts to devour the Sun and Moon but is prevented from doing so by human threats, treaties, and propitiations. Eclipsed heavenly bodies are in the dragon's mouth. In ASTROLOGY, the dragon's head (*caput draconis*) is the moon's north node or point where she crosses the *ecliptic* northward; the tail (*cauda draconis*) is her south node, crossing to the south.

draughtsman
A gaming piece or counter for backgammon or draughts, cast of metal or carved in wood, often portraying a wealthy or noble patron as a commemorative object or memento.

draw-leaf table
Usually a heavy wooden REFECTORY table, with two top "end" leaves half the length of the middle one and nestled below it. When the lower leaves are drawn out, the table is twice the length of the original top.

drawn and quartered
A criminal to be drawn and quartered was publicly pilloried on a CART OF SHAME or HURDLE sled, drawn through town as a warning example to possible malefactors, then hanged and finally cut into four pieces.

dream vision
(Or dream allegory) A popular MACROBIAN literary genre in which a PERSONA falls asleep, dreams a vision of past, present, or future love, religion, or politics; or a literary ALLEGORY, such as Dante's *Divine Comedy,* Chaucer's *Book of the Dutchess* and *Parliament of Fowls,* and the ALLITERATIVE REVIVAL poems *Pearl* and *Piers Plowman.*

dressed stone
Smoothly finished stone ornamenting corners, doors, windows, and other APERTUREs of buildings.

dreydle
A four-sided spinning top usually fabricated of wood or ivory, used in symbolic gambling games at the Jewish festivals of HANUKKAH and PURIM.

drollerie
A fanciful, playful, humorous adornment. In literature, a drollerie might appear in a characterization, CARICATURE, or SATIRE; in art, it occurs in the MAR-

GINALIA of MANUSCRIPTs and in ornamental carvings on MISERICORDs.

dromond
A large, single-sailed ship powered by rowers, important in war and trade.

drone
A musical instrument's pipe, sounding a continuous single base BURDON, as in a BAGPIPE or HURDY-GURDY.

druid
A member of the pagan Celtic priesthood.

drypoint
The INTAGLIO incising and graphic-art printing process in which a BURIN or needle or jewel point directly inscribed a design on a copper or zinc plate, thus leaving slightly ragged edges or BURRs that created subtle lines and apparently spontaneous tonalities of shade, light, and dark.

duckbill shoes
Exaggeratedly wide-toed leather shoes succeeding the fifteenth century's dramatically pointed POULAINES.

ductia
A thirteenth-century instrumental musical form in vigorous stamping dance rhythm, related to the Provençal ESTAMPIE.

duecento
The thirteenth century.

dulcian
An early BASSOON.

dulcimer
A trapezoidal stringed musical instrument struck with hammers held in each hand, unlike the PSALTERY, which was plucked.

dümmling
(German, little fool) In literature, an apparently stupid, ridiculous, NICE young fool whose ignorance truly is innocence and whose willingness to take words literally humorously reaffirms the sanctity of word. Nonsensical childhood honesty was sign of the elect: before questing for the Holy GRAIL, the knight Percival is only slowly wise.

dump
An English dance; the best known was My Lady Carey's Dump.

dun
A small Scottish hill fort.

dunce
A punctilious, pedantic, hair-splitting follower of thirteenth-century scholastic theologian John Duns Scotus; later, a stupid, thick-witted, incapable student worthy of wearing the pointed hat of shame, the dunce cap, often confused with the JUDENHUT.

dyke
An EARTHWORK ditch.

E

eagle
In ALCHEMY, MERCURY after sublimation; because of its volatility and its voraciousness, like the imperious eagle devouring lesser birds, mercury destroys, consumes, and reduces gold to its first matter.

earmark
To identify as attributed property, as farmers notch ears of cattle as mark of ownership.

earthly paradise
A place between heaven and earth, inhabited by Enoch and Elijah, the only two persons ever to leave this world without dying (Genesis 5:24; 2 Kings 2:11).

earthwork
Protective concentric rings of ditches, usually surmounted with pointed wooden stakes. The removed earth and stones piled high on the inside edge of the sloping bank were often reinforced with wood or stone REVETMENTS.

earwigging
(Anglo-Saxon *ear-wicga,* an ear crawling insect) Whispered sharing of privileged information; or private scolding.

ease
Relief or sexual gratification: old January's wife, lusty May, in the *Canterbury Tales* wants to give lovesick Damyan "ease"; the Wife of Bath says that genitalia are for "ease" of engendering; Pandarus tells Troilus (*Troilus and Criseyde* 3:197) that he will bring the lovers together to "ease your heart."

easement
A grant of right to use land, obtained in four ways: express grant, reservation, implication, and PRESCRIPTION.

Easter
The most solemn celebration of the Christian liturgical year, the feast commemorating Christ's RESURRECTION (superseding pagan spring festivals), the date determined by the PASCHAL full moon, between March 21 and April 25. The feast is preceded by LENT.

Easter Even
HOLY SATURDAY.

ebony
A jet-black, dense, smooth-grained hardwood, durable but difficult to carve, used in furniture, decoration, and INTARSIA.

ecarlate
Particularly fine woolen cloth manufactured at Ghent, prized by nobility for ceremonial and processional robes, particularly SCARLET.

Ecce Homo
(Latin, Behold the man!) Pilate, to pacify the high priests and absolve himself of blame for Christ's CRUCIFIXION, said "Behold the man!" at which moment an image of Jesus crowned with thorns appeared (John 19).

eccentric
In PTOLEMAIC geocentric astronomy, an orbit not having the earth precisely in its center; in COPERNICAN heliocentric science, an orbit not precisely center-

ing on the Sun. Ptolemy invented an imaginary eccentric orbit to account for the apparent forward and backward motion of a planet in its orbit as seen from the Earth and the epicyclical movement of planets.

echtra
An old Irish tale of adventure in which a hero visits the Celtic OTHERWORLD, beholding wonders and enduring tests. The genre probably influenced ARTHURIAN ROMANCE adventures, portraits, and narrative motifs, as in the twelfth-century works of Chrétien de Troyes.

ecliptic
The apparent yearly path of the sun projected onto the CELESTIAL SPHERE and inclined to the celestial equator by about 23 degrees; the sun crosses the equator at the equinoxes.

ecuelle
A porridge bowl.

edda
Either one of two types of Icelandic books. The *Elder Edda* was a collection of old Icelandic anonymous narrative and didactic poetry on heroic, historical, and mythological subjects, with an alliterative stressed line. The *Younger Edda* was a prose INSTRUCTION BOOK for young SCALDs, teaching KENNINGS and verse forms, written by Snorri Sturluson in the thirteenth century.

Edict of Milan
Roman Emperor Constantine's decree in 313 of the toleration of Christianity, stimulating development of magnificent BYZANTINE architecture and art works.

egg-and-dart border
A continuous band of juxtaposed ovoid shapes and arrowheads carved in HIGH RELIEF, often on CAPITALS, ENTABLATURES, and furniture.

Egyptian days
In ASTROLOGY, the unlucky, inauspicious days of the year, usually two every month.

eight Beatitudes
Christ's promises of future rewards, in the SERMON ON THE MOUNT, to the blessed who are the salt of the earth and the light of the world: the poor in spirit, those who mourn, the meek, those who hunger and thirst for righteousness, the merciful, the pure in heart, the peace makers, and those persecuted for righteousness.

eight canonical hours
The Christian prayer regimen punctuating the day every three hours: the CANONICAL HOURS.

eight orders of clergy
In ascending order of rank: ostiarius, lector, exorcist, acolyte, subdeacon, deacon, priest, and bishop.

eisel
A sour wine, resembling vinegar (*vin aigre*), added to a dish to sharpen taste, making it pungent or "pointed."

eiseddfod
(Welsh, assembly) A benevolent organization sponsoring meetings and contests for Welsh MINSTRELS, BARDs, poets, singers, and musicians.

election
The astrological method for choosing the exactly perfect time for a particular enterprise, such as business, travel, medical ministration and surgery, marriage, intercourse for creating a marvelous child (via a CONCEPTION TIME MIRROR), and other human acts under the INFLUENCE of heavenly bodies.

eleven thousand virgins
According to the GOLDEN LEGEND, 11,000 young women who had accompanied Saint Ursula, daughter of a Christian king of Brittany, on PILGRIMAGE to Rome became martyrs when on their way back to Cologne they were slaughtered by Huns.

elixir
A potent liquid medicament or APHRODISIAC potion; the elixir of life, ardently sought by alchemists, philosophers, and physicians. Paracelsus thought it could confer not only immortality but a release from PRIMA MATERIA (original substance), leading to personal perfection on earth.

ell
A measurement of length standardized in certain towns and countries, but not universally, derived from

Members of the eight orders of the clergy, including a cardinal, mitred bishops, and others, attend the canonization of Birgitta of Sweden; one cleric reads with eyeglasses. (From a manuscript by Ulrich von Richtenthal, *Beschreibung des Constanzer Conziliums*, German, c. 1450–70)

an average of the length of an ulna bone; or, an arm's length from tip of the middle finger to the elbow.

Elysium
The EARTHLY PARADISE.

emblem
(Latin, *emblema,* inlay or insertion) A sign, SYMBOL, or ATTRIBUTE for a person or abstract idea, sometimes accompanied by a motto.

embossing
Decorative raising of a design into BAS-RELIEF by thrusting it forward or hammering it from behind (REPOUSSÉ); when working from the back of the (usually) metal surface either with hand tools or a pair of matched dies, the relief die would strike from beneath onto the INTAGLIO die on the obverse.

embrasure
The space between uprights on a BATTLEMENT wall.

embroidery
The embellishing of fabric by stitching on it ornamental figures, designs, and inscriptions, such as the exquisite OPUS ANGLICANUM, the BAYEUX TAPESTRY, or ORPHREYS on secular and ecclesiastical costumes that rarely degenerated into TAWDRY.

emerald tablet
Thirteen alchemical precepts engraved on a green stone and attributed to Hermes Trismegistus, and said to be the foundation of the art of ALCHEMY.

enamel
A vitreous porcelain or CERAMIC glaze applied to a metal or pottery surface for decoration, fused in a

furnace or kiln, sometimes after CLOISONNÉ or CHAMPLEVÉ techniques, yielding a smooth, lustrous, durable, jewel-like finish.

enamelry
Decoration with ENAMEL.

encaustic tiles
Decorative floor tiles made of red clay, with stamped print cuts in relief; the hollows were filled with white clay, and the whole then glazed, decorated with foliage, heraldic DEVICEs, human and fantastical figures, or geometric patterns, and fired.

enchiriadis
(Or enchiridion; from Greek, hand) A handbook or manual, generally musical or theological.

endura
Voluntary starvation, a type of HOLY ANOREXIA, an efficient deprivation of bodily desires leading to death, practiced by the PERFECTI of the CATHARI and the ALBIGENSES.

energumens
(Greek, agitated) Human beings possessed by demons and malign spirits.

enfances
The childhood educational adventures of a hero or heroine that portend later qualities, actions, and fate.

enfeoffment
The feudal bestowing of land, of a building, or of revenues (as a bridge toll) by a LORD on a subordinate, originally in exchange for military service, counsel, and aid, later in exchange for rent, SCUTAGE, and loyalty.

English
Between its INDO-EUROPEAN origins and CHAUCER'S ENGLISH, five successive cultural forces (excluding the mysterious Picts) directly affected variety and versatility of the English language: the Celts (Gaelic ancestors of the Irish and Scots, and Brythonic descendants of the Welsh); the Romans (from the invasion of Julius Caesar in 55 B.C. through the end of Roman rule in 410); the Angles, Saxons, and Jutes (beginning in 449); the Danes (beginning in the eighth century, subdued by King Alfred in the 9th, but maintaining intermittent control until 1016); and the NORMANs (with William the Conqueror from 1066).

English subtleties
Subtilitates anglicanae, the disparaging name fourteenth-century French critics attributed to the complex Oxfordian ideas in philosophy, mathematics, science, and theology, which they believed to be polluting French thought at the University of Paris.

engraving
A graphic art INTAGLIO process of incising a design or inscription onto a metal plate with a graver or BURIN for surface ornamentation or for transferring the design to a print; partially superseded in the Renaissance by ETCHING.

enhanced
A heraldic ORDINARY or CHARGE placed above its usual position; opposite of ABASED.

en ronde boss
A popular fourteenth-century Parisian jewelry technique in which white and colored, opaque and translucent, ENAMEL was applied to previously roughened gold leaf.

ens and entia
An entity in existence, as opposed to a mere attribute or quality. Paracelsus distinguished among five entia or principles causing bodily disturbances and illness: *ens astrorum* (astrological star power); *ens veneni* (poison); *ens naturale* (natural physical constitution); *ens spirituale* (spirituality); and *ens dei* (God's will).

entablature
In the CLASSICAL ARCHITECTURAL ORDERs, the three essentials of horizontal beams above columns are: ARCHITRAVE (the lowest division, the main beam resting upon the abacus on the CAPITAL of a column); FRIEZE, (the central section); and CORNICE (the projecting upper part).

entail
The legal settlement of a landed estate restricting the ways in which it may be bequeathed by specific fixed

rules of CADENCY, descent, and devolution; opposite of FEE SIMPLE.

entasis
An architectural swelling on vertical columns to counteract the optical illusion that causes vertical parallels to appear curved inwards.

entomology
The study of insects, significant not only in bestiaries but in practical medical books and natural histories; in 1147, the physician-nun and convent-founder Saint Hildegard of Bingen discovered SCABIES mites.

entrelacement
The ARTHURIAN ROMANCE technique of interlacing episodes, one beginning at the dramatic high point of a previous incident but interrupted to sustain narrative vigor. This technique differed from EPIC RETARDATION and the FRAME TALE. Interweaving allowed harmonious juxtaposition among narratives otherwise disjunct in character, time, and action, as in the gigantic Old French *Prose Lancelot.*

entremet
(French *entre mets,* between messes, dishes, or courses) An edible sculpture of pastry, spun sugar, MARZIPAN, or fruit and flowers, placed on table or paraded around the banquet hall to signal entry of a special course. SUBTLETIEs graced the most elaborate feasts while entremets sufficed for the less lordly, but both were to entertain or edify, uniting DOCERE ET DELECTARE.

envoy
A short final stanza to a BALLADE, the concluding lines of a literary work that serve as final refrain, brief address to a patron, indulgence in the HUMILITY FORMULA, or practical send-off to the work of art.

epaule de mouton
ARMOR for the inside of the forearm.

epic retardation
The artistic device of intruding an apparently irrelevant or unnecessary event, character, or memory of the past to interrupt, and thus to retard, narrative action while sustaining dramatic tension.

epigonation
(Greek, thigh) A progress of social diminution: less illustrious successors to more distinguished forbearers; or an elaborate embellished diamond-shaped symbol used by bishops of the Eastern Orthodox Church, as in the ATTRIBUTE of Saint Gregory, fourth-century Bishop of Constantinople, advocate of the NICENE CREED.

epiphany
(Greek, manifestation) A Christian feast on January 6, after its eve, TWELFTH NIGHT, creating a triadic celebration of Christ's manifestation of divine powers: Christ's BAPTISM (Mark 1), marking Him as the Son of God; the journey of the Magi to Bethlehem (Matthew 2), manifesting Christ as the prophesied King; and the miracle of the wedding at Cana (John 2), demonstrating His divine prerogative to make miracles. The feast day is also called THEOPHANIA and HYPAPANTI.

episcopal
Christian church government by BISHOPs, their dignity and authority superior to that of PRIESTs, PRESBYTERs, and DEACONs.

epistle
A letter, particularly from one of the TWELVE APOSTLES, as in the New Testament. In liturgy, it is the first reading in the MASS, sometimes taken from the Acts of the Apostles or Revelation.

epitoga
A wide, unbelted robe with bell sleeves, important as an academic gown; sometimes called an epomine hood.

epomine hood
An EPITOGA.

equatorium
An unmotorized computational instrument for planetary astronomy, indirectly related to the ASTROLABE, ASTRARIUM, JACOB'S STAFF, and CLOCKWORK.

equestrian figure
(Latin *equus,* horse) A real, supernatural, or fabulous figure mounted on a horse that is stylized or represen-

tational, usually fitted with saddle, bridle, BELLS, and CAPARISON.

erased
In HERALDRY, a head or limb torn from the body, indicated by a jagged edge.

erect
A heraldic animal, normally horizontal but depicted vertically, facing or proceeding upward.

erg
A summer pasture or dairy farm; it is a common suffix in English place names of Scandinavian origin, as in the DANELAW.

ergotism
A disease caused by fungal changes in rye grain seed; thought to be the origin of the DANCING MANIA and SAINT VITUS' DANCE.

ermine
The pure white winter FUR of the smallest weasel, with a blacktipped tail. It adorned royal and legal robes, often as an heraldic BADGE. LAITICE or letice, resembling ermine, edged the neck, sleeves, and wide trailing hems of women's gowns, the width of the fur indicating rank. In HERALDRY, it describes a silver (white) field with SABLE (black) spots.

ermines
The heraldic FUR; white spots on black field is ERMINE reversed.

erminois
In HERALDRY, a FUR, resembling ERMINE, with black spots on gold.

eryngium
In botany, *eryngium campestre,* a fragrant herb famous in English folklore as lad's love or boy love; thought to be a mystical APHRODISIAC, it was used as stuffing in a PILLOW FACE on SAINT JOHN'S DAY.

Erziehungsroman
(German, book of instruction) A literary narrative of a hero's or heroine's education, the progress from simplicity and innocence, as the DÜMMLING, to sophistication and worldly wisdom, with the ENFANCES portending later accomplishments. Numerous ARTHURIAN ROMANCES chronicle the educations of heroes.

escarbuncle
The gem thought to have inherent and emanating rays of light, the CARBUNCLE.

eschapins
Light flat shoes, ornamentally slashed or pierced on top.

eschatology
Theological, philosophical, literary, or artistic study of four last subjects of the ESCHATON: death, judgment, heaven, and hell.

eschaton
The Final Time; The End; the subject of ARS MORIENDI and MEMENTO MORI.

escheat
Reversion of land to an overlord (or the state) from whom it has been held in TENURE by a TENANT dying without heirs.

escheator
A guardian of lands due to the king via ESCHEAT.

escoffion
A woman's headdress of a silk or gold-thread trellis net; or an elaborate velvet or satin reticulated cap covered with a bejeweled gold net.

escrow
A security system allowing a third person to hold money, personal property, a deed, or other legal document to be released only upon performance of a contract condition or contingency or receipt of full payment; sometimes called an escrowl.

escuage
(Latin, *scutum,* shield) Shield service. In return for land held in TENURE, a knight joined the king at war for 40 days at his own cost, or sent a substitute, a SCUTAGE.

escutcheon
A heraldic field on which ARMS are emblazoned; sometimes the term for COAT OF ARMS. A blot on an escutcheon is a stain on the bearer's reputation.

espera
The legal duration of time in which an event must take place, as payment of a debt, production of a promised document, or performance of an action.

esquire
A young nobleman finishing apprenticeship as a PAGE, serving a knight as shield-carrier, comparable to a JOURNEYMAN in a crafts GUILD.

essentia
The chemical and astrological essence, the active virtuous principle in things, as opposed to a poison.

estampie
(Or estampida) A rigorous, vigorous, rhythmically exciting and textually complex Provençal stamping dance, such as *Kalenda Maya,* by the TROUBADOUR Raimbaut de Vacqueras.

estate in land
A possessory interest in land measured by time, a feudal TENURE system traceable to William the Conqueror's requirement to repay debts by granting use of land but retaining ALLODIAL ownership to assure TENANTS' future services and duties. Major divisions were *freehold* and *non-freehold.* Non-freehold had no SEIZIN, as rents and leases. Freehold had seizin, consisting of: FEE SIMPLE, the highest and best right of ownership and possession, lasting indefinitely, which could be willed to heirs and grantees infinitely; FEE TAIL, requiring land be kept within a family, inheritable only by its successive eldest sons; and LIFE ESTATE, which granted possession of land for the life of the tenant, but reverting thereafter to the donor or another.

estate of inheritance
Types of ESTATES IN LAND in feudal TENURE were the non-heritable (the life estate, created either voluntarily or by operation of law), and the heritable FEE SIMPLE (both FEE SIMPLE ABSOLUTE and FEE SIMPLE DEFEASIBLE) and the FEE TAIL.

estocade
A dance step from the BUFFON.

estoppel
(Old French *estouper,* to bar, to barricade, or to block) A legal doctrine barring renewed litigation or renewed allegation of a past right. Differing from RES JUDICATA, which bars relitigation of a claim, collateral estoppel is issue preclusion, forbidding retrial of issues within a claim.

estrain
Hat straw.

estray
In law, an unowned but not wild animal.

etching
A graphic art INTAGLIO process and ARMOR ornamentation technique; a process of chemical corrosion of a surface design on a metal plate by a MORDANT that bites through a thin coating of acid-resistant etching-ground upon which the drawing is made with a steel etching needle; differing from ENGRAVING.

etrog
The citrus fruit, citron, paired with the palm, myrtle, or willow branch, the LULAV, for ceremonial and symbolic use in the Jewish harvest festival SUKKOT.

etui
A storage or traveling container for practical necessaries as scissors, BODKINS, needles, and medical or surgical instruments.

Eucharist
(Greek, I give thanks) The major act of Christian thanksgiving in the celebration of the MASS, commemorating Christ's LAST SUPPER. The bread or wafer represents by TRANSUBSTANTIATION the body of Jesus Christ in the service of COMMUNION, and generally is held in an elaborate PYX or CIBORIUM decorated with sacred EMBLEMS and DEVICES.

euphuism
Extraordinarily floriate and sweet circumlocutory language of sixteenth-century John Lyly's *Euphues*; excessive stylistic refinement at the expense of subject; cloying preciosity.

eureka
An exultant joyous cheer of success, emulating the ARCHIMEDEAN Greek epithet "I have found it!" which the elated Syracusan scientist shouted when discovering the method by specific gravity for de-

termining the proportion of base metal in a golden crown.

Eva-Ave antithesis

In literature and art, woman was portrayed as embodying eternal Judao-Christian opposites: Eva, lusty temptress and herself tempted and Ave (Maria), the Blessed Mother Mary, virgin, perfect, and peerless. A woman descendant of Eve, a creature of nature, was a seducer, corrupter, earth-bound lust-monger who by wile and guile stimulated men to bodily pleasures, sin, ruin, and damnation, while a lady follower of the Virgin Mary was imperious, just, unobtainable, spotless, by inspiration and grace stimulating men to blessedness on earth and promising sanctification thereafter. Intellectually, woman must be shunned and castigated (though enjoyed sexually when necessary) but the lady must be praised, exalted, and revered. This convenient, absurd dichotomy influenced by ARISTOTELIANISM and celibate clerics' preoccupation with WOMEN'S SECRETS, affected lives of WOMEN AT WORK, WOMEN WRITERS AND POETS, WOMEN PHYSICIANS AND SURGEONS, LADY BOSSES, CRAFTSWOMEN, and WHORES.

evangeliary

A richly ornamented, illuminated MANUSCRIPT containing the FOUR GOSPELS, such as the exquisite eighth-century INSULAR *Book of Kells*; also, a book containing only the portions of LITURGY read at MASS, arranged according to the liturgical calendar.

evestrum

In ALCHEMY, a prophetic spirit capable of interpreting signs of coming events.

ewer

A pitcher used in liturgical services for wine, and in secular banquet halls for drinks like wine, water, ale, and beer. In kitchens or at table, it often was raised on a tripod BLANDRETH base to allow hearth coals to heat the liquid before its service.

Exaltation of the Holy Cross

HOLY CROSS DAY, a Christian feast on September 14, commemorating the rediscovery of the TRUE CROSS in Jerusalem in the seventh century by Emperor Heraclius.

Excalibur

The name of King Arthur's magical sword, derived from the legend of its origin: only the elect could draw it from a stone, *ex cal* (*ce*) *libre* (*are*) ("to free from a stone"); or named after the Old Irish invincible sword Caledvulch or Caladbolg.

ex cathedra

Papal pronouncements made from the throne, thought infallible in matters of faith and morals.

excommunication

The rite of expulsion from the community of Christians on earth and the implied rejection from the community of salvation after death unless the individual is sanctified by God's GRACE; the act of ecclesiastical censure performed with BELL, BOOK, AND CANDLE.

excursus

A formal, lengthy digression, a rhetorical device comparable to EPIC RETARDATION. In *The Romance of the Rose,* the doddering yet sexually exuberant harridan interrupts her own learned discourse with a rambling excursion into animals' sexual habits, thus linking human with bestial passions and reaffirming procreation's place in the GREAT CHAIN OF BEING.

exedra

The upper surface of a VAULT or arch; or a semicircular bench, raised upon steps, aside an EPISCOPAL throne.

exegesis

Explanation and interpretation of Holy Scriptures. The THREE-FOLD INTERPRETATION of Origen and the FOUR-FOLD INTERPRETATION of Cassian and Saint Gregory insisted that for nearly every literal meaning of a text there are also spiritual, moral, inspirational, symbolic, and prophetic significances.

exemplum

An illustrative story or example in pulpit literature, sermons, moral and pedagogic disquisitions, and story collections as the GESTA ROMANORUM. From Scripture, classical AUCTORES, contemporary history, or bawdy truth or art, examples intruded into the text to teach by analogy, often dramatic, entertaining, gruesome, or shocking. A form of creative distraction, it temporarily removed attention from an uncomfortable important point, skirted around it, then, its intended victim unaware, sharply thrust it home. Related to the rhetorical EXCURSUS, it often pleasantly instructed and educationally delighted: as in DOCERE ET DELECTARE.

Expectation Sunday

The Sunday between ASCENSION day and WHITSUNDAY, commemorating the APOSTLES' expectation of the descent of the HOLY SPIRIT after Christ's ascension.

extract

A concentrated, semisolid medication or GALENICAL, which the patient took diluted in wine, water, or fruit juice.

extreme unction

The final of the SEVEN SACRAMENTS: for a baptized believer at the point of death, a priest performs the final anointing accompanied by ritual prayers.

eyeglasses

Corrective lenses in a bridge-clinging nosepiece to aid damaged vision. The earliest lenses antedate the thirteenth century. Magnifying and colored glass spectacles were sold by thriving lens makers in Nuremberg by 1482.

F

fabliaux
Lewd tales depicting ebullient philanderers, bed-hopping with exuberance. Stock characters in dramatic situations include the SENEX AMANS (old lover) cuckolded by his lusty young wife and her sexually athletic lover; the MILES GLORIOSUS (braggart soldier) whose boasting undoes him; lascivious clerical lovers with willing women congregants; and bold bawdy wives of sexually senescent men. FABLIAUX WOMEN oppose the idealized DOMNA of the EVA-AVE ANTITHESIS.

fabliaux women
A fifteenth-century alphabetical catalog describes them as "able, ardent, audacious, amorous, baiting, bored beauties, carnally curious, cuckolding coquettes, daring in their duping of doddering husbands, engagingly effervescent in feisty philandering."

facade
A building's external facing.

facet
One of many small-cut and polished faces of a gem or other hard surface for the effects of reflecting and refracting light.

faggot
A bundle of sticks, twigs, and wood bound for sale or for burning in cook fires, camp fires, or the pyres of heretics and WITCHES, or for piling against a besieged castle's wooden gate to set it afire.

faience
Tin-glazed earthenware, originally manufactured in Faenza, Italy, important for table and banquet gear and decorative ostentatious objects, both secular and liturgical. DELFT and MAJOLICA potteries produced distinctive contemporary wares.

falcon
A bird of prey trained to pursue game, one of the more popular sportbirds of noble men and women.

falconry
(Or hawking) The elaborate ceremonial technique of hunting game with birds of prey, such as falcons and other hawks. The birds were trained to the wrist, HOODWINKed, held by gesses, and let fly to ceremonial musical calls, as much for a courtly exercise and entertainment as for acquisition of kitchen fowl. A famous INSTRUCTION BOOK for the art was Frederick II's *Tractatus de arte venandi cum avibus.*

faldstool
A folding stool used as seat or as a LECTERN for a kneeling BISHOP.

false sleeves
Long fabric or FUR panels, falling from the lower part of the garment's sleeves, sometimes extending from elbow to ankle. Detachably sewn or hooked to the sleeve, the panels were in complementary or contrasting textiles, and could be bestowed as love tokens and CIMIERS in COURTLY LOVE affairs and tournaments.

familiarity breeds contempt
Chaucer said it: *over gret homlinesse engendreth dispreisinge.* Often said of a brave warrior's danger because of too-frequent closeness with death.

fan
A fashion rage in twelfth-century Italy, fans were imported from Asia Minor, Egypt, and the East. Made of peacock, ostrich, parrot, and Indian crow feathers affixed atop jeweled and enameled ivory handles.

fancy
A popular Renaissance instrumental composition for an ensemble. Of English origin, its composers included William Byrd, Thomas Morley, and Alfonso Ferabosco.

fanfare
A short melody for trumpets signaling a ceremonial, military, hunting, culinary, or festive event. It consisted usually of the tones of the triad only.

fantasia
A Renaissance instrumental composition, a popular variety of the learned, strictly contrapuntal RICERCARE.

farandole
A popular Provençal dance performed by a long chain of men and women holding hands and following the leader through a variety of steps and figures to PIPE AND TABOR music.

farce
(Latin *farcire,* to stuff) A light-hearted, formulaic, dramatic INTERLUDE, derived from the repertory of the JOCULATORES, with such stock episodes as the SENEX AMANS (old lover) in a love triangle, interspersed among serious scenes of MYSTERY and MIRACLE plays; also, artistic padding.

farris
A woman blacksmith.

Fastingong
A SHROVETIDE festival, CARNIVAL, MUMMING play, and FASTNACHTSSPIEL.

Fastnachtsspiel
A SHROVE TUESDAY or SHROVETIDE CARNIVAL play, often a MUMMING incorporating pagan fertility and sword dances, such as MORESCA, MATTACHIN, and MORRIS DANCE.

Fata Morgana
King Arthur's sister, Morgan le Fay, the fairy consort and deceiver of Merlin the Magician, who had taught her his supernatural arts. The mirages observed over the Straits of Messina were thought to be her home.

fauteuil
An armchair.

feast and fast, fast and feast
The Christian calendar alternates culinary correlatives; New Year's festival, SAINT JOHN'S DAY, and the FEAST OF FOOLS ecclesiastically sanction excess; feasts release restraint, reaffirming boundaries of self control between festivals. Fasts, such as LENT and ASH WEDNESDAY, require an avoidance of meat to stimulate piety. The learned and practical distinction between flesh and fish bifurcated animals such as the beaver, whose

While royal feasters sit at sideboards, an aumbry behind, servitors and musicians in doublets and poulaines serve the crowned host. (From M. Wohlgemuth, *Der Schatzbehalter*, Nuremberg, Koberger, 1491; courtesy of Metropolitan Museum of Art)

body was deemed flesh but whose delicious tail was classified as fish.

Feast of Feasts
EASTER, the most solemn, significant Christian holiday, more sacred than any of the TWELVE GREAT FEASTS.

Feast of Fools
A church and town celebration, near January 1 and the FEAST OF THE CIRCUMCISION. Hierarchies of church and world were turned upside down such that minor insignificant officials of CATHEDRALS assumed the titles of BISHOP and cardinal, ceremonials were parodied, persons and liturgy were mocked, yet ultimately the canons of order were reaffirmed. The leader for that day was a LORD OF MISRULE.

Feast of the Circumcision
The eighth day after CHRISTMAS, January 1, celebrating Christ's ritual circumcision.

Feast of the Dedication
The Jewish festival of lights: HANUKKAH.

Feast of Weeks
PENTECOST.

fee
(Anglo-Saxon *feoh,* cattle or property) Either moveable property, such as goods and money, or an immovable FIEF.

fee simple
A feudal ESTATE IN LAND consisting of two types: FEE SIMPLE ABSOLUTE, the highest and best ownership and possession rights, a freehold estate lasting indefinitely; and FEE SIMPLE DEFEASIBLE, an estate in land cut short when and if certain events occur. It was a land transfer with no conditions attached and no ENTAIL except that it be valid in general under the statutes of the realm.

fee simple defeasible
An interest or ESTATE IN LAND, a feudal TENURE, that could last forever as a FEE SIMPLE absolute, but might be cut short. If causing an automatic reversion to the grantor or heir, it was called a fee simple determinable. The tenure might be fee simple upon condition subsequent, causing a non-automatic reversion of possession to grantor or heirs, or fee simple subject to an executory interest, causing a remainder to a third person.

fee simple subject to executory limitation
Created by the STATUTE OF USES (1536), a FEE SIMPLE DEFEASIBLE with rights retained not by the grantor but by a third person, a future interest ESTATE IN LAND held in freehold TENURE.

fee tail
In COMMON LAW, in order to keep land in TENURE in the family, eldest sons must inherit from one another, each receiving only the equivalent of a LIFE ESTATE. This process of inheritance was created in a will by the magic words "AND THE HEIRS OF HIS OR HER BODY."

feinte
A dance step from the BUFFON.

felix culpa
(Latin, happy fault) The fortunate sin, Adam's and Eve's fall from grace in the Garden of Eden upon eating the forbidden fruit which led to the necessity for mankind's redemption and salvation by the sacrifice of Jesus in the CRUCIFIXION. If Eve had not sinned in the Garden of Eden, there would have been no necessity for a SECOND EVE, the Virgin Mary. The act of consuming holiness in the form of the EUCHARIST undoes the original evil caused by eating.

fellow
A good fellow or a NICE GIRL: an ignorant rascal, an untrustworthy lascivious young man or woman.

fel vitri
Glass gall, a white salt scum resulting from the fusion process in glass-making.

femme sole
(French, woman alone) An independent businesswoman or CRAFTSWOMAN responsible by law for her own professional practice, profits, purchases, and business debts. Married women, not only SPINSTERS, had legal protection against financial incursions of greedy relatives or HUSBANDS.

fenester
A window.

fer de moline
(French, mill iron) An iron support for a moving millstone; a MILLRIND.

feretory
A portable, though commonly stationary, SHRINE or TOMB for saints' RELICs ornamented with enamelry, carvings, and precious adornments.

fermail
A small BROOCH, like the AGRAFFE; a fastener for a TUNIC, gown, or cape at the garment's throat.

ferment
A substance that causes the catalytic action of another. Alchemists considered it a universal vivifying spirit, exalting all materials with which it combined. As yeast, it was a kitchen ferment; to the physician Avicenna, it was sophic SULFUR.

ferruginous glaze
A brown, iron-rust-colored GLAZE, containing particles of rusted iron, used to coat FLAGONs, FLASKs, and storage jars.

fess
(Latin *fascia,* a band, a fillet) A horizontal band crossing the middle of a heraldic field, one-third the shield's width; coordinated with a vertical pale to make a CROSS IN HERALDRY.

festoon
A festive decorative design of carved or painted garlands of fabric or leaves, flowers, and fruits arranged in a pendant scallop or loop between two points, set off by ribbons, chords, or vines; similar to a SWAG.

fetlock
A horse's leg-lock preventing its escape while allowing restricted movement for grazing; or the tuft of hair on a horse's leg or a person's head.

Fetter Dienstag
(German, Fat Tuesday) SHROVE TUESDAY or MARDI GRAS, the expression derived from the culinary custom of eating eggs and fat otherwise prohibited during LENT.

feud
(Latin *feudum,* a fee or reward) A FIEF or land held in feudal commitment.

feudalism
In Western Europe, particularly Germany, the contractual system exchanging land for military service, developing from the Germanic war band or COMITATUS and Roman land TENURE. In England, the political-social order William the Conqueror introduced by purchasing the loyalty of chief nobles with land grants so that the nobles would support him politically and provide fighting men. The nobility protected their VASSALs, who provided labor and manpower. Each class was linked to each by rights and responsibilities, by loyalty and dependency, in a political GREAT CHAIN OF BEING, an ORDO MUNDI sanctioned by the Church and epitomized in the FEUDAL PYRAMID.

feudal pyramid
Representing the intricate interrelationships among land holders, the king or state was the ALLODIAL owner at the apex, followed below by the TENANT IN CAPITI, then, by the process of SUBINFEUDATION, the sub-tenants. Each level had responsibility for services and feudal INCIDENTS to the landholder one level above.

Fibonacci series
A sequence of numbers, each of which, after the first, is the sum of the two previous: 1, 1, 2, 3, 5, 8, 13, 21, 34, 55, etc. It was recognized by important Italian mathematician Leonardo Fibonacci, writer of a standard algebra and arithmetic, *Liber abaci* (1201), and a geometry and trigonometry, *Practica Geometriae* (1220).

fibula
An ornamental BROOCH or clasp, often decorated with ENGRAVING or precious stones.

fichets
Slits in the sides of a SURCOAT, allowing the hands to pass through.

fief
(Latin *feudum,* a fee or a reward) In FEUDALISM, land or an estate possessed and worked in exchange for service and homage to an overlord who owns it.

figura coeli
(Latin, shape of heaven) A scheme or table showing disposition of the heavenly bodies at a particular time, used in ASTROLOGY, GENETHLIALOGY, and CHRONOPHYSICA for plotting times of nativity, disease, and daily hours.

filigree
Delicate, finely interlaced threads of silver, gold, or precious metal wire decorated with tiny balls or grains of metal. Filigree embellished secular CHALICES, jewelry, liturgical objects, and costumes.

Filioque
(Latin, and from the Son) A Christian doctrine vigorously defended by ninth-century Photius, patriarch of Constantinople, asserting that the HOLY SPIRIT was equal to the Father and to the Son and emanated from both, in the DOUBLE PROCESSION of the HOLY GHOST. It was an important controversy between the Eastern and Western churches.

fillet
A woman's stiff linen CIRCLET popular as a foreheaddress.

fimbriated
In costumery and HERALDRY, the bordering of an edge with a fringe or a narrow band.

finalis
The note on which a melody ends in the CHURCH MODES.

fin amors
Refined love in the Provençal tradition of COURTLY LOVE, sometimes PLATONIC, rarely sexual, unlike AMOR DE CON; a mannered passion celebrated cerebrally as love from a distance, AMOR DE LONH.

finial
A terminal or pinnacle decoration to an architectural element or piece of furniture or jewelry, sometimes sculptured in HIGH RELIEF, as a human or divine figure, or formed as a geometric shape, or merely a knob or KNOP.

fioretto ordinario
(Italian, an ordinary flourish) An elaborate, elegantly integrated hand-and-foot movement in sixteenth-century Italian dance.

fire of the philosophers
In ALCHEMY, adepts considered the creation and the perpetuation of a bright intense fire the critical element of their art, the sun which could destroy the corruption of philosophical chaos: the disorders and imperfections inherent in base metals and impure chemicals.

first female martyr
According to the apocryphal Acts of Saint Paul, Saint Thecla of Iconium had been converted to Christianity by Saint Paul and because of her dedication to her newfound faith was condemned to be burned, then thrown to lions and bears. Both persecutions failed, and she lived as a recluse in a cave, performing healing miracles. At age 90, again persecuted for her healing powers, she was saved when the rock of her cave opened to enclose her, her MARTYR's faith ever steadfast.

fishing nets
Ordinances determined fishing seasons for specific varieties of fish, specified places for fishing, and decided types, sizes, and meshes of nets, as well as when, where, and how they were used. In England, common nets included the kyddle, tromekeresnet, pursnet, draynet, stakenet, forestat, stalker, coanet or codnet, smeltnet, hebbyngnette, treinke, and weir.

five books of Moses
The Old Testament PENTATEUCH.

five elementary principles
Thought to compose all material substance of the universe: MERCURY, ether, or spirit, plus the FOUR ELEMENTS: earth, air, fire, and water.

five glorious mysteries
In Christianity, the RESURRECTION; ASCENSION; Descent of the HOLY GHOST at PENTECOST; ASSUMPTION; and the CORONATION OF OUR LADY.

five metrical feet
Poetic and prose rhythmic patterns that describe emphasis and duration of syllables in words, commonly

expressed as long and short, the long twice the duration of the short, approximating a musical half-note versus a quarter-note. In romance languages, the five basic patterns each create a particular mood and esthetic effect: *iambic* (short/long); *trochaic* (long/short); *dactylic* (long/short/short); *anapestic* (short/short/long); and *spondaic* (long/long).

five senses
Allegorically represented as beautiful women with appropriate ATTRIBUTEs: Hearing with a LUTE or PORTATIVE ORGAN; Sight with a mirror; Taste with fruit or sweets; Smell with flowers and perfume; Touch with a prickly hedgehog or smooth ERMINE. The exquisite Lady with the Unicorn tapestries of Cluny may exemplify all these.

Five Ways
The QUINQUE VIAE.

fixation
The chemical and metallurgical process by which a naturally volatile substance is rendered fixed, nonvolatile, and resistant to fire.

fixed signs
Taurus, Leo, Scorpio, and Aquarius, so called because the seasons or the weather are reasonably "fixed" when the sun enters those signs. Tempers of those born under them are believed stable and their creations durable, such as a tree planted, house built, or city founded. Opposite to the MUTABLE SIGNS.

fixed star
As opposed to the sun, moon, and the planets, a heavenly body that always appears to occupy the same position in the heavens, having no periodic revolution around the sun.

flagellants
Lay fraternities of self-punishing Christians in Italy, France, and Germany that flourished during the BLACK DEATH; itinerant sufferers of emotional or psychophysiological diseases, such as SAINT VITUS' DANCE, they whipped and scarified their own bodies as well as those of their fellow believers, instigated pogroms against Jews, exhorted pious self-abnegation for salvation, and terrorized towns.

Flagellants use scourges to beat their flesh. (From anonymous woodcut, 1493)

flageolet
A RECORDER-like wind instrument with four finger-holes in front, two on back.

flagon
A jug, pitcher, or pouring vessel, often embellished by paint, ENAMEL, INTAGLIO, INLAY, or APPLIQUED gold and silver adornments.

flail
An agricultural implement whose beating edge for threshing wheat or grain is connected to a long handle by a joint.

flame stitch
An embroidery technique: BARGELLO WORK.

flask
A storing or pouring vessel, related to the COSTREL, often with small wing handles that have been pierced with holes for a chord or thong in order to carry or suspend in storage. For cosmetics, medications, and drinks, chemical names or insignia usually were painted or incised on the surface.

flax
A long silky fiber from a linum plant used in weaving linen: SCUTCHING flax is one of the TWELVE LABORS of the months.

A mounted servitor with crested flagon in his left hand and a hanap in his right (far right) serves the assembled feasters while a mounted surveyor of ceremonies wields his serving wand. (From *Landeshauptarchiv*, Koblenz, 1330)

flèche
(French, arrow) A sharply pointed, lead-covered, wooden spire of a CHURCH or CATHEDRAL.

fleeming
One of three significant PHLEBOTOMY techniques, along with CUPPING and LEECHING, for BLOODLETTING.

flesh hook
A long-handled, curved metal implement for turning and grasping large pieces of meat in butcheries and kitchens.

flesh-shambles
A slaughterhouse or butchery with freshly killed carcasses on display. Men and women butchers cut and trimmed before selling the meat of such animals as sheep, pig, cow, ox, deer, beaver, whale, porpoise, boar, bear, and hare; also called a SHAMBLES.

fleur-de-lis
The stylized lily, an official royal EMBLEM of France since twelfth-century King Louis VII, though used by Charlemagne and the CAROLINGIANS; an important heraldic BADGE, often FLORY COUNTERFLORY.

fleuret
Both a GALLIARD and PAVAN dance step described in Arbeau's ORCHESOGRAPHY; it requires three steps in the time allowed for two.

flieder
The German Jewish woman's fashionable CORNALIA.

florilegia
(Latin, a gathering of flowers) Anthologies of selected literary passages compiled to instruct by example in the fine points of rhetoric and philosophical disquisition, usually representing classical AUCTORES whose works were studied in the TRIVIUM of the SEVEN LIBERAL ARTS.

flory counterflory
Heraldic decoration with FLEUR-DE-LIS alternating pointing inward and outward.

flos campi
The flower or rose of Sharon, asphodel (from the Song of Songs 2:1); one of the perfections and VIRTUES OF THE VIRGIN.

flourishings
Embellishments and glazes on breads, pastries, meats, poultry and fish, as a culinary artistic phenomenon including GILDING (the process of utilizing egg yolk and saffron to create the illusion of gold, thus AUREFICTION, not AUREFACTION, of ALCHEMY); also, artistic decorations in architecture, sculpture, furniture, and jewelry that emphasize form not function.

flowers of red wine
The yeast fungi blooms left over from wine-making, used in recipes to enhance taste.

flugel
Long, open, ground-trailing sleeves for fifteenth-century German garments, edged with fur and brocade.

flush work
Decorative wall construction combining halved flintstones, called knapped-flint, plus DRESSED STONE.

flute
A musical wind instrument. The transverse flute was held horizontally, the air blown across a hole; pitch was determined by covering and unstopping holes; known in Europe since the twelfth century and initially used more for military than artistic purposes, as was the endblown flute, the RECORDER.

fluting
In music, playing a RECORDER or early transverse FLUTE; in art and architecture, channelling, furrowing, grooving and chamfering, decorative semicircular grooves or cuts in wood or stone that feigned the appearance of fabric folds, especially important in fifteenth-century LINENFOLD carvings on furniture and interior and exterior doors.

flying buttress
An exterior stone BUTTRESS composed of a propping arch, its upper end against the high main wall, its lower against a PIER, with a stabilizing PINNACLE on the pier to accept the transmitted thrust. Flying buttresses were used as external structural reinforcement of interior unfettered space, permitting the grand, vertical skyward thrust of the interiors of GOTHIC CATHEDRALS.

folia
A fifteenth-century fool's dance, its steps comparable to the MORESCA and MORRIS DANCE.

foliate
Leaf-shaped; describing ornaments in a foliate spray, graceful botanical shoots, or flowering fine-leaved plants joined together.

folio
(Latin, *folium,* leaf) A sheet of paper, VELLUM, or PARCHMENT, with front (*folio recto*) distinguished from back (*folio verso*) by color, texture, or numbering; a book of sheets folded only once and therefore large size, in contrast to a QUIRE.

folium
A red vegetable coloring agent, like litmus, changing color according to acidity or alkalinity; an indicator by color: in neutral solution, violet; in acid, red; in alkaline, blue.

fons hortorum
(Latin, fountain of the gardens) An epithet for Mary, from the Song of Songs (4:15), one of the VIRTUES OF THE VIRGIN; a celebration of the flowing water of perfect purity, an element in GARDEN and HORTUS CONCLUSUS (enclosed garden) scenes; in art and literature, the source of the stream into which the UNICORN dipped his horn.

food for worms
In the fourteenth century TRANSI TOMBS, MEMENTO MORI, ARS MORIENDI, and sermons, the slow, inexo-

rable consumption of a human dead body by worms was considered as the just humiliation of the cadaver punished for the live being's worldly pride. Contrasting life's splendor with death's decay, diverse worms, toads on the head, and snakes in the eyes, ears, and nose desecrate and destroy bodily substances.

food painting
Natural and edible dyes were added to food for art, not for taste, and included parsley's green, rose petal's red, saffron's amber, heliotrope's blue, violet's purple, as well as mint, mallow, and hazel's aqua and green.

fool
A clown, jester, or intelligent courtier hired for entertainment and allowed impertinent statements for the sake of truth; jokingly serious, earnest in jest, he, among the flatterers, was paid to tell the truth. Fools were costumed usually in MOTLEY plus CAP AND BELLS.

Forest's thumb
The celebrated medical malpractice suit in fifteenth-century England brought by William Forest against his eminent London and Oxford University surgeons for disfiguring his hand by CAUTERY to prevent his bleeding to death. After a long court trial before judge and jury with expert witnesses, the verdict exonerated the surgeons, and attributed the hand hemorrhage and resulting scar to the patient's physical constitution, the nature of the wound, and the malevolent astrological sign of dark and bloody Aquarius.

forfeiture
A TENANT guilty of treason or breaking an oath of allegiance forfeits land held in TENURE to an overlord.

fork
Generally used as a preparatory and lifting implement in kitchens and barnyards but disdained at table as foolish and foppish and not generally accepted in culinary cutlery until the seventeenth century. Elaborate finger choreography allowed the diner tactile pleasures of eating without metallic intervention.

formes fixes
Three major poetic and musical styles: BALLADE, VIRELAI, and RONDEAU; their major elegant exponent is fourteenth-century poet-composer Guillaume de Machaut.

Fortune
Chance, fate, and luck: an active agent in human affairs. Unpredictable and mutable, Fortune was usually allegorized as an imperious, fickle woman arbitrarily raising up or casting down people on her wheel of fortune: the higher in worldly blessing, the harder and longer the fall to TRAGEDY. Religion and BOETHIAN fortitude were the only human weapons mitigating her power.

fosse
A man-made, walled channel, moat, or deep ditch for a natural water course or for defense.

Four Ages of Humankind
Youth, Prime, Old Age, and Senility; they were depicted in MINIATURES, BOOKS OF HOURS, court BERGAMASCAs, culinary SUBTLETIES, dances, and COSMOLOGICAL DIAGRAMS.

Four Ages of the World
Golden, Silver, Bronze, and Iron Ages; derived from Latin poet Ovid's *Metamorphosis,* depicting gradual decay of civilization from perfection after the initial EARTHLY PARADISE, resembling the Judeo-Christian Garden of Eden.

four cardinal virtues
Justice, Prudence, Fortitude, and Temperance, derived from Plato's *Republic.* Together with the THREE THEOLOGICAL VIRTUES, they formed the SEVEN CARDINAL VIRTUES.

four classes of music
MUSICA MUNDANA, harmony of the universe; MUSICA HUMANA, human bodily harmonies and soul rhythms; MUSICA VOCALIS, animal and natural voices; and MUSICA ARTIFICIALIS, human vocal and instrumental sound; derived from fourteenth-century Theodoricus de Campo's classification of music based on the BOETHIAN THREE CLASSES OF MUSIC.

four contraries
Hot, cold, moist, and dry, the opposing qualities characterizing all aspects of the created universe. Gen-

erally paired, they inhere in the FOUR ELEMENTS, FOUR HUMORS, FOUR SEASONS, and FOUR AGES OF HUMANKIND.

Four Daughters of God
Misericordia, Mercy; *Justitia,* Justice; *Pax,* Peace; and *Veritas,* Truth; the four virtues associated with Christ's appearance on earth. The most significant was Mercy, supreme godly charity.

Four Daughters of Time
Mercy, Truth, Righteousness, and Peace; Truth was considered the principle and true daughter of time, *veritas filia temporis.*

Four Doctors of the Church
Saints Ambrose, Jerome, Augustine, and Gregory the Great, although the title sometimes is applied to others.

four elements
Earth, air, water, and fire; associated with the FOUR HUMORS, FOUR CONTRARIES, FOUR AGES OF HUMANKIND, and FOUR SEASONS.

Four Evangelists
Matthew, iconographically represented as a man; Mark, a lion; Luke, an ox; and John, an eagle; their images derived from the vision of the prophet Ezekiel (1:5) and the four BEASTS OF THE APOCALYPSE in REVELATION 4:6; the saintly authors of the FOUR GOSPELS, associated with the FOUR DOCTORS OF THE CHURCH and the FOUR MAJOR PROPHETS.

four-fold interpretation
Holy Scripture and some secular ROMANCES and epics were interpretable on four levels of meaning: literal (superficial, surface denotation of words or tale); allegorical (abstract ideas personified); tropological (morally and ethically instructive); and anagogical (mystically uplifting or eschatological). John Cassian, Saint Gregory the Great, and Saint Augustine were the great interpreters of four-fold analysis, based on Origen's THREE-FOLD INTERPRETATION schema. Saint Augustine's celebrated distich explains: *littera gesta docet quid credis allegoria; quid agis moralia, quo tendis anagogia* (The literal teaches the facts; the allegorical, what you believe; the moral, what you are to do; the anagogic, where you are going).

Four Horsemen of the Apocalypse furiously ride, trampling king and commoners. (From Albrecht Dürer's *Apocalypse*, Nuremberg, 1498)

four Gospels
The four New Testament books—Matthew, Mark, Luke, and John—that give accounts of the life of Jesus Christ and His teachings and miracles.

Four Horsemen of the Apocalypse
The Conqueror, War, Famine, and Death, who ride horses, respectively, white, fire-red, black, and pale; the four riders from Saint John the Evangelist's Book of Revelation (6:1–8).

four humors
Blood, phlegm, choler, and black bile, causing, respectively, the sanguine, phlegmatic, choleric, and melancholic personalities, temperaments, and physiques. The four humors were associated with the FOUR STAGES OF LIFE, FOUR SEASONS of the year, FOUR ELEMENTS, and FOUR CONTRARIES.

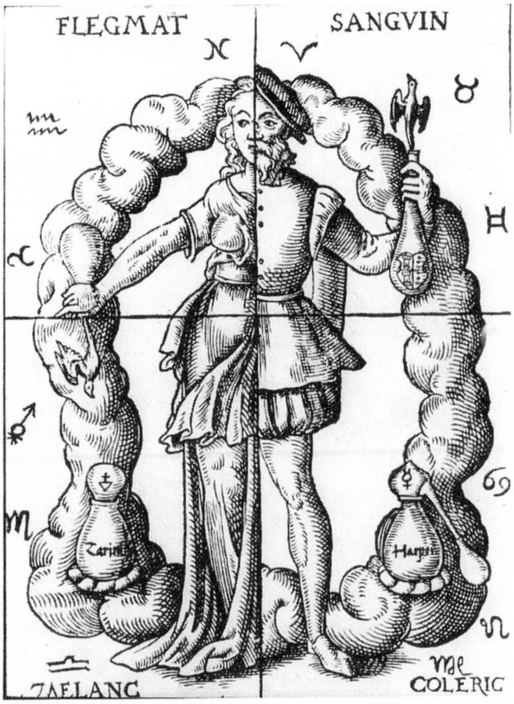

The four humors inhabit the hermaphroditic alchemical figure. (From an engraving in L. Thurneysser's Quinta Essentia, 1574)

four kings of Eleanor of Aquitaine

Four rulers whom Queen Eleanor of Aquitaine either bedded or birthed. She was first queen consort and co-ruler with King Louis VII of France; then married the Plantagenet king of England, Henry II and was by him mother of King John and King Richard I, the Lion-Heart.

Four Major Prophets

Isaiah, Jeremiah, Ezekiel, and Daniel; distinguished from the TWELVE MINOR PROPHETS.

four musical dialects

In Western CHURCH music: GREGORIAN CHANT (Roman); AMBROSIAN CHANT (Milanese); GALLICAN CHANT; and MOZARABIC or Visigothic chant.

four orders of friars

CARMELITE, AUGUSTINIAN, DOMINICAN, and FRANCISCAN, four MENDICANT brotherhoods dedicated to preaching the Gospel, to poverty, and to earthly virtue *in imitatio Christi* (in imitation of Christ). Chaucer's hypocritical, wanton, merry Friar of *The Canterbury Tales* is the best beggar in all four orders.

four parts of the world

Europe, Asia, Africa, and America, usually depicted with specific ATTRIBUTES: Europe (crown, scepter, temple, horse, and CORNUCOPIA); Asia (flowers, jewels, perfume censer, palm, and camel); Africa (black-skinned people, coral, scorpion, lion, elephant); and America (feather headdress, bow and arrow, caiman, crocodile).

four rivers of Hades

Styx, Acheron, Phlegethon, and Cocytus (really a frozen lake); sites in the *Divine Comedy* for punishments of souls in hell (Cantos 3, 8, 14, and 31 of the *Inferno*). Contrast the FOUR RIVERS OF PARADISE.

four rivers of Paradise

Tigris, Euphrates, Phison, and Gehom, flowing from the Garden of Eden (Genesis 2:11–14), symbolic of the FOUR GOSPELS. Contrast the FOUR RIVERS OF HADES.

four seasons

Associated in COSMOLOGICAL DIAGRAMS with the FOUR AGES OF HUMANKIND, FOUR ELEMENTS, and FOUR CONTRARIES, the seasons grace not only sculpture, manuscript ILLUMINATION, and literary and philosophic disquisitions, but also banquet SUBTLETIES.

four stages of life

Infancy, Youth, Prime, Old Age.

four sufferers in Hades

Ixion, Sisyphus, Tantalus, and Tityus.

fourteen stations

The STATIONS OF THE CROSS.

four temperaments

Melancholic, phlegmatic, choleric, and sanguine. Each is produced by one of the FOUR HUMORS.

Four Virtues of Christ's Coming

Mercy, Justice, Peace, and Truth, the FOUR DAUGHTERS OF GOD.

Four Winds
Boreas, the rough North Wind; Notus, the South Wind; Euros or Argestes, the East Wind; and Zephyr or Zephyrus, the mild West Wind; they are siblings of the stars, children of the Greek Goddess of Dawn Eos (the Roman Aurora) and Astraeus. In Chaucer, Zephirus's sweet breath inspires the fields, forests, and heaths to flower, and men and women to go on PILGRIMAGES.

four women governors of earth world
Nobility, Wisdom, Wealth, and Chivalry, the four gorgeous queens who convened in outer space in order to govern the earth; from Christine de Pizan's didactic, encyclopedic ALLEGORY, *The Road of Long Studies.*

foutra
Sexual intercourse, a favorite FABLIAUX word.

frame tale
A narrative, structural device in which one overarching or frame story incorporates many smaller, otherwise disjunct stories, characters, techniques, and styles. Chaucer's *Canterbury Tales,* Boccaccio's *Decameron,* Sercambi's *Novella,* and *The Tales of the Arabian Nights* exemplify such simple narrative frames, as in Chaucer's gathering for a pilgrimage diverse, sundry folk and themes, a brilliant ploy for violating classical canons of decorum and the three unities of time, place, and style, and for juxtaposing such artistic diversities as courtly ROMANCE, EXEMPLUM, BEAST EPIC, and FABLIAUX.

franche
In HERALDRY, a small, semi-circular projection at the juncture of several lines, as in a CROSS's arms meeting.

Franciscans
The Order of Friars Minor, or Minorites, a MENDICANT order founded by Saint Francis of Assisi in the thirteenth century, one of the FOUR ORDERS OF FRIARS. Activities included preaching, INQUISITION, reforms, care of sick and poor, and missions to Africa and Asia.

frankalmoigne
A spiritual TENURE: in return for an ESTATE IN LAND, a clergyman or ecclesiastical corporation distributed alms or said MASSes or prayers for the grantor; lay tenures included freehold and villeinage.

frappe-talons
A dance step striking heels together to make ankle bells ring in a MORRIS DANCE.

freedom
A noteworthy generosity of spirit subsuming personal desire while celebrating a larger good, a COMMON PROFIT; also, exemption from taxes, duties, and services; immunity from an otherwise applicable law, or a right not given to others; a privilege of membership in a corporation, as a freedom of the city; a territory of a city having particular rights and immunities.

fresco
A nearly indestructible indoor MURAL or wall painting utilizing chemically inert pigments on a fresh-laid plaster surface, the colors absorbed by capillary action into the wall's matte surface. Frescoes often depict monumental civic and ecclesiastical subjects that easily inspire veneration.

fret
A woman's headdress made of gold or silver trellis work or netting, reticulated, jeweled, and spangled.

frets
Ridged lines across the fingerboard of a stringed instrument as the LUTE or viol, marking positions for stopping the strings to create particular notes.

fretwork
Interlaced or perforated patterns in ornamental woodwork or stonework, lines usually intersecting at right angles forming a continuous band of design.

friar
(Latin, *frater,* brother) A member of a religious MENDICANT community, one of the FOUR ORDERS OF FRIARS: CARMELITES (White Friars), AUGUSTINIANS, DOMINICANS (Black Friars), and FRANCISCANS (GRAY FRIARS, MINORITES, or Friars Minor). Important in democratizing religion, friars were figures of malice in satires, living in convents but actively working with the populace in a town or city. They were distinguished from MONKS monastic (called "fathers"), such as the BENEDICTINES and CARTHU-

SIANS, whose members were fixed in one place (*stabilitas loci*), dedicated to praying in isolation and retreat, not teaching and preaching.

Friars Minor
The Gray Friars, Minorites, or FRANCISCANS, one of the FOUR ORDERS OF FRIARS.

frieze
In architecture, the central section of an ENTABLATURE surmounted by the CORNICE, underpinned by the ARCHITRAVE.

frise
(Or frieze) A sturdy woolen cloth with a shaggy or frieze pile, popular in the fourteenth century.

frittour
A fried, finger-food consisting of apple, pear, turnip, or parsnip dipped in a beer batter, sautéed until golden, and sprinkled with brown sugar, a delicacy gracing courtly banquet boards or cottage TRESTLE TABLES.

frock
A garment, usually a long hooded gown worn by monks and peasants, often girdled at the waist with rope, also called a cowled frock.

frons
The poetic stanza consisting of two PEDES followed by a CAUDA in the virtuosic three-part poetic song of the TROUBADOURS, TROUVÈRES, and MINNESINGERS.

frontlet
A forehead ornament worn by women when exaggeratedly high, wide foreheads were fashionable (the forehead of Chaucer's Prioress is a span wide), consisting of a small pendant loop of velvet, silk, or precious metal attached to the edge of the under cap, the CALOTTE worn beneath the HENNIN, often to indicate rank or wealth. A gold loop suggested a substantial yearly income.

frottola
An Italian poetic and musical secular song; stanzas preceded and followed by a refrain, a *ripresa,* similar in form to the BALLATA and VILLANCICO.

fullage
Money paid to a FULLER, LAVER, or LAVENDER for cleansing cloth.

fuller
A cloth craftsperson responsible for FULLING fabrics and garments.

fuller's earth
A fabric and FUR cleanser, a hydrous compound of silica and alumina.

fulling
Cleansing and thickening newly woven fabric by beating and washing, making it shrink-resistant and well shaped; the process sometimes used FULLER'S EARTH and was paid for by FULLAGE.

fumigation
Burning herbs, minerals, spices, or powerful narcotic substances, for their fragrance and fumes. Physicians administered analgesics, soporifics, and ANAESTHESIA; astrologers and magicians prepared incantations; perfumers transmitted aromatic essences; Christian and Jewish liturgies used ceremonial CENSERS; and philosophers relieved stress and aroused contemplation (as did Marsilio Ficino in *De vita coelitus comparanda*), stilling the mind for meditation.

fumositee
(Or fumosity) Flatulence-causing qualities of foods, or their bony or hairy excrescences which might annoy, injure, or discommode a feaster: sinew, skin, hair, crop, feather, head, pinion, and small bones. Those remains were usually removed by kitchen and banquet hall servitors who were supervised by the SURVEYOR and CARVER.

fundament
The underlying substructure of a building; or the lower orifice of human anatomy, the rectum or anus, which figured in hilarious scatological passages in Chaucer and in FABLIAUX.

funnel bowl
A cone-shaped vessel fitted at its point with a tube for conducting a liquid or powder through a small opening, used in kitchens, pharmacies, and chemical laboratories.

fur

SUMPTUARY LAWS allocated particular animal skins to specific social ranks, such that common city WHORES who wore the fur hoods of noble ladies forfeited their garb before being clapped into jail. Lining, edging, and cloak furs included squirrel, fox, marten, beaver, and LAITICE (white imitation ERMINE). Courtly garments generally used gris vair, budge, and ermine, while beaver, otter, hare, and fox graced the lower nobility and middle classes, leaving for common people lamb, wolf, goat, and sheepskin. In HERALDRY, patterns of certain COLORS, METALS, and shapes: as ermine, ERMINOIS, SABLE, and VAIR.

furlong

A measure of distance, a furrow long, the distance eight oxen in a plow-team can work without rest; also, one side of a 10-acre square.

furnace of the philosophers

An ATHANOR.

fustian

A sturdy cotton fabric, or cross-woven cotton with FLAX or linen, hailing from Egypt's Fustat or Cairo, and used especially for undergarments and cape and coat linings. Fustian equally napped and smooth on both sides was called BOMBAZEEN.

G

gabelle
A tax or customs duty, levied mainly on salt.

gaberdine
A loose-fitting smock or frock; a coarse-grained fabric garment worn by men, women, and children, and important in Jewish costume.

gable
A cable or rope; in architecture, the vertical triangular wall piece at the end of a ridged roof, or over a DORMER window.

gadroon
A decorative edge or border consisting of a row of multiple convex curves (virtually inverse FLUTING), on metal worked from the back by REPOUSSÉ, and on wood, often to embellish rounded moldings.

Galenical
A drug; or a specific medication ascribed to second-century Greek physician Galen, either a SIMPLE, the subject of pharmacognosy, the knowledge of natural substances in natural forms, or a COMPOUND of several substances, such as THERIAC. Galenicals include DECOCTIONS, TINCTUREs, fluid extracts (a concentrated liquid preparation with alcohol as solvent and preservative), EXTRACTs, and COLLYRIA. Galen distinguished between drugs that today would be called pharmacodynamic, affecting the total body, influencing the FOUR HUMORS, and changing the course of illness or disease, and drugs thought chemotherapeutic, changing not the host but the agent causing the illness such as treatments for lice worms.

galile
A popular English diamond-shaped headdress for women, entirely concealing the hair, usually worn with WIMPLE and GORGET.

galilee
A porch or chapel at a CATHEDRAL's west end, outside the CHURCH proper.

gallery
In silver and goldsmithery, an ornamental PARAPET railing running along the edge of a tray or ceremonial object; in architecture, an interior balcony or partial upper story with a view into the main hall or room, such as a MUSICIANS GALLERY.

galley
A large, oar-propelled war- or trade ship. Contrast COG and DROMOND.

galliard
A leaping dance in moderately fast triple time, and including such steps as the CINQ PAS, CAPRIOLZ or capriole, and SAUT MAJEUR. Some of the earliest have been preserved in Attaingnant's *Quatorze Gailliardes.* The galliard was usually performed after a PAVAN.

Gallican chant
The mainly Provençal PLAINSONG and rite used in the churches of Gaul before the ninth-century CAROLINGIAN reform and partly incorporated into GREGORIAN CHANT. Examples include the HYMN *Crux Fidelis* and the IMPROPERIA; eleventh-century manuscripts preserve several melodies.

galliochios
(Or galoshes) Gaulish shoes, wooden-soled shoes with leather straps protecting fine undershoes from rough stone pavement, mud, and water.

gallipot
A tall, elegantly proportioned wine or ale jug.

galloon
An ornamental finishing braid in costumery and upholstery, usually of cotton, silk, velvet, or gold or silver cording.

Galluslied
A tenth-century German song with Latin text, one of the two oldest non-liturgical German songs.

Gamaliel
Saint Paul's teacher, the great rabbi of RABBI GAMALIEL'S DREAM.

gambeson
In ARMOR, a military TUNIC, usually padded, made of leather or heavy cloth, worn alone or under a HABERGEON.

gambrinus
A bibulous epicure, after the thirteenth-century Belgian Duke, Jan Primus, a stupendous drinker, called the King of Beer; a prototypical toper.

gang-days
An alternate title for three rogation days: Monday, Tuesday, and Wednesday before ASCENSION Day.

garbage
Animal viscera and entrails that were considered delicacies, not detritus, and were baked into elaborate pies, to be served not only to commoners but also to noble feasters.

garde corps
A unisex, loose, and flowing hooded garment replacing the SURCOAT or worn over it, often sleeveless or with wide short sleeves.

garde-manger
A locked food-storage cabinet or culinary security area in a kitchen.

Gardeners carefully tend plots of herbs and flowers while indoors the lady of the house, wearing a hennin, observes two noblemen, one wearing a chaperone and liripipe. (From a manuscript by Petrus Crecentius, 15th century; courtesy of the Pierpont Morgan Library, New York)

garden
A literary setting for ALLEGORY, DREAM VISION, LYRIC, and ROMANCE, often naturalistically depicted, with a HERBER and alley. Symbolically, a place of delight or LOCUS AMOENUS, an earthly paradise, suggesting the first garden of Eden; or the site of false happiness pursuing transient fleshly delight rather than God's eternal verity; or the virginal HORTUS CONCLUSUS.

garderobe
A closet, wardrobe, or clothes storeroom; or a privy or NECESSARIUM.

gardevin
A wine cellar, cabinet, or closet for storing wine.

garget
Folded lengths of fabric wound around the head, part of a CHAPERONE.

gargoyle
A rainwater spout, projecting from a roof gutter to direct water away from the building's wall; it was often grotesque with an open-mouthed animal, human or fantastical figure.

garnache
A warm over-robe or super-TUNIC similar to the HOUSSE and to the TABARD, with short cape-like sleeves falling down to the elbows.

garnement
The collective elements of a ROBE; a garment.

garter
The BADGE of the highest order of English knighthood, Knights of the Garter: a dark-blue velvet ribbon, edged and buckled with gold, with the French motto embroidered in gold: *honi soit qui mal y pense* (evil to him who evil thinks). It was worn below the left knee. Froissart attributes its creation to King Edward III, about 1344; dancing with a woman (Seldan in 1614 identifies her as the Countess of Salisbury) who then dropped her garter, the King gallantly donned it saying, "Evil . . . ."

garters
Bands made of wool, leather, or cotton, often fringed, either to hold up stockings or CHAUSSES or to fix knee BREECHES to the leg.

gassenhauer
(German *Gasse,* alley) A popular, vernacular street song, as in Egenloff's *Gassenhauerlin und Reutterliedlein.*

gate house
The building over a castle's or town's defensive perimeter-wall. Fortified, it was a gate tower.

Gate of Ivory, Gate of Horn
The two traditional gates through which true (horn) and false (ivory) dreams come; the MACROBIAN *Commentary* on Cicero's *Dream of Scipio* was a popular dream discourse that analyzed possible deceptions as well as guidances from an active imaginary night-life and from DREAM VISION.

gathering
A particular number of MANUSCRIPT or book leaves placed one inside the other, making a QUIRE.

gat-toothed
A space between the two front teeth, a DIASTEMA; according to PHYSIOGNOMY, it was a sign of the natal star Venus and a lusty, lascivious, sexually prodigious being. Chaucer's Wife of Bath celebrated her own animal spirit by this oral EMBLEM of lust.

Gaudette Sunday
The third Sunday in the festival of ADVENT, when the clergy wear rose-colored VESTMENTS.

gaukler
Comparable to the French JONGLEUR, a German wandering MINSTREL.

gauntlet
The usually hinged, flexible metal glove-armor. To throw it at the feet of an enemy was to pledge battle.

gavelkind
English SOCAGE TENURE allowing land to descend by will to several sons simultaneously, not simply to the eldest.

gavotte
A French dance resembling the BRANSLE.

geis
A TABOO, important in Old Irish literature, including the tales of Cuchulainn and stories of the *Yellow Book* and *Red Book*. A forbidden word or gesture led to dire consequences; both the prohibitions and their effects were similar to folk motifs and MÄRCHEN in many cultures: a prohibited word, spoken, transforms man to WEREWOLF or maiden to tree.

Geisslerlied
(German, scourging song) A fourteenth-century German religious folksong, with a four-line stanza, sung by FLAGELLANTS during penitential marches.

geldyng
A castrated horse or man; also, a eunuch, demonstrating in physiognomical deprivation some past sexual sin of self or parents. The Wycliffe Bible of 1382

made it punishment for deflowering a virgin, incest, or other sexual aberration (Deuteronomy 23:1). Chaucer's Pardoner, a noble ecclesiastic, is a geldyng or a mare.

Gemarrah
The Hebrew and Aramaic commentary and supplement to the MISHNAH, together forming the TALMUD, compiled in Babylon and Jerusalem in the third through fifth centuries.

gematria
In KABALLAH and earlier methods for interpreting Hebrew scriptures, words were translated according to the numerical value of their letters in the Hebrew alphabet, and numbers according to their alphabetic value, using addition and multiplication. This technique was possible in Hebrew, Sanskrit, Greek, and other languages whose letters have numerical equivalents.

gemelle
Twins; in HERALDRY, twin BARS.

genet
The FUR of a small European spotted cat common in France, Spain, and Greece, used as an ornament in costumery.

genethlialogy
The science of forecasting by ASTROLOGY the physique, temperament, intellectual capacities, emotional behavior, and prospective profession of a person from a map of the heavens at the moment of birth.

geniture
Configuration of the heavens at the exact moment an infant is born, investigated by GENETHLIALOGY, and recorded by a BIRTH TIME MIRROR.

geniza
A lumber room. In the ninth century, the Cairo Geniza, adjacent to the main SYNAGOGUE, contained a remarkable garbage heap of letters from Jewish traders and merchants: contracts, accounts, court proceedings, business ledgers, family letters, personal jottings on odd scraps, preserved because according to Jewish law anything bearing the name of God must be buried, not destroyed. A treasure trove of miscellaneous practical details of Mediterranean Jewish culture, the documents now are housed at Cambridge University, the Jewish Theological Seminary, and other sites.

genouillieres
Knee-cap ARMOR.

genre painting
The figures and subjects derived from daily life and the domestic ordinaries, rather than from historical or religious subjects, imaginatively imitating nature for VERISIMILITUDE.

gentilesse
Inherent nobility of spirit expressed in action, ideally associated with noble birth. In COURTLY LOVE's FREEDOM, the self must be subservient to a higher COMMON PROFIT, as Dantè's GENTILEZZA in his *Convivio.*

gentilezza
Italian equivalent of English GENTILESSE, inherent ethical courtesy in all acts of life.

geographia
Table of latitudes and longitudes of 8,000 places, devised by Ptolemy of Alexandria in the second century. The table was comprised of a world map of the known continents and oceans and 26 regional maps, with the distances calculated mathematically. Inexact but influential, it was translated into Latin in the fifteenth century; the 1460 Ebner Codex, from Florence, is one such famous MAPPA MUNDI.

geomancy
The magical art of divination by signs from the earth: a figure formed by a handful of dirt thrown down on a surface, or lines or figures formed by random jottings of dots on paper; also associated with PYROMANCY and HYDROMANCY.

gernon
(Norman French *quernone,* upper lip hair) A mustache. The English family name Algernon derives from an ancestor of the Dukes of Northumberland, Sir William de Percy, who had the NICKNAME Algernon because of his moustache; also, from Count Eustace of Boulogne, the name Auxgernon.

gertrude
A long unisex TUNIC, named for thirteenth-century Saint Gertrude of Saxony, known earlier from the CAROLINGIANS; also an infant's flannel undercoat.

Gesellschaftslied
A secular, middle-class, usually polyphonic, German song differing from songs of the court (HOFLIED) or folk (VOLKSLIED). Written by Isaac, Senfl, and Hofhaimer, it was comparable to the Italian MADRIGAL and French CHANSON.

gesso
A white thick chalk, gypsum, or plaster bound with glue or gelatin to wood panels as a smooth, nonporous undercoat for painting; *gesso grosso,* or coarse gesso, filled in cracks of porous or uneven surfaces; *gesso sotile,* or fine, thin, sleek gesso, neither hid defects nor concealed fine carving.

Gesta Romanorum
(Latin, deeds of the Romans) Title of a thirteenth- or fourteenth-century anthology of Greek, Oriental, and Roman stories with moral applications; a manual of EXEMPLA for meritorious instruction by classical example.

geste
A great deed performed by a hero. It was celebrated in Old French verse epics, the CHANSONS DE GESTES, the Spanish *El Cid,* and pseudo-historical, moral-didactic works as the GESTA ROMANORUM.

get
The Talmudic term for the Jewish writ of divorce, by which a husband and wife dissolve their marriage.

Gethsemane
The garden in which Christ was arrested after his betrayal by Judas.

gibberish
Ridiculous, babbled, nonsensical words, probably in imitation of the language and incantations of the famous Muslim alchemist Geber.

gibecière
A man's leather or fabric pouch attached to a GIRDLE, hung next to his DAGGER or eating knife, containing necessaries and cash.

gigue
(French *gigot,* ham) A ham-shaped or pear-shaped stringed instrument, usually bowed, such as the REBEC.

gilding
Covering with GILT.

gill
A small liquid measure; ranging from a modern shot-glass to one-quarter of an American pint.

gillie
An Anglo-Saxon rawhide shoe, tongueless and laced with a thong.

gilt
Gold-lustered, covered with gold paint, GOLD LEAF, or, as in cookery, egg yolk, saffron, or dandelion paint for AUREFICTION.

gippon
A padded, quilted, short TUNIC, a tight-fitting and buttoned undergarment attached to BREECHES, a DOUBLET.

gipsere
A leather shoulder satchel.

girdle
An ornamental belt for emphasizing the waistline or hip curve, and for holding gown folds together; an essential accessory for decorative display and for carrying a CHATELAINE or GIBECIÈRE; also, in ARMOR, metal clasps over the hips.

girl
An adolescent male or female person. Chaucer's repulsive, reprehensible Summoner knows the secrets of all the girls of the town, since all young people and good FELLOWS were required to confess before absolution.

gisant
A recumbent sculpture, a tomb effigy representing a corpse, as in a TRANSI TOMB, MEMENTO MORI, and ARS MORIENDI.

glair
Frothed, beaten egg white used as a medium for binding paint or reactive pigments for coloring MANUSCRIPTS and for application of GOLD LEAF. To prevent putrefaction and an obnoxious odor, red sulfide of arsenic, REALGAR, was added to the glair container, sometimes just half an eggshell covered with the other half.

glaze
A glass coating over the surface of fired pottery, consisting of sand, flint, or sandstone mixed with a flux, such as lead, potash, or borax, making the clay surface of the vessel impervious to liquid, shiny, and ready for further decoration or protection of design under the glaze. Colored by metallic oxides, shades and variations were obtained by raising or lowering the firing temperature or the amount of kiln oxygen.

glebe
A small piece of cultivatable land; specifically, part of a clergyman's living.

glee
A musical entertainment; a secular or pious song.

gleeman
Like the Anglo-Saxon SCOP, a song-maker; groups singing glees become a glee club.

Gloria in Excelsis Deo
(Latin, Glory to God on high) The HYMN celebrating God, the greater DOXOLOGY or ANGELIC HYMN, sung in morning prayers and after the KYRIE of the MASS on certain feast days.

Gloria Passionis
(Latin, the glory of the Passion) The glory of Christ's passion; the demonstration of perfect patience in suffering and impeccable obedience and piety; an example for a MARTYR or saint who desired a life of AGERE ET PATI (to do and to endure); a heroic ideal of suffering.

Gloria Patri
(Latin, Glory to the Father) The beginning of the lesser DOXOLOGY: *Gloria Patri et Filio et Spiritu Sancto* (Glory to the Father and to the Son and to the Holy Spirit), praising the three members of the holy TRINITY. This formula, often ending HYMNS, is part of the DIVINE OFFICE and distinct from GLORIA IN EXCELSIS DEO.

gloss
A marginal or interlinear commentary on the Bible, usually from the Church Fathers; or interpretive comments on CANON LAW or other literature.

Glossa Ordinaria
A standard GLOSS on the Old or New Testament, also called *Glossa Communis.*

glove
A utilitarian hand cover and protector, and an important article of fashion from the twelfth century on. Popular fabrics were cotton, silk, velvet, or soft animal skins (deer, dog, buck, chicken, sheep, beaver, and doe). Rings were usually worn on or over gloves. Thirteenth- and fourteenth-century cuffs were deep and buttoned, often slashed, dagged, and ornamented with BELLS and jewels.

gnoff
A rascally, foolish, and rich old codger, comparable to the Hebrew *ganav,* like the CUCKOLD John the Carpenter in Chaucer's "Miller's Tale" and miscellaneous FABLIAUX husbands.

gnomic literature
Short, sententious, proverbial sayings within larger literary works or gathered groups of aphorisms, usually more instructive than pleasing, more *docere* (to teach) than *delectare* (to please). Such sayings were significant in Anglo-Saxon epics such as *Beowulf,* as well as in DEBATES, elegies, and literature adhering to Saint Paul's dictum, everything written is for our instruction.

Gnosticism
(Greek, *gnosis,* knowledge) A religious movement that influenced the Jewish KABALLAH and early Christianity, characterized by a revealed knowledge of God and the redemptive destiny of the select; it distinguished the Demiurge or Creator God who emanated from the more remote, dispassionate Divine Being. Three classes of created beings were those of the spirit, of the psyche, and of matter.

God bless you
Said not only to wish good health (German, "gesundheit," WASSAIL), but to counteract when sneezing the opening of the nostrils or NOSETHIRLes, passages for the soul to exit or the devil to enter; also, a quick benediction to avoid malefaction.

godchild
A newly baptized person responsible to GODPARENTs.

godor
An Icelandic ruler or chief convening the legislative ALTHING.

godparent
A witness to Christian BAPTISM, responsible for the adherent's or GODCHILD's faith, obedience, and renunciation of damnable activities.

godron
A high, frilled, or pleated collar of starched muslin, a ruff worn by both men and women in the early Renaissance.

gods' and goddesses' Greek and Latin names
In art and literature, classical allusions sometimes interchange particular gods' and goddesses' names in the Greek and Roman pantheons (Roman names are given first in each pair): Aesculapius = Asclepius; Aurora = Eos; Bacchus = Dionysus; Ceres = Demeter; Cupid = Eros; Diana = Artemis; Hercules = Heracles; Juno = Hera; Jupiter = Zeus; Latona = Leto: Luna = Selene; Mars = Ares; Mercury = Hermes; Neptune = Poseidon; Proserpina = Persephone; Saturn = Cronus; Sol = Helios; Venus = Aphrodite; Vesta = Hestia; Vulcan = Hephaestus; Ulysses = Odysseus.

Golden Fleece
From the classical myth of Jason and the Golden Fleece, the Order of the Golden Fleece, the fraternity established by the Duke of Burgundy in the fifteenth century to defend the faith, promote chivalry, and further peace. England's King Edward the IV was a prominent knight of the Order. Its EMBLEM or insigne was a gold lambskin-shaped medallion worn as a pendant from a heavy chain around the neck.

Golden Legend
Spectacularly popular and influential, the LEGENDA AUREA was a calendric compilation of saints lives composed by the thirteenth-century DOMINICAN friar, Jacobus de Voragine, later Archbishop of Genoa. It was characterized by lugubriously detailed martyrdoms and punctiliously described virtues of canonized and locally-worshipped sufferers for Christ's word. Caxton published the first English version in 1483.

golden mean
The perfect point between two extremes or excesses. Horace called it *aurea mediocritas* (*Odes* 2.10:5), after the Greek mathematical and architectural statement of perfection. Dividing a FIBONACCI SERIES number by the previous integer in its series approximates the mean.

golden sequence
The HYMN VENI SANCTE SPIRITUS.

golden thumb
Sign of one skilled and DEXTEROUS in cheating customers of grain or minerals; Chaucer's Miller has one, as do others in the grain and mining trades.

gold ground
Spatially neutral gold background for MOSAICs, panel paintings, and MINIATURES. GOLD LEAF was applied to the backs of transparent glass TESSERAE, so that refracted light reflected by gold was refracted again, brilliantly.

gold leaf
Beaten gold obtained by CUTCHING was applied in thin sheets to MANUSCRIPTs, jewelry, indoor architectural ornaments, ceilings, doors, furniture, and wooden COFFERs, usually over SIZE plus dull red BOLE.

golem
A quasi-human Kaballistic creature, usually with the word *emeth* (truth) emblazoned on the forehead. Removal of the initial letter *E* caused death (*meth* in Hebrew meaning he is dead).

Golgotha
(Aramaic *galgaltha,* skull) The hill of the CRUCIFIXION, CALVARY.

Goliardic literature
Satiric, anti-clerical, erotic, often lewd, Latin and vernacular verse written and performed by itinerant GOLIARDS, educated students familiar with church ritual and prayer. Wittily sophisticated, ingeniously punning, it celebrates wine, women, and sexual pleasure.

Goliards
Wandering scholars of the twelfth and thirteenth centuries, such as the ARCHIPOETA, who sang, studied, taught, and whored their way from university to university. They were also writers of notable poems and songs such as the CARMINA BURANA and other GOLIARDIC LITERATURE.

gonelle
An early, long TUNIC worn by men and women, both secular and ecclesiastic. The soldier's style reached only halfway down the leg to allow for mounting of horses.

gong
A privy. Chaucer's Parson, who hates prostitutes, likened them to a communal gong wherein men perch their MEMBERS.

Good Friday
The Friday in HOLY WEEK that commemorates the PASSION and CRUCIFIXION of Christ. A day of fasting, penitence, and abstinence, the only day of the liturgical year that MASS is not celebrated.

good wine needs no bush
Excellent labeled vintage or other merchandise required no further advertisement: a vintner's IVY and bush-shaped sign distinguished a winery from an ale house.

goose is cooked
Frustrating, utter ruin. From the putative mockery of Scandinavian warrior Eric XIV of Sweden: fool-hardy though courageous town dwellers besieged by Eric's forces chose to hang a goose on the pole rather than

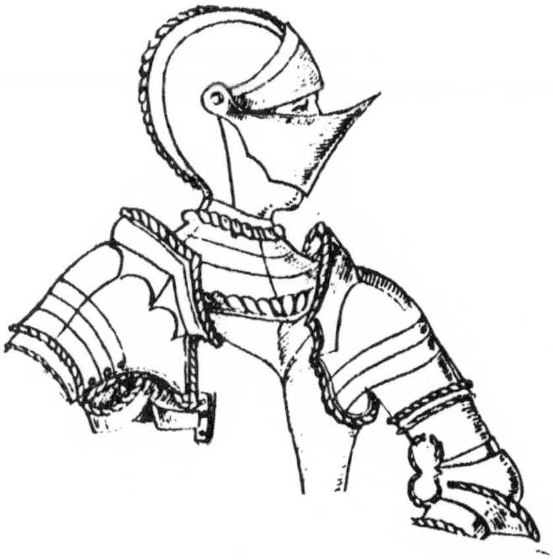

A gorget. (From the arms of Justin de Rudshield, Yorkshire, England, c. 1437)

the flag of surrender; Eric cooked the goose as he burned down the town.

gorget
Ornamental or practical neck and throat ARMOR; or a necklace or jewelry BADGE or EMBLEM suspended from the neck, pendant on the breast.

gorgias
A gauze covering a woman's cleavage in the dramatic décolleté of fifteenth-century gowns, ultimately "gorgeous."

gospel
(Anglo-Saxon *godspel,* good news) The "good tidings" of Jesus Christ's doctrine and teachings of redemption; in LITURGY, the rite of the EUCHARIST; one of the FOUR GOSPELS.

gossip
(Anglo-Saxon *god sib,* sister in God) A good, friendly woman companion for conversation.

Gothic
In architecture, the INTERNATIONAL STYLE characterized by a vertical skyward thrust, pointed arches, and lavish use of STAINED GLASS that dominated Europe from the twelfth through fifteenth centuries, exemplified by magnificent churches and cathedrals with extravagant VAULTS, SPIRES, LANCETS, ROSE WINDOWS,

OGEE ARCHes, stone TRACERY, RETICULATED TRACERY, and FLYING BUTTRESSES to prevent SPALLING; sumptuous RELIQUARIES, MONSTRANCES and other ceremonial objects. In CALLIGRAPHY, the MANUSCRIPT hand marked by thick, vertical, modeled penstrokes, especially for religious texts; in ethnology, a Germanic people and their dialect, recorded from the eighth through tenth centuries. During the Renaissance, a disparaging designation for the earlier, seemingly crude "barbarian" Germanic style versus the "civilized" ROMANESQUE or Italian style.

go to pot
By choice or circumstance, to slowly disintegrate, the whole broken to pieces, standards drastically diminished or abandoned. The expression derived from the culinary pleasures of stew-making, as MORTREWS, HODGE-PODGE, or SALMAGUNDI, with the ingredients diced and minced small.

gouache
Opaque water color applied in manuscript ILLUMINATION and MINIATURE painting, especially for highlights and special effects.

goûte à pois
A popular, woven, stained, or embroidered spotted fabric, the dots singly strewn or in clusters.

gown
(Anglo-Saxon *gunna,* a garment for women) A long and loose-fitting, sleeved ROBE for men or women.

grace
God's generous divine assistance to mankind, whether or not deserving this blessing. Tertullian called it Divine Energy working in the human soul; Saint Augustine considered it God's mercy to prevent damnation caused by ORIGINAL SIN. It is conveyed in or through the SEVEN SACRAMENTS. Also, a prayer of thanks before or after meals.

gradual
(Latin *gradus,* step) The melodically florid second element of the PROPER of the MASS, a responsorial CHANT originally sung from the AMBO's steps and called *responsorium graduale*; the text is taken mostly from the PSALMs.

Grail
A legendary bowl, CHALICE, or dish thought to be used by Christ at the LAST SUPPER and by Joseph of Arimathea for collecting Christ's blood at the CRUCIFIXION. The literary quest for the Holy Grail appeared in numerous ARTHURIAN ROMANCES: Chrètien de Troyes' *Perceval*; the *Prose Lancelot*; Robert de Boron's *Estoire du Graal*; *Perlesvaus*; the Welsh *Peredur*; Wolfram von Eschenbach's *Parzival*; and the English *Joseph of Arimathie.*

grain of salt
A story or allegation taken *cum grano salis* is accepted gingerly, its truth needing test before belief, just as in the wine or beer tasting service of CREDENCE; Pliny added a grain of salt to suspect liquor to counteract possible poison (a BEZOAR works better).

gramalla
A long outer garment reaching from neck to toes; in the fourteenth century, John I of Aragon required all Jews under his jurisdiction to wear it in addition to the JEWISH BADGE and special hood.

Grande Chartreuse
In the Alps near Grenoble, the architecturally exquisite mother house of the CARTHUSIAN order, founded by Saint Bruno; each hermit-monk had a separate cell with a garden opening on to a communal CLOISTER.

grand magisterium
The alchemical numerical configuration 1, 4, 3, 2, 1, used in procedures of SEPARATION and volatilization, and depicted in art.

granulation
Like BEADING, a decorative surface ornamentation using small grains or balls of silver, gold, or other metal in rows or at particular points within a FILIGREE or open-work design.

grapes of wrath
In Isaiah 63, God expresses his wrath against the nations. The speaker from Edom in CRIMSON garments, red as a vintner's coming from a WINE PRESS, answers "I have trodden the wine press . . . in my anger and trampled them [the grapes] in my wrath; their life blood is sprinkled upon my garments. . . . I trod down the peoples in my anger . . . and I

poured out their life blood on the earth." Important in Christian ICONOGRAPHY, the grapes of wrath in TYPOLOGICAL SYMBOLISM prefigured the agonies of Jesus Christ in the CRUCIFIXION: Christ crushed in the wine press, the STIPES representing the CROSS.

Gratian's Decree
The lawyer-jurist-churchman Gratian's ordering of the chaos of conflicting CANON LAW: he arranged about 4,000 texts by subject, recognizing and resolving contradictions. His *Decretum Gratiani* or *Concordantia Discordantanium Canonum* (1140) was the model for later compilations of DECRETALS and pronouncements by church councils.

graver
A metal instrument, a BURIN, with a sharp square or LOZENGE-shaped point for cutting furrows in copper plates for ENGRAVING.

grave riverenze
A sixteenth-century Italian bow in a dance sequence.

gravoire
A curved, knife-shaped, hair parter or coiffeur arranger, often made of ivory or precious metal and encrusted with jewels and ENAMELS. Its handle or hilt was decoratively carved.

Gray Friars
The FRANCISCANS or Friars Minor, one of the FOUR ORDERS OF FRIARS.

great chain of being
A TOPOS expressing the glorious interrelatedness of all elements in the world order, ORDO MUNDI, with God positioned at the top, followed by choirs of ANGELS, cherubim and seraphim, man and woman (in the middle), beasts, plants, then stones. Human ability to ascend to the level of angels, using reason and rejoicing in soul, is balanced by human tendency to descend towards bestiality in indulging carnal pleasures.

great coat
A short, loosely fitting, full-sleeved outer garment decorated with gold and elaborate stones, a PALETOT.

Greater Antiphons
The SEVEN O-ANTIPHONS.

Great Year
A popular Stoic doctrine, frequently debated, important for astrological prediction and GENETHLIALOGY, and officially condemned as illogical in 1277: an astronomical event with practical effect was supposed to occur every time the sun, moon, and five planets return to the same position relative to each other. At that time, all events, pleasurable and perilous, of the previous Great Year configuration would be repeated identically.

green lion
A mineral substance used by alchemists to unite it with MERCURY, creating a RED LION (or EAGLE), in procedures of SUBLIMATION and SEPARATION.

Green Thursday
(Latin *dies viridium,* green day) MAUNDY THURSDAY, because penitents who had made confession on ASH WEDNESDAY were to carry green branches that signified their reception into full COMMUNION.

gregor
A cacophonous instrument, a ratchet-rattle noisemaker, like the CRACELLE, twirled by Jews on PURIM to obliterate sound of the name of hated Haman, uttered while reciting the Book of Esther.

Gregorian calendar
The calendrical reformation in 1582 by Pope Gregory XIII. It superseded the Julian calendar, originated by Julius Caesar in 46 B.C., to account accurately for the earth's 365¼ days' passage around the sun. An error of ten days had accumulated by the sixteenth century, so that the Papal Bull *Inter gravissimas* decreed leap years as *century years* divisible by 400: as the years 1600 and 2000.

Gregorian chant
The Roman liturgical PLAINSONG or CHANT traditionally thought arranged and codified in the seventh century under Pope Gregory I. It is one of the FOUR MUSICAL DIALECTS of the Western Church.

grenade
(French, pomegranate) The fifteenth-century ball-shaped hand grenade filled with gunpowder and metal particles named after the POMEGRANATE. King

Louis XIV's special military units for hurling the weapon were called *grenadiers.*

greve
Shin ARMOR; or a slightly pugnacious kicking step in a GALLIARD.

griffin
A fabulous animal popular in BESTIARIES: with the head and wings of an eagle, and the body and behind of a lion. It is a vigilant guardian, especially of gold.

grille
An ornamental and protective iron grating enclosing a chapel or tomb.

Grimm's Law
A systematic explanation of medieval linguistic affinities by the nineteenth-century German philologist-compiler of fairy tales. He recognized correspondences between consonants in Germanic and other INDO-EUROPEAN tongues, such as Sanskrit, Greek, and Latin: for example, Latin *pes* became English *foot*; Latin *tres* became English *three*; and Latin *centum* became English *hundred,* as voiceless stops (*p, t,* and *k*) evolved into spirants (*f, th,* and *h*). This Germanic sound shift was further refined by WERNER'S LAW.

grimoire
The grammar of black magic.

grisaille
A technique in painting, ENAMELRY, and STAINED GLASS that created delicate gray-green, black-brown delineations of figures, facial features, and drapery. The effect was achieved by fusing a fired mixture of crushed glass with iron or copper oxides, cobalt, and other pigments in a liquid medium.

groined vault
An architectural intersection of two VAULTS.

grotesquerie
Decorative painting and sculpture representing unnatural, fantastic, and extravagant combinations of human and animal forms, sometimes ludicrous, comic, scatological, or absurd, usually ingenious and charming.

Animal grotesquerie forms an initial letter "S." (From Jean Fevrier, Paris, 15th century; courtesy of Galeria Medievalia, Tenafly, New Jersey)

gruppo
A sixteenth-century Italian musical ornamentation, comparable to a trill.

gueridon
A small circular candlestand, table, or column supporting a tray. King Louis XIV supposedly imitated in sculpture a famous Moorish slave called Gueridon who was popular in Provençal songs.

Guidonian Hand
GUIDO'S HAND.

Guido's Hand
The eleventh-century Italian BENEDICTINE monk Guido D'Arezzo's clever mnemonic for remembering musical pitch of the HEXACHORD by using the five digits of the hand. The hand of a singer became a modulator with each tip and joint of each finger having an allotted note; the singer then could practice and exercise at any time. Guido's SOLMIZATION system is taught today.

guild
A craft organization, a proto-union controlling many aspects of professions such as weaving, shipbuilding, medicine, and surgery. The guilds were charged with training, preparing for licensing, and regulating the practitioners of each industry; master guildsmen and guildswomen supervised JOURNEYMEN and trained apprentices. Such activities served triple benevolent purposes: providing to the craftsman or CRAFTSWOMAN unemployment, accident, and death benefits; serving the profession by preventing malpractice and regulating competition; and affording to the town or city handsome or subsidized town halls, fountains, and cultural events as MYSTERY PLAY cycles. Some guilds were exclusively male, some solely female, some mixed. Women, for instance, monopolized France's silk industry; married or unmarried craftswomen worked as FEMMES SOLES.

guilloche
A metal jewelry and furniture border design resembling twisted ribbons interspersed with rosettes.

guimp
A WIMPLE, a light veil surrounding a woman's face, often worn by a nun.

gularon
Also called *collet* and *patte,* the part of the CHAPERONE hat covering the shoulders.

gules
In HERALDRY, the COLOR red; one of the SIX TINCTURES.

gull
To deceive with false information.

gum arabic
A stronger binder for pigments than GLAIR, used for MANUSCRIPT ILLUMINATION. The gum originally was taken from acacia trees or from cherry, plum, or almond trees, and was soluble in hot water.

gum tragacanth
A binder for pigments for painting, very deliquescent, taking up prodigious amounts of water: one ounce absorbed the amount of water sufficient for one gallon of thin jelly in making fine light tones. The gum was obtained from a shrub native to Asia Minor.

gun stalk
A wooden support on which a fifteenth-century gun barrel was mounted or, on shipboard, against which a cannon barrel was leaned.

gymel
(Latin *cantus gemellus,* twin songs) A two-part musical polyphonic melody based on parallel thirds.

gypsum
Lime sulfate, important in GESSO, sculpture casting, and decorative arts.

H

habergeon

In ARMOR, a sleeveless CHAIN MAIL coat, lighter than a HAUBERK.

habit

Men's or women's garments, often referring to the clothes of ecclesiastics.

Haftorah

A selection from the prophetic books of the Old Testament, read in a SYNAGOGUE on Sabbaths and festivals after the reading from the FIVE BOOKS OF MOSES, the PENTATEUCH.

Haggadah

A ritual book retelling the biblical story of Exodus, often with magnificent ILLUMINATIONS and decorations, delineating the order, SEDER, of Jewish prayers and praises for the festival of PASSOVER.

Hagia Sophia

(Greek, Holy Wisdom) A superb example of a BYZANTINE BASILICA, the Church of the Holy Wisdom in Constantinople was built in a mere five years (begun 532) during the reign of Justinian; an exquisite, monumental, unified space surmounted by a central DOME and ornamented by MOSAICs.

Hagiographa

(Greek, sacred writings) The third part of the Old Testament, after the PENTATEUCH and the Prophets, consisting of Psalms, Proverbs, Job, Song of Solomon, Ruth, Lamentations, Ecclesiastes, Esther, Daniel, Ezra, Nehemia, and Chronicles.

Hagiography

The life histories of saints. One of the most popular literary compilations was the GOLDEN LEGEND, LEGENDA AUREA, of Jacobus de Voragine.

haincelin

A short HOUPPELANDE with embroidered sleeves, named after King Charles the VI's FOOL, Haincelin Coq.

hair

Length, color, texture, and abundance of hair on the head was believed to signify personality, temperament, sexuality, and social state, according to PHYSIOGNOMIES such as Rudolphus Goclenius's *Physiognomica et Chiromentica*. Long, soft, finely-textured, reddish or yellow hair indicated effeminacy and lack of virility; the sparser the hair, the more cunningly deceptive its owner. Hairline also was considered an indicator of intelligence and social class (Chaucer's Prioress's forehead is a span broad, signifying well-born intellect). Ingeniously designed hair tweezers created by illusion what nature neglected, and scruffy eyebrows and dandruff had to be treated with the herb hellebore and borscht or beet soup. Balding had four piliating "remedies": aloe, caraway, southernwood or artemisia, and madonna lily.

hair of a mad dog

A remedy for a perilous injury from a rabid dog's bite was a wound dressing or compress incorporating a piece of the mad dog's hair into a healing salve or ointment, a MEDICAL SIMILARITY or complimentarity, as opposed to treatment by medical contrary. According to the FOUR CONTRARIES, the cold, moist nature of the rabid animal required a hot, dry plaster to counteract its effects and neutralize them. Sympathetic magic and superstition suggested that working with, not against, a poison could lead to a faster cure.

hair perfume
Dr. Trotula of Salerno suggested a fine recipe which delighted noble Salernitan men and women: the odor of musk, DECOCTIONS of herbs, roses, particularly DAMASK, and other floral essences sprinkled on head, brush, comb, or hatband.

Halakhah
Laws of Jewish religious daily life uniting laws of the TALMUD with post-Talmudic rabbinic rulings and interpretations.

halberd
A military spear-battle-ax, its sharp-edged blade ending in a point, good for smashing helmets.

halcyon days
The calm two weeks of the winter solstice, poetically important because, as the nesting time of the kingfisher on the sea's surface, it was thought calmed by the bird's magic powers; a time of blessedness and good luck.

half-timbered
A popular building technique: timber framework with bricks, tile, or lath-and-plaster filling spaces between timbers.

Hallel
(Hebrew, praise) A Jewish title for the PSALMs (usually numbers 112 through 118) sung at special festivals, particularly PASSOVER.

Hallenkirche
(German, a hall church) A German variety of a GOTHIC edifice with AISLEs as high as the NAVE, essentially eliminating the CLERESTORY and FLYING BUTTRESSes.

hallmark
An identifying mark or insigne stamped inconspicuously on a silver, gold, pewter, or other metal object. In England, the practice was probably begun by the goldsmith's company assaying and stamping objects to attest to their purity and quality. Some hallmarks included the maker's initials or DEVICE, the town and year of manufacture, and the assay and tax status.

halo
An AUREOLE.

hammer beam
One of a pair of wooden half-beams supporting a trussed roof, often terminated by an ANGEL BEAM.

Hammer of Witches
DOMINICAN inquisitors Kramer and Sprenger's stunningly popular fifteenth-century book, MALLEUS MALEFICARUM defining the nature, corrupting power, and seditious habits of WITCHes. Their information was derived from the pseudo-science of natural philosophers and the misogynist tradition of the thirteenth century, especially Pseudo Albertus Magnus' WOMEN'S SECRETS, the ideological basis for the conclusion that women prone to witchcraft deserve death.

hanap
A double cup whose cover also is a cup.

Hanukkah
The eight-day Jewish Festival of Lights that celebrates the rededication of the Temple by the Maccabees, and often concurrent with CHRISTMAS. The MENORAH, an eight-branched candelabrum, often elaborately designed and embellished, is the holiday's most familiar ritual object, one of Judaism's earliest, most dependable insignia.

hare
Considered a fine banquet food, the mammal in ICONOGRAPHY represented a woman lover. The small, fertile, furry animal of Venus was an object of the HUNT OF LOVE.

harlot
A lower class man or woman, not necessarily roguish, nasty, or sensual. The modern sexual distinction and sensual aspersion, as with GIRL, was a fifteenth- and sixteenth-century PEJORATION.

haroset
A tasty, fragrant mixture of apple, cinnamon, nuts, and wine prepared and eaten at the Jewish PASSOVER

meal, the SEDER, symbolizing the mortar and strawless brick that the Jews made during their Egyptian bondage. The twelfth-century physician-philosopher Maimonides suggested a splendid recipe.

harpy
A fabulous, filthy, ferocious monster, with a female face, breasts, and upper body, with the wings and claws of a vulture or eagle; also, a minister and messenger of vengeance.

harquebus
See ARQUEBUS.

Hasidism
A popular twelfth-century mystical teaching of morality from the Jewish KABALLAH, exemplified in the *Book of the Pious* (*Sefer Hasidim*) of the three Kalonymous rabbis: Samuel, Judah, and Eleazar.

haslet
An ILLUSION FOOD, consisting of fruits and nuts, strung on a cord, dipped in batter, and sautéed. It was disguised to emulate the choice morsels of DAINTIES, the genitalia of large hunted animals, a culinary delicacy reserved for noble leaders of a hunt.

hasp
A latch or fastening on a door or hinged lid of a COFFER or chest; in erotic poetry and FABLIAUX, the impediment to free passage, the resistance requiring unlatching by charm, reason, or force.

hatching
Parallel or crossed lines giving texture, shade, and spatial depth in ENGRAVING.

hatchment
In HERALDRY, the ACHIEVEMENT displayed for seven days at the house of a dead knight or lady, and thereafter for a year and a day in the parish church.

hauberk
In ARMOR, a flexible CHAIN MAIL military TUNIC.

haut boy
An oboe.

havdalah
The service concluding the Jewish Sabbath, celebrated with prayers and a symbolically woven candle, elegantly dividing the sacred day of the week from the secular, distinguishing the holy from the profane.

haye
(Anglo-Saxon *hege,* a hedge or fence; or French *haie,* a hedge) A dance figure associated with the BUFFON, sometimes performed in a round, or with many dancers aligned in two hedge-like rows that wove figure eight patterns. The style probably derived from serpentine pagan fertility and solstice dance rites.

hazzan
The Jewish CANTOR or singer of the CHANTs and songs in the SYNAGOGUE's Hebrew LITURGY; some *hazzanim* served Christian courts as music masters and DANCE MASTERS.

head rail
An oblong linen or cotton headdress usually with a chin strap and held in place by a FILLET or crown.

health manual
An INSTRUCTION BOOK for lay people and physicians, arranged by logical anatomical descent from head to toe, or by diseases and injuries, or by animal, plant, and mineral families of medicines. Examples include the TACUINUM SANITATIS, Platina's *On Honest Indulgence,* and Konrad Gessner's *Tierbuch, Fischbuch,* and *Fogelbuch.*

hectoring
Loud bullying and offensive, mocking assertiveness, named after Trojan warrior Hector, familiar in ROMANCEs and dramas about the Trojan War. Hector was often portrayed as crude, foul-mouthed, boisterous, and blaring.

hedge
A gambling technique: betting on both of two likely possibilities to diminish risk and assure some winning.

hell mouth
The graphic representation of the entrance to Hell as a monstrous mouth exuding flames and stench,

guarded by demons who toss sinners into the gaping hole.

helm
Metal or leather military headgear.

hemiola
(Greek, one-and-a-half) Musical pitch or MENSURAL NOTATION relationships with the arithmetic ratio of 3:2; also, the musical interval, the fifth, or the time values expressed in blackened notes of *tempus perfectum*.

henge
In England, a Neolithic circle of wood or stone uprights, such as Stonehenge, encircled by a bank outside a ditch. Such a structure probably was used for ceremony and astronomy.

hennin
A pointed, conical headdress for women, popular in fifteenth-century France and Burgundy, usually of stiffened silk or velvet with a vail flowing from the pinnacle. Probably brought to France by Isabelle of Bavaria in the fourteenth century, it was also called the steeple; its extravagant height required regulation by SUMPTUARY LAW. The height ascended according to the woman's social rank.

herald
An announcer of identity; a tournament, court, or town official required to recognize members of a HOUSEHOLD by the heraldic EMBLEMs and DEVICEs displayed.

heraldic
Pertaining to identifying and ceremonial qualities of HERALDRY.

heraldry
The art of announcing, representing, and explaining the ARMS of a noble HOUSEHOLD, GUILD, province, university, organization, or person by generally accepted figures, particularly animals (such as the LION or YALE), positions (COUCHANT, RAMPANT, DORMANT), COLORs, TINCTUREs, and FURs. Identifying BADGEs, EMBLEMs, and DEVICEs initially were embroidered on a COAT OF ARMS, but later embellished all types of possessions. Heraldry theorists were influenced by BARTOLISM. Though probably imported to England by the NORMANs, the first heralds' college or COLLEGE OF ARMS was chartered by Richard III in 1483.

herb
A wild or cultivated leafy plant Charlemagne called "the friend of physicians and the praise of cooks." Every plant had a medical or culinary use, and almost every disease or disability an herbal prevention, palliator, or cure depicted in medical texts known as HERBALs and HEALTH MANUALS.

herbal
A book describing plants and their medical and culinary uses, blending empirical observation with tradition descended from Dioscorides' *De materia medica* and Pliny's *Natural History*. Some lavishly illustrated herbals added animals and minerals to the fruits, vegetables, grasses, and grains to make a HORTUS SANITATIS or garden of health or a medicinal menagerie.

herbarius
A HERBAL health and hygiene text such as the HORTUS SANITATIS (*Garden of Health*) containing medical and culinary instructions: mineral, vegetable, and animal, for protecting health, preventing illness, and curing disease or injury of both body and mind.

herber
An arbor or a shady bower in a GARDEN.

hereos
The consuming disease, love sickness. A form of MELANCHOLY, it was thought to be caused by a lover's distance, an imperfect AMOR DE LONH, rejection, or by social impedimenta, such as impossibility of access.

herigaute
A HOUSSE or GARDE CORPS, open at the side and similar to the DALMATIC.

hergeat
War gear, horse, ARMOR, and weapons given by a lord to a man in feudal TENANCY, in addition to the land.

heriot
A death TALLAGE, usually the best animal or finest part of crop paid by a VILLEIN to the overlord; originally HERGEAT or war gear.

herm
A stone heap or CAIRN; a pillar depicting the fertility figure Priapus as an extravagantly large, erect phallus attached to the torso or displayed on a pedestal. In architecture, furniture, and metalwork, other representations included a head of Mercury on a quadrangular pillar, or a three-quarter-length figure on a pedestal.

Hermes Trismegistus
NeoPLATONIC devotees of ALCHEMY and mysticism applied that name to the Egyptian god Thoth, the putative author of alchemical doctrine.

herringbone perspective
Projection lines converging not at the VANISHING POINT but at a picture's central vertical axis.

hersismus
Stinking armpits. In the eleventh century, the woman physician and surgeon Trotula of Salerno, suggested a deodorizing herbal remedy of mint and wild strawberry.

heterophony
Two or more versions of the same melody, performed simultaneously with ornamentations by singers or instrumentalists.

hexachord
The six-note scale, represented in GUIDO'S HAND, the important musical structure of six diatonic tones separated by a semitone interval: C, D, E, F, G, A. Guido d'Arezzo's emendation of the earlier TETRACHORD theory in the eleventh century anticipated the modern heptachord system and the octave.

Hiberno-Saxon
The art style that flourished in England, Ireland, and Scotland from the seventh through the ninth centuries. It was characterized by RECTILINEAR and CURVILINEAR decorative schemes, animal INTERLACE, labyrinthine undulations, CARPET PAGES, full-length symbols of the FOUR EVANGELISTS (rather than evangelists' beasts). MANUSCRIPTs were produced on chamois-surfaced VELLUM, and were written with INSULAR letters, the major pages beginning with DIMINUENDO. Examples include the books of Durrow, Lindisfarne, Echternach, Saint Willibrord, and Kells.

High Holy Days
The pair of significant New Year's celebrations in Judaism: ROSH HASHONAH and YOM KIPPUR.

high relief
Carved or molded sculpture raised from a flat or curved surface to create a genuinely three-dimensional figure visible at least half "in the round." The technique embellished architectural elements such as a FRIEZE, BATTLEMENT, or FINIAL, and adorned useful objects such as a CHASSE or COFFER.

high table
A banquet table set on a dais at which the most noble or honored guests were seated in order to see and to be seen by all other feasters seated and served at SIDEBOARDs according to social status.

Hillelites
Followers of the great first-century Jewish rabbi Hillel, more tolerant than the SHAMMAITES. Their disputes were recorded in the TALMUD.

Hippocampus
A fabulous marine monster having a horse's forequarters and the hind parts of a fish. It was sometimes a seahorse drayer of the classical chariots of Neptune and of Galatea, sometimes the great fish LEVIATHAN that swallowed Jonah.

hippocras
An aromatic wine, named after Hippocrates' Sleeve, a cloth strainer in which sweet basil, cinnamon, sage, clove, ginger, rosemary and other spices were mixed, red wine poured through, then heated, creating the celebrated digestive and banquet beverage.

hirsute
Hairy, characteristic of the WILD MAN.

Hispano-Moresque
Describing the culture of Islamic Spain which brilliantly united Arabic, Jewish, and Christian influences

Acrobats and grotesques intertwine in an historiated initial "W." (From *The Illuminated Alphabet*, ed. Theodore Menten, Dover Publications, Inc., New York)

in its literature, music, astronomy, medicine, weaponry, winery, architecture, art, and commercial crafts. Silk-making and weaving centers like Almeria, Malaga, Seville, Granada, and Saragossa exported lustrous fabrics decorated with ARABESQUES and Arabic-inspired or Kufic border inscriptions. Fine LUSTER WARE ALBARELLOS and CHARGERS from Malaga, Paterna, and Valencia inspired competition with Italian MAJOLICA.

historiated

In MANUSCRIPT decoration, representational ornament, rather than mere attractive design, serving a narrative or pedagogic purpose. Historiated initials often begin important paragraphs or sentences in BOOKS OF HOURS, ANTIPHONALS, and PSALTERS.

hoarding

A covered wooden gallery attached to a wall or on its top, permitting the dropping of stones and boiling oil on besiegers of a castle or town.

hobby horse

A wooden horse, with a sculptured head on a pole, placed between the legs for "riding." Derived from a pagan representation of a summer solstice sacrificial victim to assure agricultural fertility, the hobby was associated with the MAYPOLE, MORRIS DANCE, and MUMMING plays, particularly in MIDSUMMER EVE festivities.

hocket

A polyphonic musical ornamentation separating the melodic line into short, sometimes single note, staccato fragments sung by alternating choirs. A technique frequently railed against by scandalized ecclesiastics, it seemed to resemble hiccoughs.

hocktide

The second Monday and Tuesday after EASTER, celebrated with donations of money and goods to church and parish, merrymaking, music, revelry, and amusements; also called Hock Monday and Hock Tuesday.

hodge-podge

Or a hotch pot, a succulent, serendipitous stew, though one recipe suggests beef, veal, lentils, carrots, dates, apricots, and currants as basics. It was made in a kitchen cauldron or BLANDRETH by adding leftovers to soup stock, so that all tastes and textures were blended at a week's end.

Hoflied

A courtly song such as MINNESANG, as opposed to the bourgeois GESELLSCHAFTSLIED and the folksong or VOLKSLIED.

höhe minne

Noble love of the MINNESINGER for a high-born, imperious lady, similar to the DOMNA of the TROUBADOURS. A Germanic variation on COURTLY LOVE ideals, höhe minne was opposite to NIEDERE MINNE, a contrast particularly exploited in the songs of Neidhart von Ruenthal.

hokus-pokus

(from Latin *hoc est corpus domini*, This is the body of the Lord, from the CANON of the MASS) A ridiculous, deceptive magical incantation. Quack physicians were sued by irate patients or by offended physicians' and surgeons' GUILDs for using verbal charms and TALISMANs of nonsensical Latin in fraudulent cures.

holograph
A document written wholly by the author's own hand, not a scribe's or secretary's.

holour
An old letcher. Chaucer's Parson describes superannuated, sexually senescent men who can leer and kiss, but cannot produce, like dogs who lift their legs to PISS but cannot.

holy anorexia
Intentional starving to test the self, prove piety, expiate sin, demonstrate holiness, or suffer martyrdom, a form of self abnegation and pious humiliation practiced by church reformers and holy mystics such as Catherine of Sienna, Veronica Giuliani, and Margaret of Cortina. Daughters of God lived and died by personal visions of perfection, like the CATHARI who starved themselves to death by ENDURA. Their aversions to food were precursors of modern anorexia nervosa and bulimia.

Holy Cross Day
A Christian feast celebrated September 14, also called EXALTATION OF THE HOLY CROSS.

Holy Family Feast
Celebrated on the first Sunday after EPIPHANY.

Holy Ghost
The Third Person of the Christian Godhead: the HOLY SPIRIT.

Holy Innocents
A Christian feast celebrated December 28, commemorating the massacre of the children of Bethlehem two years old and younger by Herod the Great in his attempt to destroy the infant Jesus.

Holy Kinship
The extensive family of Saint Anne, Mother of the Virgin Mary, which, according to the GOLDEN LEGEND, had TRINAL TRIPLICITIES, yielding THREE MARIES. Anne married three successive husbands: with Joachim, she had a daughter Mary, who later married Joseph, and gave birth to Jesus; with Cleophas, she had another daughter Mary, who married Altheus, and produced four sons: Simon, Jude, Joseph the Just, and James the Less; and with her last husband she had still another daughter Mary, who married Zebedee, and bore James the Greater and John the Evangelist.

Holy Maccabees feast
A Christian feast, usually August 1, commemorating the Jews' sufferings and deaths described in Maccabees 7 and Hebrews 11:35. Jews celebrate those events in the festival of HANUKKAH.

Holy Name
Christ's NOMEN SACRUM.

holy orders
One of the SEVEN SACRAMENTS: taking holy orders empowers the individual to administer divine GRACE to the faithful by other sacraments, such as the EUCHARIST, and by the word. A spiritual power is conferred after training, preparation, and consecration, for proper adherence to ecclesiastical and liturgical duties.

Holy Saturday
The vigil or day before EASTER Sunday, commemorating Christ's resting in the tomb, and anticipating the RESURRECTION; also called EASTER EVEN.

Holy See
The Roman Catholic Pope's governmental headquarters at Rome, the royal or EPISCOPAL seat of dignity, authority, and jurisdiction.

Holy Spirit
The Third Person in the Christian TRINITY, coequal and coeternal with the Father and the Son, a member of the HYPOSTATIC UNION.

Holy Thursday
MAUNDY THURSDAY, the Thursday before EASTER, another name for ASCENSION Day.

Holy Trinity
A feast celebrating the TRINITY with recital of the ATHANASIAN CREED, beginning with the emotional QUICUMQUE VULT.

holy water font
A wood, stone, or metal vessel, usually ornamented with religious scenes and symbols, containing water for ritual purification, and used in rites and devotional acts such as BAPTISM, asperging, exorcism, and burial.

Holy Week
The calendar week preceding EASTER, devoted to celebration and the reenactment of Christ's PASSION with prayers, drama, and LITURGY, particularly the solemn events on GOOD FRIDAY that omit a MASS, all to anticipate the commemoration of Christ's RESURRECTION.

homage and fealty
Personal obligation of a TENANT holding land TENURE to an overlord.

homespun
A simple fabric, woven, dyed, and fulled at home.

hometz
Foods containing leaven, forbidden to Jewish celebrants of Passover in commemoration of the events of Exodus 21:15–20.

homily
A short, simple sermon, whose moral is indirectly stated through a familiar holy or practical event, usually from the Bible. It is a homely, honeyed message easier to accept, harder to ignore, than a straight sermon on ontological doctrine; similar in effect to the EXEMPLUM and the BIBLIA PAUPERUM.

homme arme
(French, armed man) A fifteenth-century French folksong frequently used as a TENOR melody in polyphonic MASSes.

homo bonus
The twelfth-century good man, in Italian the OMO BUONO.

homo signorum
The graphic depiction of an ASTROLOGICAL MAN.

homo silvestris
A WILD MAN.

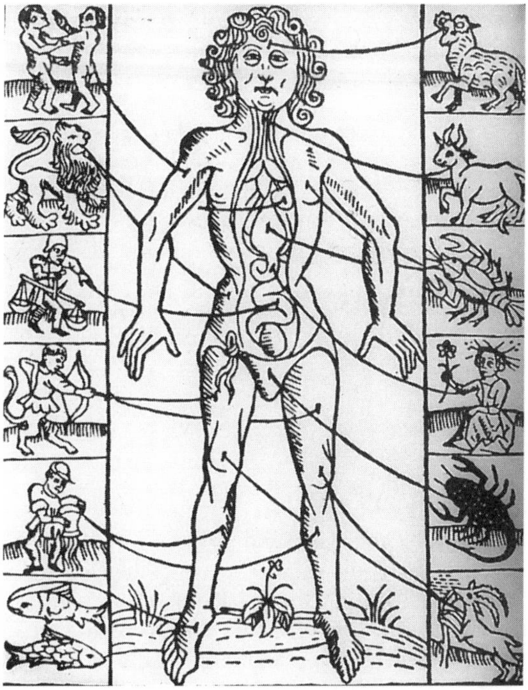

This *homo signorum* associates astrological signs with internal and external organs. (From *Bloodletting Calendar*, England, 15th century; from the collection of Professor Harry Bober, NYU Institute for Fine Arts, courtesy of Galeria Medievalia, Tenafly, New Jersey)

honeymoon
Uniting MEAD, ASTROLOGY, and marriage bliss: the fermented honey wine with supposedly APHRODISIAC powers was drunk by the bride and groom for a month after the wedding to stimulate CONCEPTION TIME for a child. If luck and stars allowed, a year later the couple would BRING HOME THE BACON.

hood mold
A molding projecting from the wall over an arch, door, or window to serve as ornamentation as well as to divert rainwater.

hoodwink
To deceive as if by blindfolding. From a FALCONRY technique of placing a hood over the head of an eager hawk to prevent jitteryness, flying off the hunter's wrist prematurely, or eating its own prey.

hope
One of the THREE THEOLOGICAL VIRTUES.

hope's crow
This ATTRIBUTE of hope defined her optimism for tomorrow; a crow's cawing sounds like *cras, cras,* (tomorrow, tomorrow), as in, "Tomorrow there will be OPPORTUNITY if FORTUNE allows."

hoqueton
(from Arabic *alcoton,* a variety of cotton) A tight-fitting padded cotton TUNIC similar to the GAMBESON.

horae canonicae
The eight CANONICAL HOURS.

horizontal arches
An unusual architectural and masonry form for Brunelleschi's fifteenth-century CUPOLA of the Florentine CATHEDRAL Santa Maria del Fiore. The design required the invention of special equipment and techniques for the elegant soaring shape.

horned headdress
An ATOUR.

Horns of Moses
Michaelangelo's powerful sculpture of Moses with two horns crowning his head culminated an earlier tradition depicting Jews as horned, an image traceable to fourth-century Saint Jerome's mistaken confusion of Hebrew *qeren,* scintillating with rays of light (Exodus 34:29), with Latin *cornuta,* horned. Horns had been symbols of honor in ancient, barbarian, and ANGLO-SAXON arts, particularly when on warriors' helmets; later, they became EMBLEMs of infamy, demonic ATTRIBUTES of Satan and of Jews. Christian theologians associated Moses's horns with the horns of the BISHOP's MITRE, the two peaks representing the Old and New Testaments (according to Robert Paululus and Petrus Cantor in the twelfth century), or signs of God's resplendent brightness and truth (according to William Durandus, Bishop of Mende in the thirteenth century).

The horned Moses and Aaron observe the destruction of an enemy camp. (From the *Old Testament,* Cologne, Germany, 1479)

horologium of Richard of Wallingford
The fourteenth-century English ABBOT's clock, built though his brethren and King Edward III criticized his work on the sumptuous machine while he neglected his church. The horologium was an astronomical clock with trains of gears, mechanical linkages, a dial, indexes, a rotating lunar globe, wheel work for tracing heavenly body motions, and a bell.

horoscope
(Greek, hour observer) In ASTROLOGY, the depiction of the configuration of the ZODIAC SIGNs at the moment of a person's birth thereby predicting by GENETHLIALOGY the future life activities, temperament, PHYSIOGNOMY, and fate.

horoscopy
The study of a HOROSCOPE to predict the future.

hortus conclusus
(Latin, the enclosed garden) A symbol of virginity. One of the VIRTUES OF THE VIRGIN adopted for secular allegories, such as the *Romance of the Rose* and numerous GARDEN sites of DREAM VISIONS.

Hortus Deliciarum
(Latin, garden of delights) An illustrated encyclopedia compiled from many Church Fathers and other sources in the twelfth century by the ABBESS-scholar-physician Harrad of Landsburg for instructing her nuns at Hohenburg; she wrote: "I, the bee, draw sap of diverse flowers (FLORILEGIA), inspired by God, and construct by my love for you a honeycomb for sweetness and light. . . ."

Hortus Sanitatis

(Latin, garden of health) A spectacular HERBAL, a natural historical compendium describing medicinal properties of vegetable, animal, and mineral foods, and remedies such as hot baths.

Hosannah

(Hebrew, Save us, God) A Jewish supplication translated to Greek, and applied to the Christian PALM SUNDAY proclamation of Jesus as Messiah. In the Christian LITURGY, *Hosannah in excelsis,* Hosannah in the highest, is part of the SANCTUS.

hose

Cotton, wool, or leather stockings, sometimes fitted with a thin leather sole, making shoes unnecessary. As garments became shorter, hose became longer or higher, covering from the waistline to the toes. Hose became an important sartorial companion of the DOUBLET.

host

(Latin *hostia,* sacrifice) The consecrated bread or wafer of the Christian MASS, eaten by the celebrant and penitent worshippers who have confessed and have been absolved of sin. The host is offered to God as a sacrifice during the EUCHARIST.

houppelande

A popular fourteenth- and fifteenth-century ROBE for men and women. It was full and richly ornate in fabric, belted at waist or hip, and had exceedingly long, FUR-lined, funnel-shaped sleeves, and a funnel-shaped collar, the CARCAILLE. The sleeves and the collar both had DAGGING.

hourd

A timber gallery on the summit of a tower or PARAPET of a fortified castle. It surmounted MACHICOLATION.

house

In ASTROLOGY, one of the 12 compartments into which the circle of the heavens is divided, moving from north to south along the horizon; the ZODIAC sign in which a planet has most INFLUENCE.

houseaux

Tall, thick-soled leather boots ranging in height from beneath the knee to mid-thigh. They often had an open toe or heel.

household

The social order of a family or organization. The complete domestic hierarchy included all attendants and servants, often as many as hundreds or thousands. All personnel wore a distinctive LIVERY, from the SURVEYOR, PANTLER, CARVER, BUTLER, SQUIRE, CHAMBERLAIN, and SERGEANT AT ARMS, to the CHILDREN IN DOMESTIC SERVICE, and the PAGES.

housel

(Anglo-Saxon *husl,* holy) The EUCHARIST.

housse

A long, wide shawl buttoning at the breast, trimmed with FUR at the neck and hem.

Hrosvithan

Related to the works of Hrosvitha von Gandersheim, the learned poet, scholar, playwright, and BENEDICTINE NUN of Gandersheim in Saxony. Her Latin writings imitated Terence, Virgil, and Horace, and dramatically praised women's chastity and fortitude. She was celebrated in her own time for her *Dulcitius, Sapientia,* and *Paphnutius.*

Hufnagelschrift

(German *huf,* hoof) The horseshoe-shaped musical notation NAGELSCHRIFT.

humidity of the philosophers

A viscous, vaporous, or unctuous liquid that was the result of chemical and alchemical procedures.

humility formula

An author's statement of humility, as "If this book offends, don't blame me. I am but a paltry human fool. If it pleases, praise God whose inspiration I cherish." Self-deprecating invocations written by Chaucer, ARCHIPOETA, or Caxton, minimizing their art, were artifice and MENDILOQUENCE, the required literary exoneration of self from pride, political embarrassment, or danger.

Hungarian stitch

BARGELLO WORK.

hunting horn music

Because some horns played only a single pitch, the call depended on rhythm, length, and intensity of sound. *Mote* was blown at uncoupling of the hounds; *rechete,* to recall dogs or to urge them to the kill; *mane* and *pryse,* rhythmically portended the animal's calm in the banquet hall, since harmonious hunting prefigured healthful eating. Hunt music inspired the CHASSE, CACCIA, and CATCH, early forms of POLYPHONY, in which music of the ceremonial pursuit of the animal was transferred to the pursuit of the desired lover.

hunting manuals
Hunting INSTRUCTION BOOKS, often magnificently illustrated, written by Gaston Phebus, King Frederick of Sicily, and others depicted the ceremony and sport, methods of tracking, chasing, killing, and carving the prey. Many include sections on FALCONRY, animal husbandry, HUNTING HORN MUSIC, and medical uses of animals in the treatment and cure of disease and injury.

hunt of love
Imitating popular HUNTING MANUALS, love allegories use language of the chase for depicting the arts of COURTLY LOVE; poems and songs such as the CHASSE, CACCIA, and CATCH express passion via the rhetoric of the hunt and HUNTING HORN MUSIC. FABLIAUX writers and devotees of AMOR DE CON particularly exploit connections between sexuality and hunting.

huppah
The Jewish wedding canopy under which the bride and groom stand during the marriage ceremony; it is simultaneously symbolic of their temporal home and their place in God's universe.

huque
A flowing robe, short or long, worn as military and civilian costume, often edged with FUR or embroidered with precious stones.

hurdle
A low, flat, sled-like vehicle on runners drawn through the town by a horse or person, to which a malefactor or criminal is tied for punishment by shaming.

hurdy-gurdy
An unbowed, mechanical, stringed instrument with a keyboard. A revolving wheel cranked by a handle

A fraudulent baker convicted of selling underweight bread is punished by carriage through town ignominiously tied on a hurdle. (From Assisa Panis, 14th century; courtesy of the Guildhall, London)

touched internal strings and a set of stopping rods to sound several bass strings as a DRONE or BURDON, while other strings were activated by keys struck for melody. Also called a wheel fiddle or VIELLE A ROUE.

hurly-burly
Excited, noisy commotion. *Macbeth*'s witches and the loud noise of the *hurlu-berlu* in Rabelais are similar to the stylized keening and noisy wailing of ancient Irish mourners at funerals, the CORONACH.

husband
(Anglo-Saxon from Scandinavian *hus-bondi,* a person bound to the HOUSEHOLD) An agricultural land worker, or property holder. The female equivalent was HUSSY.

hussy
(Anglo-Saxon *hus-wyf,* a HOUSEHOLD-bound woman) A housewife, comparable to HUSBAND. *Housewife* shortened to *hussy,* but only in the later Renaissance did it become a term of opprobrium, as with HARLOT, by the process of PEJORATION.

huve
A projecting headdress with many folds, it was anchored to each side of a woman's head by long pins and BODKINS.

hydromancy
Divination by water signs: tides, ripples, currents, swirls, and whirlpools.

hyleg
In ASTROLOGY, the sign or planet, also called the APHETA, which influences a person's longevity; when it reaches the ANARETA, the person dies.

hymn
A song of praise adoring God, comparable to biblical PSALMs and CANTICLEs.

Hypapanti
EPIPHANY.

hypocaust
An underground furnace room which distributed, by ducts, warm air to the rooms and spaces above, centrally heating them. The system was used also in indoor baths and health SPAs.

hypostatic union
In the single person of Christ, the joining of two distinct natures: God and Man.

I

iamb
One of the FIVE METRICAL FEET, consisting of a short followed by a long beat.

ichnography
Drafting by rule and compass for creating or copying floor plans, designs, and experiments in PERSPECTIVE and ANAMORPHOSIS.

icon
A devotional panel painting portraying Christ, the Virgin, or saints. The icon is venerated in Eastern Orthodox churches; also, an element in an ICONOSTASIS.

iconography
The study of meaning in seemingly simple works of art contrived with hidden pictures, SYMBOLs, ALLEGORIES, ATTRIBUTEs, and covert layers of representation, often requiring the FOUR-FOLD INTERPRETATION; also, the application of ICONOLOGY to art.

iconology
Knowledge of ATTRIBUTEs and EMBLEMs, particularly representations of mythological and holy figures, as INSTRUMENTS OF CHRIST'S PASSION and SAINTS AND THEIR ATTRIBUTES.

iconostasis
A partitioning screen with many tiers of ICONs separating the sanctuary from the main section of an Eastern Orthodox CHURCH.

idiophone
A self-sounder, a practical rather than artistic musical instrument, such as a clapper, bones, bell chime, gong, GREGOR, CRACELLE, and noise maker. It was used to alert people to danger, to announce an entrance, or to stimulate animals to run or to fight.

I H S
The sacred cipher representing the Greek initials for Jesus Christ, the Savior; also, the first three letters of the name Jesus in Greek. The initials also represent the Greek word for fish, *ichthus,* SYMBOL of Christ's sacrifice and role as fisher of men requiring salvation. Interpreted also as abbreviations for: *Iesus hominum salvator* (Jesus, the savior of men); *in hoc salus* (in this Cross is salvation); and IN HOC SIGNO (in this sign you will conquer).

ilech
In ASTROLOGY, the star associated with medicine; in ALCHEMY, a compound of salt, sulphur, and MERCURY.

iliaster
In ALCHEMY, the first chaos of the universal matter, said to consist of silver, salt, and MERCURY, the prime principle.

ilk
(Anglo-Saxon *ilke,* equivalence, similarity, identity) Of the same type.

illuminated
Of a book of MANUSCRIPT with ILLUMINATIONS; or a person intellectually or spiritually enlightened, after learning the QUINQUE VIAE.

illumination
The art of decorating MANUSCRIPTs with MINIATUREs, elaborate initial letters, HISTORIATED capitals, and elegant borders, often with plants, animals, GRO-

TESQUERIES, and ARABESQUES, painted in watercolor, brilliant TEMPERA colors, and burnished gold and silver. Spiritually, illumination means understanding, knowledge of God's radiance ("In Your light we see light"), and is the second of the THREE STAGES OF BERNARDIAN MYSTICISM.

illusion food
Edibles crafted by painting or sculpture to appear other than what they seem; to surprise guests into admiration: golden apples (veal and dill meatballs wrapped in gold-tinted pastry with green MARZIPAN leaves), appreylere (beef and lamb baked in pastry shaped and painted to seem an elegant wine pitcher), or blackbird pie (four-and-twenty live blackbirds safely tethered within the crust are later liberated into the hall).

imagines clipeatae
Portraits of the FOUR EVANGELISTS decorating CANON TABLES.

imago pietatis
A portrait of Jesus Christ designed to encourage meditation on His sacrificial death.

imbricated pattern
A decorative ornament whose leaves or scales overlap.

Immaculate Conception
The flawless conception of the Virgin Mary in the womb of her mother Anne, allowing Mary to be born exempt from ORIGINAL SIN; hence her ability likewise to conceive without sin her son Jesus. The concept was argued by Saint Augustine, Saint Ambrose, Saint Jerome, Saint Bonaventura, the FRANCISCAN Dun Scotus, and other Church Fathers. Other Maries of the HOLY KINSHIP are not so pure as this MADONNA IMMACULATA. The term often is misunderstood as the conception of Christ by Mary.

impasto
A thick, oil-based paint applied to a canvas or panel to create relief, solidity, and emphasis for figures or objects.

impresa
(Italian, enterprise) An EMBLEM or DEVICE, such as CANTING ARMS, plus a motto, used to identify a person by commemorating a significant personal quality or past event. The device could be purposefully enigmatic, yet allusive and intelligible to those of a similar social class and education. For example, after France's King Louis XII in 1499 had invaded Italy, he created as impresa a spiny PORCUPINE with *cominus et eminus:* "I fight hand-to-hand and at a distance." Judges, ecclesiastics, artists, bakers, and great banking families such as the Medici and Farnese had impresas applied to their ceilings, tapestry borders, jewel CASKET covers, personal jewelry, and ceremonial costumes.

Improperia
(Latin, reproaches) Roman liturgical CHANT of three sections of the Old Testament Prophets. It was derived from one of the FOUR MUSICAL DIALECTS of the church, the GALLICAN CHANT, sung on GOOD FRIDAY morning.

Incarnation
Christ's assumption of human nature: the second person of the TRINITY, the Word, made flesh, to dwell among people (John 1:14). The divine and human nature united in a single person were in perfect HYPOSTATIC UNION: the invisible, incomprehensible, and timeless God, with a visible, understandable, temporal but sinless man.

Incarnation initials
The Greek letters XPI, Christ's NOMEN SACRUM (holy name), often depicted in DIMINUENDO in MANUSCRIPT ILLUMINATION.

incidents
Feudal responsibilities owed to an overlord in land TENURE, such as HOMAGE and FEALTY, AIDS, FORFEITURE, RELIEF, and ESCHEAT.

incipit
(Latin, it begins) The beginning, the first word of a MANUSCRIPT, document, GREGORIAN CHANT, liturgical text as sung by the CANTOR before the chorus joins in, or CANTUS FIRMUS MOTET.

inconjunct
Describing independent and simultaneous ideas that do not influence one another; in ASTROLOGY, two

planets' positions not in conjunction, so that neither affects operation of the other.

incremental repetition
Repetition within the progress of a story. A powerful rhetorical and structural element of early English and Scottish BALLADs, the technique built suspense and hypnotically reinforced emotion by repeating phrases, lines, or epithets, adding at each successive expression small though significant changes.

incubus
An imaginary male demon, an evil spirit believed to attack sleeping women sexually, and recognized by ecclesiastical and civil law as causing pregnancies. The female counterpart was called a SUCCUBUS.

incunabula
(Latin, cradle or swaddling) The initial version, earliest form of an art or craft; specifically, the first books and pamphlets printed with movable type, before 1501. Between ten and twenty million volumes were printed on paper, VELLUM, and PARCHMENT in this infancy of printing.

indenture
A tangible, material object signifying a debt or contract, attesting to ownership and preventing either side from altering the record: a notched wooden stick, halved, half held by debtor, half by creditor, or a written contract, halved, with serrated edges. Also, the temporary serfdom of a freeborn man, woman, or child, who owed service and labor in exchange for learning a craft, as an APPRENTICE.

Index Librorum Prohibitorum
(Latin, List of Prohibited Books) The official list of books the Roman Catholic Church prohibits its members to read or own, first compiled by an INQUISITION council under Pope Paul IV in 1557.

indigo
A deep blue dye derived from Indian plants. Highly prized and priced, it influenced trade, exploration, politics, banking, and, because ships were necessary transport vessels, stimulated construction of the seaworthy COGs, DROMONDs, and GALLEYs.

Indo-European
The family of languages considered to be related by descent and progressive differentiation, commonly divided into two sub-groups, CENTUM and SATEM, the Latin and Avestan words for "one hundred." Nine principal language classes: Indian, Iranian, Armenian, Hellenic, Albanian, Italic, Balto-Slavic, Teutonic (including English), and Celtic have certain words in common, such as epithets for winter, snow, and the names of trees (e.g., beech) and animals (e.g., bee), suggesting a unity of expression of diverse peoples and elemental ideas. Discoveries of Hittite and Tokharian added two new language groups to the original nine.

indulgences
The church's granting of pardon for sins confessed and forgiven. Plenary indulgences were rewards for participation in the CRUSADES. Sales of indulgences by pardoners were among the abuses criticized by leading writers of the Reformation.

infanticide
Population control, emphasizing the reduction in the number of female babies by murder, abandonment, and laying-over, the smothering of a baby in bed by rolling over it.

influence
The astrological effect of the motions of the heavenly bodies and their zodiacal configurations upon human events and the human body. Planets and HOUSEs in malign conjunction, such as Jupiter and Saturn in Scorpio in 1484, were thought to have caused pandemic syphilis; other configurations were believed to have caused such public health disasters as the PLAGUE and epidemic upper respiratory disease or flu, short for influenza.

infula
The LAPPET or ribbon on a BISHOP's MITRE.

inglenook
An enclosed wall-seat beside a fireplace.

ingress
Entering a field, church, or idea; the astrological entrance of an orbital body into a sign of the ZODIAC, a quadrant, or one of the three HOUSEs.

In hoc signo vinces
(Latin, In this sign, you will conquer) The words emblazoned on a banner in the vision of Constantine the Great that inspired his (and the empire's) formal conversion to Christianity, and led to the LABARUM.

inhumation
Burial. In chemistry and biological experimentation, it was the placing of a soluble substance into dung for purposes of dissolution, or for developing an embryonic substance already germinating.

inlay
A design created on a surface by precisely inserting into shallow depressions thin pieces of wood, metal, tile, stone, shell, or ivory. The whole piece is then sanded and polished flat, as in MOSAIC, MARQUETRY, and INTARSIA.

in nomine
(Latin, In the name of God) An instrumental composition based on a CANTUS FIRMUS. One of the earliest was composed by John Taverner (d. 1545).

Inquisition
Juridical prosecution of heresy by Christian ecclesiastical courts, begun in the thirteenth century by a secular edict of Emperor Frederick II; it was soon followed by Pope Gregory IX's establishment of DOMINICAN and FRANCISCAN inquisitors. Torture and death via AUTO DA FE eliminated large numbers of CATHARI, ALBIGENSES, medical women accused of practicing WITCHcraft and sorcery with WOMEN'S SECRETS, and Jews, especially the MARRANOS and MORISCOS of Spain in the fifteenth century.

In an Inquisition mass burning, Jews and Protestants are tortured. (From a woodcut, Nuremburg, 1493; courtesy of the Jewish Museum, New York)

INRI
The acronym for Jesus of Nazareth, King of the Jews. It was the mocking inscription Pilate fastened to the CROSS: *Iesus Nazarenus Rex Iudaeorum* (John 19:19).

insigne
An EMBLEM or DEVICE used for identification in HERALDRY, on a COAT OF ARMS, and on ecclesiastical VESTMENTS.

instruction books
Didactic texts for educating people in many aspects of life, professions, and behaviors. MIRRORS OF PRINCES taught leadership to the nobility; other subjects could be learned via HUNTING MANUALS, sex manuals, treatises on the ARS AMATORIA and COURTLY LOVE, dance and etiquette books, such as ORCHESOGRAPHY and the SIX REQUISITES, religious rule books for ANCHORITES and ANCHORESSES, especially BENEDICTINES, INSTRUCTION BOOKS FOR WOMEN, even arts of dying well, the ARS MORIENDI. Pictorial didactics included sculptured funerary "books," the TRANSI TOMBS, MORALIZED BIBLES, and BIBLIA PAUPERUM.

instruction books for women
Education by INSTRUCTION BOOKS for substance and style in a profession or craft, or for practical skills and etiquette, as *Ancrene Rewle* for celibate churchwomen; *Ménagier de Paris* for young wives of older men; and Christine de Pizan's *Book of the Three Virtues,* for the welfare and honor of all women.

instrument
A musical, agricultural, or functional implement; in a sexual context, genitalia: Chaucer's Wife of Bath calls her husband's penis his beloved instrument.

instruments of Christ's Passion
In art and ICONOGRAPHY, objects associated with the suffering and PASSION of Jesus Christ included: nails, hammer, lance, sponge, column with chord, scourges for flagellation, crown of thorns, chalice, Pilate's

An interlaced "ITA" is formed of mammals, birds, fish, and flowers. (From the manuscript Book of Kells, Trinity College, Dublin, Ireland, c. 9th century)

washbasin, the arresting soldier's lantern, rope, club, sword, pincers, the purse with 30 pieces of silver, Christ's seamless garment, the soldier's dice, the ladder to remove the body from the CROSS, the sun and moon, a vat of vinegar, an ointment jar with embalming spices, a heart with five wounds, the ear of Malchus, the cock of Saint Peter's denial, and such sacred MONOGRAMS as INRI and IHS.

insular
The distinctive artistic style of ILLUMINATION for MANUSCRIPTS characterized by INTERLACE and CARPET PAGES, flourishing in Ireland, Scotland, and England's MONASTERY of Lindisfarne in the seventh, eighth, and ninth centuries, as the Books of Kells, Durrow, Armagh, and Lindisfarne.

insuration
Chemical saturation of a substance with liquid in order to dissolve it, or to facilitate its purification; also, saturating with a desiccator, as salt, before SUBLIMATION.

intaglio
An incising technique in the graphic arts, jewelry, and the decoration of metal objects, such as ETCHING or ENGRAVING; the opposite of RELIEF.

intarsia
The decorative technique of inlaying small pieces of wood veneer, usually in contrasting colors, grains, and textures, into a wood surface. Related to MARQUETRY, this technique depicts deep PERSPECTIVE in elaborate town scenes, musical instruments, and streets and roads "in the distance" on wall panelling, furniture, COFFERS, and chests.

intercessor
One who intercedes between a human supplicant and God, either Jesus Christ as ADVOCATUS or the Virgin Mary, who was celebrated as AUXILIUM CHRISTIANORUM (the support of Christians) and ALMA REDEMPTORIS MATER (Gracious Mother of the Redeemer).

interdict
An exclusion of a person, group, city, or nation from participation in Christian spirituality, usually imposed by the Pope or a local BISHOP, and rescinded after sufficient penance.

interlace
A Celtic artistic technique gracefully intertwining animal shapes, alphabet letters, leaves, and fanciful figures in an elegant geometric design; important in

Celtic and INSULAR MANUSCRIPTs such as the Book of Kells and the Lindisfarne Gospels.

interlude
A musical or mimed entertainment between a series of MYSTERY PLAYS or MORALITY PLAYS; or an entertainment, comedy, or FARCE performed between courses of a feast, accompanied by SUBTLETIES or ENTREMETS.

international style
The late fourteenth- and early fifteenth-century qualities of GOTHIC art: linear elegance, fashionable, contemporary costumery, graceful swaying figures, scintillating color, and elegant exoticism paired with punctilious realism. Best exemplified in the works of the Limbourg Brothers, Ghiberti, Broederlam, and Lorenzo Monaco, the style pervades panel painting, sculpture, MANUSCRIPT ILLUMINATION, carving, metal work, and architecture.

intrados
An arch's or VAULT's underside.

introit
The ornate, ANTIPHONAL first CHANT of the MASS.

Irish script
The distinctive sixth- and seventh-century CALLIGRAPHY of INSULAR manuscripts, using both MAJUSCULE and MINUSCULE letter forms, influenced ANGLO-SAXON script and manuscript decoration.

isocephaly
Artistic arrangement of figures so that all heads are seen at the same height.

isorhythmic
Repeated, identical musical rhythmic patterns called TALEAE, as in a liturgical CANTUS FIRMUS of fourteenth-century MOTETs.

ispahanis
A precious fabric, made by Moravids in Spain from the eighth through eleventh centuries, and in Antioch in the twelfth century.

istoriato
Historical, mythical, biblical, or genre scenes, more decorative than didactic, on MAJOLICA, MANUSCRIPTs, and other art forms.

ivy
(Anglo-Saxon, *ifig*, ivy, the climbing five-angled evergreen) A shrewish woman. The climbing evergreen plant on a pole, called an ale-pole or ALE-STAKE, signified a tavern selling beer and ale; an ivy bush indicated a wine bar. "Good wine needs no ivy-bush" meant, a quality drink required no advertising.

J

jack
A quilted, padded, military DOUBLET, usually sleeveless and tight-fitting, worn over a HAUBERK, or itself armored with small, interdigitated, metal leaves. It later developed into the JACKET.

jackanapes
The *jack o'naibs,* a face card in an Eastern game popular in western Europe; or the "Jack Napes," an ape or monkey pet or zoological curiosity; or the ridiculing NICKNAME of William de la Pole, Duke of Suffolk.

jacket
A man's close-fitting, upper-body garment derived from the JACK. Since it was also considered lower-class or peasant garb, its name probably derives from the common country name *Jacques.*

Jacob staff
An important observational instrument used in astronomy and navigation for several centuries, it was invented by fourteenth-century Jewish astronomer Levi Ben Gerson. It consisted of a crosspiece slid along a calibrated staff until two stars could be observed in the night sky. The angular distance between them was determined by calculating the ratio of the length of the crosspiece to its distance from the eye.

Jacob's well
A resting place at a spring between Judea and Galilee where Jesus met a Samaritan woman and said, "Whoever drinks the water I give will never again suffer thirst" (John 4:13), a subject common in paintings.

jakes
(Or john) A NICKNAME for a toilet or bathroom, from John Harrington's ingenious *Metamorphosis of Ajax,* a discourse on a flush toilet.

jaloux
The jealous husband of COURTLY LOVE tradition, deceived and feared by lovers in TROUBADOUR songs.

jambeau
Protective leg ARMOR.

Janus
The two-faced Roman god, protector of doorways and gateways, often depicted in the TWELVE LABORS OF THE MONTHS as the symbol of January.

jape
A trick, illusion, or joke performed by a juggler, jester, or magician who worked in town fairs or market squares, derived from the tradition of the JOCULATORES.

jardin de deduit
The pleasure GARDEN, a LOCUS AMOENUS.

jaseran
Fine CHAIN-MAIL body protection or a fabric JACK sewn with metal plates.

Jericho
Blackmore Priory, the favorite trysting place and resort for sexual escapes from statecraft for England's King Henry VIII. His courtiers' excuse that the King had gone to Jericho implied that, like Joshua, he was

fighting battles to break down walls of maidenly resistance or anatomy.

jerkin
A padded JACKET or GAMBESON derived from the earlier COTE-HARDIE; a short upper garment worn by men. The woman's equivalent was the jerkinet.

jersey
A fifteenth-century knitted shirt or TUNIC for sailors and fishermen of the islands of Jersey and Guernsey.

jesse
In FALCONRY, the light leather or silk thongs or straps temporarily tying a HOODWINKed falcon to a perch, and also used for identification; in decorative art, the JESSE TREE.

Jesse Tree
Arboreal representation of Christ's genealogy from the root of Jesse, father of David, a representation of Christ's Old Testament heritage and the venerable family tree.

jester
A professional entertainer using mimicry, humor, buffoonery, and satire; a court FOOL, dressed in MOTLEY, derived from the JOCULATORES tradition; sometimes, a chanter of CHANSON DE GESTES.

Jewish badge
A DEVICE to distinguish Jews and thereby ostracize them. Taking many shapes and colors: in the Papal states, a yellow fabric patch (for men), yellow-and-blue striped (for women); a yellow or red circle, in Barcelona; a particolored circle, yellow and red, worn on men's breasts and women's foreheads, in Rome; a blue insigne shaped like the Greek letter *tau,* in Sicily and Naples; a yellow star, in Verona; a coin-size red cloth worn over the heart, in Spain. Elsewhere the badge was shaped as a tablet or star. In the form of the letter *O,* it was called the ROWEL or ROUELLE. The badge was worn in addition to or as substitute for the JUDENHUT.

jig
A popular early sixteenth-century English dance, usually accompanied by PIPE AND TABOR.

joculatores
Late Roman itinerant theater players and entertainers who performed at markets, fairs, and church festivals, affecting drama and later COMMEDIA DELL'ARTE. Their formulaic characterizations with inevitable actions offered pleasure of the familiar and reestablishment of ORDO MUNDI. Stock characters included the SENEX AMANS (old lover) and his young, sexually exuberant wife; the GOSSIP, a shrewish, loquacious wife of an UNGUENTARIUS or ointment seller; and the MILES GLORIOSUS (boasting soldier). The players provided humor for EASTER liturgical plays, SHROVETIDE festivities, MYSTERY, MIRACLE, and MORALITY plays.

joie
Superb love celebrated in TROUBADOUR lyrics, as written by William of Aquitaine and Bernart de Ventadorn, and courtly ROMANCE, as those of Lancelot or Tristan. Joy voiced in song should express the lyrical harmony of affection itself; as Saint Bonaventura said, "Union of a good and beautiful subject with a delightful object leads to joy which creates song."

jolif mestrier amourous
Love's merry business, sexual foreplay and intercourse, a FABLIAUX pleasure.

jongleur
An entertainer in the JOCULATORES tradition; before the twelfth century, a juggler, mime, acrobat, and performer with trained animals such as bears and monkeys; later, a singer of TROUBADOUR songs, sometimes also a composer and a poet, and reciter of CHANSONS DE GESTES.

jordan
A URINE FLASK used for UROSCOPY; in a bedroom, a covered chamber pot for urination and defecation, sometimes disguised as a chair; a NECESSARIUM.

journade
An elaborate parade CLOAK that was a flowing cape with wide slit sleeves.

journeyman
(French *journée,* a day's work, wages, or travel) A craftsman hired out for daily wages, ranking higher

Wearing Judenhuts, Joshua and his warriors blow down the walls of Jericho. (From the *Psalter of Saint Louis*, Bibliothèque Nationale, Paris)

than an APPRENTICE but lower than a MASTER in the well-regulated GUILDs.

joust

A formal, ritualized, martial exercise in which mounted knights competed for prizes, or ransoms, as in war; a war game often with legal outcome but without actual battles. The events were often enhanced with elaborate ARMOR, horse CAPARISONs, music, art, food, and festivity. "Love-jousting" was sexual intercourse.

jube

An ornamental CHOIR SCREEN; or a silk or wool overshirt with elbow-length sleeves, decorated with needlework or braid.

Jubilate Sunday

The third Sunday after EASTER, so-called from words of the MASS: *jubilate deo omnis terra,* All the earth, rejoice in the Lord (Psalm 100) or from the INTROIT (Psalm 66).

Jubilee

(from Hebrew *jobel,* the ram's horn or *shofar* and Latin *jubilum,* a joyous shout) The fiftieth year, the year after seven sets of seven years of work, a celebration of sacred sevens prescribed in Leviticus 25 as a

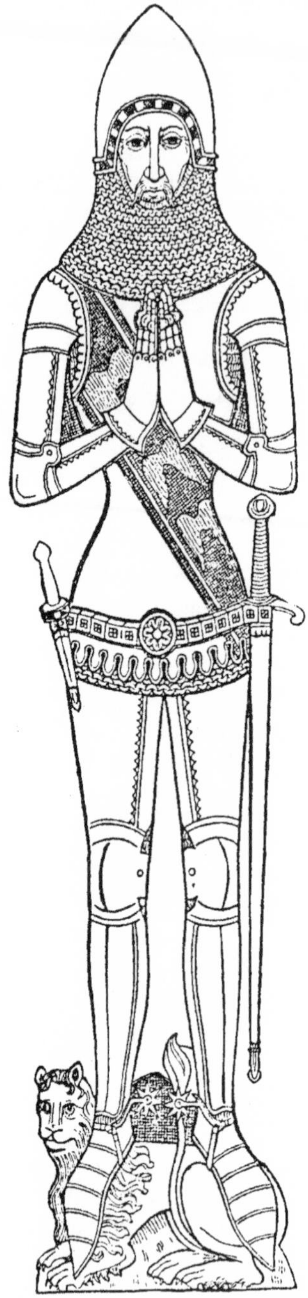

A knight wears a jupon crossed by a baldric and a bassinet with camail. (From a brass rubbing of Sir John Wingfield, Letheringham Church, Suffolk, England, c. 1400)

joyous rest for the earth and for humankind, and dedicated to praising God, emancipating slaves, restoring property to owners and heirs, and celebrating order.

jubilus
A long exuberant MELISMA sung to the final *A* of an ALLELUIA.

Judaicae pelliciae
Fur-trimmed garments, lavish Jewish clothing.

Judenhut
(German, Jews' hat) A pointed hat or DUNCE cap, which Jews were required by law to wear with the JEWISH BADGE or ROWEL or ROUELLE in many parts of Europe. Old Testament figures often were so depicted.

Judica Sunday
(Latin, *Iudica,* Pass judgment upon me) The fifth Sunday in LENT, named for the opening words of the Latin MASS from PSALM 43: Judge me, sentence me, Oh God. Also called PASSION SUNDAY.

jugum Christi
(Latin, the yoke of Christ) A SCAPULAR.

Julian calendar
Julius Caesar's calendrical configuration, later superseded by the GREGORIAN CALENDAR.

jupe
(Arabic *djuba*, a short jacket) A loose-fitting jacket.

jupon
A tight-fitting padded DOUBLET worn beneath a HAUBERK; later, a sleeveless SURCOAT of elaborate fabric and heraldic ornament.

jus tertii
(Latin, right of the third) A legal defense asserting that only a third party can bring a lawsuit, not the current defender or plaintiff; or a case brought for the benefit of a third party.

K

Kaballah
The Jewish esoteric tradition sharing elements with both Greek and Christian mysticism and closely akin to GNOSTICISM in theology, cosmology, angelology, and magic. From the twelfth century onward, Kabalistic spirituality, explained and transmitted by such graphic schema as the SEPHIROTIC TREE, affected Christian philosophy, theology, art, and architecture.

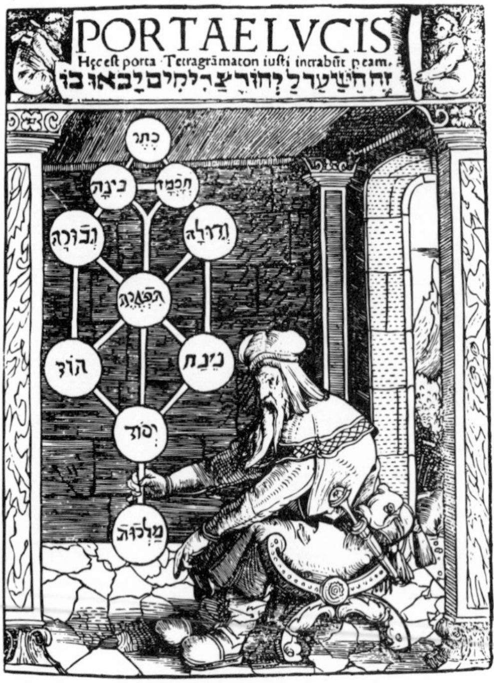

An adept at Kaballah holds the sephirotic tree. (From an engraving, Ricius, *Portae Lucis*, 1516)

kaddish
The great Jewish DOXOLOGY, mostly Aramaic, partly Hebrew, originally recited both before and after a TORAH reading in SYNAGOGUE, and later added to the end of mourning prayers for the dead.

kagoule
A peasant's short, hooded cape of cloth or FUR.

kalansuwa
A Persian hat worn by Jews, Christians, and other non-Muslims, crafted only of certain COLORS and adorned with two special button-shaped EMBLEMS or BADGES.

kameah
(Hebrew, good luck charm) Worn as protection against evil, an amulet inscribed with sacred names, blessings, SIGILS, and signs; or a luck charm affixed to a house or room; sometimes a MAGIC SQUARE containing the numbers equivalent to the name of a propitious planet or spirit, as in GEMATRIA.

kantorei
(Latin *cantor*, singer) A group of singers employed by a church or court; or the paid or volunteer musicians of a community.

kappe
A short hooded CLOAK worn by the leader of a Jewish SYNAGOGUE, and by German Jewish bridegrooms.

kappel
A skullcap or *yarmulke* of a religious Jew.

keep
A castle's inner stronghold or defensive tower, surrounded by one or more walls, with a BAILEY between them.

kenning
The ANGLO-SAXON and Old Germanic poetic technique of describing something without naming it, achieved by joining two or more of its major qualities: the ocean as "the whale's road"; a high-prowed sailing ship as "a foamy-necked floater"; a well-wrought sword as "hammer leavings."

kermes
A brilliant red insect dye, like the English CRIMSON, extracted from female insects living in European evergreen oaks. The dye was important in fabric coloring, inks, and medicine.

kerry
A hooded black CLOAK, traditional in Ireland and central Europe.

kersey
An important thirteenth-century woolen cloth, firm, pliable, somewhat coarse, and ribbed. Originating in the village of Kersey in Suffolk, England, it was used for stockings.

ketubah
(Hebrew, the written document) A Jewish marriage contract, usually embellished with ILLUMINATIONS, detailing the partners' rights and responsibilities (even sexual ones) and the husband's financial obligations towards the wife, including his promise to return her DOWRY if he dies and to pay her a sum of money if he divorces her without reason.

keystone
An arch's central stone, which keeps it from collapsing. The last stone to be placed, it was often carved with ornaments.

kiddush
The Jewish benediction chanted each Sabbath and festival eve and morning, at home over a cup of wine and loaf of bread. Kiddush cups of gold, silver, pewter, ivory, or porcelain usually were embellished with floral and geometric designs or biblical scenes.

kinnor
King David's stringed instrument, probably not a harp but, rather, a LYRE, with a trapezoidal frame and 5, 7, or 9 strings.

kirtle
In ANGLO-SAXON texts, a long TUNIC worn by men or women; later, an outer garment or coat, often of velvet, silk, taffeta, or satin, with elaborate trimming and close-fitting sleeves buttoned hand to elbow.

kiss of Judas
Judas's kiss of betrayal that identified Jesus to the guards in the garden of GETHSEMANE, the act ultimately leading to the CRUCIFIXION (Luke 22).

kittel
The Jewish costume also called SARGENES.

knight
(Anglo-Saxon *cniht,* youth) A military associate of a king or nobleman, holding land in TENURE called KNIGHT'S TENURE, in exchange for providing military service; in feudal rank, a social position below an earl and baron. The KNIGHT owed double HOMAGE AND FEALTY to the LORD: to God and to the overlord; and to the LADY: his beloved secular DOMNA and to the church's exalted Lady Mary.

knight's tenure
A knight holding land in TENURE from an overlord or king owed him military services and feudal INCIDENTS. Obligations included HOMAGE AND FEALTY (political and economic obligations); AIDS (emergency financial services, such as ransom payments, mandatory gifts at knighting of overlord's son or marriage of daughter); FORFEITURE (if the tenant was found guilty of treason or breach of an oath of fealty, he forfeited possession of the land); death payments, as WARDSHIP (if the tenants's heir was a minor, under age 21, the overlord took full possession, rents, and profits); MARRIAGE (the overlord had the right to choose a bride for the tenant's heir, or to sell the right); RELIEF (a tenant's heir paid for the right to possess inherited land); and ESCHEAT (if a tenant died without heirs, the property reverted to the overlord).

knock on wood
A superstitious tapping of a wooden object when in fear that either something bad will happen or some-

thing good will cease. The custom was derived from pagan propitiation rites performed to inspire spirits dwelling in wood or trees, such as the MAYPOLE, or to awaken them after winter slumber, as with the divinities affecting agriculture and human life. Simultaneous whistling and knocking demonstrates the petitioner's purity by emitting malign spirits or preventing their entry, as in the ritual of saying "GOD BLESS YOU" to one who has just sneezed.

knop
A small knob or protuberance for either embellishment or use.

knot garden
Formal flower beds edged with low growing hedges and planted in elaborate geometric patterns with dwarf shrubs, rosemary, and attractive herbs, the open spaces within the designs filled by TOPIARY.

knuckle bow
A knuckle guard on a sword hilt.

Kol Nidre
(Hebrew, all our vows) The exquisite, often misinterpreted, Jewish formula and ceremonial song requesting absolution from an unfulfilled promise, vow, or word in the past and forthcoming year, recited on the eve of the HIGH HOLY DAY of Atonement, YOM KIPPUR.

korn-jude
A virulently anti-Semitic coin minted in Germany and Austria during fifteenth-century famines, accusing Jews of withholding necessary grains or AFFEERING, thus inciting pogroms against Jewish communities. On the obverse was: "The people curse him who holds back grain; but blessing is on the head of him who sells it," from Proverbs (11:26). On the reverse, a grotesque grain merchant, a BADGER carrying a heavy meal sack trailing grain through a hole pierced by a devil.

kosher
(Or kashruth) Ritually acceptable daily food according to Jewish dietary laws based upon proscriptions found in Leviticus and HALAKHAH. MORALIZED BIBLEs elaborately depicted Old Testament food laws, attributing to them new Christian, moral purposes, with forbidden birds and beasts likened to human foibles and sins. Ritual butchers and food handlers performed the practical tasks of slaughtering and preserving while chanting appropriate prayers, thereby to join dictates of religion to hygiene.

krummhorn
(German, bent horn) A slender, oboe-like instrument, curved at its end to fashion a *J*-shaped horn. In French, it was called *cor morne,* mournful horn, because of its nasal, strident, yet lamenting tone. Also called a CROMORNE, it is sounded by a double reed in a capped mouthpiece.

kuttrolf
A distillation bottle with entwined neck tubes for allowing water or fluid to flow drop by drop; or a storage bottle for rare herbal and floral TINCTUREs.

kyrie
(Greek, O, Lord!) A triple supplication to God sung three times as the first element of the ORDINARY of the MASS, at the end of CANONICAL HOURS, and elsewhere in LITURGY: *kyrie eleison, christe eleison, kyrie eleison:* Lord have mercy, Christ have mercy, Lord have mercy.

L

labarum
The battle insignia adopted by Constantine the Great after he experienced a vision of a banner displaying the expression IN HOC SIGNO VINCES (In this sign you will conquer): a golden lamb with a cross surmounted by the CHI-RHO.

label
In HERALDRY, to indicate CADENCY, a first son's sign on a COAT OF ARMS, a BEND, sometimes with a tassel, drawn upon the upper portion of the shield, sometimes with three dependent points.

labor
In most contexts, work; in sexual context, amorous ardor: in Chaucer's "Merchant's Tale," senescent January labors all night in lovemaking, which his young wife May finds worthless. Work was also payment of TALLAGE; and celebrated in the TWELVE LABORS OF THE MONTHS.

lace
To embellish milk or cider with wine (as CAUDLE or METHEGLIN); or to float cinnamoned apples on WASSAIL; or to spice and add herbs to wines for taste and health.

laches
(Latin, *laxus,* loosened) Culpably lax in not asserting the rights people must use or lose; often controlled by a STATUTE OF LIMITATIONS.

lacquer
A lustrous hard-polished surface decoration originating in the East. Multiple successive layers of resin or lac (from an Indian insect, *rhus vernicefera*) are applied to wood or another surface, and each coat is filed, sanded, and smoothed.

lac virginis
(Latin, milk of a virgin) A milky fluid in chemical and metallurgical actions.

Ladino
Spanish as spoken by Jews flourishing in Spain before their expulsion in 1492. It was written in Hebrew characters and contained Hebrew and Aramaic words.

lady
(Anglo-Saxon *hlaef-dige,* bread-loaf-maker or loaf-kneeder) The bread-loaf maker whose male counterpart, LORD, was the bread-loaf protector; also, the female ruler of a HOUSEHOLD or the wife of a KNIGHT.

lady bishops
Women church leaders responsible directly to the Pope in Rome. They had vast ecclesiastical privileges and responsibilities: they presided at sacred ceremonies, heard confession, performed COMMUNION, distinguished miracles from frauds (as did the ABBESS Hilda of Whitby), accepted men and women religious as monks and nuns, built churches, hired priests, collected TITHEs and rents, and directed the care and the repair of buildings in convent communities and COEDUCATIONAL MONASTERIES.

lady bosses
Not only great queens, such as Eleanor of Aquitaine, whose lands and expeditions demonstrated her passionate talent for ruling kingdoms, but also lesser ladies directed large manors and HOUSEHOLDs, their staffs, workings, and protection. In the church,

learned influential women like Eloise of Paraclete administered ABBEYs for nuns, directed COEDUCATIONAL MONASTERIES, lands, hospitals, scriptoria, and schools, and functioned as LADY BISHOPS.

Lady chapel
A CHURCH or CATHEDRAL chapel dedicated to the Virgin Mary, usually the eastern extension of an AISLE.

Lady Day
The feast celebrating Gabriel's ANNUNCIATION to the Virgin Mary, March 25.

Laetare Sunday
(Latin, *laetor,* to exult) The fourth Sunday in LENT, named from the opening words of the MASS: "Rejoice with Jerusalem. . . ." It is celebrated with relaxations of Lenten penitential observances.

lai
A lyric or narrative poem filled with magic, marvels, TRANSFORMATIONs, and mystery, usually celebrating love and its vicissitudes. Sung by MINSTRELs, TROUBADOURs, or JONGLEURs, the lai was based on the so-called BRETON LITERATURE, and associated with Old Irish *loid* and German LIED, both meaning "song." The twelfth-century poet Marie de France wrote many lais; Chaucer adopted the style in his "Franklin's Tale."

laisse
An Old French stanzaic form of various lengths and metrical patterns in a CHANSON DE GESTES, as the *Song of Roland.*

laitice
An imitation ERMINE fur.

Lamb of God
(Latin, *Agnus Dei,* Lamb of God) A symbolic representation of Christ, according to the APOCALYPSE, leading the faithful flock of TWELVE APOSTLES, who are portrayed as sheep.

lambrequin
A knight's decorative helmet scarf, the COINTISE or CIMIER.

lambswool
A spectacular WASSAIL combining roasted apples, raw sugar, grated nutmeg, and shaved ginger with warm, strong ale, and served with tiny sweet cakes floating on its surface. It was a drink for November 1 to celebrate the spirits presiding over fruits and seeds of the Day of the Apple ("la mas ubal," pronounced "lamasool," later "lambswool"). Another possible origin is LAMMAS YULE, the summer festival celebrated on August 1 when lambswool was enjoyed.

lamen
An amulet and good luck charm, a geometrically shaped, magical disc or seal of metal, wax, or pure white paper whose auspicious shape and inscribed occult names would connect the wearer to the spirit or planet whose astrological INFLUENCE was sought. It was worn on the forehead as a phylactery or suspended from a neck chain at the level of the heart.

Lamentations
The Old Testament book of the Lamentations of Jeremiah, mourning the destruction of Jerusalem, the defilement of the temple, and the miseries of the Jews. It was often depicted as typological PREFIGURATION of the PIETÀ. Musical settings of select passages are sung in the Roman LITURGY for MATINS, one of the CANONICAL HOURS, on three days of HOLY WEEK.

Lammas
(Anglo-Saxon *hlaf,* breadloaf plus *mass,* loaf-mass, then "lammas") The early English church's harvest festival of consecrating loaves of bread formed from first ripened grain. Lammas Day was August 1, when Lammas-fields and Lammas-lands were exchanged; private arable land became common pasturage until spring planting time. Sometimes called Lammas YULE.

lance
A martial weapon, a pointed iron or steel head on a long wooden shaft, wielded when charging full speed on horseback.

Lance of Longinus
The long-pointed weapon used by the Roman soldier Longinus to pierce the side of the crucified Christ to make sure he was dead before allowing the disciples

to bury him. It was reputedly kept at HAGIA SOPHIA until 1241, when Saint Louis of France built the Saint-Chapelle to house it and the CROWN OF THORNS.

lancet
A small LANCE; or a double-bladed pointed surgical scalpel; or a tall, narrow, sharply pointed window in English GOTHIC architecture, recalling the martial and medical instruments.

Landini cadence
An important musical feature in ARS NOVA, particularly in the works of Guillaume Machaut and Burgundian composers, a musical cadence named after Francesco Landini: the sixth degree (A) is inserted between the leading tone (B) and the octave (C), with the altered fourth (F sharp) serving as a leading tone to the dominant (G).

langue d'oc
The language of the Provençal TROUBADOURS, from its word for "yes" (*oc*), in contrast to the northern French LANGUE D'OIL. As *Languedoc,* it designates the country south of the Loire River, as opposed to France in the north.

langue d'oil
French, the language of the TROUVÈRES, from the word for "yes" (*oil*), as opposed to the LANGUE D'OC of the Provençal TROUBADOURS.

lantern
A glass TURRET on a tower, DOME, or rooftop, allowing light to enter the interior of a building; also, a small portable light.

lapidary
A treatise on the origin, color, practical purpose, and mystical property of precious gems and semiprecious stones. AGATE, TOPAZ, TOADSTONE, LAPIS LAZULI and SOLACE STONE are typical minerals and gems used in medicine, divination, decoration, and jewelry.

lapis lazuli
A semiprecious, bright blue gemstone, consisting of a complex sulfur-containing silicate, important as a jewel, amulet, and a source for the expensive, vivid blue pigments for painting: AZURE and ultramarine. The stone is often confused with AZURITE.

lapis philosophorum
The PHILOSOPHERS' STONE.

lappet
Flat lace ribbons or pendant fabric strips usually worn in pairs, and attached to a MITRE, cap, crown, or clerical headdress.

larding knife
A knife for inserting lard or fat into meat before cooking to tenderize it and enrich flavor. The technique and instrument are credited to the cook of fifteenth-century Pope Felix V.

larga
In fourteenth- and fifteenth-century MENSURAL NOTATION, the largest values: the MAXIMA or multiples of it.

Last Supper
Christ's celebration in Jerusalem of the Jewish PESACH or PASSOVER meal, the SEDER, with his TWELVE APOSTLES, foreshadowing his betrayal. In consecrating the bread and wine, he initiated the first COMMUNION, a first EUCHARIST, which is liturgically commemorated during the TRIDUUM SACRUM.

lather
(Anglo-Saxon, washing soda—modern lye) The white bubbly foam of soap; or the anguished fury of the ireful.

Latin literature
Despite nationalistic and artistic triumphs of vernacular languages, Latin literature flourished throughout the Middle Ages: sacred works, history, poetry, epic, song, satire, panegyric, MIROIRS DE PRINCES, and ROMANCE were written in Latin, utilizing the learned classical TOPOS and popular characterizations of JOCULATORES. Especially influential works were John of Salisbury's *Policraticus,* a treatise on statesmanship; the poems of Walter Map; histories and chronicles by Giraldus Cambrensis, Geoffrey of Monmouth, and William of Malmesbury; GOLIARDIC verse; and hilarious satires such as Nigel Wireker's *Dan Burnel the Ass.*

latten
A yellow metal alloy resembling BRASS, probably composed of copper and zinc, and used in thin sheets for CROSSes, candlesticks, and RELIQUARIES.

lauda
(Or lode) Italian HYMNs of penitential praise, often associated with Saint Francis of Assisi.

laudario
A HYMN collection.

Lauda Sion
Saint Thomas Aquinas's SEQUENCE summoning the church to adore the EUCHARIST—a concise, philosophical, magnificent HYMN.

lauds
(Latin *laudare,* to praise) The second hour of the DIVINE OFFICE, named from Psalms 148, 149, and 150. One of the EIGHT CANONICAL HOURS, its prayers, PSALMs, and CANTICLES are usually sung at dawn.

laurel
An evergreen SYMBOL of victory and of immortality, derived from the classical custom of crowning athletic and intellectual heroes with laurel wreaths. Adopted by Christian ICONOGRAPHY as a sign of chastity, the laurel signified triumph over temptations of this world.

lavabo
(Latin, *lavare,* to wash) A washbasin for cleaning hands or objects; also, the ceremony of washing the celebrant's hands at the OFFERTORY of the MASS.

lavatorium
A large basin for washing bodies of the newly dead; also, the room containing the LAVABO—a washroom.

lavender
A CRAFTSWOMAN responsible for laundering or FULLING fabric. The female counterpart of a LAVER, her profession affected the family names of her progeny via MATRONYMICS.

laver
A water pitcher or AQUAMANILE used with basin and towel for domestic or liturgical hand-washing; in the fabric trades, a FULLER or launderer, whose female equivalent was a LAVENDER.

laverer
The court servant in charge of ceremonial hand-washing with fragrant, spiced water poured from an AQUAMANILE.

lavolta
(Italian, to turn) A popular English dance intermittently banned because of its seeming indecency. In its tamest form, the man would lift and turn his lady high in the air, her flying skirts displaying her undergarments or anatomy. The dance was a variation of the GALLIARD.

laxative
HERBALs and DIETARIES recommend foods, minerals, and herbs to relieve constipation and to purge the body. Bad dreams could be so cured: Chaucer's coquettish, learned hen, Pertelote, counsels her terrified husband Chaunticleer to forget his frightful premonitory dream of being caught by a fox and to take a laxative.

laystall
(Or laystowe) A public defecation depot or latrine.

lead
The heaviest base metal, dull pale gray, soft, and maleable. In ALCHEMY, lead was the heavy, lusterless primal substance to be turned by chemical TRANSMUTATION and "spiritual maturation" into gold: ***aurum philosophorum est plumbum,*** "the philosophers' gold is lead."

lectern
A sloping desk made of wood, metal, or stone, at which one stood for writing, reading, or singing. An eagle with outspread wings frequently embellished those either secular or ecclesiastic. In a CATHEDRAL, the lectern was the place from which the EPISTLE was read during MASS.

lector
(Latin, reader) Second of the MINOR ORDERS, a reader of portions of the Old Testament and other texts in the LITURGY.

leech
(Anglo-Saxon *laece,* a healer) A physician, surgeon, or medical practitioner.

leechcraft
Medical science and the art of healing; also the PHLEBOTOMY technique of LEECHING.

leeching
Application of live leeches to PHLEBOTOMY POINTS for BLOODLETTING or PHLEBOTOMY.

leffas
An occult vapor of the earth; plant sap.

Legenda Aurea
(Latin) The GOLDEN LEGEND.

leich
A Germanic musical-poetic form resembling the LAI, expressing pious or secular love; also, a dance melody of unequal stanza-lengths.

Leise
German HYMNs, begging songs, or folksongs with the refrain *Kyrie Eleison,* derived from the LITANIES, and named after the suffix *leis* in *eleison.*

leman
(Middle English *lief,* dear, plus *man,* person) A wife or husband, but usually a mistress, concubine, or paramour; a woman or man vigorous in sexual play. The term sometimes was used for "beloved" in mystical praises of Christ.

Lent
The spring season's 40-day Christian fast from ASH WEDNESDAY to EASTER Eve, commemorating Moses's, Elijah's, and Christ's 40 days' fasting in the wilderness. Lent was preceded by SHROVETIDE CARNIVALs and MUMMING plays.

leopard
The sinuous feline described in bestiaries as a cross between *leo* (lion) and *pard* (panther), a creature which never can change its spots (from Jeremiah 13:23). Human beings are superior because they can change their spots: a repentant sinner can be cleansed by absolution from the "spotting" of sin and saved thanks to God's GRACE.

leper
A person ill with the degenerative systemic disease now known as Hansen's disease, leprosy; or a sufferer of a dermatological illness, the "disease of the soul" expressed cutaneously. Isolated and treated in a LEPROSARIUM, the patient had to say and sound *noli me tangere* (Touch me not!) by shaking a rattle or CRACELLE.

leprosarium
An isolation hospital that quarantined LEPERs or a clinic that treated them.

let
To hinder, interfere, or stop. The term is preserved in modern tennis jargon.

Leviathan
A gigantic sea creature that ate, and then disgorged, Jonah. It was thought to be a giant noble fish (not a mammal), the whale, or a crocodile, dragon, or HIPPOCAMPUS.

lewd
Lay and secular, rather than ecclesiastical or clerical, an unlearned, unlettered layman not having benefit of clergy and not having taken holy orders; only later vulgar or obscene, by the process of PEJORATION.

librarius
A MANUSCRIPT dealer, bookseller, a university's authorized textbook producer and seller.

lick into shape
A metaphor for necessary completion, transforming the inchoate into the actual, derived from BESTIARY bear-lore: bear cubs, born blind and incompletely formed, require the mother bear's caressing, creative tongue to complete the bear-shaping. This trait also is ascribed to the LION and associated with Christ's necessary care for Christians.

Lied
A Middle High German song, particularly a COURTLY LOVE lyric, similar to the Provençal CANZO.

Liederbuch
A German song collection, as the *Glogauer, Lochamer,* and *Münchner* song books.

lierne
A short RIB between principal ribs in a GOTHIC VAULT.

life estate
A feudal ESTATE IN LAND whose duration is measured by a person's life, providing all the rights and privileges of ownership except transfer by sale or at death.

ligature
A square-shaped musical notation modifying the NEUME, with rhythmic importance in early POLYPHONY: two notes sung on the same syllable, ascending or descending, and forming a unit.

lilium inter spinas
(Latin, The lily among the thorns) An epithet for the Virgin Mary (Song of Solomon 2:2) or the perfect chastity of a woman emulating the VIRTUES OF THE VIRGIN.

Limbo
The place where souls of Old Testament saints await Christ's RESURRECTION. In Dante's DIVINE COMEDY, it is the dwelling of Jewish heros and saints, classical eminences, unbaptized newborn Christians, and others whose fault was not active sin but birth too early in the dark beginnings of time to know the illumination of Christianity's radiance.

limewood
A fine-grained, light wood from the lime or linden tree, popular for carving.

Limoges enamels
Masterly twelfth- through fourteenth-century French CHAMPLEVÉ art adorning CRUCIFIXes, CHASSEs, RELIQUARIES, ecclesiastical jewels, and secular objects, following the inspiration of MOSAN ENAMEL painters. Later fifteenth- and sixteenth-century enamelers, such as Jean de Court, Suzanne de Court, Pierre Raymond, and Pierre Courtois, created essentially secular decorative art.

linenfold
A wood-carved, raised, ornamental pattern resembling folds in linen. The design was popular on wall panelling, chests, and furniture, particularly in fifteenth-century Flanders, England, and France.

lintel
A horizontal stone or timber slab bearing the wall's weight above a window or door.

lion
King of beasts, a BESTIARY animal with three major traits, according to *Physiologus:* the ability to cover its tracks; to sleep with open eyes; and to LICK INTO SHAPE its unformed cubs. The lion was also associated with Christ's life and RESURRECTION. The most common beast in HERALDRY, its major positions include COUCHANT (lying down, head raised); DORMANT (lying, head on front paws); PASSANT (walking, right forepaw raised); PASSANT GARDANT (passant, but head towards viewer); PASSANT REGARDANT (passant, but head looking backwards, to SINISTER side of shield); RAMPANT (rearing up on hind legs, weight on the left); SALIENT (reared up as if for a leap); SEJANT (sitting on haunches, forelegs on ground); and STANJANT (body in profile, face towards viewer). A lion's whelp, a LIONCEL, is also common in heraldry.

lioncel
A heraldic figure, a baby LION, often appearing several per shield.

lion rampant
The heraldic beast portrayed facing the right of the shield, the LION rearing or standing with forepaws in the air, right paw above left, a posture suggesting its aggressive, fierce high spirits.

lira da braccio
(Italian, an arm LYRE) A bowed VIOL.

liripipe
The extravagantly long fabric tail of a CHAPERONE hood, wrapped around the head or neck or swung over the shoulder (usually the left) and ornamented with BELLS, fringe, or decorative semiprecious stones. Its length often signified social rank.

lisp
A congenital, learned, or affected inability to pronounce the letter *s* as a sibilant sound, resembling instead a *th*. In erotic poetry, an indicator of sensuality in women and homosexuality in men. In FABLIAUX, in homoerotic poems of twelfth-century Spain's Samuel Ha Nagid, and in Chaucer, whose Pardoner lisps "to make his English sweet upon the tongue," a lisp as a sexual indicator was as dependable as a GAT-TOOTHED smile or a well-placed NEVUS to identify Venus's elect.

lister
A dyer, primarily a color craftsman for yarn and fabric, using vegetable and organic dye sources like MADDER for red, WELD for yellow, WOAD for blue.

lists
Jousting fields enclosed by barriers, usually surrounded by spectators' boxes and pavilions.

litanies
(Greek, supplication) Prayers of petition for peace, unity, protection from plague, or good harvest, followed by a response such as "Lord have mercy." They are often said during processions and before the ASCENSION.

litanies to the Virgin
Popular responsorial supplications celebrating the VIRTUES OF THE VIRGIN, with invocations like "Star of the Morning," "Star of the Sea," "Queen of Angels," to which the response is, "Pray for us!"

litotes
The prevalent ANGLO-SAXON literary technique to express a positive by stating the negative of its opposite, resulting in mild or wild understatement. "Beowulf's life-days were not completely valuable to his enemies" means they despised him and lusted to kill him. Petrarch, desiring to exercise his readers, said, "I do not wish the public to read entirely without effort what I have written not entirely without effort."

litre
A CHURCH's ornamental, painted wall-band of the COATS OF ARMS of founders and patrons.

liturgical colors
Correct colors for liturgical items varied according to season, century, and nation. Usually VESTMENTS, banners, ALTAR frontals, and other fabric decorations are white for CHRISTMAS, EASTER, CORPUS CHRISTI, MAUNDY THURSDAY, ASCENSION, and feasts of virgins and unmartyred saints; red for PENTECOST, HOLY CROSS DAY, the Precious Blood celebration, and martyred saints' days; green for days after TRINITY and EPIPHANY; purple for ADVENT and LENT; blue for feasts of Mary; and black for funerals and requiem MASSes.

liturgy
(Greek, public service) A public religious service of the CHURCH or synagogue, the Christian EIGHT CANONICAL HOURS, and celebration of the EUCHARIST.

livery
(French *livree,* a gift) The contractually or customarily guaranteed costume and clothing gift from a feudal overlord to the HOUSEHOLD retainers. The livery bore identifying heraldic COLORS and EMBLEMS with subtle distinctions among fabric and FUR that indicated social rank and were affected by SUMPTUARY LAWS. A professional uniform identified members of craft GUILDs, such as the ostentatious guildsmen's finery in Chaucer's *Canterbury Tales.*

livery cupboard
An upright chest for storage of food or clothes, generally with PIERCING to let in light and air.

livery of seizin
A ceremony in which a symbolic clod of earth was transmitted with or without a written deed to a TENANT taking possession of a freehold ESTATE IN LAND and assuming all rights and responsibilities of TENURE.

locus amoenus
(Latin, pleasant place) A conventional but idealized, shaded, secluded GARDEN, almost always with trees, flowers, spring, and singing birds. Imitating Virgil, later poets made it the locale for COURTLY LOVE and other amorous adventures, such as the pleasure garden in the *Romance of the Rose.*

loggerheads
Long-handled iron heating rods, similar to CAUTERY IRONs, used to heat wine by their immediate transfer from fire to flagon, causing sizzling sounds and an aromatic burst of spices and herbs. By analogy, seethingly angry people are said to be "at loggerheads."

loggia
In architecture, the space formed by the ground floor set back from the road, as well as the arches that support the front part of the upper stories; or an arcaded, colonnaded balcony.

Logos
(Greek, word or reason) In Judaism, the creative power of God's Word; in Christianity, the second person of the TRINITY, the Christ Incarnate.

Lollard
(Dutch *lollaerd*, mutterer and mumbler) A follower of fourteenth-century English theologian John Wycliffe, who insisted that the Bible must be read in English translation to stimulate true understanding of pious words of praise, not mere PATTER, to permit personal interpretation by each Christian. Lollardy's development into a heresy became a precursor of the Reformation.

Lombard style
Northern Italian pre-ROMANESQUE architecture and art, or its imitations.

longa
A musical notational symbol indicating a very long note, perhaps equivalent to four modern whole notes.

lord
(Anglo-Saxon *hlaef-weard*, breadloaf ward or guardian, whose female equivalent is LADY, loaf kneader) the male ruler of a HOUSEHOLD; a feudal upper-class man, owner of a FEE or manor.

Lord of Misrule
The boisterous leader of the FEAST OF FOOLS.

Lord's Day
A Christian liturgical name for Sunday.

Lord's Prayer
Taught by Jesus Christ to the APOSTLES in the SERMON ON THE MOUNT (Luke 11:2), the prayer invokes God and then consists of 7 petitions, 3 celebrating God, and 4 requesting human physical and spiritual necessities, such as daily bread. Tertullian called this prayer the GOSPEL's epitome, ***breviarium totius evangelii.*** Often called PATERNOSTER, because of its first words in Latin, it became on the tongues of the ignorant a mere PATTER.

love-days
Special yearly times for resolving civil or personal disputes and settling debts; in a sexual context, those times for excelling in amorousness.

love knot
A design for jewelry, for HAIR, or for a clasp of a robe, CLOAK, or coat, resembling a figure eight and representing the uninterrupted continuity of perfect love: the eternal intertwining of two bodies, two souls, or two spirits.

Low Sunday
QUASIMODO SUNDAY.

lozenge
A shape important in ornament and structure having four equal sides, two acute angles, and two obtuse angles, such as a diamond or rhomboid; in HERALDRY, the shape in which a COAT OF ARMS of a LADY is placed; also a heraldic device within a coat of arms.

lozengiers
(Or losengers) Flatterers, scandal mongers, and backbiters of the COURTLY LOVE tradition, feared by lovers, encouraged by the JALOUX or jealous husbands, and frequently lambasted in TROUBADOUR lyrics.

Lucidarium
Title of a late-thirteenth-century musical treatise on plain or unmeasured music by Marchettus of Padua.

Lucifer
The "light bearer," the ANGEL who pridefully thought himself God's equal, which diabolical presumption caused him to be cast down from the

The lozenges of the horse's caparison enclose the letters AMOR for this joust of love. (From the Manesse Manuscript, Heidelberg, 14th century)

heavenly realm of light into the perpetual darkness of Hell. He is identified with Satan because of a misreading of Isaiah 14:12. Sometimes Venus, the Morning Star (as in Psalm 109:3 and in 2 Peter 1:19); and lightbringer, without satanic implication, is applied also to Christ.

lulav
A Jewish ceremonial palm branch forming a cluster with myrtle leaves and willow, which, with the citron, ETROG, is used in celebrating the harvest festival of SUKKOT.

luminaries
Natural light-givers, especially the sun and moon.

lunation
A lunar month, exactly 29½ days, the time from one new moon to the next.

luncheon
From NUNCHEON, the noon quench.

lunette
(French, little moon) A light-admitter: a small VAULT within a larger one that admits light; or a window, often semi-circular, above a square-headed or rectangular window or door; or the decorative paintings in such space.

Lupercalia
A Roman fertility festival observed on February 15, superseded in the fifth century by the Christian PURIFICATION FEAST on February 2.

lushburg
Base metal coins from Luxembourg. When Chaucer's Monk gives Venus her payment "but not in Lusscheburghes," he satisfies a sexual DEBT by successful intercourse, a metaphorical payment in good coin.

lust
Either merry, exuberant, and sybaritic, as in "lusty folk" at a party; or, as Chaucer's Wife of Bath celebrates her gift of Venus, one of the SEVEN DEADLY SINS, LUXURY—lechery.

luster
A thin metallic GLAZE producing a rich, usually irridescent pottery surface, as in HISPANO-MORESQUE pottery and MAJOLICA.

lustermädchen
(German, light maiden) A Germanic or Scandinavian chandelier composed of animal antlers, a flying female form, and candleholders.

lusterware
Pottery painted and glazed with irridescent jewel-like colors, a technique probably originating in Persia, reaching magnificence in the HISPANO-MORESQUE.

lute
Derived from the Arabic *oud,* a plucked stringed musical instrument. Its body shaped like a pear half, its neck long and flat, having multiple FRETS, a pegboard perpendicular to the neck, and strings running parallel to the body. Its melodies were written in TABLATURE.

luxury
(Latin *Luxuria*) Lechery, one of the SEVEN DEADLY SINS.

LXX
(Roman numeral for the number 70) The SEPTUAGINT.

lynchet
(Or linch) A small earthen bank or narrow unplowed strip serving as a boundary between fields.

lyre
A stringed instrument, either plucked or bowed, brought west from Byzantium.

lyric
A poem to a musical accompaniment, or a song. The ALBA, BALLADE, CANZO, PASTOURELLE, PLANH, and SIRVENTES were sung by MINSTRELs, courtly lovers, TROUBADOURs, GOLIARDS, TROUVÈREs and MINNESINGERs, and ranged in style and content from refined to bawdy.

M

macaronic verse
Poems introducing Latin or other "foreign language" words or phrases for refrains, comic effects, or learned affectations.

mace
A heavy spiked staff or club with a metal head; or a secular scepter of authority or sovereignty resembling the weapon.

machicolation
Floor openings in a castle's overhanging sentry walks or PARAPETS, useful for dropping flaming or heavy missiles on an enemy below.

machicotage
A fashionable, late-fourteenth-century Parisian musical ornamentation of GREGORIAN CHANT. Into the melody sung by the choir, several performers would insert flourishes and improvise grace notes.

macquette
A sculptor's preliminary sketch in such impermanent material as wax or clay to serve as a model for the final work of art in painted plaster, stone, or bronze; a BOZETTO.

macrobian
Pertaining to dreams, their theory, causes, and effects, as described by fifth-century author Macrobius in his popular commentary on Cicero's *Dream of Scipio,* important for the genre of DREAM VISION.

macrocosm
The great created universe, made of the FOUR ELEMENTS and FOUR CONTRARIES; those qualities of the ORDO MUNDI are reflected in the human being, the creation-in-small, the MICROCOSM.

madder
A popular red coloring substance made from BRAZIL WOOD, and used in painting, fabric dyeing, and yarn tinting for cloth and TAPESTRIES.

Madonna Immaculata
The Virgin Mary, referring to her IMMACULATE CONCEPTION, the doctrine that all ORIGINAL SIN was excluded from her soul from the first moment of her creation by God's singular GRACE and privilege.

madrigal
A short love poem and its contrapuntal setting for several (usually five or six) voices singing polyphonically.

Magi
The first Gentiles to worship Christ (Matthew 2:1–12), they came from the East to Bethlehem bearing gifts of gold, frankincense, and myrrh. Only after the sixth century were they named and numbered the THREE MAGI.

magic circle
In ALCHEMY and ASTROLOGY, a symbol of creation; also, a circle of holy names and SIGILS painted, incised, or tiled on the floor which protected a magician standing in its center from attack by the spirits he attempted to command.

magic planet
Saturn. Board games, poetic structures, architectural components, and divinations favored the number 15 because of Saturn's propitious conjunctions with

other heavenly bodies, as in numerical calculations reducible to a MAGIC SQUARE.

magic square
Numbers from 1 to 9 arranged in a square so that the sum of each row, column, and corner diagonal is equal:

8	1	6
3	5	7
4	9	2

The sum 15 is significant in ASTROLOGY, as it is approximately one-half of the synodical period of 29.46 years of Saturn, the MAGIC PLANET. A SIGIL square was constructed from letters of a spirit's name.

magnelia
Particularly efficacious medical remedies because of inherent divine or occult powers.

Magnificat
(Latin, glorify, extol) A CANTICLE of the Virgin praising the Lord for the ANNUNCIATION: *Magnificat anima mea dominum,* My soul glorifies the Lord (Luke 1:46–55). Daily sung with special ANTIPHONs at VESPERS, one of the eight CANONICAL HOURS.

magnum opus musicum
(Latin, the great musical work) A prize-winning work, a crowning achievement in musical composition or performance; also, the collective name for the 516 musical compositions by the sixteenth-century composer Orlando di Lasso.

Magnus Liber Organi
(Latin, the great book of the ORGANUM) A collection of the ORGANUM composed for MASS and DIVINE OFFICE at Notre Dame of Paris by Leonin and Perotin.

mahoitre
Cylindrical pads for extending shoulder width on such men's garments as the GIPPON and the extravagantly wide POURPOINT. The effect was complemented by a tightly cinched waist.

maidenhead
Either spiritual or anatomical maidenhood or virginity.

mail
A coat of CHAIN MAIL.

mainpernor
A surety for a person under arrest.

maislin
A common bread of mixed wheat and rye grains.

maîtrise
A French CATHEDRAL's choir and choir school building directed by the *maître de chapelle,* choirmaster.

majolica
Tin-glazed earthenware or LUSTERWARE, particularly from Valencia, Spain, usually transported by ships registered in Mallorca.

major orders
In Christian hierarchy, formally codified by thirteenth-century Pope Innocent III, in descending order, BISHOPS, PRIESTS, DEACONS, and sub-deacons were considered superior in authority to members of MINOR ORDERS.

majuscule
Very large MANUSCRIPT writing for group reading, as in ALTAR BOOKS.

make no bones
To directly discuss, without euphemisms. In a late-fifteenth-century English AKEDAH tale, Abraham, about to kill his son "made no manier bones ne stickyng"—made no bones, gave no interference to God's will—and told Isaac exactly what he was going to do. Possibly derived from culinary (no fish bones in the throat, no choking on the words) or gaming (no chancy dice in the hand, no hidden meanings in the words) lore.

maker
A poet, creator, or maker of ideas, illusions, and language. Chaucer was one of the finest makers and "finders" of this fair language English, and, like Dante, he celebrated the vernacular.

Three witches prepare a Sabbath, as in the Malleus Maleficarum. (From a woodcut by Hans Baldurg Green, German, 1510; courtesy of Metropolitan Museum of Art, New York)

Malchut Shamayim
(Hebrew, Kingdom of Heaven) Referring to God's sovereignty in human daily existence, and reaffirming significance of human life in God's glorious GREAT CHAIN OF BEING.

Malleus Maleficarum
(Latin, *Hammer of Witches*), a pernicious, pseudoscientific fifteenth-century treatise by DOMINICAN inquisitors Heinrich Kramer and Jacob Sprenger, based upon ARISTOTELIAN and thirteenth-century natural philosophical attempts to comprehend the universe and the place of women and of men within it. The HAMMER OF WITCHES contained rules for detecting witches and noted punishable magic practices; it became a standard legal text for witch trials.

Maltese cross
A CROSS IN HERALDRY, a cross-moline with eight points, the badge of the sovereign military Order of Malta.

mamzer
A bastard.

mancheron
A half-sleeve, usually of silk, velvet, or fine cotton, showing through the wider or slashed sleeves of an overgarment, HOUPPELAND, or DOUBLET.

manchet
A fine-grained white bread, often baked with currants and glazed fruit; important in England, along with PANDEMAYN, SIMNELL, MAISLIN, and WASTLEBREAD.

mandatum novum
(Latin, new commandment) The first words of the ceremony for the washing of feet, celebrated in the MAUNDY THURSDAY LITURGY.

mandilion
A TABARD, an open-sleeved, hip-length garment with heraldic EMBLEMS, worn by civilians and by knights over their ARMOR.

mandorla
(Italian, almond) An almond-shaped or oval frame enclosing a portrait of Christ at the ASCENSION, or the oval-shaped pallet upon which the Virgin Mary was carried to Heaven at the ASSUMPTION. The almond shape was associated both with the Virgin's womb and Christ's wounds; also called VESICA PISCIS, an elliptical AUREOLE.

mandrake
(Or mandragora) A plant with a forked root resembling human legs, thought to shriek in pain when pulled from the earth. A potent APHRODISIAC traceable to Reuben's mandrake (Genesis 30), it was also widely celebrated as a medicinal emetic, narcotic, and anesthetic, especially in DECOCTION for ANAESTHESIA in orthopedic surgery.

Manicheans
A Christian heretical sect that was GNOSTIC, dualistic, austere, severely ascetic, and vegetarian. Founded in

the third century by Manes or Manichaeus, Manicheanism was based on a philosophical belief in divine forces of Light versus satanic powers of Darkness; also, the perfect Elect were to be supported by the more worldly Hearers. The movement doubtlessly influenced the ALBIGENSES and the CATHARI.

maniple
An embroidered linen or silk scarf worn by priests and other clerics on the left hand or arm as part of the liturgical VESTMENTS.

mannered music
Melodically eccentric, rhythmically complex, and notationally extreme fourteenth-century music, as written by Guillaume Machaut.

Man of Sorrows
A depiction of the suffering and agonies of the crucified Christ, often with dramatic, lugubrious realism, emphasizing His CROWN OF THORNS, anguished facial expressions, sweat, blood, and tears. Particularly popular in the late Middle Ages in art of Spain, England, and Germany, such emotionalism often was associated with religious mysticism, as in the writings of Saint Francis of Assisi and Saint Bridget of Sweden.

manteline
A short over-ARMOR parade MANTLE, often hooded and elaborately decorated.

mantle
A semi-circular or rectangular CLOAK clasped at neck or shoulder with an AGRAFFE or FIBULA and sometimes embroidered and bordered with braid or fur. Also called a *manthe* or *manteau*.

manum inicere
(Latin, to lay a hand on) In a religious context, the arrest of Jesus Christ before his CRUCIFIXION; in medicine, laying on the hands of healing.

manuscript
A handwritten text, often enriched by MINIATURES, ILLUMINATIONS, and decorative MARGINALIA. Bound in a volume, it became a CODEX.

maphorion
A long great CLOAK or cape.

mappa mundi
(Latin, map of the world) A world map, incorporating not only all known, supposed, and mythological landmasses and seas, but also symbolic or fantastic animals and plants. Most versions were associated directly or indirectly with the maps in Ptolemy's GEOGRAPHIA.

marcasite
Crystallized iron pyrites used in jewelry and ALCHEMY.

märchen
Folklore themes that were transformed in literature. Chaucer's racy FABLIAU, "The Miller's Tale," consists of two such folklore themes: the man made to fear Noah's flood, and the misdirected kiss.

marchpane
Marzipan: almonds in sugar paste, a confection easily molded into ornamental shapes, significant for banquet SUBTLETIES and ENTREMETS.

Mardi Gras
(French, Fat Tuesday) The period of revelry preceding the self-abnegations of LENT for Christians; called FETTER DIENSTAG in Germany.

marfors
A long narrow veil covering a woman's head and pendant to her shoulders.

marginalia
The decorations surrounding the text on pages of MANUSCRIPTS and early printed books. Embellishments could be colored or monochrome, painted or line-drawn, secular or religious, fantastic or realistic, moral or obscene. Originally, anything marked in margins, as comments, corrections, GLOSSes, or subheadings.

Mariolatry
(*Maria* plus the Greek *latrein,* worship) Enthusiastic, exaggerated, excessive praise and worship of the Virgin Mary in twelfth- and thirteenth-century Europe, particularly by mystic theologians and saints, such as Bernard of Clairvaux, whose allegorical commentary on the Song of Songs stimulated erotic ardor for the VIRTUES OF THE VIRGIN, and the mystic visions of Saints Catherine of Siena and Bridget of Sweden.

Mary as the Blessed INTERCESSOR became preeminent and CHURCHes and CATHEDRALs were dedicated to *Notre Dame,* Our Lady.

Mariology

Systematic study of the life of the blessed Virgin Mary, especially her IMMACULATE CONCEPTION and the INCARNATION of Jesus.

marque pied

A dance step in the BRANSLE, TORDION, and MORRIS DANCEs, with the toe of the free foot placed next to the standing foot.

marquetry

A furniture, COFFER, or paneling surface decoration made of pieces of colored wood or ivory fitted and glued into a VENEER, a larger thin sheet of background wood; both were then applied to the surface awaiting decoration. Marquetry is related to INLAY and INTARSIA in appearance, but different in technique.

marramas

A CLOTH OF GOLD made in fourteenth-century Lucca but Oriental in origin, celebrated for ecclesiastical adornments on VESTMENTs and ALTARs.

marranos

Fifteenth-century Jews in Spain forcibly converted to Christianity. They usually practiced Judaism in secret, and were brutally persecuted by the Spanish INQUISITION.

marriage

One of the SEVEN SACRAMENTS, conferred by spouses upon each other. MATRIMONY is a contract or agreement, not requiring DOWRY, DOWER, or MORGENGABE. A feudal INCIDENT after death of a KNIGHT or TENANT holding land in TENURE was the right of the overlord to choose the bride for the dead tenant's heir.

marriage by consent

Though CHILD MARRIAGE was common, theologians and exponents of CANON LAW, such as Gratian, insisted on marriage by consent of the partners: the usual age was 12 years for a boy, 14 years for a girl. Some apparent adultery actually was CLANDESTINE MARRIAGE as recognized by CANON LAW.

marriage group

G. L. Kittredge's modern name for structural unity and pervasive themes in Chaucer's *Canterbury Tales:* the husband-wife DEBATE over the MASTERY QUESTION in marriage (the Wife of Bath's thesis: woman's mastery over man; the Clerk's antithesis: man's sovereignty over woman; and the Franklin's synthesis: power vested in both and neither); also, the issues of GENTILESSE and TROTH in relationships.

martel

A hammer, especially a *martel de fer,* or war hammer; often the INSIGNE of a blacksmith.

marten

A FUR-bearing animal related to the ERMINE. Its fur was important in costumery and in HERALDRY.

martlet

In HERALDRY, the footless swallow, martin, or small black bird, a sign of CADENCY for a fourth son (perhaps because the son had no footing in ancestral lands); also, a small MARTEN.

martyr

(Greek, witness) A believer who dies for the faith in a violent demise at the hands of persecutors. Saint Thecla was the FIRST FEMALE MARTYR, Saint Stephen the PROTOMARTYR.

martyrium

A chapel or shrine honoring a MARTYR, built over the martyr's RELICS and often located at the western end of a CHURCH.

marzipan

MARCHPANE.

mask

(Hebrew, cover) Used in costumery, court theater, MASQUERADEs, MUMMING plays, and sometimes MORESCAs, the mask was made of fabric or *papier mâché* to disguise the face of a performer and to create an illusion. A mask was often used outdoors to protect a delicate complexion against sun rays.

masque
A noble entertainment with a mythological, allegorical, or political subject, combining music, poetry, dancing, mime, acting, costumery, and sets, for court participation and performance.

masquerade
A masked entertainment: participants disguised in fantastical or imaginative garb dance, declaim, and disport themselves for pleasure and, sometimes, for political purposes. The masquerade was associated with the MORESCA and the MORRIS DANCE. Flammable costumes could cause disasters, such as the BAL DES ARDENTS.

mass
The liturgical celebration of Christ's LAST SUPPER, the EUCHARIST, and the CRUCIFIXION. The name was derived from the concluding benediction: *Ite missa est congregatio,* Go, the congregation is dismissed. Structurally, the Roman Catholic mass consists of the PROPER, the varying elements, and the ORDINARY, the constants: INTROIT (P); KYRIE (O); GLORIA (P); GRADUAL (P) plus ALLELUIA (P) or Tract (P); CREDO (O); OFFERTORY (P); SANCTUS (O); AGNUS DEI (O); COMMUNION (O); *Ite Missa Est* or BENEDICTUS (O).

Massey, John, of Cotton
A contemporary of Chaucer associated with John of Gaunt, John Massey may well have been the author of the superb ALLITERATIVE REVIVAL poems in the Cotton Nero manuscript: *Sir Gawain and the Green Knight, Patience, Pearl,* and *Saint Erkenwald.*

master
A skilled craftsman or craftswoman deemed qualified to practice the profession, to teach APPRENTICES, to employ JOURNEYMEN, to wear the GUILD LIVERY, and to pass judgment on a MASTERPIECE before an artisan could be approved for guild membership or recommended for licensing.

masterpiece
The GUILD requirement for a piece of work demonstrating the professional competence required of a JOURNEYMAN before licensure as a MASTER.

mastery question
A common literary ploy requiring a hero's choice between impossible opposites, thus yielding mastery to the questioner. Chaucer's ferociously ugly hag in "The Wife of Bath's Tale" asks her handsome young husband-knight how he would prefer her: fair and faithless, or foul and faithful. In the *Confessio Amantis,* John Gower elaborated the choice: fair by day and foul by night, or foul by day and fair by night. The hero incapable of choice so gives mastery to the woman, but then receives as reward the impossible unities of perfection.

matassin
A sixteenth-century elaborately costumed dance: participants were disguised as armored knights or allegorical figures in dance and mock combat. A MATTACHIN apparently had related but different choreography.

Mater Maria Dei
(Latin, Mary, the Mother of God) The appellation for Mary, specifically referring to her own IMMACULATE CONCEPTION, her miraculous conception of Christ, and her dolorous parenthood, life events celebrated in the various Marian heresies and MARIOLATRY. Other Marian maternal appellations include THEOTOKAS, DEIPARA, and DEI GENITRIX.

matières
The THREE MATTERS OF ROMANCES.

matins
(Or mattins; Latin *matutinum tempus,* morning time) The first and longest of the eight CANONICAL HOURS liturgically presenting the DIVINE OFFICE. Usually celebrated between midnight and 3 A.M., the night hours, all others being day or diurnal hours.

matrimony
MARRIAGE, one of the SEVEN SACRAMENTS, with the double purpose of uniting a man and woman for procreation and preservation of the species, and for comfort, companionship, and satisfaction. Its essential religious properties are unity and indissolubility. However, CLANDESTINE MARRIAGE permitted an essentially private, non-liturgically-blessed union until the sixteenth century.

matronymics
The tracing of family name and heritage through the mother's lineage and profession. The name *Baxter* comes from a female professional baker; *Webster,* from a weaver (the male version is *Weaver* or *Webber*); *Brewster,* from a wine or ale brewer; and *Lavender,* from a fabric launderer or FULLER (the male equivalent being *Laver*). CRAFTSWOMEN's sons and daughters often were identified by their mother's profession and family name.

mattachin
A mimed battle dance, often containing a stylized symbolic beheading and resurrection, as in the MORRIS DANCE (probably different from the MATASSIN).

Matter of Britain
One of the THREE MATTERS of heroic ROMANCE, celebrating the adventures of King Arthur and the knights and ladies of AUTHURIAN ROMANCE.

Matter of France
The CHANSON DE GESTES; one of the THREE MATTERS OF ROMANCE.

Matter of Greece and Rome
The ROMANCEs of Troy, the Trojan War, and Alexander the Great; one of the THREE MATTERS OF ROMANCE.

matula disc
A circular chart used for medical diagnosis and prognosis by URINALYSIS. The technique involved the association of color, texture, smell, and taste with the FOUR HUMORS, the FOUR TEMPERAMENTS, the patient's state of digestion, the time of the onset of the illness, age, and other variables.

matutine
Pertaining to the morning.

matzo
Unleavened bread ceremonially baked and eaten at PASSOVER to commemorate the speed of Exodus and hardship of travel. Usually round or square, matzos sometimes were whimsically shaped as birds or beasts.

Maund
MAUNDY THURSDAY in the Christian calendar, named either after Jesus Christ's MANDATUM NOVUM, new commandment, or the maund, the alms basket used to distribute food to the poor.

Maundy Thursday
The Thursday preceding EASTER, the day in HOLY WEEK commemorating the LAST SUPPER and the institution of the EUCHARIST. The name derived from MANDATUM NOVUM, the first words of the ceremony for the washing of feet. BELLS are silent after MASS on that day until the ALLELUIA during the vigil of EASTER EVEN on HOLY SATURDAY.

mausoleum
A monumental TOMB.

maxima
The longest musical note value in MENSURAL NOTATION.

maypole
A tall, ceremonial wooden idol decked with leaves, mayflowers, and long streamers which were held by dancers who interwove in circular patterns meant to imitate the sun's course. Derived from pagan summer solstice rites celebrating the god of vegetation in a tree, the festivities usually included MORRIS DANCEs, MUMMING plays, and ROGATION PROCESSIONS.

mazer
A burled or well-grained hardwood drinking bowl, plain or footed, and elaborately carved or fitted with INLAYs or ORMOLU mounts; or a similarly fashioned porcelain, glass, or metal vessel.

mead
A sweet, aromatic, honey wine, in and out of fashion throughout Western Europe, for healthful and elegant drinking and for celebrating a HONEYMOON. Mead was an ANGLO-SAXON staple sometimes disdained by courtly followers of French taste and Anglo-Norman cuisine.

mead hall
In Germanic epics, the ruler's political meeting and MEED hall where thanes feasted and drank MEAD.

The hall Heorot in the ANGLO-SAXON epic *Beowulf* is an example.

meane
In music, the tenor and alto parts, midway between treble and base; a middle part of a polyphonic vocal or instrumental composition.

medallion
A large decorative or identifying medal, often a portrait or geometric design. It might have been worn pendant on a chain around the neck as jewelry, or incorporated into a carpet, book title page, or heraldic decoration.

medical licensure
Physicians and surgeons were examined before being licensed in order to maintain excellence of the craft. In twelfth-century Salerno, King Roger's dicta were models for malpractice legislation, and Frederick II of Sicily reaffirmed licensing strictures in 1240. In England and France, men and WOMEN PHYSICIANS AND SURGEONS were governed by strict legislation that determined rights and responsibilities of patients, practitioners, and professional GUILDS.

medical similarities
A homeopathic notion based on the theory *similia similibus curentur,* let like be cured by like. For instance, HAIR OF A MAD DOG was considered a cure for a rabid bite, and small amounts of a potent poison were thought to counteract debilitating effects of large doses.

medium coeli
In astronomy and ASTROLOGY, the mid-heaven or zenith.

meed
Reward, wages, hire, recompense; in sexual context, requiting passion in a love DEBT.

megillah
A scroll or ROTULUS, usually associated with the tale of Queen Esther and King Ahashuerus of the Jewish holiday PURIM. Five Old Testament books traditionally are termed *megillot:* Ecclesiastes, Esther, Song of Songs, Ruth, and Lamentations.

Meistersingers
German poets-composers-guildsmen, middle-class perpetuators of the aristocratic MINNESINGERS' song tradition.

melancholic
(Greek *melanos,* black) One of the FOUR TEMPERAMENTS, indicating a personality that was contemplative, intellectual, introspective, fatalistic, and gloomy, a disposition produced by a preponderance of black bile, one of the FOUR HUMORS.

melancholy
The psychopathological state of those people predisposed by astrological inheritance to an abundance of black bile, one of the FOUR HUMORS. Such people were thought to possess traits ranging from stupidity to genius, and tendencies from depression to frenzied mania. Three kinds of melancholy were derived from the Aristotelian, Hippocratic, and Galenic traditions: cerebral affliction; bodily affliction that sympathetically affected the brain; and hypochondria, vapors that affected the brain. Major disease varieties manifesting melancholia were lycanthropy, cynanthropy, and *hereos,* love sickness. Galen considered sexual abstinence a major precipitating factor of melancholy.

melee
A MELLAY.

melisma
A musically florid, emotionally expressive vocal elaboration of a single syllable of text in GREGORIAN CHANT and thirteenth-century POLYPHONY. Contrast SYLLABIC STYLE.

mellay
A hand-to-hand battle of military combatants.

members
In sexual contexts, genitalia.

memento mori
(Latin, Remember that you must die) A remembrance of death, gracing literature, art, and personal jewelry. For instance, a bracelet's exquisitely carved ivory or boxwood skull, neither morbid nor lugubrious, was a reminder in midst of frivolity or pleasure that life's

A memento mori, a skeleton with a viol takes hold of a young lover. A dancing skeleton playing a cornetto regales unwilling listeners. (From *Der Toten Dantz,* Jacob Meydenbach, Mainz, 1492)

higher purposes or temporal shortness must temper joy in earthly delights.

mendicant
An individual religious, or a monastic community, begging ALMS, usually one of the FOUR ORDERS OF FRIARS.

mendiloquence
Artful lying.

Mene, mene, tekel, upharsin
(You have been weighed, measured, and found deficient) The mysterious writing on the wall at BELSHAZZAR'S FEAST, from the Book of Daniel (5).

Menestrandise
The Parisian GUILD of professional MINSTRELs and musicians, founded in 1321.

menorah
A seven-branched candlestick or oil lamp, often gorgeously decorated, used for symbolic and practical purposes in Jewish homes and SYNAGOGUEs. The HANUKKAH candelabrum has eight vessels plus a starter or servant light, the SHAMOS.

menstruum
In anatomical context, the secretion produced in the womb discharged at monthly periods; in chemical jargon, a solvent dissolving a liquid substance.

mensural music
Thirteenth- through sixteenth-century polyphonic compositions with every note having a strictly determined rhythmic value, opposed to GREGORIAN CHANT or PLAINSONG's free rhythms.

mensural notation
The system of musical notation codified by Franco of Cologne, developed in the thirteenth century, with fixed time relationships among note values, as in *minima, maxima, longa,* and *brevis.* In the earlier PLAINCHANT's notational system, with NEUMES, a note indicates a tone's pitch but not its duration.

Merchant Adventurers
Founded in fourteenth-century England, a merchant company so powerful that governments granted it self-rule. It fluorished in import and export trade in the Low Countries, Antwerp, Bruges, and Hamburg.

Merchants of the Staple
English wool and cloth exporters, one of the highest mercantile ranks, who held a government monopoly in raw wool. Calais was one of their major ports.

merchet
A marriage tax that a VILLEIN paid as TALLAGE to the manor LORD for permission for the villein's daughter to marry a man from outside the manor.

mercury
Quicksilver, the silvery white, brilliantly lustrous metal. In ALCHEMY, it was one of the FIVE ELEMENTARY PRINCIPLES composing all material substances; it was also called spirit or ether.

Merkabah
In early KABALLAH, the mystical tradition stressing visions of God's heavenly halls, chariot, and throne, and the THIRTY-TWO WAYS OF WISDOM.

merlon
On a BATTLEMENT or fortified PARAPET, the upright or "tooth" alternating with the "gum" or EMBRASURE in CRENELATION.

mermaid
A sea creature with the upper half of a woman and the lower half of a fish, and often consort to a MERMAN.

merman
A water creature, half man, half fish. Triton the Merman was the son of the sea god Neptune and his consort, Amphitrite. The female equivalent is a MERMAID.

metals
In HERALDRY, the COLORS silver (ARGENT) and gold (*or*).

metanalysis
The incorrect linguistic analysis of where an *n* belongs, either to the preceding indefinite article or to the noun: ***a nadder*** became ***an adder***; ***a napron, an apron.***

metaphor
An artistic comparison for intensifying meaning and effect, omitting the word of comparison: her lips are red roses. Metaphor is more abstract than SIMILE, less than ALLEGORY.

metathesis
The linguistic phenomenon in which *r* and vowels reverse places in pronunciation and spelling: the *thridde brid arn* on the *gaers!* (The third bird ran on the grass.)

metheglin
(Welsh *methaeg,* physician and *lyn,* elixir) A honey wine, related to MEAD, and celebrated in medical clinics and banquet halls.

mezzo-relievo
(Italian, middle relief) Works of art sculptured in relief, projecting halfway between HIGH RELIEF and BAS-RELIEF.

mezzuzah
A Jewish ceremonial object affixed to the right-hand doorposts of houses and individual rooms. It is a small, embellished vessel containing a calligraphed scroll with passages from the Bible, usually Deuteronomy (6:4–9; 11:13–21), plus one of the names of God.

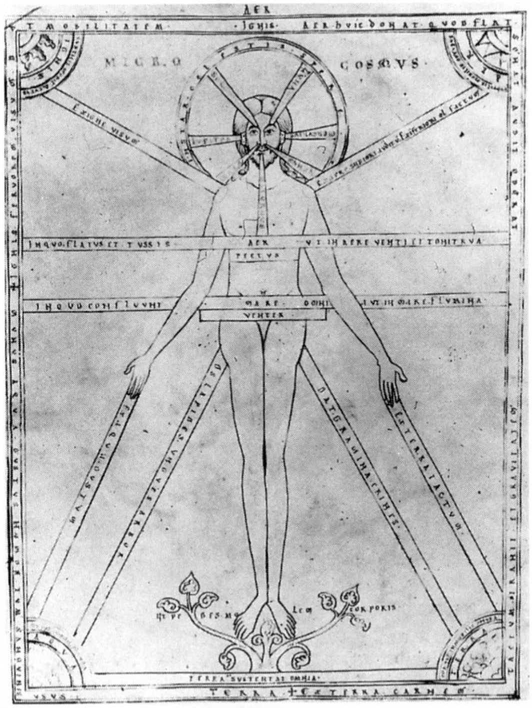

The microcosm incorporates the four elements and four humors plus Luna, the moon, and Sol, the sun. (From *Byrthferth's Manual,* 12th century; courtesy St. John's College, Cambridge, England)

Michaelmas
The Christian feast celebrated September 29 honoring Saint Michael the ARCHANGEL.

microcosm
The human being as a miniature reflection of creation, the MACROCOSM. The FOUR ELEMENTS and FOUR CONTRARIES definable in the body's FOUR HUMORS were thought to demonstrate the spectacular interunities of God's divine plan.

middle
The MIDRIFF, waistline, or exposed space between breast and hips, celebrated as erotic in PHYSIOGNOMIES, particularly if graced by a NEVUS.

Middle Ages
The thousand years between the Fall of Rome in the fifth century and the Renaissance in the fifteenth. An epithet superior to the ridiculous term DARK AGES, it implies the marking of a mean between extremes, not a benighted millennium. The Middle Ages were characterized by Germanic, not Roman, ethics; tribal, not administrative, units; and particular local customs and precedents prevailing, not general legal principles nor written universal codes. Internecine warfare was a hallmark of the age, stimulating magnificent defensive architecture in castles and cities, powerful armaments and consequent innovation in chemistry, metallurgy, and physics, and both philosophical and theological inquiries into the personal, national, and global effects of war and peace.

Middle English
The English language used during the years 1100 through 1500, derived from ANGLO-SAXON dialects, among which CHAUCER'S ENGLISH of the fourteenth century became standard. The four major dialects were Northern, Midland, Southern, and Kentish.

midriff
(Anglo-Saxon *middhrif*, womb place) An elaborately decorated waistline or diaphragm section of a man's or woman's garment.

Midsummer Eve
An originally pagan celebration on the eve of the summer solstice, about June 21. Festivities included revelry, divinations, rogations, BONFIRES, MUMMINGS, and dancing sometimes vigorous enough to stimulate DANCING MANIA.

mier
A handmill equipped with cranks, gears, and blades (or stones) for crumbing stale bread.

mikvah
A Jewish ritual purification bath, used monthly by women, and at other times by converts to Judaism, requiring ritual ablution comparable to BAPTISM. The elaborate architecture and embellishments of the baths were comparable to Roman and Christian ceremonial baths and health SPAs.

milchglas
(German, milk glass) Semi-translucent or opalescent cryolite glass.

miles gloriosus
The boasting soldier of the JOCULATORES tradition, a stock character in early drama and TROPES; a guard for Christ's tomb in MYSTERY and EASTER plays depicting the RESURRECTION.

millefiori
(Italian, a thousand flowers) An all-over decorative, floral design, MILLEFLEURS.

millefleurs
(French, a thousand flowers) A continuous, all-pervasive pattern consisting of countless flowers, adorning the backgrounds of TAPESTRIES or MANUSCRIPT MARGINALIA.

millrind
An iron support for the rotating millstone of a water-powered or wind-driven mill mechanism; also, a heraldic DEVICE.

mimesis
The theory that art imitates life.

minaret
A mosque's tower.

mince matters
(Latin *minutia,* trifles) To chop anything into small pieces or to ameliorate nasty truths. The expression

derives from the culinary technique of mincing meat, vegetables, or fruits for AFFORSING.

miniature
(Latin *miniare,* to color with *minium,* red lead) Minium or red lead with CINNABAR pigments along with other hues were used to paint VELLUM, PARCHMENT, or paper for illuminating liturgical and secular MANUSCRIPTS and early books. Lustrous colors were laid on GESSO bound with GLAIR, and complemented with gold and silver. Miniatures also sometimes were painted on ivory, metal, and wood.

minim
Equivalent in music and dance to a one-half note, a relatively quick beat used as the CROCHET or quarter note today. In CALLIGRAPHY, it is the smallest upright element of MINUSCULE (lowercase) characters, as *i, n, m,* and *u*.

ministeriales
Especially in Germany, the social class of the knighthood bound to the service of an overlord or ruler. Serving as managers of villages or manors, and performing important tasks at major courts, this class of knights developed into a nobility based on administrative skill and princely protection, not on land holdings and loyalty of retainers.

Minnekastchen
(German, a love casket) A love COFFER, for storing jewels, letters, and small precious objects. Larger coffers accommodated linens and lingerie in advance of marriage, like CASSONEs.

Minnelied
A Middle High German love song, a MINNESINGER's LIED celebrating either HÖHE MINNE or NIEDERE MINNE.

Minnelieder
(German, love songs) A collection of love songs of German MINNESINGERs. The MINNELIED emphasized a knight's adoration of a LADY and a woman's passionate yearnings for her lover. Love songs and other songs adhering to the tripartite structure of BARFORM include superb examples of the crusading song, HYMN to the Virgin, the political SPRUCH, TAGELIED, and LIED written by Walther von der Vogelweide, Hartmann von Aue, Reinmar von Hagenau, Dietmar von Eist, and Neidhart von Reuenthal.

Minnesinger
A twelfth-, thirteenth-, or fourteenth-century COURTLY LOVE composer and poet of noble descent, or of the MINISTERIALES, the Middle High German equivalent of the TROUBADOUR and TROUVÈRE, who wrote MINNELIEDER.

Minorites
Brothers of the MENDICANT religious order, the FRANCISCANS, one of the FOUR ORDERS OF FRIARS, as distinct from the Capuchins and the FRIARS MINOR Conventual.

minor orders
In ecclesiastical hierarchy, porters, LECTORS, exorcists, and acolytes rank below members of MAJOR ORDERS.

minstrel
A professional poet-musician, itinerant or court-based, including the JONGLEUR and SCOP. A minstrel might be employed by a feudal HOUSEHOLD or be a member of a musical craftsmen's GUILD, such as MENESTRANDISE.

minuscule
Very small MANUSCRIPT writing used in POCKET BOOKs and some BOOKS OF HOURS; particularly fine INSULAR examples are the Book of Mulling and Book of Armagh.

minyan
The group of ten adult males, the quorum of worshippers for Jewish communal prayers. Not only in towns and cities but also while traveling, Jews were expected to find brethren for prayers. Though Jews were under edict of expulsion from England, King Henry IV gave safe conduct to his illustrious Jewish physician, Dr. Elias Sabot, who had been a doctor to popes and bishops, to move freely about the country, accompanied by ten members of his HOUSEHOLD.

mi-parti
(French, divided in the middle) A popular fifteenth-century male and female fashion in garments and stockings, with fabrics of two contrasting colors

paired vertically, either front and back, or left side and right side. In noble LIVERY, the heraldic colors of the HOUSEHOLD graced the servitors' legs and their DOUBLETS.

miracle play

A drama about non-biblical but religious subjects: wondrous deeds, devotion, and martyrdom of the saints. The plays were derived from the readings in the church service of saints' lives from the GOLDEN LEGEND, such as the tale of Saint Nicholas and the THREE BALLS. Associated genres were MYSTERY and MORALITY plays, all influenced by the JOCULATORES tradition.

miroirs de princes

See MIRRORS OF PRINCES.

mirror of Narcissus

A water mirror, a SPECULUM, meticulously yet seductively reflecting reality. As in the myth of Narcissus, the gazer falling in love with his own reflection in a pool of water and trying to capture and embrace it, drowned.

mirrors of princes

INSTRUCTION BOOKS for responsible, courtly, humane rulers, as well as practical guides to etiquette, derived from the classic treatise of Isocrates (*Ad Nicoclem,* 374 B.C.). One of the most common literary genres, these manuals exercised the minds and the pens of significant thinkers, such as the Neoplatonists John of Salisbury (in his *Policraticus*), William Perrault, Hugh of Fleury, and Aegidius Romanus. Popular in myriad versions and translations not merely for princes but also for courtiers and townsmen imitating habits of nobility, the books were also called *miroirs de princes* (French) and *specula princepis* (Latin).

misericord

(Latin *misericordia,* mercy, compassion, pity) The underside shelf of a raisable choir-STALL seat, often humorously or grotesquely carved. The shelf propped up the standing, weary, officiant at sacred service. It was also the name of a dagger used for a merciful coup de grace, or a room of a MONASTERY where certain rules were relaxed.

A misericord carving depicts an ale wife carried by a demon being tossed into a Hellmouth. (From a drawing of a wooden misericord, 14th century, Ludlow Church, England; courtesy of M. P. Cosman, *Fabulous Feasts: Medieval Cookery and Ceremony,* George Braziller, New York, 1976)

Mishnah

The second-century Hebrew compilation and codification of Jewish oral law, arranged by subject (such as agriculture, festivals, and marriage) and attributed to Rabbi Judah the Patriarch.

missal

A book of texts for celebrating MASS, containing the CANON of the mass and a calendar of major church festivals with directions for the priest. The main parts are the ORDINARY (said at every mass), the PROPER of time (additions according to liturgical season), the proper of saints (for saints' feasts) and the common of saints (for the feast of the APOSTLES, the text is given once, not twelve times). The missal was often gorgeously illuminated, traditionally with scenes of the CRUCIFIXION and Christ enthroned in majesty.

misura

(Italian, measure) A dancer's ability to keep good time, one of the SIX REQUISITES FOR A GOOD DANCER.

miton

Also called a *moufle,* a fingerless glove used both in elaborate costumery and in hunting and rough work. The miton was often an extension of the sleeve or attached to it by lacing.

mitre
A BISHOP's tall, deeply cleft hat or headdress, from the front resembling in outline a pointed arch, from the side, the two HORNS OF MOSES (though sometimes positioned vice-versa). Made of linen or satin fabric, the mitre often was embroidered and bejeweled. Permission to wear a mitre was also granted to ABBOTs and ABBESSes of important monasteries.

mitzvah
A commandment, both a blessing and an obligation, a duty imposed by the TORAH on a practicing Jew. The TALMUD lists 613 biblical mitzvot regulating daily existence and demonstrating piety and righteousness. Also, any good and charitable deed.

mixne
A dung hill.

Mixolydian
The seventh CHURCH MODE, beginning on G, one of the four AUTHENTIC MODES (D, E, F, G).

mizrach
(Hebrew, East) A Jewish amulet, scroll, MANUSCRIPT page, or metal plate hung on the East wall of a SYNAGOGUE or dwelling, and often decorated with Psalm 67 written in the shape of a MENORAH.

moat
A deep, defensive ditch, usually filled with water, surrounding a fortified town or castle wall.

mode
One of the eight musical CHURCH MODES or early scales; a repetitive, rhythmic musical pattern named after verse patterns TROCHAIC, IAMBIC, DACTYLIC, ANAPESTIC, SPONDAIC, and tribrachic) and typical of early MENSURAL MUSIC.

modus
Either a CHURCH MODE or rhythmic MODE.

Mogen David
(Hebrew, David's Shield) The six-pointed Star of David, an identifying BADGE or DEVICE for Jews. It was the generally welcomed, though sometimes nefariously imposed, symbol of the Jewish people by the fifteenth century.

mohel
A ritual surgeon performing the Jewish rite of circumcision with traditional ceremonies.

molding
Ornamental carving on projections or recessions of a wall or column, including billet molding, hood, cover, bolection, and cable molding.

molding board
A professional public baker's long, flat kneading table used for shaping dough loaves brought by customers for baking; also, an instrument for stealing dough when fitted with a small trap door so that a servant hidden beneath could scrape out dough from loaves above. The pilfered produce became new breads for sale, a larceny that in fifteenth-century London landed some women bakers on the THEWE, and men on the PILLORY or HURDLE.

Moll
The diminutive, friendly, NICKNAME for Mary. It was the affectionate name for one of the THREE MARIES, and for favored animals: the DAYE in Chaucer's "Nun's Priest's Tale" owns three cows, three sows, and a sheep named Moll.

monastery
(Greek *monasterion,* a place to live alone) The house of a religious community of MONKs, nuns, or the coeducational house for both, living according to the BENEDICTINE RULE or similar regulation requiring obedience.

monasticism
The individual or communal quest for Christian perfection in isolation, in a MONASTERY, or in the world. The NUN or MONK is committed to THREE COUNSELS OF PERFECTION, THREE VOWS, the celebration of the DIVINE OFFICE, manual labor, and adherence to the BENEDICTINE RULE or to the MENDICANT life practiced by the FOUR ORDERS OF FRIARS.

monk
A member of a male religious community usually living in a MONASTERY under THREE VOWS of poverty, chastity, and obedience.

monochord
A single-string musical instrument consisting of a long wooden resonator along which a moveable attached ridge varies the vibrating lengths of string; also, a scientific instrument for investigations and demonstrations of acoustical laws.

monody
Music for solo singer.

monogram
A cipher or set of letters representing an artist's signature, or a royal or holy personage, as the CHI-RHO, I H S, and ALPHA AND OMEGA insignia of Christ.

monstrance
A partially transparent devotional vessel carrying the HOST in processions and for certain devotions before the altar. The vessel is sometimes CRUCIFORM, or towered and turreted with gold or silver CRENELATIONs, and elaborately embellished with jewels, ENAMEL, or NIELLO.

month's mind
A REQUIEM MASS celebrated on the 30th day after a Christian's death or burial.

mont joie
A battle cry; or a MONSTRANCE.

mood music
Melody, rhythm, or MODE used intentionally to influence emotions, particularly manipulating mood for medical or psychiatric effect. Mood music was played at health SPAs, clinics, courts, outdoors for processions, and widely practiced on BOETHIAN authority.

moot
An ANGLO-SAXON speaking-meeting, a legislative or parliamentary gathering, comparable to the Icelandic ALTHING.

morality play
An allegorical drama in which personified VIRTUEs and VICEs compete for the hero's soul, as in *Everyman, The Castle of Perseverance, Mundus et Infans,* and the numerous precursors to the Faust plays. Contemporaneous with MYSTERY and MIRACLE PLAYS, like them the morality owes some characters and incidents to the JOCULATORES.

moralized Bible
Non-liturgical laymen's scriptures, retelling Bible stories with commentary crafted to instruct while pleasing with vivid graphic representation of text and ALLEGORY. One fourteenth-century *bible moralisée* having 5,000 small paintings seemed more an exuberant cartoon book than holy text.

mordant
A metal-corrosive chemical for ETCHING ARMOR or plates for prints.

moresca
(Italian, Moorish) One of several types of dramatic dance entertainments: miming, costumed sword dances on allegorical or humanistic subjects similar to MASQUERADEs; acrobatic WILD MAN or savage dances; dance battles between Christians and Saracens; and lascivious skits imitating the manners and dialects of Moors, such as Orlando di Lasso's *Moresche* (1555). Morescas were allied with MORRIS DANCEs, English and European agricultural fertility rituals, and MATTACHINs.

morganatic marriage
When a king, ruler, or nobleman married a commoner, he bestowed on the spouse a substantial MORGENGABE to assure that neither the wife nor their children would have any interest in his estate after death, not inheriting title, arms, or further assets.

morgengabe
(German, morning gift) The substantial gift from a husband to his wife, usually substituting for her future testamentary rights to his assets. Either the gift literally was presented the morning after their first night together, its substance and magnitude having been determined in advance by contract, or the gift was symbolically transferred before witnesses at the church door after marriage. A MORGANATIC MARRIAGE celebrated this DOWER.

Moriscos
Fifteenth-century Muslims converted from Islam to Christianity, particularly in Spain, where they were persecuted by the INQUISITION.

morning star
The planet Venus, also called LUCIFER, the light bringer, when appearing in the eastern sky before sunrise. As the Star of the Morning (*Stella Matutina*), it was considered an ATTRIBUTE of the Virgin Mary. As a weapon, it was an ironical name for a spiked MACE resembling a rayed star.

Morpheus
(Greek) God of Dreams, son of Sleep (Hypnos), one of the TWO SONS OF NIGHT; grandson of Night (Nyx).

morris dance
A popular country, sword, and stamping dance in England. Participants usually wear ankle bells and flowing scarfs or head wreaths. Ultimately derived from pagan fertility rites and ritual renewals of spring, the morris dance was associated with the MAYPOLE, MUMMING plays, and the MORESCA.

morse
(Latin *modere,* to bite) A clasp or fastening for a cape or CLOAK, usually wrought in gold or silver and set with stones.

mortar
A large cup-shaped vessel of sturdy material (such as marble, BRASS, wood, or heavy glass) for pounding food or pharmacy ingredients with a pestle to pulverize them; or an early artillery weapon of similar shape.

mortrews
(French *mortreuil,* mortar) A savory stew, the meats, vegetables, or herbs of which were ground in a MORTAR. Chaucer's guildsman's Cook is famous for this dish.

mosaic
A floor and wall decoration in which variously colored marble, stone, glass, or pottery cubes (tesserae) were set in a cement or glue matrix and the total surface then smoothed, polished, and lustered. The designs might be secular, whimsical, or ecclesiastic, and the technique was particularly celebrated in BYZANTINE architecture.

Mosan enamels
Vigorous, expressive, CHAMPLEVÉ ENAMELS created in the twelfth century in the Meuse Valley by artists as Nicolas of Verdun and Godefroid of Huy, inspired by wealthy clerical patrons like ABBOT Suger of St. Denis and Abbot Wibald of Stavelt. Mosan enamels influenced LIMOGES ENAMELS.

motet
An unaccompanied choral composition with three groups of vocalists singing simultaneously one or more sacred texts intended for performance in church LITURGY, especially at VESPERS. It was a popular polyphonic musical pattern from the thirteenth century on, with numerous secular and solo subtypes.

motet-chanson
A fifteenth-century French CHANSON with Latin text.

Mothering Sunday
LAETARE SUNDAY.

motley
A LIVERY or costume with variegated, checkered, or multicolored juxtaposed fabrics. Often amusing or

A jester dressed in motley blows his horn. (From a woodcut by Albrecht Dürer in Sebastian Brant, *Stultifera Navis,* Basel, Johann Bergmann, 1497)

incongruous, these were the clothes of a jester or FOOL when worn with CAP AND BELLS, but without them, considered fashionable among courtiers.

motte
An earthen mound surrounded by a BAILEY, for fortified defense of a castle tower or KEEP.

moucheture
Tiny slashings and DAGGINGs in clothing, shoes, gloves, and CLOAKs.

moveable feasts
Annual Christian ecclesiastical festivals falling on dates that vary according to rules governing the lunar or solar calendar, such as EASTER, which falls on the first Sunday after the full moon of the vernal equinox, thus anytime between March 21 and April 18.

Mozarabic
The particular art, LITURGY, music, poetry, and culture of Spanish Christians, especially in Aragon, Castile, and Leon, living under Muslim rule. Mozarabic CHANT is one of the FOUR MUSICAL DIALECTS of Christian liturgy.

mullet
A prevalent food fish; or a type of forceps, tweezers, or pincers used by physicians, apothecaries, and weavers; or in HERALDRY, a star of (usually) five triangular rays, sometimes six (like the MOGEN DAVID) or more.

mullion
A vertical bar of wood, stone, or metal, separating multiple window panes or door panels. Paired with TRANSOM bars, mullions support GOTHIC STAINED GLASS windows, often surmounted by TRACERY.

multi vallate
Having many RAMPARTs.

mumchance
A mimed MASQUERADE dance, also called a mummenschantz.

mumming
The performance of a masked, mimed play, usually performed by mummers, preserving an ancient agricultural fertility rite of beheading and resurrection, much like the MORRIS DANCE and MAYPOLE festivities.

Mummers wearing bird masks entertain the feasters as musicians play. (From woodcut, Hans Burgmair; courtesy of Metropolitan Museum of Art, New York)

mural
A wall or ceiling painting, integrated into the architectural setting, and executed with some permanent or imperishable material, such as stone, glass, or ceramic MOSAIC, colored cement, or porcelain ENAMEL. The technique was usually for outdoor wall decoration; interior mural technique is FRESCO.

murrain
A dreadful, contagious disease of sheep characterized by ulcers, maggots, and painful death; also plague, in general.

musica artificialis
(Latin, unnatural music) Vocal and instrumental music, one of the FOUR CLASSES OF MUSIC proposed by fourteenth-century theorist Theodoricus de Campo based on the BOETHIAN THREE CLASSES OF MUSIC; in contrast to natural music of PULSE and the rhythms of the heavenly spheres.

Musica Enchiriadis
The important late-ninth-century musical treatise describing POLYPHONY in connection with the then newly introduced PORTATIVE ORGAN.

musica ficta
The performer's introduction of musical changes not indicated in the written score (chromatic or nondiatonic tones, tones converted into semitones, and semitones into tones).

musica figurata
Polyphonic music in which the rhythm is not indicated and is open to the performer's interpretation. Contrast PLAINSONG and GREGORIAN CHANT.

musica humana
Rhythms of the human PULSE, periodic fevers, monthly menstrual cycles, and other indicators of the harmonies of the body with the music of the spheres; one of the THREE CLASSES OF MUSIC as well as one of the FOUR CLASSES OF MUSIC.

musica instrumentis
Music played on instruments or sung, the only one of the THREE CLASSES OF MUSIC actually heard by human ears.

musica mensurabilis
MENSURAL MUSIC, or MUSICA FIGURATA.

musica mundana
(Latin, world music) Planetary patterns and zodiacal rhythms, the music of the spheres, one of the THREE CLASSES OF MUSIC as well as one of the FOUR CLASSES OF MUSIC.

musica plana
PLAINSONG or GREGORIAN CHANT, as opposed to polyphonic and measured music.

musica reservata
A sixteenth-century elegant, eccentric chamber music, both secular and religious, and uniting passion of sound with meaning of word, especially in the Netherlands, Germany, and Italy.

musica sacra
Sacred music.

Musica Transalpina
The first printed collection of Italian MADRIGALs with English texts, published by Nicholas Younge in 1588.

musica vocalis
Animal and natural sounds; one of the FOUR CLASSES OF MUSIC.

musica vulgaris
Secular, vernacular music.

musicians gallery
A raised balcony in a banquet hall or great hall from which musicians played FANFAREs that signaled the serving of courses, and later played digestive music crafted for proper metabolism of the menu. Trumpets, pipes, BELLS, and a PORTATIVE ORGAN generally introduced a feast; CORNETTOs and SHAWMs concluded it.

mutable signs
The four astrological signs characterized by changeable, moveable nature and consequent instability of people ruled by them: Gemini, Virgo, Sagittarius, and Pisces. Contrast the FIXED SIGNS.

mutation
A linguistic sound change produced in an accented root vowel or diphthong by a sound in the following syllable, making irregular plurals for certain nouns: for example, the original *mani* became men; *foti,* feet; *tothi,* teeth; *gosi,* geese. *Mutation* is also a term for a musical transition between two interlocked HEXACHORDs, groups of six melodic tones.

myrrhophores
The women myrrh carriers, the THREE MARIES at Christ's tomb discovering His RESURRECTION (Mark 16:1).

mystery play
A drama on a biblical subject. The term *mystery* refers to God's or Christ's intercession in the human world: the Creation, the Fall of Mankind, the Flood, the

CRUCIFIXION, and the Redemption of Mankind. Many were organized into dramatic cycles which ranged in topic from the Creation to the APOCALYPSE. Christ's specific life history was the subject of the PASSION PLAY, individual saints' lives of the MIRACLE PLAY, and the ALLEGORY and battling for man's soul of the MORALITY PLAY. The English Wakefield, York, and Chester plays were written and performed by craft guildsmen on moveable pageant wagons so that the productions could triumph town after town.

N

nagelschrift

(German *Huf,* hoof, *nagel,* nail, *schrift,* writing) Fourteenth- and fifteenth-century musical notation NEUMEs, resembling horseshoe nails; also called GOTHIC NEUMES.

nap bow

A NAPPER's implement in the cloth trades for lifting and smoothing nap on fabric's surface.

napper

A cloth craftsman responsible for raising the nap on a fabric surface using a NAP BOW and TEASLE. Napping usually followed FULLING.

Narragonia

Fool's Paradise, the goal of the ridiculous voyagers on Sebastian Brandt's NARRENSCHIFF, the Ship of Fools.

Narrenschiff

(German, Ship of Fools) Title of Sebastian Brant's fifteenth-century satire on human folly and VICE. It inspired such works of art as Hieronymous Bosch's *Garden of Terrestrial Delights,* and such literature as Erasmus's *Praise of Folly.*

narthex

A VESTIBULE or PORTICO situated at the western end of a CHURCH or a BASILICA. The narthex is divided from the NAVE by a screen, railing, or wall, for the CATECHUMENs or penitents.

narwhal

A single-spiral-horned marine animal, a cetacean hunted for its apparent resemblance to the UNICORN. The horn was used in powders and ELIXIRs that were thought to be powerful erotic stimuli.

native

In ASTROLOGY, a human being born under a particular planet or sign, the subject of a horoscope and predictions by GENETHLIALOGY.

Nativity of Saint John the Baptist

A Christian feast, June 24, celebrating his miraculous birth (Luke 1).

natural necessity

The ARISTOTELIAN idea that inexorable and orderly movements of the celestial machinery make every earthly and human event occur precisely when it does. Astrologers, philosophers, and astronomers, like Nicole Oresme in the fourteenth century, compared necessary celestial regularity to clockwork.

natureingang

(German, nature introduction) A sylvan site used as a literary device in charming, seemingly ingenuous MINNESINGER songs that set the spring mood for praising nature's glory and eliciting erotic desire.

nave

(Latin *navis,* a ship) The main body of a CHURCH or CATHEDRAL, excluding the CHANCEL and TRANSEPTs.

Nebuchadnezzar's children

Crazy people suffering from congenital madness, MELANCHOLY, HEREOS, or other mental disease. King Nebuchadnezzar, a prototypical madman in literature and art, and other wild men are portrayed in one of three conventional ways: as mad sinner, as unholy WILD MAN, or as holy wild man. These representations exemplified God's triple uses of madness: to punish the damned, to purge sinners, and to prove the virtue of saints. Wild men were frequent figures in drama, ROMANCE, and MANUSCRIPT ILLUMINATION.

necessarium
A privy; a building with toilets, sometimes heated and equipped with niches for candles for good light.

necromancy
Divination by the study of entrails of corpses, or by summoning of the dead. Necromancy is also called the black art, conflating *necro* (pertaining to death) and *niger* (black).

needle
Usually made of wood, ivory, or metal, and used to ply thread in fabric trades, sewing, medicine, and PHLEBOTOMY. Steel needles and BODKINs were introduced to the West by the Moors. Cluny manufactured needles extensively, though by 1370, Nuremberg had an active industry.

nef
A ship-shaped SALT.

neomenia
The new moon, and the festivals imitating ancient Greek and Jewish celebrations beginning lunar months.

nepotism
The bestowing of ecclesiastical preferment and church benefits upon close relatives and friends; jobs given for family patronage and pay, not for the appointee's piety or ability.

Ner Tamid
In Judaism, the ceremonial Eternal Light, kindled perpetually before the holy ARK, the ARON HA-KODESH, symbolizing the perpetuity of God's love, human faith, and intellectual learning.

nest of weights
Nesting cup-shaped metal weights housed in a box or master cup, itself the largest weight and equal to the sum of the smaller cups stored concentrically within it, or each larger weight twice that of the smaller, the nests ranging from several pounds down to a fraction of an ounce. Used by merchants, money changers, goldsmiths, jewelers, and cooks requiring accurate measurements of products, weights exactly calibrated, marked and regulated according to town, country, or international standards. Particularly popular in Nuremberg and exported from there to all of Europe, the nests were often decoratively incised with geometric designs, hunt scenes, and secular love motifs.

Nefs on the banquet table emulate the elaborate ship in the feast pantomime of Crusaders' capturing Jerusalem. (From *Grandes Chroniques de France,* 15th century; courtesy of the Bibliothèque Nationale, Paris)

Nestorians
Followers of Nestorius, a Christian ABBOT of Antioch, later patriarch of Constantinople. Nestorius insisted that the Virgin Mary ought not be called MATER MARIA DEI, Mother of God, because she bore Jesus

A nest of weights from 15th-century Nuremburg is stamped with maker's marks, has incised hunting scenes, and, as the handle, two aspectant dolphins. (Courtesy of Galeria Medievalia, Tenafly, New Jersey)

as a human being; he also denied her IMMACULATE CONCEPTION, his doctrine declared heretical by the COUNCIL OF EPHESUS. In Antioch, Arabia, and Egypt, the Nestorians were effective transmitters of ecclesiastical doctrine and scientific ideas.

neuma
(Greek *pneuma,* breath or spirit) An extended melismatic passage (see MELISMA) in GREGORIAN CHANT or PLAINSONG, sung to a single syllable or a vowel sound to express a spiritual feeling more significant than mere words. In the ALLELUIA, it is called the JUBILUS. Neuma also refers to the pedagogic melodies for illustrating characteristics of each CHURCH MODE.

neume
A square or diamond-shaped musical notational sign, also called NAGELSCHRIFT, for writing PLAINSONG. Important from the eighth through fourteenth centuries, this musical marking was superseded by MENSURAL NOTATION.

nevus
A flat, black or pigmented mole or beauty mark. Like the DIASTEMA and LISP, the nevus was considered a sign of voluptuousness and eager sexuality.

newel
The center pillar from which winding stairs radiate, or the post of a stairway's handrail.

nice
(Latin *nescius,* ignorant) A ridiculous, SILLY, disreputable rascal, or one simply foolish.

nickname
By DISSIMILATION from *an eke name* to *a neke name* and thence *a nick name,* a familiar additional name, usually a contraction, diminution, or variation of a given name, family name, or epithet, such as *Jim* for James, or *JACKANAPES* for the fifteenth-century Duke of Suffolk.

niedere minne
(German, lower love) Common love or lesser love expressed by the MINNESINGERs in praising country pleasures, especially the unspoiled pastoral beautiful woman's exuberantly sharing lips and body; opposite to HÖHE MINNE.

niello
An ornamental jewelry technique in which a black compound of sulphur or alloy of silver, copper, or lead was brushed into a design that had been incised on metal, then fired and polished to a beautiful luster.

nihil ex nihilo
(Latin, nothing out of nothing) Aristotle's maxim: nothing comes from nothing, or something cannot be made out of nothing. The saying defines the limits of the paltry, material world and the human creativity within it, contrasted with God's supernatural creation of matter.

nimbus
A luminous circle or AUREOLE, though occasionally CRUCIFORM or triangular, surrounding the head of a saint or holy personage, functionally similar to a MANDORLA or VESICA PISCIS.

nine heroes

Noted in the fourteenth-century courtly poem, *Vows of the Peacock* by JONGLEUR Jacques de Longuyon, the three pagan heroes: Hector, Alexander, and Julius Caesar; three Hebrew heroes: David, Joshua, and Judas Maccabeus; and three Christian heroes: King Arthur, Charlemagne, and Godfrey of Bouillon. Their counterparts were the nine heroines and the NINE SCIENTIFIC WORTHIES; all exemplified in the earthly world the reflection of heavenly TRINAL TRIPLICITIES.

nine Muses

Goddesses of the arts dwelling on Mount Parnassus. Daughters of Zeus and the Titaness Mnemosyne (Memory), the Muses were: Cleo, muse of history; Euterpe, music and lyric poetry; Thalia, comedy and pastoral poetry; Melpomene, tragedy; Terpsichore, dance and song; Erato, lyric and love poetry; Urania, astronomy; Calliope, epic poetry; and Polyhymnia, heroic hymns.

nine orders of angels

SERAPHs, CHERUBs, Thrones, Dominions, Virtues, Powers, Principalities, ARCHANGELs, and ANGELS.

nine scientific worthies

Three ancient scientists: Pliny, Ptolemy, and Galen; three Arab scientists: Avicenna, Abu Mashar, and Averroes; and three Hebrew scientists: Maimonides, Profacius (Don Profat Tibbon of Marseilles, or Jacob Ben Machir), and Abraham Bar Hiyya. Like the NINE HEROES, they exemplified on earth the power of TRINAL TRIPLICITIES.

nodes

One of the two astronomical points marking the intersection between a planet's orbit and the ECLIPTIC.

noeane

Miscellaneous syllables of unknown meaning found in tenth-century treatises of music theory that described short melodies with the characteristics of various CHURCH MODES.

noli me tangere

(Latin, Do not touch me) Christ's saying "Touch me not" to Mary Magdalene, one of the THREE MARIES, when he appeared before her as she wept beside his sepulcher after the RESURRECTION. LEPERs and patients with communicable diseases were compelled to state this phrase, to wear a BADGE signifying it, to sound their horn, clapper, or CRECELLE, and to maintain an ambulatory quarantine.

nomen sacrum

(Latin, Holy Name) The Greek letters *XPI,* a sacred MONOGRAM, from Christ's genealogy in the Gospel of St. Matthew, *Christi autem generatio:* However, the birth of Christ. It was also the INCARNATION INITIAL in HIBERNO-SAXON and other MANUSCRIPTS.

Norman

Describing the Norsemen who invaded Normandy in the tenth century, adopted Christianity, and thereupon substituted adventure and commerce for piracy. They conquered England in 1066 (the NORMAN CONQUEST), which transformed the conqueror William, Duke of Normandy, into William I, King of England. In court custom, church, and language, ANGLO-NORMAN superseded ANGLO-SAXON. While Norman architecture was ROMANESQUE in influence, the Normans in England introduced massive proportions, the rounded arch, sparsely adorned stonework, CRUCIFORM CHURCHes with monumental square towers at the CROSSING, blind ARCADES, and GROTESQUERIE in sculptural adornment, such as the CATHEDRALS of Winchester and Peterborough, the ruined French ABBEY of Jumièges near Rouen, and numerous buildings in Apulia and Sicily.

Norman Conquest

Duke William of Normandy's triumph over English King Harold in 1066. King William the Conqueror then introduced to England NORMAN ideas, language, architecture, agriculture, jurisprudence, food, and FEUDALISM. The Conquest also affected ecclesiastical learning and Christian zeal through the writings of Lanfranc and Saint Anselm, and sweepingly changed court, civil, and country life. The BAYEUX TAPESTRY depicts the crucial battle.

norroy

In England, the chief HERALD charged with arranging funerals and HATCHMENTs for dead knights north of the Trent River; contrast SURROY OR CLARENCEUX.

nosethirl
A nostril, or nose hole, the facial orifice through which spirits travel. The danger was that the benign spirits might leave, and the malign might enter, requiring the wishful blessing at a sneeze: "GOD BLESS YOU!"

notiricon
In KABALLAH, a mystical ACROSTIC demonstrating hidden correspondences in names. A thirteenth-century example: the letters of the name *Adam* (Alef, Dalet, Mem) which could also spell *David* and *Messiah*.

Notre Dame school
The spectacular twelfth- and thirteenth-century church music center at the CATHEDRAL of Paris, Notre Dame. The school was important for its experiments in COUNTERPOINT, like the ORGANUM, and was home to such composers as Leonin and Perotin (Perotinus Magnus).

nun
A woman consecrated to the religious life, living in a MONASTERY, a CENOBITIC or EREMITIC community for women or a COEDUCATIONAL MONASTERY, or in spiritual isolation with other ANCHORITES AND ANCHORESSES; her VOWS incorporate the THREE COUNCILS OF PERFECTION.

nuncheon
(Anglo-Saxon *non* noon plus *scencan,* to pour fluid) The noonquench or noon drink, a payment in wine or ale to workers to lubricate the afternoon's labors. The ceremony later became associated with food and evolved into the modern luncheon.

Nunc Dimittis Domini
(Latin, Now, Lord, You can dismiss your servant) Simeon, destined not to die until seeing the Savior, said this after viewing the infant Jesus at the PRESENTATION and PURIFICATION in the Temple (Luke 2:29).

O

obeying signs
In ASTROLOGY, the six ZODIAC SIGNS Libra, Scorpio, Sagittarius, Capricorn, Aquarius, and Pisces; opposite of COMMANDING SIGNS.

oblate
(Latin *oblatus,* one offered) A child given to a MONASTERY for upbringing, or a layman living in a monastic community without having taken religious vows.

oblation
(Latin *oblata,* offerings) The gifts of bread and wine offered in the Christian EUCHARIST, or a donation at MASS for use by the clergy, the poor, or the infirm.

oblatorium
A side APSE in a Christian BASILICA or CHURCH in which the eucharistic bread and wine are blessed.

O-blessings
The SEVEN O-ANTIPHONS.

obstetrical contraction stimulators
A preparation of coriander seed inserted into the vagina, and a jogging table to bounce the patient into contractions were among the medicinal and mechanical devices from Greek, Roman, and Arabic sources usually translated for the West by Jewish medical scholars and physicians.

obstetric hoop
In order to relieve the woman's back burden during pregnancy, a hoop that circumnavigated the base of the belly and the upper back and was supported on the shoulders.

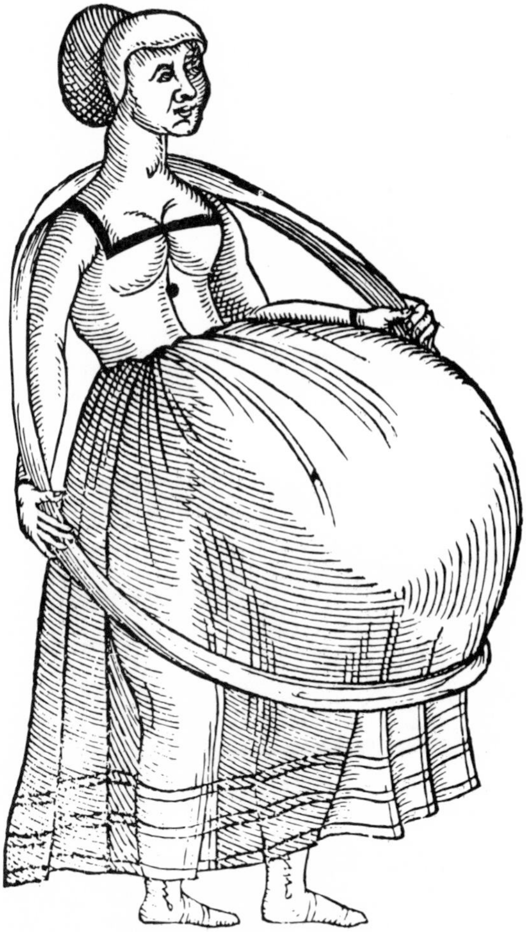

A woman uses an obstetric hoop to relieve the burden of her multiple gestating babes. (From Amboise Paré, *Oeuvres* [1575], National Library of Medicine, Bethesda, Maryland)

occult virtue
Inexplicable, inherently powerful elements affecting human existence. They were thought to reside in herbs, stones, animal flesh, and astronomical phenomena as comets and eclipses. Agrippa in his *Philosophy of Natural Magic* maintained that human intellect and reason alone could not discern causes of potent qualities but PHILOSOPHERs could discover them by experience and intuition.

Ockham's razor
A logical instrument for cutting through cant to truth: the tenet that of all possibilities, the simplest explanation fitting the evidence is best. The theory developed from William of Ockham's rational economy in resolving quandaries of choice; comparable to an ARUDSHIELD.

octave
(Latin *octava dies,* the eighth day) Either the eighth day after an ecclesiastical feast, or an eight-day observance period of a feast.

oculus
A building's eye to the sky, a circular window, such as a ROSE WINDOW, decoratively admitting light at the top of a pediment or surmounting a main door in a CHURCH or CATHEDRAL.

odhecaton
(Greek, *ode* or song, plus *hecaton,* 100) A collection of 100 songs; specifically, Petrucci's printed collection of 100 popular songs (actually 99) of secular polyphonic music composed between 1470 and 1500.

offertory
Part of the PROPER of the MASS, sung after the CREDO, as the PRIEST offers an OBLATION of bread and wine.

office
The DIVINE OFFICE, the service of the eight CANONICAL HOURS, as opposed to the liturgical celebration of the MASS.

ogee
In architecture and the decorative arts, a continuous double curve, convex above, concave below, thus shaped like an *S* lying on its side. Two ogees juxtaposed as an arch create the OGEE ARCH.

ogee arch
A pointed arch with a double curvature: the upper level is convex and the lower portion is concave. Popular in England from the thirteenth century onward for both secular and ecclesiastical GOTHIC doorways, window frames, and furniture decoration.

oil of iron
Red alchemical SULFUR.

old dance
The DANCE OF LOVE: sexual play climaxing in intercourse. Pandarus in Chaucer's *Troilus and Criseyde* knows its every step, making him a good go-between for lovers.

Old Hall Manuscript
A superb collection of 148 polyphonic musical compositions performed in the royal household chapel in fifteenth-century England, a precedent probably initiated by King Henry IV. The compositions included settings of the ORDINARY of the MASS, ISORHYTHMIC MOTETs, and ANTIPHONs.

Old Man of the Mountains
The thirteenth-century Muslim leader of the ASSASSINS, Sheik al-Jabal, who commanded fanatical obedience from his followers and devotees.

oleum et operam perdis
(Latin, You waste oil and toil) An inscription found on several alchemical portraits. This quote from Cicero suggested the vanity of attempts to transmute base metals into gold, AUREFACTION, or to find the ELIXIR of eternal life.

Omobuono
(Italian, fine man) The twelfth-century good man, or HOMO BONUS, who, once wealthy and worldly, gave all his goods to the poor; his earthly saintliness was recompensed by canonization. A prototype for such *imitatio christi* was depicted in paintings and decorations in Venice and Cremona.

onager
A heavy artillery war machine: mobile with an open frame, a winched, single-springed, single-armed catapult. It succeeded the Roman cheiro-ballistra.

on the carpet
(French, *sur le tapis,* on the carpet) A subject up for discussion. The expression is derived from the customary use of oriental carpets as SANAPs, covers for the banquet table, a common center of conversation.

opicinus
A heraldic beast in a COAT OF ARMS (like the Surgeons Guild of London): body and legs of a LION (for boldness), neck and head of an eagle (for keen vision), tail of a camel (for patience), and wings of a GRIFFIN (for swiftness).

Opportunity
The ALLEGORY of optimism often associated with FORTUNE in literature and art. Known variously as Chance or Possibility; often depicted as a strong young man with a shock of forehead hair, so that opportunity might be seized by the forelock.

opus anglicanum
(Latin, English work) A kind of superb English needlework, EMBROIDERY, and delicate, woven handwork, usually executed in the split-stitch, with a tiny center stitch holding a long outline stitch to the background.

opus araneum
(Latin *araneum,* spider's web) Handmade lace imitating in pattern an intricate web.

Opus Dei
The DIVINE OFFICE.

oralia
A headdress veil with two blue stripes, required by thirteenth-century law for Jewish women, later superseded by the extravagant horned CORNALIA.

orans
A figure, usually the Virgin Mary, praying, particularly for departed souls.

oratory
A small chapel or CHURCH.

orb
A sphere or globe, an INSIGNE of Christ PANTOCRATER; in ASTROLOGY, the space on the celestial sphere in which the INFLUENCE of a planet, star, or ZODIAC house acts.

Orchesography
The superb dance manual preserving PAVANs, BASSE DANSEs, GALLIARDs, and BRANSLEs, by Thoinot Arbeau, pseudonym for clergyman Jehan Toborot. Cast as a dialogue or DEBATE, the manual is an INSTRUCTION BOOK for townsmen and women who desired advice on dance performance, etiquette, and deportment.

ordinary
The unchanging staples of the Christian MASS, as opposed to its PROPER. In HERALDRY, an early, simple, common CHARGE or DEVICE, like a FESS, BEND, BAR, CHEVRON, CROSS, or SALTIRE.

ordo
(Latin, order) A musical indication of the number of times a rhythmic pattern is repeated without interruption.

ordo mundi
(Latin, the order of the world) The blessed interrelatedness of all created things, God's divine plan for perfect order in the universe. The world as MACROCOSM possessed FOUR ELEMENTS and FOUR CONTRARIES harmoniously reduced in the human being, the MICROCOSM. The GREAT CHAIN OF BEING, COSMOLOGICAL DIAGRAMs, and ZODIAC MEN graphically represented these hierarchic interdependencies.

orfèvrerie
(French, goldwork) Pure gold decorative and practical objects such as CHALICEs, RELIQUARIEs, RETABLEs, daidems, earrings, and bracelets; in cookery, AUREFICTION.

organistrum
A HURDY-GURDY.

organ portative
A small, secular organ either worn about the player's neck (a keyboard played by the right hand, with the left hand working a triangular feeder bellows) or set upon a stand (one person playing, another working the bellows from behind). The scales were not regularly diatonic or chromatic but selective, omitting

notes unusual in particular types of music. The organ had as many keys as pipes and contained no stops.

organum
An early type of polyphonic music, its first stage described in MUSICA ENCHIRIADIS. There were four types in its development: parallel organum (ninth and tenth centuries), free organum (eleventh and twelfth centuries), melismatic organum (twelfth century), and measured organum (thirteenth century).

oriel window
An upper story's bayed window, surmounting CORBELS.

orientation
Facing East: the direction of the axis of a Christian CHURCH, a pagan monolith HENGE (such as Stonehenge), and a Jewish SYNAGOGUE or MIZRACH.

original sin
The Christian belief in the human tendency to repeat Adam's sin in the Garden of Eden, a fall from GRACE which, though fortunate as the FELIX CULPA, requires BAPTISM to wash away the taint, vigilance to prevent further sinning, and sacramental reconsecration. Of all humankind, only the Virgin Mary was born free from original sin because of her IMMACULATE CONCEPTION.

orison
A prayer or magical incantation.

orle
(Latin *ora,* border, margin) A narrow heraldic band that bordered a shield, a knight's helmet, or a woman's headdress or CHAPLET, and represented the wearer's identifying COLORS.

ormolu
(French *d'or moulu,* ground gold) A GILDING for BRASS, BRONZE, or base-metal objects or ornaments, prepared from ground gold or from GOLD LEAF.

orphrey
An embroidered panel, usually of a vertical rectangular shape, either sewn to or worn over ecclesiastical COPES, CHASUBLES, and VESTMENTS, as well as royal garb. The panel was often jeweled and bordered with precious fringe and lace, depicting holy scenes, SYMBOLS, or saints and their ATTRIBUTES.

orpiment
A yellow paint pigment important in MANUSCRIPT ILLUMINATION, particularly HIBERNO-SAXON, related to REALGAR.

osculatory
A sacred object for kissing, such as a PAX.

ostensory
(Or ostensoir) A transparent holy vessel, PYX, or MONSTRANCE displaying the HOST or RELICS for worshippers' veneration.

ostinato
(Italian, obstinate) In thirteenth-century and later music, a clearly defined melodic phrase persistently repeated throughout a composition.

ostler
An oat merchant.

otherworlds
Past worlds, future worlds, and sites of afterlife were settings for imaginary voyages in DREAM VISIONS, such as Dante's DIVINE COMEDY, Christine de Pizan's *Road of Long Study,* and the Irish Saint Brendan's *Voyages.*

ounce
A panther-like feline beast appearing in BESTIARIES, sculpture, and painted decorations. The name originally was *lounce,* but lost the "l" through METANALYSIS.

out-Herod Herod
Pompous and loud shouting. Shakespeare propagated the expression taken from MYSTERY PLAYS in which Herod was portrayed as a loud, bombastic, stentorian-voiced man.

ouvert
(French, open) An ending for a repeated section in fourteenth-century musical forms such as BALLADS, ESTAMPIES, and VIRELAIS.

overpaint
A finishing layer creating fine shades of color, texture, and minute detail, applied after a preliminary layer or underpaint had established the artwork's form and design.

oviform
Egg-shaped.

ovolo
A decorative MOLDING design of convex quarter-round or quarter-ellipse elements in succession; contrast CAVETTO molding.

oxymoron
The paradoxical unity of opposites, usually in human emotion; for example, pleasurable pain and painful pleasure. ARS NOVA poet-composer Guillaume Machaut describes love as sweet suffering; TROUBADOURS, TROBARITZ, and MINNESINGERS expressed such simultaneous antitheses of affection in COURTLY LOVE.

oyez!
(Norman French, Hear Ye!) A crier's command for the audience's attention to the arrival in court of the judge, a jury's verdict, or a public proclamation.

P

page
A boy or youthful assistant to a servant, or a young knight in training to learn the arts and crafts of CHIVALRY. A page was also one of the CHILDREN IN DOMESTIC SERVICE before becoming a SQUIRE. Particular titles ranged from page of the stable, of the scullery, and of the NECESSARIUM, to page of honor and page of the back stairs.

palfrey
A civilian saddle horse for riding, not warfare, often covered with an ornamental CAPARISON.

paletot
A short GREAT COAT.

palinode
A retraction of what has been written, sometimes paired with the HUMILITY FORMULA. It was common as a religious, political, or professional protection against antagonism, censorship, jail, death, or danger to soul, for writing satirical or bawdy works, as Chaucer's in the *Canterbury Tales,* Jean de Meun's in the *Romance of the Rose,* and Andreas Capellanus's in his *Art of Courtly Love.*

palisade
A castle or fort's defensive fence of stakes.

pall
Originally a full cloak worn by a PHILOSOPHER; later, an ecclesiastical VESTMENT, often worn by an ARCHBISHOP, or an ALTAR-cloth, or a CHALICE cover at the EUCHARIST, or a coffin shroud at a funeral.

pallettes
ARMOR armpit protectors, steel plates shaped like saucers.

palmette
Stylized palm leaf ornament, in imitation of the classical anthemion decorative leaf and flower.

Palm Sunday
The Sunday before EASTER in HOLY WEEK, commemorating Christ's exultant entry into Jerusalem, just one week before his RESURRECTION. Penitents in procession carry palm fronds that symbolize Christ's victory and represent his protection.

paltoch
A PAGE's JACKET, a short fitted DOUBLET laced to HOSE, or to CHAUSSE and CODPIECE.

panacea
A universal medication, like THERIAC, thought to ameliorate a wide variety of symptoms, and used to treat and cure diseases ranging from the common cold to BUBONIC PLAGUE.

Panagia
(Greek, all holy) An Eastern Church title of veneration for the Virgin Mary. It is also the name for a small devotional amulet-portrait of the Virgin worn by Greek BISHOPs, and for a celebratory bread blessed in the Virgin's honor.

pandemayn
A daily bread, commonly made of white wheat, both eaten and used for TRENCHERS.

panderer
Lovers' friendly go-between, who arranged their assignations, sometimes for cash. The prototype is Pandarus, Troilus's friend and Criseyde's uncle, in Chaucer's poem *Troilus and Criseyde.*

Pange Lingua
(Latin, Sing, tongue) Either of two famous Latin HYMNS: one by Venantius Fortunatus in the sixth century, and the other by Saint Thomas Aquinas in the thirteenth century, who took the first line and TROCHAIC meter from Venantius and embellished them magnificently.

pannychis
An all-night VIGIL, a liturgical preparation for a feast in the Eastern church.

pan perdu
(French, *pain perdu,* lost bread, or *pain pour Dieu,* bread for God) Circlets of bread soaked in egg yolk, sautéed until golden, and sprinkled with cinnamon and sugar.

pan pipe
The SYRINX played by the God Pan, a prototype of the wind instrument in the PIPE AND TABOR.

pantaloon
The costume combining men's stockings and BREECHES, common in fifteenth-century Venice, and named after Saint Pantaleone. Later, the name referred to a character so garbed in Italian comedy, COMMEDIA DELL'ARTE.

pantler
A banquet hall and HOUSEHOLD servitor responsible for service of bread, preparation of TRENCHERS, and managing the SALT. He or she carried a SALT PLANER as EMBLEM as well as practical implement.

Pantocrator
(Greek, All Mighty) A portrayal of Christ, particularly in BYZANTINE art, as the creator of all the universe. Dignified and solemn, his right hand is raised in blessing, his left hand holding the GOSPELS or an ORB.

pantry
A room, closet, or cabinet for storing bread and creating TRENCHERS.

paper making
An industry which flourished in Spain and France in the twelfth century, and in Italy in the thirteenth century. Paper replaced PARCHMENT and VELLUM as the primary material for European MANUSCRIPTS by the late fourteenth century, and for printing in the fifteenth century. The paper craft was invented by the Chinese earlier than the Han Dynasty in the second century (the paper of Ts'ai Lun was made of tree bark, hemp, rocks, and fish net) and the process monopolized by the Arabs from the eighth through the twelfth centuries, usually in the form of CHARTA BOMBYCINA (Bagdad and Damascus, the major paper trade centers).

papsi
(French *passe-pied,* pass the foot) A dance particularly popular in Brittany; its rhythms affected contemporary instrumental music composition.

parable
A teaching tale with an explicit moral, similar to the EXEMPLUM. Examples include the WISE AND FOOLISH VIRGINS, the UNMERCIFUL SERVANT, and the PRODIGAL SON.

Paracelsan
Pertaining to the sixteenth-century physician, chemist, and ALCHEMIST Theophrastus Bombastus von Hohenheim, called Paracelsus. He vigorously opposed GALENICALS and medical applications of the FOUR HUMORS, and advocated use of MERCURY to treat syphilis and venereal diseases. Writing primarily in German not Latin, his popular books include *One Hundred and Fourteen Experiments and Cures.*

paradise
(Old Persian *pairidaeza,* a walled garden) A secure, eternal GARDEN, a perfect place of peaceful refreshment after long tribulation or after life.

paranomasia
The rhetorical art of punning. Words with double meaning often were half bawdy or scatological.

parapet
A defensive barrier wall of earth or stone at the edge of a RAMPART, balcony, roof, or platform, to prevent outsiders or enemies from seeing in or gaining entrance, and for preventing those walking on a high roof or dangerous balcony from falling off; a parapet often is bordered by a BALUSTRADE.

parcel gilt
A decorative technique GILDING only certain portions of a surface or carving.

parchment
Sheep or goat skin specifically prepared for writing and painting. Good quality parchment came from Pergamum in Asia Minor. The superior, more elegant variety was VELLUM, a major material for MANUSCRIPTS, finally superseded by PAPER MAKING.

par close screen
A screen dividing a CHANTRY chapel or tomb from the rest of the CHURCH.

pargetting
Ornamental patterned plasterwork.

parochet
The Jewish ceremonial curtain or veil protecting or decorating the holy ARK.

parody mass
An early sixteenth-century technique for a liturgical MASS that freely borrowed preexisting secular materials, not merely the CANTUS FIRMUS but whole compositions.

parousia
(Greek, presence or arrival) Christ's SECOND COMING.

partial signature
A musical technique used before the year 1500 allocating a musical signature (usually B flat) to some but not all voices in a polyphonic composition.

parti-colored costume
As in MI-PARTI, a garment vertically divided with the COLORS of two fabrics joined. In LIVERY, heraldic colors identified the HOUSEHOLD of the wearer; the jester or FOOL'S MOTLEY was parti-colored.

parti-colored hose
A fashion for men's tights or HOSE, each of the two legs wearing a different color; similar to MI-PARTI.

partimen
A Provençal TROUBADOUR DEBATE poem resembling the TENSON.

Jews at the first Passover eat the paschal lamb before leaving Egypt with their walking sticks for the desert. (From a German edition of the Old Testament, Cologne, 1479)

Pasch
(Aramaic and Greek, Passover) Both the Jewish PASSOVER or PESACH and the Christian EASTER.

paschal
(Greek form of Hebrew *Pesach,* Passover) Pertaining to the Christian feast of Christ's RESURRECTION. Celebrating the PASSION, death, and resurrection, Christ is depicted as the PASCHAL LAMB. A paschal candle symbolizing the risen Christ is lit on HOLY SATURDAY in a special candelabrum placed on the Gospel-side of the ALTAR. In Judaism, the word PASCHAL refers to PASSOVER and the symbolic foods of the SEDER.

paschal lamb
The lamb eaten at the Jewish PASSOVER or PESACH meal, the SEDER; or the Christian AGNUS DEI, Christ as sacrificial, PASCHAL Lamb of God. "Christ is the true lamb who has taken away the sins of the world, who by dying has overcome our death and by rising again has restored our life." (I Corinthians 5)

pas de brabant
A vivacious leaping dance related to the GALLIARD, ALTA DANZA, and SALTARELLO.

passa mezzo
A type of light PAVAN with a moderate tempo.

passant
A heraldic animal depicted as walking, with the right forepaw raised.

passant gardant
A heraldic animal PASSANT, with head turned towards spectator, as in the ARMS of England, which would be described as "GULES, three LIONS passant gardant in pale *or*."

passant regardant
A heraldic animal PASSANT, but looking backward towards its tail, to the SINISTER of the shield.

passementerie
Ornamental braiding on theatrical, secular, ecclesiastical, and military garments. It was often made of precious metals, with embroidery, beads, fringe, and BELLS.

passe pied
(Or passe papsy) An energetic, strenuous leaping dance with multiple cross-steps and back-steps.

Passion
(Latin *pati,* to suffer) The sufferings of Christ culminating in His CRUCIFIXION through which Christians are redeemed. Some INSTRUMENTS OF CHRIST'S PASSION depicted in art include nails, crown of thorns, lance, sponge, scourge and pillar, hammer, rope, dice, the head of Judas, hands (that struck Christ), rooster (that crowed after Peter's denial), and Saint Veronica's VERNICLE. The Passion is liturgically commemorated on GOOD FRIDAY and the TRIDUUM SACRUM.

Passion play
A drama concerned with the PASSION, CRUCIFIXION, and RESURRECTION of Christ. An example is the still popular German Oberammergau Passion play.

Passion Sunday
The fifth Sunday in LENT, also called JUDICA SUNDAY, the beginning of PASSIONTIDE and ending on HOLY SATURDAY. CRUCIFIXes, sculptures, and images in the church are veiled in purple.

Passiontide
The final two weeks of LENT, from PASSION SUNDAY to HOLY SATURDAY.

Passover
The Jewish harvest festival, PESACH, celebrating God's "passing over" the houses of the Israelites in Egypt whose doorposts protectively were marked with lamb's blood.

pastel
A fragile, impermanent, delicate painting technique using colored chalk. The pigment is mixed with just sufficient aqueous binder, like GUM TRAGACANTH, to allow its holding and transfer to the surface.

pastiglia
Ornamental imitation carving, mock BAS-RELIEF or REPOUSSE achieved with thick GESSO modeled, tooled, painted, or GILDED. Pastiglia was used on furnishing, panelling, and MOLDING, and sometimes for raised halos or wings decorating paintings.

Pastoureaux
(French, shepherds) The early fourteenth-century northern French peasant revolt, which promoted a pilgrimage to the Holy Land, the burning and pillaging of castles and towns, attacks on Jewish communities with special ferocity, and insurrections against the Church at Avignon. The revolt was suppressed when Pope John XXII excommunicated the participants and encouraged their destruction.

pastourelle
A thirteenth-century northern French or Provençal poem detailing sexual dalliance between a knight and shepherdess, celebrating country pleasures and natural erotic delights. If forced to seduction, the woman often humiliatingly outwitted the man.

paterae
Small, flat, circular or oval ornaments, either decorated with ACANTHUS leaves, or themselves depicting a stylized rosette.

Pater Noster
(Latin, Our Father) The first words of the LORD'S PRAYER. Often used as a PATTER by the seemingly pious or ignorant.

patina
A metal's or other medium's decorative and protective surface film, color, or texture, such as oxidized copper's "weathered" green copper carbonate; or the lacquers, polishes, and varnishes applied to surfaces

to retard corrosion, protect the surface, or create an artistic effect.

Patripassian
The third-century theologian Noetus of Smyrna believed that Christ was both God and Father, thus proposing that the major paternal element of the TRINITY suffered death in the flesh. This belief caused fierce debate and resulted in Noetus's excommunication. The issue was later resolved with the doctrine of Christ's dual nature as divinity and sufferer embodying AGERE ET PATI.

patronymic
A family name derived from the father's profession, place of origin, or particular personal quality. Contrast MATRONYMIC.

patten
A thick-soled, high-heeled shoe popular in Spain, Italy, and France, usually made of decorated leather, CUIR BOUILLI, or velvet, and worn over a slipper. When fitted with a blade, it was an ice skate.

patter
(Latin, *Pater Noster*) First words of the LORD'S PRAYER, "Our Father who is in heaven . . ." Gradually, the words became associated with the notion of a rapid repetitive recital of familiar words, sometimes nonsensical.

pavan
An elegant, stately processional dance performed by couples progressing in a circle or processing down a long hall or path. Popular in Italy, Spain, France, and England, it probably derived from the six basic steps of the BASSE DANCE. The pavan often was paired and alternated with the GALLIARD.

pawnbroker's balls
The three golden balls that are a SYMBOL for a pawnshop. The sign was derived either from the three bags of gold Saint Nicholas miraculously produced as a DOWRY for deserving young women, or from the three balls or PILLs of the Medici family, a pun on that medicinal PATRONYMIC.

pax
(Latin, peace) A silver, gold, bronze, ivory, or glass tablet or plaque, round, square, or rectangular, with a carrying handle behind. The front displayed a sacred scene such as the CRUCIFIXION or PIETÀ, and was kissed by the priest celebrating MASS, or carried in a procession, then passed to other clergy and the congregation for kissing and obeisance; an OSCULATORY.

peacock
A SYMBOL of immortality and of Christ's RESURRECTION because its flesh is thought not to decay. The peacock was also a fabulous feast dish, an ILLUSION FOOD: first carefully defeathered, then roasted with cumin, then refeathered, it looked alive. Its claws and beak GILDED, and cotton wool pressed into its beak ignited, the ardent bird appeared to breathe fire. Stimulating amorous inclinations, the dish was listed as a potent APHRODISIAC in medical texts and ARS AMATORIA.

peacock's tail
In ALCHEMY, the many-colored surface of a metallic chemical reaction, resembling the plumage of a PEACOCK.

pear
A beautiful fruit for eating and cookery, also considered an APHRODISIAC. It was an important Christian SYMBOL, and an emblem of sexuality. The pear was associated with the POMEGRANATE and the Garden of Eden's apple in the transmission of sexual knowledge. In literature, the pear-lust of a pregnant woman made the PEARTREE both symbol and site for sexual intrigue.

peartree
A tree bearing the succulent fruit thought to be an APHRODISIAC. Its limbs supported arboreal orgies (such as Chaucer's lusty May proved to her aged husband January in the "Merchant's Tale"). *Peartree* was a euphemism either for intercourse or a penis: FABLIAUX WOMEN who longed to pick a pear from a peartree actually lusted after male MEMBERS.

Peasants' Revolt
The sixteenth-century uprising of German peasantry because of economic and religious grievances expressed in the TWELVE ARTICLES. The ruthless, lawless mob was brutally exterminated by armies of Lutheran princes.

peasecod-bellied doublet
Worn by men with HOSE or CHAUSSE, an extravagantly wide and padded DOUBLET with a wooden or bone armature shaping the front section covering the genitals, the CODPIECE.

pecia
The piece or unit of work, usually a GATHERING, by which a copier of university texts was paid.

pedes
(Latin, feet) The two sections of the major stanza, the FRONS, of the tripartite courtly song of the TROUBADOURS, TROBARITZ, TROUVÈREs, and Italian writers of the DOLCE STIL NUOVO, followed by the CAUDA.

pedestal
A base supporting a column or sculpture.

pedule
A Northern European rawhide boot worn by men and women, sometimes laced to BREECHES.

pejoration
Progressive semantic development of a word's meaning from mild and decent to harsh and dreadful; for example, HARLOT originally meant a man with unknown occupation, an idler; opposite of AMELIORATION.

pele
A long-handled paddle for conveying bread, pies, and pastries to and from ovens.

pele tower
A fortified tower generally built on borderlands to protect castle and town against raiders.

pelican
Because the pelican was believed to pierce her breast to feed her young with her blood, the bird symbolized Christ's sacrifice for mankind's salvation through the act of His CRUCIFIXION. A DISTILLATION device used in chemistry and ALCHEMY.

pelicon
A woman's FUR-lined silk, wool, or fine fabric overTUNIC, usually knee-length and unbelted, sometimes adorned by a hip-GIRDLE and pouch.

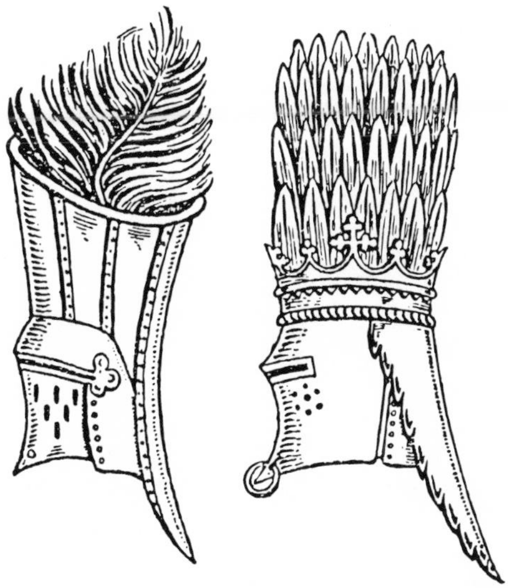

Penaches adorn the helmets. (From the helm of William de Latimer [left], and [right] Edward Courtenay, 1400; courtesy of C. H. Ashdown, *British and Continental Arms and Armour*, Dover Publications, 1970)

pelisse
A popular full-length, long-sleeved, fur-lined CLOAK worn by both men and women, resembling the PELICON, and in some countries identical to it.

pellicule
A fabric so delicate, diaphanous, and translucent yet strong, it was thought to resemble a pellicle, the membrane in an egg between its shell and the egg white.

pelta
A decorative ornament shaped like a Roman shield or a scroll-and-trumpet, often in HIBERNO-SAXON art.

penache
(Latin *penna*, feather) A feather plume or crest worn atop a helmet.

penance
(Latin *poenitentiae*, regret or repentance) In Christianity, a necessary precondition for forgiveness, a sinner's sufficient loathing of his sin as offense against God. The penitent expiates the sin by prayers and good works, such as fasting, PILGRIMAGE, and alms giving.

pentangle
(Or pentacle) A five-pointed star-like figure constructed as a continuous, endless, eternally renewable, inexorably perfect figure. It was the emblem of Sir Gawain's perfect VIRTUE and an occult sign of magicians.

Pentateuch
The five Books of Moses from the Old Testament: Genesis, Exodus, Leviticus, Numbers, and Deuteronomy.

Pentecost
(Greek, 50th Day) The Feast of Weeks, the 50th day after the Jewish PASSOVER or PESACH, commemorating both Moses's giving of the law and the first fruits of harvest. In Christianity, Pentecost is the seventh Sunday after EASTER, celebrating the descent of the HOLY GHOST to the APOSTLES. It is also called WHITSUNDAY.

pentimenti
(Italian, regrets) UNDERPAINTINGS usually with SINOPIA, demonstrati,ng an artist's changes, substitutions, reversals, and reworkings in the process of creation.

Perfecti
Especially zealous CATHARI abstaining from sex and meat, sometimes electing death by ENDURA.

pergola
A trellis-protected, shaded walkway popular in fifteenth-century Italy and England.

peristyle
A courtyard's interior COLONNADE.

perizonium
A loincloth.

pers
An exquisite, high-quality, rich, blue fabric important in Provence in the twelfth and thirteenth centuries.

persona
A fictional "I," a literary device in which the author speaks *as if* himself, using the familiar first person singular to create VERISIMILITUDE. An example is Chaucer, the erudite, personable author speaking in *The Canterbury Tales* as Pilgrim Chaucer, a rotund, shy, unintellectual gazer on the ground.

perspective
Artful representation of three-dimensional scenes on a two-dimensional surface, so that structures and figures intimate depth and natural spatial order. This illusion was the goal of experiments in ANAMORPHOSIS: by geometric plan and manipulation of light and shadow, figures and objects were depicted as if appearing to a spectator from a fixed point above, below, in front, or behind, to achieve by VERISIMILITUDE the distance, shape, proportion, and position. Variations in perspective important in art included aerial, isometrical, linear, parallel, and visual.

perspective cabinet
A box with a small hole or aperture, set on a table or stand, for viewing artistic illusions of ANAMORPHOSIS.

Pesach
The Jewish harvest festival (known also as PASSOVER) celebrating the biblical Exodus from Egypt, commemorated by a SEDER at which the HAGGADAH is read and MATZOH and HAROSET are served as symbolic foods. In Christian tradition, Pesach is remembered as Christ's LAST SUPPER.

pestle
A club-shaped, metal, wood, bone, or glass instrument for pounding, pulverizing, bruising, or mashing foods, medicinal herbs, or drugs in a MORTAR. A pestle is the ATTRIBUTE of the apothecary.

Peter's Pence
An ALMS FEE paid to the Pope, also called ROMESCOT.

petit-drap
A man's BREECHES.

Petrarchan
Associated with the fourteenth-century Italian poet Petrarch (1304–74), writer of the epic *Africa,* the ALLEGORY *Trionfi,* and exquisite sonnets celebrating his beloved Laura.

Petruslied
One of the two oldest non-liturgical German songs, dating from a ninth-century manuscript.

petticote
An undercoat worn by men and women beneath a SURCOAT. The overgarments were slashed or slit to allow the petticote's contrasting colors and ornaments to show through.

pewter
An alloy of tin with copper and antimony.

peytral
ARMOR for a horse's breast.

pfundnoten
(German, pound notes) Very long notes in the CANTUS FIRMUS of polyphonic compositions, such as the ORGANUM.

pharos
A lighthouse or marine beacon, named after Ptolemy Philadelphus's tower light at Alexandria.

philatory
A RELIQUARY shrine.

philosopher
An inquirer into the nature of things: ideas, ethics, human, and scientific phenomena; or an alchemist. Chaucer's clerk-philosopher had little gold in his coffers.

philosophers' stone
In chemistry and ALCHEMY, gold in its supreme, definitive form; or that which was able to transmute base metals into gold; metaphorically, the highest wisdom, the final achievement of emotional and intellectual perfection. Identified with an ELIXIR or PANACEA, a stone thought powerful enough to prolong life indefinitely and to cure all disease and injury.

philosophical egg
A combination of MERCURY plus SULPHUR and salt, thought in ALCHEMY important for particular chemical reaction, likened to the three essentials of a bird's egg (the white, yolk, and pellicle); or an ovoid vessel in which the mercury mixture was heated.

philtre
A potion or drug exciting sexual love, like an APHRODISIAC, or producing a magical effect, as the potion taken by Tristan and Isolde, causing their adulterous passion resulting in death.

phlebotomy
BLOODLETTING, a significant medical therapy, by one of three major techniques: FLEEMING, to create a simple incision in an artery or vein by a scalpel, a knife, or a fleem (also fleam, a LANCET); LEECHING, to apply live, bloodsucking leeches to various bodily points; or CUPPING, to place glass, wood, or porcelain vacuum cups on the body to draw blood from the nicked skin's surface. Phlebotomy was meant to diminish the patient's blood volume and reestablish equilibrium among the body's FOUR HUMORS. PULSE music directly or indirectly determined efficacy of

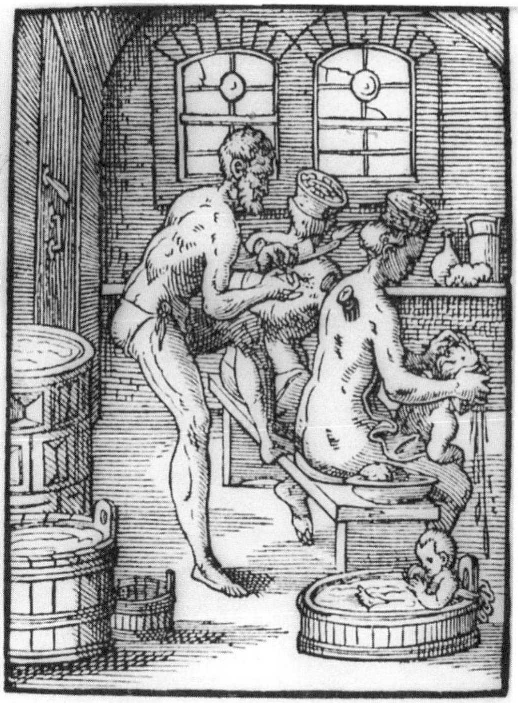

For phlebotomy by cupping, a bathhouse attendant lights the match for a cup while the patient washes one child's hair and watches the baby safely strapped in a bath. (From *Master of the Housebook*, German, 15th century; courtesy of Galeria Medievalia, Tenafly, New Jersey)

A physiognomy depicts foreheads signaling the irascible, vain, salacious, and vicious. (From engraving, Barthelemy Cocles, *Physiognomia*, Le Petit Bernard, Lyons, 1549)

bloodletting. Specific PHLEBOTOMY POINTs were indicated on a VEIN MAN or ZODIAC MAN.

phlebotomy point
An exact position on the human body from which arterial or venous blood could be drawn at specific seasons for general hygiene, for particular purposes to treat diseases or injuries, or to serve as an adjunct to medication or surgery. In BLOODLETTING calendars and PHLEBOTOMY manuscripts, the points were depicted upon an anatomical figure, the VEIN MAN (closely related to the ZODIAC MAN) and comparable to CAUTERY POINTS.

phlegmatic
A person possessing an overabundance of one of the FOUR HUMORS, phlegm, and therefore of slow, lethargic temperament, as depicted by PHYSIOGNOMY and predicted by GENETHLIALOGY.

phoenix
A centuries-old, gorgeously-plumed, unique, fabulous bird, consumed yet renewing itself by fire, dying to be reborn, its end its beginning. A classical beast described by Ovid, Herodotus, and Pliny the Elder, the phoenix was an important Christian SYMBOL of Christ's RESURRECTION, and used as a tomb adornment suggesting the possibility for life's renewal through death. Because solitary and self-sustaining, the phoenix was also an ALLEGORY for Chastity: no lust fires can consume her.

phonascus
The person charged with giving the musical tone or pitch and the timing beat in liturgical choirs.

Phrygian
One of the CHURCH MODES, having E as the tonic FINALIS.

phrygium
A white, woollen Papal cap worn at non-liturgical ceremonies, influencing the shape of the Papal TIARA.

phylacteries
Jewish symbolic, ceremonial, liturgical objects, bound to the forehead and the arm by observant celebrants, containing four VELLUM strips with passages from Exodus (13:1–16) and Deuteronomy (6:4–9 and 11:13–21).

physiognomy
The science associating human physical features with temperament as well as spiritual condition, based on GENETHLIALOGY and ASTROLOGY; a book or treatise, usually illustrated, describing the relationship between physique and personality.

physiologus
A moralizing BESTIARY in which natural history, empirical observation, and scientific thought are joined to ALLEGORY, religious instruction, and exuberant imagination. For example, as the beautiful pure-white CALADRIUS bird found in Jerusalem is said to possess

so benevolent a gaze that, if looking at a sick patient, it acquires the human illness and flies toward the sun, burning up the infirmities and curing the patient, so Christ "our Savior, all white," like the caladrius, turned His face to humanity and took upon Himself all the ills of the world.

piazza
A formal open space surrounded by buildings, approached through archways.

picardy third
In music around 1500, an interval of a major third used in the final chord of a composition in minor key.

pie powder courts
(French *pied poudre,* powder foot) Merchants' courts that adjudicated cases concerning those attending merchandise markets and produce fairs. The courts were so named because of the itinerants' dusty boots (thus, powdered feet).

pier
A solid masonry support for sustaining vertical pressure, as in a FLYING BUTTRESS; or a pillar for supporting an arch, gate, or door; or the wallspace between windows.

piercing
An ornamental design cut through wood, metal, leather, or ceramic ware, leaving an open-work pattern, allowing light to pass through.

Pietà
A representation of the crucified Christ who has been removed from the CROSS, often in the arms of the sorrowing Virgin, and surrounded by the THREE MARIES and various saints.

pietra dura
Rare marble and stone INLAY design, smoothed and highly polished for decorating tabletops, cabinets, jewel COFFERS, and small ostentatious objects.

pig
One of the most common domestic animals in Western Europe, often depicted in the TWELVE LABORS OF THE MONTHS for November (feeding on acorns) and December (being slaughtered, then salted, for winter food stores).

pigaches
Fashionable eleventh- and twelfth-century shoes with long, upturned, pointed toes, similar to the classical *calceus rependus.* They were a prototype of the extravagant POULAINES or CRACOWES.

pike
An important food fish and banquet staple on FEAST AND FAST menus; also, a martial weapon, comparable to the HALBERD, a sharply pointed metal head on a long wooden shaft.

pilaster
A square, rectangular, or rounded column anchored into a wall from which it projects with its own capital and base.

pilgrimage
A journey to a holy site either distant, like Jerusalem, or local, like the shrine of Saint James at Compostela, Spain. Pilgrimages were undertaken for several reasons: petition for aid, as in curing an illness; PENANCE imposed for sins committed or in hope of absolution; salvation insurance, accumulating good deeds early in life as later jewels in a heavenly crown; fulfillment of a secular vow, promise, or RASH BOON; safe travel, securing protection against violent acts of men (robbers and murderers) or nature (sudden storms); or opportunity to meet new friends or, for Chaucer's Wife of Bath, new spouses.

pilgrim's flask
A traveler's flat, stoppered bottle: a canteen for transporting liquid, with rings near the neck for carrying-cords that attach to arm, GIRDLE, or horse's saddle.

pilgrim's shell
The scallop shell, the BADGE or EMBLEM of pilgrims to Compostela, Spain, the shrine of Saint James the Greater. By the twelfth century, the shell was an INSIGNE for all pilgrims.

pill
(Latin, *pilula,* little ball) A small ball of medicine for swallowing whole; in HERALDRY, an EMBLEM or IMPRESSA in CANTING ARMS, as for the Medici family.

pillory
A public shaming device for criminals or accused malefactors, binding the head and hands to a pole, or thrusting them through boards cut to fit and restrain them. The punishment, usually lasting for a period of hours or days, exposed the offender to weather, ridicule, and attack. For women's marketplace larcenies, a THEWE was used.

pillow face
A form of DIVINATION, a pillow so punched and arranged that its creases seemed to form hidden faces or serendipitous heads that would foretell the future, as in Albrecht Dürer's *Six Pillows* (1493). For luck, a pillow might be stuffed with ERYNGIUM.

pinnacle
A small vertical ornamental TURRET terminating a buttress, roof, or COPING of a building.

pipe and tabor
A common musical instrument pair in courts and country market entertainments. The pipe was a single reed flute or RECORDER-like instrument; sometimes two were played simultaneously, or a row of pipes united to form the PAN PIPE or SYRINX. The pitch of the pipe was controlled by the fingers of one hand; the other hand held the baton that beat the small tabor drum, or else strummed the drum with the fingers, producing simultaneous percussion and melody.

piscina
A ceremonial basin in a church CHANCEL for the priest's hand-washing after rinsing sacred liturgical objects.

pismire
An ant, whose name may be derived from the urine-like odor of the ant hill. A pismire became a routine analogy in descriptions of fury, one of the SEVEN DEADLY SINS.

piss
Urine. Literary characters and real people purged it for health, for diagnostic URINALYSIS, and for contributing uric acid to alchemical experiments.

pittance
A small food gift allowed to members of religious communities on holidays, for good behavior, or at times of illness.

piva
An Italian BAGPIPE; the fastest dance step, embellished by leaps and quick turns, of the BASSE DANCE; also, the name of the most energetic early Renaissance dances.

plagal mode
A musical mode with the AMBITUS or range beginning with the fourth below the FINALIS and extending to the fifth above.

plague
The devastating contagious diseases flourishing in the fourteenth century as PNEUMONIC PLAGUE and BUBONIC PLAGUE, or the BLACK DEATH, dramatically affecting European economy, culture, psyche, and religion.

plague saints
Saints frequently invoked against the plague to prevent it or cure it: Saint Sebastian, Saint Roch, and Saint Nicholas of Tolentino.

plague searcher
A town health official, often a woman, who examined patients suspected of BUBONIC or PNEUMONIC PLAGUE. The plague searcher risked revilement, physical attack, and even murder for posting the sign of pestilence and quarantine upon a suspected house.

plague treatises
Medical essays on the causes, modes of transmission, methods of care for patients, and cures of plague, by fourteenth-century physicians and scientists. Writing in 1348, Gentile da Foligno attributed the cataclysmic BUBONIC PLAGUE, or BLACK DEATH, to airborne poisons which affected lungs and hearts; the contagious qualities of vapors and air provided for the facile and rapid spread of the disease, man to man, nation to nation. Astrological causes included the eclipses of the moon being timed with malevolent planetary conjunctions (as between Saturn and Jupiter), thus creating the necessary effects to poison the air. GE-

NETHLIALOGY predicted who within a population would remain immune from plague and who would fall victim.

plainsong
(Latin, *planus cantus,* flat or level song) A thirteenth-century name for GREGORIAN CHANT and other monophonic, vocal, rhythmically free, melodies. It is also the generic name for the FOUR MUSICAL DIALECTS of the Western church. Plainsong scales start from D, E, F, and G.

planctus
A formalized lament, COMPLAINT, or PLANH.

planh
A Provençal lament, PLANCTUS or COMPLAINT commemorating leave-taking, or panegyrically bemoaning a death.

planisphere
A flat disc or map with a polar projection of the complete heavens visible in a particular latitude, an important component of the ASTROLABE.

plastron
A protective metal ARMOR breastplate worn by warriors and fencers; also an adornment for a peasant costume, a STOMACHER laced to the bodice.

platen
The raised and lowered top of a printing press, moved by a pulled bar. Dürer depicted it, along with ink balls, the press bed, a composing stick, frisket, dividers, shears, and fixed, as well as moveable, type in a drawing of his godfather Anton Koberger's print shop in 1511.

Platonic
Pertaining to the ideas of the Athenian Greek philosopher Plato (fourth century B.C.). His ideals of statecraft and pure Ideas discussed in the *Republic* and the *Phaedo* influenced Christian and Jewish philosophy, ethics, and pedagogy. Descriptions in some Platonic dialogues inspired portraiture of the SEVEN DEADLY SINS and SEVEN CARDINAL VIRTUES. His *Timaeus* affected ideas about substance and style, SENTENCE and SOLACE; his *Symposium* influenced COURTLY LOVE.

Pleiades
The seven stars in the neck of the bull, Taurus. They were named after the daughters of Atlas and Pleione: Electra, Alcyone, Merope, Maia, Taygete, Celono, and Asterope. Astrologers maintained that viewing those stars could cause eye injuries and blindness.

plica
(Latin, fold or plait) A musical notation sign for an ornamental tone or grace note higher or lower than the main written notes. The sign was derived from the earlier QUILISMA.

plinth
A block between the bottom of a statue and its pedestal, or between a column's base and the ground.

pluvial
A floor-length, open-fronted MANTLE, worn as a ceremonial ecclesiastical VESTMENT and coronation regalia for nobility.

pneumonic plague
An epidemic infectious disease that attacks the human lungs, causing serious breathing disabilities and death. Pneumonic plague often has been confused with BUBONIC PLAGUE and the BLACK DEATH which raged in Europe, especially in the fourteenth century.

pocket-book
A small MANUSCRIPT for personal study and easy transport, written in MINUSCULE, such as a BOOK OF HOURS, as distinct from an ALTAR BOOK.

pockets
Pockets for stowing objects were sewn into a gown or cloak's AMIGAUT opening, hood point, CODPIECE, wide sleeve, or armpit gusset opening. Also, various external pouches and bags were attached to a waistband, hipbelt, or GIRDLE.

pointing
A sand-and-cement mixture, sometimes colored, used to reinforce and finish joints between bricks after their laying.

points
Metal-tagged laces for attaching HOSE or CHAUSSE to a DOUBLET or GIPPON.

pollution
Emission of noxious substances that could foul air or water was prohibited by continental and English laws (especially under Edward III) in the fourteenth century. In a sexual context, orgasm or involuntary ejaculation. Among clerical condemnations of women was their tendency to pollute men's bodies: based on ARISTOTELIAN teachings, Albertus Magnus and other devotees of WOMEN'S SECRETS instructed men to avoid women during menstruation and after childbirth.

polychromy
Many-colored painting and embellishment.

polyphonic
The intertwining musical voices of POLYPHONY exemplified by the composers and performers of the ARS NOVA and their progeny who created extravagant embellishments upon a CANTUS FIRMUS.

polyphony
Several separate instrumental or human voices in COUNTERPOINT with one another. Consisting of simultaneously performed melodies for each of several voices or parts, the music was arranged to emphasize the importance of each part's melodic line.

polyptych
An ALTAR-piece or devotional object with more panels than a DIPTYCH or TRIPTYCH.

pomander
An apple-shaped, segmented perfume or spice container.

pomegranate
A feast fruit and adornment because of its brilliant red color and pungent taste; and a complex SYMBOL. Because of its many seeds, the pomegranate was a sign of regeneration (classically the symbol of Proserpine, Queen of the Underworld), voluptuousness, fertility, and progeneration (like the PEAR or apple). In liturgical context, it represented virgin purity, chastity, Christ's RESURRECTION, and the Church itself (as multiple seeds/souls enclosed by one strong skin). The pomegranate inspired names of art objects (RIMMONIM), weapons (GRENADE), and, possibly, even cities (Granada, Spain).

Pomerium
Title of the important early-fourteenth-century treatise on MENSURAL MUSIC and POLYPHONY by Marchettus of Padua: *Pomerium artis musicae mensurate.*

Pope Joan
A legendary ninth-century female Pope, learned, politically adept, her male disguise finally ruined by pregnancy.

porcupine
Because BESTIARIES depicted it shooting its quills at enemies, the porcupine was a frequent animal BADGE of warriors, such as King Louis XII (1462–1515) in his IMPRESA.

porta clausa
(Latin, shut door) The closed gate, a sign of virginity, one of the VIRTUES OF THE VIRGIN (Ezekiel 44), comparable to the HORTUS CONCLUSUS. In racy lyrics and narratives, a chaste virgin's intact hymen was often juxtaposed with the WINNOWING BASKET.

portal
An entrance door.

portative organ
An ORGAN PORTATIVE.

portcullis
A castle or town gate. Heavy, gridded, and barbed, it was raised and lowered from within the walls as an important element of defense.

portico
An entrance to a building formed by a roof-covered COLONNADE.

portolan chart
From the fourteenth through the sixteenth centuries, a navigator's chart that depicted ports, coastlines, and compass points (RHUMB LINES) for plotting courses in the Mediterranean, the Black Sea, and the Atlantic coastal waters of Europe.

portpayne
A ceremonial cloth for carrying bread in the banquet hall.

posset
Milk heated until curdling, then combined with wine, ale, or spices, and drunk for pleasure or health.

post and lintel
A basic architectural unit of two or more upright posts supporting a horizontal beam, the lintel.

postern
A back gate.

Potiphar's wife
After her unsuccessful attempt to seduce young Joseph, Potiphar's wife vindictively accused him of having attacked her. He was sent to prison, only to be released later to interpret Pharoah's dream of the SEVEN FAT COWS AND SEVEN LEAN COWS (Genesis 39).

poulaines
(French, "Polish") Shoes with extravagantly long and pointed toes, fashionable in fourteenth- and fifteenth-century France and Burgundy. Also called CRACOWES, poulaines affected the gait, dance, and etiquette of the wearer; toe points sometimes were bound by thongs to the wearer's knees or belt for freer foot function. Following Polish fashion, poulaines were derived from the earlier PIGACHES.

pounce
A fine powder preventing ink from spreading and blurring on unsized paper.

pourpoint
A man's short, ceremonial coat, popular in France from the thirteenth through the fifteenth centuries. The coat had extravagantly wide shoulders which were padded with MAHOITREs and a tightly cinched waistline. The costume was good for displaying a magnificent physique, and often worn with POULAINES.

pou-sto
(Greek, where I stand) The ideal propitious place for accomplishing great feats. Greek (Syracusan) philosopher Archimedes stated that with a lever long enough and a proper place to stand, he could move the world. With the right instruments in the right place, nothing is impossible.

poverty
The condition of being poor was considered both a VICE and a VIRTUE. In Chaucer's "Wife of Bath's Tale," an old hag lecturing her fearful lover in bed, considered it a hateful good, an elicitor of ingenuity and industry, a mirror for viewing true friendship, and a possession no one would envy or steal.

powder horn
A flask for gunpowder, originally made from an animal horn ornamentally incised and decorated with metal or leather.

precinct
A CATHEDRAL CLOSE with all its auxiliary buildings.

predella
A devotional kneeling stool or its platform, or a step beneath an ALTAR-piece.

prefiguration
TYPOLOGY. Christian scholars, artists, theologians, and craftsmen interpreted the Old Testament as predictive, prefiguring, and foreshadowing the New Testament: *Omnia in figura contingebant illis* (All things were relating to those in form). In the Old Testament AKEDAH, Abraham's incomplete sacrifice of his son Isaac prefigured the Christian God the Father's offer of His son, Jesus Christ, for sacrifice.

pregnancy prevention
Methods to obstruct pregnancy were detailed in medical texts, DIETARIES, HERBALS, and obstetric and gynecological treatises both technical and popular. The twelfth-century WOMAN PHYSICIAN Dr. Trotula of Salerno's contraceptive techniques included coitus interruptus and other forms of SEED spilling, rhythm method intercourse, and herbal decoctions, like acorn steeped in fennel wine.

presbyter
An elder or overseer of the church, sometimes a BISHOP; the original title of a PRIEST.

prescription
Obtaining the right to use land against the express desire of its rightful owner, if the use is open, notorious, adverse, continuous, uninterrupted, and under a claim of right. It was comparable in land use to

The Presentation of Jesus Christ in the Temple. (Woodcut, Peter Drach, *Der Spiegel menschlicher Behaltnis,* Speyer, 1500)

ADVERSE POSSESSION in land title, a penalty for LACHES. A rightful owner not asserting a valid right loses it (likewise in modern American land law).

Presentation of Christ in the Temple
A Christian feast, February 2, that also coincides with the PURIFICATION FEAST or CANDLEMAS.

Presentation of the Virgin Mary
A Christian feast, November 21, celebrating the presentation of the Virgin in the Temple.

pretzel
Popular double-baked bread shaped in imitation of a young scholar's arms crossed on his chest in prayer.

pricken
In an equestrian context, to spur a horse; in a sexual conquest, to fornicate lustily.

pricket
A type of candlestick, differing from the CHAMBER CANDLESTICK, that impaled a wax candle upon a long upright point surmounting the usually elaborate metal-cast or wood-carved base.

prie-dieu
(French, pray to God) A household prayer furnishing designed with a low hinged seat, suitable for kneeling, that covered an enclosure for devotional books, and a high vertical section for resting a book or hands clasped in prayer.

priest
(Greek, *presbyter,* an elder) An ordained member of the Christian clergy, subordinate to a BISHOP, who celebrates MASS and administers the SEVEN SACRAMENTS.

prima materia
In alchemical theory, the still undifferentiated primal substance, chaos, or an unconscious, initial state of soul before removal of dross.

prime
First of the eight CANONICAL HOURS, celebrated usually at 6 A.M. by the singing of HYMNS, PSALMS, and

A street baxter sells pretzels while bakers prepare round loaves for customers. (From Ulrich Richtenthal, *Concilium zu Constanz,* 1483, Germany; courtesy of New York Public Library)

lessons of the DIVINE OFFICE, welcoming the new day.

primogeniture
Legal granting of a complete estate or total inheritance to the firstborn, excluding the other children. Those siblings, in an effort to eke out a living, swelled the ranks of abbeys, nunneries, mercenary armies, and bands of CADs.

Primum Mobile
(Latin, first mover) In the geocentric PTOLEMAIC UNIVERSE, the First Mover, the tenth sphere of the ancients, supposedly beyond the sphere of the FIXED STARs (the ninth sphere) which by its own motion was thought to whirl itself and all subordinate spheres around the earth every 24 hours.

primum querita regnum dei
(Latin, First seek out the Kingdom of God) Inscribed on churches and liturgical objects, from Matthew 6.

printer's devil
A fifteenth- and sixteenth-century printer's assistant, whose hands, face, and clothing were invariably blackened by printer's ink; also, the affectionate (or pejorative) name given to the black-skinned assistant of the Venetian printer Aldus Manutius.

privity
A legal relationship, as in a buyer to a seller, a lessee to a lessor, or a donee to a donor.

privy
An outhouse or NECESSARIUM; or genitalia.

prodigal son
From Luke 15, the PARABLE of two sons, one who dutifully worked at home and obeyed his father, the other who solicited whores, gambled, and prodigally squandered his patrimony. Nevertheless, the profligate young man, returning home as a penitent, was welcomed joyously by his father because the son, who was as if dead, returned to life, the one who was lost was found. Likewise, God forgives repentant sinners.

progress
A ceremonial journey; for a nobleman, king, or queen, a movement from one castle to another to examine landholdings, to provide practical and legal oversight, and to reaffirm political control.

prohibition
An astrological frustration of two planets nearly in conjunction but with a third one interposing itself, thus affecting the fates of human beings ruled by the expected conjunction.

prolation
A musical indicator in MENSURAL NOTATION of the relationship between the semibreve and its three or two MINIMs.

Promethean
Associated with Prometheus, the heroic Greek thief of fire and transmitter of light to humankind. For those actions against the gods, he was punished by being chained to a rock, where an eagle daily fed on his liver; however, he was finally released by the hero Hercules. In *typology,* Prometheus is a PREFIGURATION of Christ, the bringer of the light of Truth who suffered but because of the FELIX CULPA was freed by RESURRECTION.

proper
The varying and changeable elements of the Christian MASS, opposite of the ORDINARY.

proportion
In musical MENSURAL NOTATION, the shortening or lengthening of note values according to arithmetic ratios.

prorogation
In ASTROLOGY, the direction of a predictor of the length of a person's life.

Protomartyr
Saint Stephen, the first martyr (Acts 6–7), stoned to death because of his vituperative address to the Sanhedrin accusing the Temple Fathers of being "stiff-necked" in their refusal to recognize Jesus Christ as the Messiah.

pryvete
Private parts or genitalia.

psalm
A sacred song or HYMN sung in private devotion, during the eight CANONICAL HOURS, or in public prayer; also, one of the Old Testament Psalms of David, contained in a PSALTER.

psalmody
In Christian LITURGY, the singing of PSALMs in one of three ways: in straight choral singing (direct psalmody) of the song; in RESPONSORIAL SINGING, alternating between chorus and soloist; or in ANTIPHONAL singing, alternating between two choirs. Psalmody is descended from Hebrew CANTILLATION.

psalmtone
One of the GREGORIAN tones or CHANTs giving musical setting to a PSALM.

psalter
A PSALM book for use both in church and in private prayer. A psalter generally contained miscellaneous other prayers, a COMPUTUS calendar, depictions of the TWELVE LABORS OF THE MONTHS, and Old Testament stories, especially those which were PREFIGURATIONs of New Testament episodes. Used for praying at the CANONICAL HOURS, it was a less comprehensive prayerbook than a BREVIARY but for some patrons was as richly illuminated as the most sumptuous BOOK OF HOURS.

psaltery
A plucked ZITHER, a common stringed instrument played not only in town and court but also, according to many artistic depictions, in heaven by ANGELS, saints, King David, and the NINE MUSES.

psychomachia
(Latin, war within the mind) A mind-battle in which conflicting ideas war for the individual's choice. The term harks back to Prudentius's *Psychomachia,* a remarkable fourth-century ALLEGORY that personified the SEVEN DEADLY SINS and other abstract ideas, later to become the important intellectual habit and art form.

Ptolemaic universe
The generally accepted concept, popularized by Ptolemy, that the planets and stars orbited around the earth in a geocentric cosmic design, guided by the PRIMUM MOBILE. This concept was superseded by the COPERNICAN REVOLUTION.

pudding-basin cut
A hairstyle for fifteenth-century men in which the neck and temple hair were shaved, leaving hair on the head in the shape of a skullcap.

pudendum
(Latin, the shameful thing) A circumlocution for vagina; also, QUEYNT, QUONIAM, BEL CHOSE, and PRYVETE.

pulpit
A raised preaching platform.

pulpitum
A gigantic stone screen separating a CATHEDRAL CHOIR from a NAVE.

pulse
Physicians metered patients' pulse at the brachial artery, wrist, and axilla, calculated the rhythm, strength, and regularity of the pulse, and compared their data against pulse music treatises by such venerable physicians as Galen (whose 16 books on pulse distinguished among 27 pulse varieties). Following Galen, Avicenna, and Peter of Abano, medical practitioners felt by TACTUS ERUDITUS (an informed touch) the *pulsus formicans* (ant-like beat), *pulsus gazellans* (gazelle-like beat), as well as such traits as consonance, dissonance, and scale. A PULSILOGIUM reaffirmed tactile accuracy.

pulsilogium
Galileo's ingenious pendulum device for counting PULSE rate. The invention developed from his discovery of the isochronal properties of the pendulum (when bored at a Duomo service, he timed the altar lampswings to his own pulse rate), and was not superseded until the eighteenth century by Sir John Floyer's portable physicians' pulsewatch.

punch
A metal tool used for CHASING and other incising of metal for decoration.

punctate
A design with minute spots, dots, or depressions, resembling punctures.

punctus
In musical MENSURAL NOTATION, a dot or point after a note adding to its value; an indicator of PROLATION; or each of the three repeated sections in the ESTAMPIE.

Purification Feast
Following Judaic tradition (Leviticus 12) of sacrificing two turtle doves and two young pigeons for ritual purification of a new mother, the Christian feast of Purification (Luke 2:22) commemorates the consecration of Christ at the Temple in Jerusalem, which rite simultaneously purified his mother, Mary. The feast is celebrated on February 2 as CANDLEMAS, with ritual processions with lighted candles.

Purim
The Jewish spring festival recorded in the biblical book of Esther, commemorating the triumph of the Jews over Persian King Ahasuerus's edict to kill them. Thanks to Mordecai's and Queen Esther's outwitting the evil Haman, the law was rescinded. The holiday is celebrated with symbolic foods, prayers, rejoicing, SIVLONOT, and sounding of GREGORS.

purpura
In HERALDRY, one of the SIX TINCTURES, the color purple; its modern spelling results from DISSIMILATION.

pursuivant
At JOUSTS, an apprentice HERALD, an announcer of ARMS and HOUSEHOLD of knights performing in battle.

putto
(Latin *putus,* pure one; plural, *putti*) A winged chubby child; if in amorous or sexual context, an AMORETTO, a little lover or Cupid; in a religious context, a CHERUB or ANGEL.

puys
Literary and musical competitions in France and Provence from the eleventh through sixteenth centuries, influencing similar artistic contests elsewhere, as among German MINNESINGERS.

pyrography
Wood burning; the art of designing or drawing on wood with a heated metallic point or cylinder burning in the lines.

pyromancy
Divination by fire, the occult opposite of HYDROMANCY.

pyx
An elaborate container or CIBORIUM for the wafer of the EUCHARIST.

Q

Quadragesima

The 40 days of LENT.

quadrant

A timing and measuring device in the shape of a quarter-circle, used by navigators, astronomers, astrologers, and physicians. Chronophysicians computed propitious moments for PHLEBOTOMY, medication, or surgery using a quadrant, ASTROLABE, VOLVELLE, or BLOODLETTING CALENDAR. A physician carried a quadrant among other equipment as a VADE MECUM.

quadrivium

The four mathematical and scientific studies: Arithmetic, Geometry, Astronomy, and Music. Combined with the TRIVIUM (Grammar, Rhetoric, and Logic), they comprised the SEVEN LIBERAL ARTS of the university curriculum.

quadruplum

The fourth musical part above the TENOR of the ORGANUM and the CLAUSULA.

quaintise

A COINTISE.

quarrel

The missile replacing the earlier arrow of the CROSSBOW.

quarternaria

A SALTARELLO.

Quasimodo Sunday

The first Sunday after EASTER, called LOW SUNDAY, the name derived from the opening words of the INTROIT of the MASS: *quasi modo geniti,* As if in the manner of a newborn.

quatrefoil

Four-leaved.

Quatrocento

The fifteenth century.

Quatro Coronati

(Latin, Four Crowned Ones) Four martyrs especially honored by stone masons. Apparently, four fourth-century stonecarvers, Simpronian, Claudius, Nicostratus and Castorius (plus a fifth, Simplicius, inexplicably excluded from honor), refused to obey the Roman emperor's command to sacrifice to the Sun god; as punishment, they were sealed alive in lead boxes, thrown into a river, and drowned.

quem quaeritis trope

A short Latin TROPE that became an important dramatic interpolation into the EASTER MASS and influenced the development of liturgical drama, including the PASSION PLAY and MIRACLE, MYSTERY, and MORALITY PLAYs. The trope started simply: the THREE MARIES arriving at Christ's tomb to anoint his body met angels asking, "Servants of Christ, Whom do you search for in the sepulcher?" (*Quem quaeritis in sepulchro o Christicolae?*) They answered, "Servants of Heaven, We look for Jesus of Nazareth, crucified!" (*Jesum Nazarenus, crucifixum, o coelicolae!*) Chanted or sung antiphonally, the scene was embellished by amusing JOCULATORES characters (like the UNGUENTARIUS and MILES GLORIOSUS) and enough bawdy and raucus elements to expell this proto-drama from the church to the market place. The trope comes from the ninth-century Saint Gall Manuscript.

querent
A questioner, particularly one requesting an astrological prediction by computation of a HOROSCOPE.

queued
In HERALDRY, a tailed beast, which may even be DOUBLE QUEUED.

queynt
A vagina. Chaucer's Wife of Bath, proud of her own voluptuous vulva, refers to it with such affectionate circumlocutions as QUONIAM and BEL CHOSE. A man making a woman's "acqueyntaunce" may simply have met her or may know her carnally. The Jewish satirist Emmanuel of Rome, a friend of Dante, magnificently punned this word.

Quia Emptores
(Latin, because the buyers) England's Parliament enacted a statute in 1290 forbidding SUBINFEUDATION of freehold estates, making all land transfers SUBSTITUTIONS. The law helped the king and overlords regain profits from land TENURE agreements.

Quicumque vult
(Latin, Whoever wishes) The initial words of the ATHANASIAN CREED, followed by *salvus esse* (to be saved).

quid pro quo
(Latin, what for what) An alphabetical table of drugs and their substitutes, or a list of poisons and their antidotes. Such practical texts common in vernacular languages were required reading in medical curricula for men and WOMEN PHARMACISTS and men and WOMEN PHYSICIANS.

quilisma
In the musical notation of PLAINSONG, a particular NEUME or sign usually falling between two notes with a third interval between, probably to be sung with trill or tremulo, later becoming the PLICA.

quillon
One of two arms of a sword's cross guard, the crosspiece dividing blade from hilt and protecting the hand holding the sword.

quince
A piquant orange-colored pear-shaped fruit, significant in desserts, meat dishes, breads, and medication. Depicted in sacred art, the quince was held by the infant Christ, as symbolic of the sweet fertility of perfect idea.

Quinquagesima
The 50 days between EASTER and PENTECOST, beginning on the Sunday before ASH WEDNESDAY and marked by an abstinence from meat, liturgical alterations, and personal deprivations of LENT.

quinque viae
(Latin, five roads or ways) Five arguments from the *Summa Theologica* of Saint Thomas Aquinas to prove the existence of God: all motion requires a First Mover; all effects need a first cause; the existence of anything mandates a necessary being to cause existence; all comparisons require a perfect standard; and the purposes of inanimate objects demand a directive intelligence.

quinta essentia
(Latin, fifth quality) The fifth principle, the quintessence or ethereal aspect of astrological, chemical, and medical substances.

quire
A GATHERING of four sheets of paper, PARCHMENT, or VELLUM folded to form eight leaves of a MANUSCRIPT; sometimes 24 separate leaves.

quistron
A kitchen boy in a large HOUSEHOLD, charged with the rough culinary work of stirring the contents of gigantic pots, moving heavy BLANDRETHs, and winching weighty cauldrons.

Qui tollis peccata mundi
(Latin, You who take away the sins of the world) Words celebrating Christ, taken from the GLORIA of the MASS. The expression was also associated with the patron saints of lost causes, Saint Jude and Saint Thaddeus.

quod libet
(Latin, what is pleasing) In thirteenth-century music and later, a melodic and textual joke combining famil-

iar elements incongruously juxtaposed, such as MOTETs with raunchy secular TROUBADOUR or TROUVÈRE melodies combined with sacred liturgical themes of GREGORIAN CHANT. Also, it was a twice-yearly rhetorical exercise in the universities, especially at Paris before CHRISTMAS and EASTER: a master disputed any question the participants demanded; the subject could be abstruse, theological, practical, or trivial. A famous example is Saint Thomas Aquinas's argument on existence of the soul.

quoins
(French *coins,* corners) External cornerstones in brick or stone architecture.

quoniam
A vagina or PUDENDUM.

Quo vadis?
(Latin, Where are you going?) Saint Peter, in flight from Rome, met Christ on the Appian Way and asked, "Lord, where are you going?" Christ answered, "I am coming to be crucified again." Peter interpreted this "second CRUCIFIXION" as Christ suffering for one of his 12 disciples, and so returned to Rome for martyrdom.

R

Rabbi Gamaliel's dream

The tutor of Saint Paul and grandson of Hillel, the great Rabbi Gamaliel appeared in a dream to the PRIEST Lucian who later discovered the RELIC of the PROTOMARTYR, Saint Stephen.

rabelin

In architecture, a castle's defensive wall angle, pointing towards the likely direction of attack.

racket

A reedy-sounding wind instrument. It was short and thick, with wooden or ivory cylinders that were pierced lengthwise by cylindrical channels arranged in a circle. The central cylinder had a blowing cup, the pirouette, of one of five sizes: treble, alto, tenor, bass, and double bass.

racking crook

An ingenious ratchet device for raising and lowering large kitchen cauldrons, pots, BLANDRETHs, and cooking vessels.

radix

(Latin, a root) The essential beginning, as *radix malorum est cupiditas,* greed is the root of all evil. In GENETHLIALOGY, it was the ZODIAC configuration visible in BIRTH TIME MIRRORs or CONCEPTION TIME MIRRORS.

rampant

Fierce, vicious, high spirited; in HERALDRY, describing an animal such as a LION rearing up on its hind legs, its forepaws extended.

A racking crook lifts a heavy cauldron for preparation of ceremonial meats. (From a 12th-century manuscript of the Old Testament; courtesy of Pierpont Morgan Library, New York)

rampart

An earthwork fortification, a mound of earth usually surmounted by a PARAPET; three ramparts together comprise a TRIVALLATE fortification.

random rubble

A wall construction technique using irregularly shaped stones.

The *radix malorum* as root of the tree of life and of sexuality. (From woodcut, Bible, Verard, French, c. 1502; courtesy of the Metropolitan Museum of Art)

rape
Abduction or kidnap. Thomas Malory's "rape" of a maiden and Chaucer's "rape" of Cecily seem to have had no sexual import, simply the unwilling transport from place to place. *Rape* was also the name of a vegetable (the turnip, radish, field-mustard, or cole-seed) eaten by people or cultivated for sheep feed and rape-oil.

rapes
A savory dish of beans and vegetables, such as turnips, lentils, or other kinds of RAPE mashed in a mortar with breadcrumbs, spices, and herbs.

rapier
A short, small sword useful for rapid thrusting.

rash boon
A rash promise or VOW; an impulsive pledge of word leading to unexpected consequences, usually dire. Important in MÄRCHEN and GEIS, a rash boon is the literary stimulus for Chaucer's "Merchant's Tale" and the actual incentive for some PILGRIMAGEs.

rath
In Ireland, a circular enclosure with earthen walls, usually fortified, sometimes the home of a warrior chief. The word is preserved in Irish place-names, though some hill forts are called Daneraths because of incorrectly ascribing them to Danish invasion, as in the DANELAW.

rauschpfeif
A small, reeded, wind instrument related to the oboe, with one finger hole in the back, seven in the front.

ray
In astronomy, a beam of light emanating from a star or luminous body; in ASTROLOGY, a beam of INFLUENCE or sympathy accompanying a star's light.

raye
A fabric popular in the twelfth and thirteenth centuries, with horizontal stripes of contrasting colors.

rayere
A tall, narrow opening for admitting light in a thick castle wall; a slender LANCET.

real covenant
A promise to do or not to do a particular thing concerning use of land.

realgar
Red sulfide of arsenic used for preventing putrefaction of GLAIR, and for fireworks.

rear-vault
A structural or decorative VAULT behind a BAY, often in a GOTHIC CATHEDRAL.

rebec
A slender-necked, stringed instrument, played held at the chest or between the knees, and bowed.

rebis
An alchemical hermaphrodite uniting male and female principles and chemical opposites.

rebras
A garment's REVERS.

reciting note
In PLAINSONG, the dominant musical note on which the intermediate words of each of a PSALM's verses are sung.

reconciliation
A ceremony of readmission of public penitents into the community on MAUNDY THURSDAY. In the INQUISITION of heretics, the ceremony of repenting and recanting error, of saving of the soul, and of allowing the body to burn in a state of grace.

recorder
A beaked whistle-FLUTE. This most popular musical instrument was fashioned in six ranges, families, or consorts: double bass, bass, tenor, alto, soprano, and sopranino.

rectangulus
An astronomical instrument created in the fourteenth century by Richard of Wallingford, ABBOT of St. Albans. It consisted of four brass rules hinged and mounted by a swivel joint atop a pillar. The lowest rule was engraved with a scale separated into sixes, demonstrating the difference between duodecimal and decimal systems.

rectilinear
Describing a decorative ornament characterized by ruler-drawn right angles. Compare CURVILINEAR.

recto
The right hand page of an open book, or the upper side of a VELLUM, PARCHMENT, or paper sheet. Opposite of VERSO.

rederijker
A wealthy burger-poet, a member of a Dutch Chamber of Rhetoric, who composed formulaic poetic and dramatic works, comparable to the German MEISTERSINGER.

red letter day
An important Christian feast or saint's day, noted in a MANUSCRIPT in red ink, by RUBRIC, as opposed to the less important BLACK LETTER DAY.

red lion
In ALCHEMY, the mineral matter remaining after the process of SUBLIMATION (also called EAGLE after a GREEN LION has been achieved). Literary references to colored beasts usually were arcane chemical names.

refectory
The dining hall of a MONASTERY, castle, or manor house. Generally it contained a dais for the HIGH TABLE, a MUSICIANS GALLERY, a TRENCHER table, AUMBRY, *banquettes,* and SIDEBOARDs.

regal
A small reed organ, the pipes of which were shaped like cylindrical clarinet beaks. The Bavarian bible regal could be folded and packed into its book-shaped bellows; when closed, it resembled a large book of Scripture.

regardant
A heraldic animal with a raised head turned to SINISTER or to the left side of a shield.

Regina Coeli
(Latin, The Queen of Heaven) A title of the Virgin Mary. She was often depicted as a crowned, regal figure, holding her child Christ, and surrounded by an entourage of 144,000 virgins. These included innocents, such as the young child in the alliterative DREAM VISION *Pearl.* Among the other VIRTUES OF THE VIRGIN was her exalted motherhood as MATER MARIA DEI (Mary, Mother of God) and SANCTA DEI GENITRIX (Holy Mother of God).

regrator
A retailer who bought merchandise or produce at wholesale and sold at a profit.

reien
Vigorous, vivacious summer songs (winter songs are TÄNZE) by MINNESINGERs such as Neidhart von Reuenthal. The songs imitated rustic dance rhythms and celebrated simple, natural, pastoral gratifications, both aesthetic and sexual.

relic
A holy, esteemed, or revered object, such as a bone, a strand of hair, an article of clothing, or a particle of a possession thought to belong to a dead saint or holy figure, and usually preserved in a RELIQUARY.

relief
In either BAS RELIEF or HIGH RELIEF, sculpture raised from a plane or curved surface for decorative, symbolic, or utilitarian purposes. In land law, it was a feudal INCIDENT, a payment to an overlord for the privilege of inheriting TENURE of land.

reliquary
A box, casket, shrine, or vessel to preserve a RELIC. Reliquaries were decorated with precious jewels, ENGRAVING, REPOUSEE, ORMOLU, NIELLO, ENAMEL, and FILIGREE, sometimes a MONSTRANCE or CROSS, and often in the shape of a hand, a head, a leg, or an anatomical part corresponding to the relic. ROCK CRYSTAL or glass permitted the object to be seen. ROMANESQUE and GOTHIC reliquaries were especially magnificent.

relish
A musical ornament used in the performance of early English lute, viol, and keyboard compositions, consisting of alternating adjacent notes or trilling successive notes.

remanieur
(French, revisor) A French or Burgundian writer of the fifteenth century who revised Old French CHANSONS DE GESTES with the morality and favored prose style of the newly wealthy middle class.

remedia amoris
(Latin, the remedies of love) In HERBALS, DIETARIES, medical texts, and ARS AMATORIA, recipes for APHRODISIACS and herbal baths either to increase or suppress libidinous interest. These included directions for assuring prophylaxis against MELANCHOLY, and adherence to Saint Paul's insistence that it is better to marry than to burn with passion. Also, the title of texts inspired by Ovid's classical treatise of the same name.

rennes
A variety of CHAINSIL cloth.

repetenda
A common musical technique in the eighth through eleventh centuries, adding PSALM VERSES (*versus ad repetendum*—verses to be repeated) to GREGORIAN CHANT when necessary to extend the music or to augment the text.

replevin
Legal recovery of possession of property wrongfully taken, opposite of TROVER.

repoussé
A metal embellishing technique, EMBOSSING, by hammering or pushing a design into RELIEF from the reverse of the sheet or object.

requête d'amour
(French, request for love) An appeal for love in a courtly LYRIC, DREAM VISION, or ROMANCE, in which hyperbolic praise of the beloved was paired with constant self-deprecation.

requiem
(Latin *requies,* rest) A text of the MASS for the dead, beginning with the INTROIT: *Requiem aeternum dona eis, domine,* Lord, give them eternal rest.

repriese
A BASSE DANCE step: a slight shaking or circular movement of the foot, first with one then the other leg.

reredos
(Anglo-Saxon, behind the back) A curtain, row of arches, painting, or ornamental decoration behind the ALTAR in a CHURCH or CATHEDRAL.

res controversa
(Latin, the disputed matter) In CIVIL LAW, a question in controversy.

rescripta
Papal answers to specific questions on church doctrine and custom, as in the DECRETALS.

res facta
(Latin, a completed work) A fifteenth-century musical composition completely written out in all parts, as opposed to an improvised fauxbourdon.

res gestae
(Latin, things done) In law, admission into evidence of an eyewitness' spontaneous, excited utterance or revelation otherwise thought inadmissible hearsay.

res integra
(Latin, a matter untouched, a thing unopened, virgin) A legal subject untouched by law court decision or dictum, considered in court for the first time.

res ipsa loquitur
(Latin, the thing speaks for itself) In law, a refutable inference of negligence or guilt from the apparently reasonable belief that an event occurred only because of negligence and could not have occurred without it.

res judicata
(Latin, matter adjudicated) The legal ban on relitigation of claims already completely and fairly tried.

res nova
(Latin, new things) In law, a new case, which may be RES INTEGRA.

res nullius
(Latin, no one's property) Property unowned, abandoned, or unownable.

responsorial singing
The performance of GREGORIAN CHANT by alternating soloist and chorus. Compare ANTIPHONAL singing.

responsorium
Liturgical CHANTs derived from responsorial PSALMODY. Solo VERSE alternates with a choral refrain, as in the early GRADUAL of the MASS and ALLELUIA.

res universitatis
(Latin, property of the whole) A common—a town or municipal property open to the use and enjoyment of its citizens.

resurrection
On the third day after CRUCIFIXION, Christ's rising from the dead and being seen by the THREE MARIES and the TWELVE APOSTLES (Mark 14:50), an event celebrated during HOLY WEEK.

retable
A rectangular stone, metal, or wood panel backing an ALTAR; a shelf or ledge supporting ornaments; or a frame enclosing elaborately painted or decorated panels.

rete
The stylized star map of an ASTROLABE.

reticulated tracery
(Latin *reticulum,* a small net) Gothic stone TRACERY with ornamental APERTUREs resembling net mesh.

reticule
A hairnet, or a net-like design.

retrochoir
Part of the CHANCEL behind the east end of the high ALTAR.

retrograde
Backward or contrary movement, as in WIDDERSHINS. In ASTROLOGY, it is the apparent movement of a planet in a direction contrary to the order of the signs.

Revelation
The last book of the New Testament, the APOCALYPSE of Saint John the Apostle. Recording his vision of the future as it appeared to him while in exile on the Island of Patmos, where he had been sent in A.D. 95 by the Roman emperor Domitian, he wrote prophecies, instructions, and warnings about the end of the world, such as the coming of the FOUR HORSEMEN OF THE APOCALYPSE, the perils of the SEVEN CHURCHES, and the breaking of the SEVENTH SEAL.

reverence
An elegant, graceful bow in a dance.

revers
The edge or border of a garment turned up or turned back, as in a coat, glove, bodice, or hat; the revers usually had a contrasting color or texture or was decorated with embroidery or braid.

revetments
Stone or timber supports or projections for protecting an EARTHWORK bank.

Rhenish potteries
From the fourteenth through the sixteenth centuries, earthenware manufacturers at Cologne, Raeren (near Aachen), and Siegburg specialized in BELLARMINEs, TIGERWARE, SCHNELLEs, SCHNABELKANNEN, and similar salt-glazed kitchen, banquet, or tavern ware.

rheno
A twelfth-century hoodless, short cloak lined with sable, ERMINE, miniver, and similarly expensive FUR. The garment was favored by the Angevin nobility.

rhetoriqueur
Like the Dutch REDERIJKER, a French or Burgundian poet experimenting with forms, stanzas, and meters that were non-courtly and morally appealing to prosperous merchants.

rhinoplasty
The surgical procedure for reconstruction of the nose by grafting, or by raising a pedicle flap of skin with inherent blood supply from the arm, for patients injured by violence, war, or accident, or congenitally disfigured or born without a nose. The procedure was initiated by father-and-son physicians, the Doctors Branca, in Sicily in the fifteenth century and popularized in the sixteenth century by the surgeon of Bologna, Dr. Gaspare Tagliacozzi.

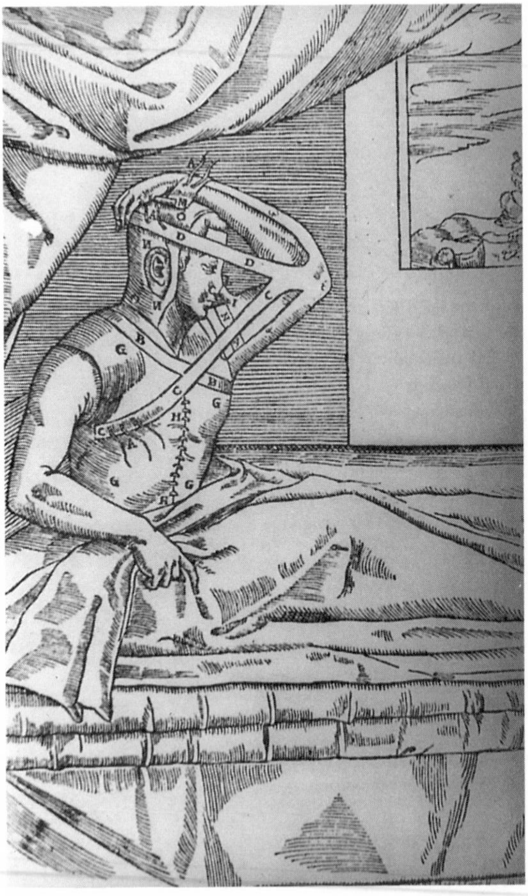

A rhinoplasty patient is immobilized with a Tagliacozzi vest. (From *The Life and Times of Gaspare Tagliacozzi, Surgeon of Bologna*, Martha Teach Gnudi and Jerome Pierce Webster, New York)

rhumb line
A navigator's compass point for plotting a course, as in a PORTOLAN CHART.

rhyme royal
Chaucer's seven-line stanza (rhyming ab, ab, bc, c) appearing in *Troilus and Criseyde*, the *Parliament of Fowls,* and in several *Canterbury Tales.* The rhyme scheme also was used by the SCOTTISH CHAUCERIANS.

rhythmic mode
A rhythmic pattern in twelfth- and thirteenth-century POLYPHONIC composition that was thoroughly consistent in each part.

rib
According to the Old Testament, the source of woman. In one account, Eve was created from a rib removed from Adam's side (Genesis 2:21,22), contradicting the account of her earlier creation in God's own image (Genesis 1:27) (the TWICE TOLD EVE). In architecture, a rib is the projecting, reinforcing band of a pointed arch or VAULT, often elaborately ornamented. A diagonal rib, in a GROINED VAULT, passes angle-to-angle to intersect another rib at the center; a transverse rib stretches from wall-to-wall; a wall rib directly adheres to a wall.

ribibe
A worn-out old woman, once sexually interested and interesting.

ricercare
(Italian, to seek out) A sixteenth-century experimental musical instrumental composition, as in Marc Antonio da Bologna's *Ricercare, Moteti, Canzoni.*

riddle
A popular ancient literary game giving metaphoric clues to an object's or idea's identity without naming

it. Riddles had elements of GNOMIC verse and the KENNING, as the ANGLO-SAXON riddles of the eighth-century *Exeter Book*.

riese
A pointed, veiled hat fashionable among German Jewish women.

riggamarole
A repetitive list-like recital of words, as in the thirteenth-century Scottish ragman's role, the oath of allegiance Scotsmen cynically signed for the English King Edward I.

right circle
The name given to the equator by astronomers and astrologers.

rigmarole
A RIGGAMAROLE.

rimmonim
POMEGRANATE-shaped silver or precious metal FINIALs, usually elaborately pierced and wrought, surmounting the rolling staves of Jewish TORAH scrolls, MEGILLAHs, or ROTULUS books.

rinceaux
FOLIATE ornament with sinuous branching scrolls, plants, and leaves.

rispetto
A fourteenth-century Italian poetic and MADRIGAL stanza, usually eight lines rhyming ab, ab, cc, dd.

ritornelle
The last two lines of a fourteenth-century MADRIGAL stanza, epitomizing its thought and musically varying its meter.

ritual blood guilt
The hysterical accusation that Jews used a Christian child's blood at PASSOVER to bake MATZOH. Such rumor caused numerous pogroms against Jews, especially after they had been implicated in England in the murders of Saint Hugh of Lincoln and Simon of Trent.

robe
All the elements of a costume, from undergarments to outer cloaks, smallest lacings, major fabrics, and FUR components. Sub-classes included: *robe deguisee* (richly ornamented, daring, new fashions), *robe de commune* (ordinary daily ware), *robe gironnee* or *a plis gironnes* (pleated, full-folded garb, belted at the waistline), and *robe longue* (an academic gown or religious order's HABIT).

roc
A woman's overgarment, comparable to a man's over-TUNIC.

rocaille
Ornaments imitating shells and other sea shapes.

rock crystal
Transparent, colorless pure silica or quartz, often used for jewelry and RELIQUARIES.

rocket
A ROQUET.

rod
A measure, originally the length of an ox goad, about 5½ yards.

rogation procession
A Christian ceremonial procession that circumnavigated a BONFIRE, a church PRECINCT, or a parish, to pray for good crops. The ritual was derived from pagan fertility and sun charms and MAYPOLE rites. The procession followed the direction of the sun and moved *contra solis* (against the sun), in reverse, only in times of mourning.

romance
Courtly fiction preciously wrought in poetry or prose, depicting COURTLY LOVE, tests of virtue, and triumphs over impossibilities. The THREE MATTERS of romance mirrored the customs and ethics of the audience while inspiring (by moralizing) and entertaining (by marvels, magic, and mysticism). ARTHURIAN ROMANCE was the principal type.

***Romance of the Rose* quarrel**
The thirteenth-century poem begun by Guillaume de Loris, but completed by Jean de Meun, *The Romance*

of the Rose was a popular ALLEGORY of COURTLY LOVE, with acerbic antifeminism as well as courtly manners. Its methods, messages, and meanings were argued by thinkers, moralists, and poets, especially the fifteenth-century writer Christine de Pizan who roundly attacked the poem's subject and style.

romanesca
A type of melody famous in fifteenth- and sixteenth-century LUTE literature, constantly varied and emended.

Romanesque
An architectural and artistic style imitative of the classical Roman and preceding the GOTHIC, while integrating both BYZANTINE and Eastern influences. Romanesque building design was distinguished by severity of line, simplicity of ornament, monumental sculpture, FRESCO paintings, a leaning towards the macabre, PIER and column alternation, massive tower-crowned WESTWORKS, and extravagant masonry VAULTS. Fine examples of Romanesque style are the CLUNIAC monasteries and churches as St. Martin's in Tours and Santiago de Compostela in Spain, France's ABBEY Church of St. Madeleine Vezeley, Germany's CATHEDRAL at Speyer and St. Mary's in Cologne, and Italy's baptistery at Pisa and Monreale in Sicily. Important frescos, bold in scale and color, are at Saint-Savin in France and Sant'Angelo in Formis, Italy. Romanesque SCRIPTORIA produced richly illuminated MANUSCRIPTs, particularly PSALTERs, and multivolumed illustrated Bibles, such as the Winchester Bible. Exquisite ecclesiastical vessels and secular objects were designed in metalwork and ENAMEL of MOSAN and LIMOGES.

Rome-scot
An ALMS FEE paid to the See of Rome as a percentage of monies collected by local churches; also called PETER'S PENCE.

rondeau
A French musical form, beginning and ending with a bipartite refrain, in monophonic TROUVÈRE songs and POLYPHONY.

rondel
In thirteenth-century France, a 13-line, three-stanza poem with much repetition and few rhymes. Variants included the RONDEAU and TRIOLET.

rondellus
In music, either the monophonic RONDEAU, or a CANON similar to a ROUND or ROTA.

rood
The CRUCIFIX.

rood loft
A gallery across an English church CHANCEL, supporting a ROOD and supported by a rood beam.

rood screen
A decorative wooden screen in an English CHURCH or CATHEDRAL between the ROOD beam and church floor.

roquet
A short, hooded, smock-like wool cape worn by commoners and PAGEs.

rosary
A series of three cycles of prayers to the Virgin Mary, celebrating the mysteries of the Virgin, with a string of beads used as a mnemonic prayer counter. It was popularized as a devotional aid and amulet either by Saint Dominic in the twelfth century or in the fifteenth century by a DOMINICAN FRIAR.

rose window
A circular stained glass window with TRACERY, resembling a rose, and typically found over the main entrance of GOTHIC churches and CATHEDRALs.

Rosh Hashonah
(Hebrew, Head of the year) The Jewish HIGH HOLY DAY celebrating the New Year. The day is marked by prayers, by sounding of the SHOFAR, and, in the LITURGY, the AKEDAH, the story of Abraham and Isaac.

rota
A musical round, derived from a circle dance.

rotrouenge
A type of thirteenth-century French poem having between three and seven stanzas, an internal refrain, and concluding with a formulaic phrase stating the poem's finish: *ma rotrouenge finira.*

rotulus
A long roll book, presented as a PARCHMENT or VELLUM scroll wound around one wooden cylinder or between two with attached handles. In Jewish tradition, the scroll is the form of the TORAH and MEGILLAH, which are usually surmounted by RIMMONIM. The rotulus was associated in Christian art with Old Testament prophets and scholars.

rotunda
(Latin *rotundus,* round) A DOME, circular domed building, or circular walkway around such a structure.

rouelle
The ROWEL or JEWISH BADGE.

rouncivale
A mannish woman, a lesbian.

roundels
Dessert platters of wood, porcelain, MAJOLICA, ENAMEL, tile, or heavy paper, decorated and inscribed with often risque poems or ditties which the feaster must sing to an improvised or popular melody. Sometimes roundels were decorated with individual scenes from mythological, biblical, or historical sagas, and the feaster would improvise a poem or sing a lyric associated with the roundel's specific theme, as with magnificent LIMOGES plates made for banquets of the Parliament of Paris depicting the Jason and Medea legend.

roundlet
A stuffed fabric circlet, a crownless underhat worn alone or covered by turban-folds of the CHAPERONE, ending in a long LIRIPIPE.

rowel
The compulsory ROUELLE or JEWISH BADGE imposed by various church councils (such as the Lateran and Narbonne) and civil governments.

ruade
A GALLIARD's backward kick.

rubric
(Latin *ruber,* red) Attention-catching devices, such as red letters or red underlining, used for identification in MANUSCRIPTS.

ruby-flash
A work of art, usually made of glass, colored a glowing, purple-tinged red, with oxides of copper, iron, lead, and tin.

ru de vache
(French, a cow's kick) A GALLIARD's kick to the side and backwards.

rule against perpetuities
To prevent excessively long vestings of contingent future interests in land, this rule specified that no contingent interest in land would be honored unless it was vested no later than 21 years after the death of a specific person alive at the creation of the interest.

rule in Shelley's case
If a freehold ESTATE IN LAND was granted in a will to an individual for his life and a remainder to his heirs, then the two holdings were merged to allow for the payment of inheritance taxes. This rule avoided a clever tax dodge, and was comparable to the DOCTRINE OF WORTHIER TITLE. Shelley's Case in 1581 stimulated Queen Elizabeth's interest and used as precedent a rule promulgated in Abel's Case in 1324.

rummer
A large commodious drinking glass.

rune
A letter of the old Germanic alphabets (like the *eth* and *thorn*), incised on stone or used in Scandinavian, ANGLO-SAXON, and MIDDLE ENGLISH texts; or a magical symbol, a secret mysterious sign or SIGIL.

russet
A coarse homespun fabric, usually dyed with tree bark to produce a reddish brown color and used by the poor and the peasants for clothing.

russetting
A country person wearing clothing of RUSSET.

rusticated
Rustic, rough, yet pure and uncorrupted, used as an adjective; as a verb, sent into the country, banished from refinements of city and court.

rutebufian

Thirteenth-century poetry that was not courtly, lyrical, nor personal (though written with PERSONAe). Seemingly artless, it created through art a naturalness of expression, as in the extraordinary VERISIMILITUDE of simplicity in works of Parisian poet Rutebeuf, a leader of public disapproval against MENDICANT FRIARs and an exponent of the masters of theology at the University of Paris.

S

sabaton
A broad-toed ARMOR foot covering or boot.

sable
In HERALDRY, the COLOR black; in costumery, a sumptuous rich FUR from the small carnivore related to the MARTEN.

sack
A popular sherry wine. The favorite drink of Shakespeare's Falstaff so inflated him that he became a huge "bombard of sack."

sackbut
(French *sacque boute,* a pull-push) An early trombone, made in three pitches: alto, tenor, and bass.

sacra conversacione
(Latin, holy discourse) Artistic representation of a sacred or holy conversation between a pair or among a group of saints attending the Virgin and Child, or at the Virgin's coronation, or at Christ's CRUCIFIXION. Sometimes the artist introduced into the scene a saint or personage otherwise improbable but important for the court, MONASTERY, or patrons who commissioned the art. Practical or political reasons for anachronisms in portraiture resemble the flattery inherent to the DONOR PORTRAIT or VOTIVE PAINTING.

sacrament
An outward visible sign of an inward spiritual GRACE ordained by Christ; one of the SEVEN SACRAMENTS.

Sacred Tunic
The garment said to have been worn by the Virgin Mary at the time of Christ's birth, the important RELIC sacred to the people of Chartres, symbol of the Virgin's palace in that French town after Emperor Charles the Bald presented it to Chartres in 876, and stimulus for building there the spectacular CATHEDRAL of Notre Dame completed in 1220, whose GOTHIC VAULTS soar 116 feet in vertical skyward thrust.

sacristy
In a CATHEDRAL or CHURCH, a storage room for liturgical vessels and clerical VESTMENTS.

saffron
An important golden dye made from the bright yellow stamens of the crocus plant and used for flavoring and coloring food, dyeing fabric (particularly fine linen and silk), and tinting hair blond.

saga
Created in Iceland and Norway, a heroic prose narrative which recounted history, as in the *Heimskringla,* and domestic disasters and deeds of noble families, as in *Njals' Saga,* the *Laxdaela Saga,* and *Eyrbyggya.*

Saint Andrew's Day
November 30, the first day of the church's liturgical year, beginning ADVENT.

Saint Anthony's fire
Erysipelas, CANKER, or venereal disease.

Saint Bartolph's Town
The name of the English town, pronounced "Boston," beautifully represented the linguistic processes of apheresis, aphesis, syncope, and apocope, as letters or syllables were dropped out, respectively, from beginning, middle, and end of the words in a regular, predictable manner: via apheresis and aphesis the

initial "saint" disappeared; via apocope "town" contracted to "ton"; syncope contracted everything else.

Saint Dunstan's tongs

A dangerous, inciting act. With fire tongs, Dunstan tweaked the Devil's nose, as did the Bishop Eloi. Like using a SPOON with a long handle for dining with the devil, Dunstan's tongs were not adequate protection from true peril.

Saint Elmo's fire

A display of static electricity at the tips of masts, tall trees, and ships' yard arms.

Saint John's bread

The ubiquitous carob, the seed pod of a locust tree. It was used as candy (tasting something like chocolate), a flavoring and coloring agent for foods, and a source of jewel-measuring. Weight of diamonds in CARATS derives from carob grains. Carob was the "locust food" sustaining Saint John the Baptist in isolation in the wilderness when he uttered his VOX CLAMANTIS IN DESERTO, the voice of one crying in the wilderness (though some interpreted his locust food as insect, not arboreal).

Saint John's Day

A Christian feast, June 24, celebrating Saint John the Baptist. The festivities were associated with pagan MIDSUMMER and summer solstice rites, such as BELTANE FIRES, BONFIRES, ROGATION PROCESSIONS, divinations with ERYNGIUM, MUMMING plays, and MORRIS DANCES.

Saint Martial school

From the tenth to twelfth centuries, the music school at the Abbey of Saint Martial in Limoges, France, important for the composition of SEQUENCES, TROPES, and the polyphonic ORGANUM.

saints and their attributes

Of the FOUR EVANGELISTS, TWELVE APOSTLES, and hundreds of saints identifiable by SYMBOLS of their excellence, life, or martyrdom, their signs decorating ecclesiastical and secular works in Western architecture and art, here is a selection (evangelists are marked by an *E*, APOSTLES by an *A*):

St. Jerome with his lion writes a manuscript in his study. (From engraving, Albrecht Dürer 1471–1528, German; courtesy of Metropolitan Museum of Art)

SAINT	*ATTRIBUTE*
Agatha	breasts or pincers
Agnes	lamb and book
Aidan	flaming torch, stag
Alban	axe and saltire
Albertus Magnus	Dominican habit and book
Aldan	gold saltire
Alexis	sea shell
Alfred the Great	harp, crown, and scepter
Alphege	battle-axe
Amator of Auxerre	hatchet
Ambrose	beehive and 2 scourges, 1 saltire
Anatole	book of mathematics
Anatolia	angel, dagger, sword, arrows
Andrew (A)	saltire
Anne	lily

SAINT	*ATTRIBUTE*
Anselm	sailing ship
Anskar	staff and cross
Anthony of Egypt	tau cross
Anthony of Padua	lilies and books
Anthony the Great	pig, lion, or staff
Antipas	axe behind a mitre
Asaph	crossed keys or crozier and key
Athanasius	triangle and pallium
Aubert	2 loaves of bread
Augustine of Canterbury	cross, lily, and pall
Augustine of Hippo	flaming heart pierced by crossed arrows
Aurea	millstone
Barbara	tower or castle ramparts
Barnabas	6 roses
Bartholomew (A)	flaying knife and book
Bartolus	leper's wounds
Basil	church
Bede	pitcher and sun rays
Benedict	broken cup and raven
Benno	fish and key
Bernard	3 mitres and book, or a beehive
Birgit	scroll with holy monogram
Blasius	teasel or wool comb, or 2 candles saltire
Bonaventure	chalice, Host, and cross, or cardinal's hat
Boniface	book pierced by sword
Botulph	chevron and cross
Brendan	ship and navigator's instrument
Brice of Cours	basket of eggs
Brigit	lamp and oak wreath, goose or cow
Bruno	crowns of Cologne or Carthusian habit
Camillus	red cross
Catherine of Alexandria	wheel
Catherine of Siena	cross and heart
Cecilia	harp or organ
Chad	cross potent and central square
Charles	crowned Humilitas
Christina	sword, or millstone and 2 arrows
Christopher	lantern and staff, or Christ on shoulder
Clare	ciborium
Clement	anchor
Columba	dove, or Iona cross
Columban	bear
Cornelius	cross and horn or sword
Cosmas	urine flask and ointment box (with Saint Damian)
Crispin	shoemaker's tools, or a shoe
Cuthbert	cross and 4 rampant lions; or swan
Cyprian	double battle-axe and crown
Cyril of Alexandria	pens and Greek scroll
Cyril of Jerusalem	money bag
Damian	urine flask and ointment box (with Saint Cosmas)
David of Thessalonica	seated lion
David of Wales	dove and cloud
Denis (or Dionysius) of Paris	cross and 4 rampant lions; or mitred head in hands
Didacus	roses and bread
Dominic	a star and a dog with a torch in its mouth
Dorothy	flaming torch, or a laden basket
Dunstan	covered chalice, or harp, or a pair of tongs
Edith	church
Edmund	rich ring
Edmund of East Anglia	crown and crossed arrows
Edward	crown and crossed sword and scepter
Edward the Confessor	cross and 5 doves or martlets, or a finger ring
Eligius or Eloi	gold horseshoe or church

SAINT	*ATTRIBUTE*	*SAINT*	*ATTRIBUTE*
Elizabeth	Maltese cross and withered leaves	James the Less (A)	saw or club
Elizabeth of Hungary	food basket, or 3 crowns	Januarius	2 bottles on a book
Erasmus or Elmo	ship, or windlass	Jerome	cross potent fitchy, or lion and cardinal's hat
Eric of Sweden	crowns and fountain or waves	Joan of Arc	crown, sword, and two fleurs-de-lys
Etheldreda	3 crowns or psaltery	John Chrysostom	beehive, or chalice on book
Eulalia	dove	John of Bohemia	palm, or finger on mouth
Faith	Holy Trinity inscription	John of God	chest of coins
Felicitas	7 swords	John of the Cross	cross moline
Fiacre	bird and flower, or garden spade	John the Apostle (A/E)	serpent and chalice, or the eagle
Florian	burning house, or eagle and flames	John the Baptist	Maltese cross
Frances of Rome	angel	Joseph of Arimathea	cross, chalice, tears
Francis of Assisi	cross and stigmata or 5 drops of blood	Joseph of Nazareth	carpenter's square and lily
Francis Xavier	baptismal font	Judas Iscariot (A)	30 pieces of silver
Frederick	sword on a book	Jude (A)	sailing ship
Gabriel	shield and spear	Julia	rope and cross
Gall	bear, bread, and staff	Julian	saltire cross, or crosslet
Genevieve	lamb	Justin	pen and sword
George	red cross, or dragon	Kentigern	fish and ring
Germaine	lamb	Kevin	book and crozier
Gertrude	7 rings or heart	Killian	cross and crossed swords
Gildas	bell or fountain	Lambert	sword on book
Giles	deer pierced by arrow	Lawrence	gridiron
Gobnata	crozier and beads	Leander	flaming heart
Gregory	epigonation	Leo	mitre and pick-axe
Gregory the Great	rampant lions and I H S monogram or dove	Leonard	crossed chains, fleur-de-lys on book
Harvey	sheet of music	Lioba	hand washing foot
Helena	true cross	Louis	crown of thorns and fleur-de-lys
Henry	crown and imperial robe	Lucia	eyes on platter, or lighted lamp
Herbert	stag with cross on head	Lucien	dolphin
Hermangild	I H S on heart	Lucy	flaming lamp and sacred cipher, or two eyes in a dish
Hilary	pen and 3 books	Luke (E)	winged ox
Hilda	3 snakes	Lydia	snail or scallop
Hildegarde	heart	Marcellina	cross
Hubert	stag and cross	Margaret of Antioch	cross and dragon
Hugh of Grenoble	hand holding flowers	Margaret of Scotland	saltire and cross
Hugh of Lincoln	swan	Mark (E)	winged lion
Ignatius	heart and I H S, or lion		
Irene	horse		
Ivo	law book		
James the Greater (A)	gold scallop shells, or pilgrim's staff and purse		

SAINT	*ATTRIBUTE*
Martha	food, cup, pitcher, and table
Martin of Tours	cross florry and saltire florry, or carbuncle, or soldier cutting his cloak in half
Mary (Virgin Mary)	winged heart pierced with sword, white lily, fleur-de-lys, mystic rose, crescent moon, Maria monogram
Mary Cleophas	with sons: Jude, James the Less, Simeon, and Joseph
Mary Magdalene	ointment jar, tears,
Mary Salome	with sons: James the Greater and John the Evangelist
Matthew (A/E)	winged man
Matthias	battle-axe and book or two stones
Maurice	seven stars, or banner with lion rampant
Michael	dragon, or trefoiled cross
Mildred	crozier and vail
Neot	deer
Nicholas of Myra	3 bezants, or 3 money bags, or 3 balls, or 3 boys in cauldron
Nicholas of Tolentino	cross and dove
Nilus	oil lamp
Norbert	ciborium
Odilia	keys; or eyes on platter
Olaf	axe and crown
Osmund	black saltire and book
Oswald	ciborium
Pantaleon	lion or medical bottle or sword with vase
Patrick	red saltire, or snakes and a shamrock
Paul	open book pierced by sword
Perpetua	dragon and ladder
Peter (A)	crossed keys and inverted cross
Peter Nolasco	radiant bell, or ship
Peter of Verona	sword and credo

SAINT	*ATTRIBUTE*
Philip (A)	cross bottony and bread
Placidus	crescent
Polycarp	burning logs
Prisca	couchant lion
Priscilla	lion
Procopius	monk with Devil on chain
Raphael	wallet and staff
Raymond	rosary
Regina	fountain, dove, lamb, or torch
Reginald	fountain
Regulus	fountain
Remigius	holy oil jar; dove
Roch	dog holding bread, or pilgrim's hat, staff, and scallop
Romuald	ladder
Rosa	roses
Rosalia	roses
Rupert	basket of eggs
Sabbas	lion
Scholastica	dove
Sebastian	arrows
Seraphina	chain
Simeon Stylites	whips and pillar
Simon (A)	fish and book, or 2 oars and hatchet
Stanislav	open purse
Stephen	3 stones and palm branch
Susanna	crown and sword
Swithin	3 green apples and raindrops
Sylvanus	cliff
Sylvester	cross patriarchal or tiara
Tabitha	gazelle or heart
Thais	scroll with inscription
Thecla	serpents and lions
Theodore	mitre over scroll
Theodorich	eagle
Theodorus Turo	horse
Theresa	radiant heart with flame-tipped arrow, or I H S
Thomas (A)	carpenter's square and spear

SAINT	*ATTRIBUTE*
Thomas Aquinas	radiant sun with eye, or star, dove or chalice
Thomas More	book, chancellor's insignia
Thomas of Canterbury	3 black birds (Cornish choughs)
Timothy	club and stones
Titus	book and broken idols
Ursula	cross on banner, or small bears
Valentine	heart
Valerian	two swords
Veronica	vernicle
Victor	spear, shield, and carbuncle
Victoria	angel, dagger, sword, and arrows
Vincent	grid-iron and dalmatic
Vojtech of Prague	palm
Wenceslas	eagle on banner
Wilfrid	7 rectangles in a triangle; or fish
Winifred	fountain
Zeno	book
Zita	keys

Saint Swithin's Day

July 15, the day considered important for weather prediction. Commemorating removal of the buried bones of the ninth-century English Bishop of Winchester, Saint Swithin, from outside his church to the new CATHEDRAL, the day's weather controlled that of the following month. Rain on Saint Swithin's Day portended 40 days' precipitation, while fair weather promised a rainless 40.

Saint Vitus's dance

Chorea, a serious central nervous system disorder caused by rheumatic fever; or, ergotism, a disease caused by fungal changes in rye bread seeds, producing frenzied bodily movements, a DANCING MANIA, with virulent outbreaks of epidemic in the Rhine and Mosel regions in Germany, and near Liège in 1374. According to chronicles, sufferers resorted to graves and desert places, lying down as if dead, throwing themselves into wells, or rolling about in filth, demanding to be beaten. Like the FLAGELLANTS, the sufferers attributed their disease to God's wrath at human perfidies.

sal

Salt; in ALCHEMY, one of the ultimate elements of all substances.

salamander

In bestiaries, following Pliny and Aristotle, a lizard-like amphibian that not only withstands fire but fights it. Its dramatic poisonous properties enabled it to kill at once: if it climbed a fruit tree, all fruits would become infected with its venom, killing anyone who ate them; if the salamander fell into a well, its powerful toxin would slay those who drank. The beast is common in the ICONOGRAPHY of evil.

Salic law

In 1328, with the cooperation of the University of Paris and representatives of the THREE ESTATES, a new law was promulgated: no woman shall succeed to the throne of France. This legitimated the crowning of King Philip V, who was only the nephew of the former king, Philip IV, whose three sons had died and whose daughter Jeanne was heir to the throne. Earlier, there had been no bar to women rulers; LADY BOSSES had thrived.

salient

In HERALDRY, a LION or beast depicted as rearing, or rampant, but with both forepaws and hindpaws held together as if for a leap.

salmagundi

A mixed, aromatic stew, combining several meats, vegetables, and piquant spices; a stylistically varied or substantively mixed work of art, comparable to a SATIRE.

salt

An elaborate, embellished, sculptured vessel containing salt at table. The salt could be shaped like a ship (a NEF), castle, or town with CRENELATIONS and parapets; elegance of the vessel signified wealth, political power, or artistic taste. The most noble and honored diners sat "above the salt," while all others sat "below" it.

saltarello
A spritely, energetic Italian dance, probably derived from the BASSE DANCE, and similar to the GALLIARD, though with smaller leaps.

saltire
An *X*-shaped CROSS, the Saint Andrew's CROSS.

salt planer
A ceremonial and practical instrument for the office of the banquet hall PANTLER charged with managing the bread and the salt. Generally made of ivory, the planer was used to shave salt from large salt blocks for filling the SALTs.

saltwick
Salt sources of Lincolnshire, England: Northwick, Middlewick, and Nantwick. Most place names with *wick* suffixes were salt marshes or mines.

Salve Regina Mundi
(Latin, Hail, Queen of the World) The greeting of Saint Nicholas of Myra to the Virgin Mary. He was so pious even in his youth that as an infant he abstained from his mother's milk on fast days.

samite
A rich, strong silk cloth, related to CENDAL, and strengthened in both warp and weft by delicately interwoven wire. This material was often used for coronation and ecclesiastical investiture robes.

sanap
A table carpet or runner, often woven TAPESTRY, AUBUSSON, or EMBROIDERY.

san benito
A yellow or black ceremonial sackcloth garment, sometimes grotesquely decorated, worn by heretics with a yellow MITRE before being executed at an AUTO DA FE during the Spanish INQUISITION.

Sancta Dei Genitrix
(Latin, Holy Mother of God) Mary as blessed progenitrix of Christ is the MATER MARIA DEI (Mary, the Mother of God) who becomes REGINA COELI (Queen of Heaven).

sanctus
The fourth element of the ORDINARY of the MASS: *Sanctus, sanctus, sanctus, . . . pleni sunt caeli et terra* (Holy, holy, holy, . . . heaven and earth are filled), and *Benedictus qui venit* (Blessed is he who comes).

sander
A vessel holding sand for sprinkling on wet ink in order to dry it quickly.

sanguine
A hopeful, ruddy skinned, optimistic person characterized in PHYSIOGNOMY by a preponderance of blood, one of the FOUR HUMORS; one of the FOUR TEMPERAMENTS.

sapientia et fortitudo
(Latin, wisdom and strength) The paired opposites in literature and in life ideally united in a single, heroic human being. While in the *Song of Roland,* Roland is *preux* (physically and martially powerful), and Oliver is *sage* (learned and wise), the ARTHURIAN ROMANCE hero Tristan displays simultaneous prowess of body and of mind. MIRRORS OF PRINCES taught the unified ideal.

sarbal
A sleeveless CLOAK or gown.

sarcophagus
A decorated tomb, such as a TRANSI TOMB, ornamented with sculptures and inscriptions.

sargenes
A white linen overgarment, with voluminous sleeves, lace collar, and matching cap and GIRDLE, worn by Jews during the HIGH HOLY DAYS (especially YOM KIPPUR), by bridegrooms, and by the leader of a SEDER at PASSOVER. The sargenes was also called a KITTEL or a *sukenis.*

sarsanet
A fine thin silk originally from the East, where it was reputedly woven by Saracens. The silk was made into gowns, capes, scarfs, LAMBREQUINs, and trimmings.

Sarum Use
The liturgical and musical practices of the English CATHEDRALs of Salisbury (*Sarum* is the ancient name

for Salisbury), Hereford, York, and others, in opposition to the Roman LITURGY.

satem
The Avestan (Persian) word for "one hundred," used to identify a sub-group of INDO-EUROPEAN languages: Indian, Iranian, Armenian, Balto-Slavic, and Albanian.

satin de chine
A costly, lustrous silk fabric with a smooth light-reflecting surface. Originally imported from China, it was used for ceremonial and parade garments in continental Europe in the twelfth and thirteenth centuries and in England in the fourteenth century.

satire
(Latin SATURA, the name of a mixed dish melding meat, vegetables, and fruits; or SATYR, a pagan man-beast) An artistic genre humorously or vituperatively depicting follies and vices in order to inspire reform, as in ALLEGORY, SIRVENTES, BEAST EPICs, and beast fables.

saucer
The courtly HOUSEHOLD servant responsible for preparing garnish sauces in order to pique the appetite. The most common sauces were white sauce, black sauce, or green sauce, which included mustard.

saute majeur
(French, important leap) A high jump or leap in a GALLIARD.

Savonarola chair
From the Italian Renaissance, a wooden folding chair in the shape of an *X* with interlacing curved slats and a wooden seat. A chair often was decorated with carving or INLAY, especially with CERTOSINA work.

Saxons
A Germanic people dwelling near the Elbe River, who conquered parts of England and contributed to the development of the ANGLO-SAXON civilization; also, a type of ROMANESQUE architecture in England.

scabbard
A case or sheath protecting the blade of a sword, dagger, or knife when not in use.

scabies
A cutaneous disease significant in medical entomology: in 1147, Hildegard of Bingen, the BENEDICTINE nun, physician, and founder of the Rupertsberg Convent, described scabies mites as the cause and the vector, not a symptom, of the disease.

scagliola
Plasterwork imitation marble.

scald
An Icelandic, Norwegian, or other Scandinavian poet, a writer or performer of EDDA, comparable to the ANGLO-SAXON BARD.

scalework
A decorative ornament resembling overlapped tiles, an IMBRICATED PATTERN.

scallop
The bivalve mollusk shell, the BADGE of pilgrims returning from Santiago de Compostela, and an ATTRIBUTE of the APOSTLE James the Greater.

scapular
(Latin, *scapulae,* shoulder blades) A narrow cloak or stole, part of most monastic HABITs, and required by the BENEDICTINE RULE; symbolically, the yoke of Christ.

scarf
Originally a sling for carrying gear, worn diagonally over the shoulder across the chest to the opposite hip; later, a protective, ornamental, or decorative sash or BALDRIC.

scarificator
A surgical instrument or LANCET for making incisions, as for BLOODLETTING.

scarlet
The finely woven, soft yet strong, red-dyed ECARLATE woollen fabric, so prized it gave its name to the rich red color associated with the cloth.

schabbes deckel
A round, floppy hat of felt or wool worn by congregants of German Jewish SYNAGOGUEs.

Schema
(Hebrew, Hear!) The first word of the Jewish celebration of God's unity: *Hear, O Israel, the Lord our God, the Lord is One!* The basic statement of the monotheistic faith.

schivah
In Judaism, the mourning period following the death of close kin.

schnabelkannen
Long-spouted jugs for pouring wines and ales, manufactured by RHENISH POTTERIES.

schnelle
(German, quickly) A tall beer, ale, or wine tankard designed by RHENISH POTTERIES for speedy quaffing.

schola
A church choir led by a CANTOR.

Schola Cantorum
(Latin, school of singers) A papal choir and singing school, probably founded in the fourth century by Pope Sylvester and revivified in the sixth century by Saint Gregory. The school was instrumental in the dissemination of Roman LITURGY and CHANT.

Scholastica's House
The first BENEDICTINE nunnery, founded in the fifth century near Monte Cassino by Saint Scholastica, the twin sister of Saint Benedict.

Scholasticism
Formal theological teaching of the twelfth through fifteenth centuries. Scholasticism adopted both PLATONIC and ARISTOTELEAN doctrines. Major theorists were Peter Abelard, Thomas Aquinas, Bonaventure, and Albertus Magnus.

schul mantel
A Jewish costume worn on the Sabbath, a CLOAK without an opening for the right hand to pass through as reminder for the wearer not to carry any forbidden object on the Sabbath.

sconce
An ornamental bracketed candlestick or lantern, often with a protective screen against draft or wind.

scone
(German, *schonbrot,* fine bread) A round bread cut into quadrants made of wheat, oats, or barley, common in northern England and Scotland. A scone is similar to BANNOCK, though finer, and often embellished with raisins, dates, or glazed fruit.

scop
An ANGLO-SAXON poet, harpist, and singer, who composed and performed for courtly and aristocratic audiences songs of historical events and adventures of heros. He was similar to the GLEEMAN, a song maker.

scordatura
Unusual and peculiar tuning of stringed instruments such as LUTEs for facilitating difficult passages and chords.

scot-ale
A meeting specifically for ale drinking, in which the expenses for beverage and entertainment were shared by the participants. The scot-ale was not always convivial or voluntary: Giles of Bridport, Bishop of Salisbury, in 1256 forbade them because unscrupulous foresters and landholders compelled others to be their guests in order to extort money from them by requiring exorbitant payments for a drink or a "shot," so that no one was allowed to go "shot" or "scot" free.

Scottish Chaucerians
Scottish writers who, in the fifteenth and sixteenth centuries, imitated Chaucer's ideas, characters, and poetic forms. Among the poets were Robert Henryson, William Dunbar, Gavin Douglas, and King James I (James VI of Scotland).

scriptorium
A MANUSCRIPT "factory" noted for a careful division of labor among copyists, rubricators, illuminators, and binders. Some were secular, others were attached to such ecclesiastical organizations as ABBEYs and COEDUCATIONAL MONASTERIES.

scudulle
A small bowl with a broad horizontal rim.

scutage
(Latin *scutum,* shield) In feudal law, a fine or tax a TENANT holding a knight's FEE owed to an overlord

for refusal to or an inability to provide military service in return for land TENURE; also called ESCUAGE. The monetary rent paid for land or a building by a lord or knight to an overlord in an ENFEOFFMENT.

scutching
Cleansing and refining fibrous material such as flax, hemp, cotton, silk, or wool by beating out its impurities or imperfections. Flax scutching was a commonly depicted rural LABOR, one of the TWELVE LABORS OF THE MONTHS.

scythe
An agricultural harvesting implement with a long curved blade attached to a long handle, sometimes for use single-handed, otherwise two-handed.

Second Adam
An epithet for Christ as the new First Man of redeemed humanity, because of the FELIX CULPA. Adam of the Old Testament was considered a typological PREFIGURATION of Christ.

Second Coming
Christ's return to earth in glory and judgment at the world's end. This event, portended in the LITURGY of ADVENT, stimulated popular belief in the emergence of ANTICHRIST figures. It is also called PAROUSIA.

Second Eve
The Virgin Mary, MATER MARIA DEI (Mary, mother of God), whose coming was the result of the FELIX CULPA. In TYPOLOGY, Mary is parallel to the first Eve of the Old Testament, as Christ is to Adam, so Mary is the second person of the EVA-AVE ANTITHESIS.

secretaire à abattant
(French *abattoir,* to pull down) A desk for writing and for storing papers and books, with a fall front or hinged panel that could be pulled down to form a convenient writing surface.

Secretis Mulierum
WOMEN'S SECRETS.

seder
The order of service for the ceremonies (such as reading the HAGGADAH) and ritual foods (such as MATZOH and HAROSET) of the Jewish holiday PASSOVER, commemorating the events in the biblical book of Exodus.

sedilia
Three stone seats for use by the clergy. Either movable or recessed, the seats were often elaborately ornamented with canopies and niches. They were usually placed on the south side of the CHOIR near the ALTAR.

seed
In agrarian context, the small planted elements from which crops, flowers, and trees grow; in sexual situations, semen. Chaucer's Wife of Bath mischievously queries celibacy and abstinence: "If no seed is sown how can praised virginity grow?"

seizin
In COMMON LAW, a right to possession of a freehold ESTATE IN LAND held in TENURE, usually transmitted by a ceremony or LIVERY OF SEIZIN.

sejant
Sitting up. Usually describing a four-legged animal in HERALDRY, a LION, YALE, or other animal sitting with its forelegs upright.

sen
(French, sense) The intention and meaning behind the subject-matter of Old French ROMANCEs. Chrètien de Troyes' ideal unity of *sen et matière* is comparable to the indivisible unity between meaning and manner, SENTENCE and SOLACE, in the works of Chaucer.

sendelbindel
The German Jewish CORNALIA.

senex amans
(Latin, the old lover) A foolish codger whose folly causes him to become a CUCKOLD. He was a stock character in FABLIAUX, drama, and narrative poetry, derived from the JOCULATORES tradition.

senjal
In COURTLY LOVE, a lover's code name to retain secrecy and avoid scandal.

sentence
Substance and meaning in literature, as opposed to SOLACE, the techniques for pleasing. Literary perfection was the unity between DOCERE et DELECTARE, teaching and pleasing. The tale incorporating "best sentence" with "most solace" would win the Canterbury pilgrims' prize supper. Compare SEN.

separatio
In early chemistry, an analytic and extraction process for separating the components of substances.

separation
In ASTROLOGY, the departure of one planet from another.

sephira
In the Jewish mystical philosophy, KABALLAH, the 10 emanations or attributes that associate the infinite with the finite, graphically represented as a TREE OF LIFE, the SEPHIROTIC TREE.

Sephirotic Tree
The Kaballists' graphic depiction of the structure of creation. Progressing downward in SEPHIRA from the infinite to the finite, it showed a geometric arrangement of ten emanations (*sephirot*) of the divine will, each a lightning flash of divine wisdom: *keter* (the crown), *chochniah* (wisdom), *binah* (understanding), *chad* (mercy), *gevorah* (sincerity), *tipherat* (beauty), *netach* (eternity), *hod* (splendor), *yesod* (foundation), and *malkut* (the kingdom).

Septuagesima
(Latin, seventieth) The 70 days beginning with the third Sunday before LENT and ending with the Saturday before EASTER.

Septuagint
(Latin, seventy) The important third-century B.C. Greek translation and emendation of the Hebrew Old Testament by 72 translators commissioned by Ptolemy Philadelphus of Alexandria. The work included the PENTATEUCH and the books of the APOCRYPHA, and abandoned the conventional triple separation of the Bible into Law, Prophets, and Writings or HAGIOGRAPHA.

sequence
One of the most significant types of liturgical GREGORIAN CHANT TROPES, attached to the ALLELUIA, either invented or popularized by Notker Balbulus, a tenth-century MONK of St. Gall.

seraph
The highest celestial being in the NINE ORDERS OF ANGELS, usually represented as having six wings.

sergeant-at-arms
In England, an armed officer in a HOUSEHOLD; or one of a martial band of 24 required in attendance on the king or a nobleman to keep order and arrest troublemakers or traitors.

sergeanty
A feudal land TENURE providing personal service to the king; grand sergeanty, "touching defense of the country," supplied the king's marshal, banner-bearer, attorney, or CORNAGE; and petit or petty sergeanty provided culinary and wood-gathering services.

Sermon on the Mount
Christ's promises and teaching of the EIGHT BEATITUDES (Matthew 5:1–12).

serpentine
Resembling a serpent's skin or sinuous movement; an ornamental stone, rock, or mineral, essentially magnesium silicate.

service of love
In COURTLY LOVE, the lover's double allegiance to his beloved and to God, or to the God of Love. Such dual commitment was comparable to the feudal double allegiance of a knight to his overlord and to the Lord God. Through acts of self-abnegation, the lover could prove himself worthy to receive the sacrament of love as well as his investiture with its insignia (the portrait of the beloved, his lady's sleeve, or LAMBREQUIN). This allegiance in French literature was *service d'Amour* and in German, *Minnedienst.*

sesquialtera
A musical term (used by Johannes de Tinctoris) to describe the proportional relationships among musical notes; similar to the HEMIOLA.

setons
Threads or slender linen bands inserted under the skin through incisions for ailments of the testes, anus, loins, navel, spleen, stomach, spine, and eyes. Roger of Salerno's *Surgery* suggested the use of setons with CAUTERY and PHLEBOTOMY.

set-square
An instrument for measuring right angles, used by carpenters, architects, and builders. The tool also was an ATTRIBUTE of the APOSTLE Saint Thomas, of Joseph (the father of Jesus), and of allegorical representations of Geometry and MELANCHOLY.

settle
A seat, generally with a high wooden back.

Seven Ages of Man
The seven life phases: infancy, adolescence, youth, prime, elder age, dotage, and, finally, death.

The Seven Deadly Sins lead to infernal punishments. The envious are immersed eternally in ice cold water. (From Nicolas Le Rouge, *Le grant kalendrier et compost des Bergiers*, Troyes, 1496)

Sloth as one of the Seven Deadly Sins leads to infernal punishment by snakes in a hellish snakepit. (From Nicolas Le Rouge, *Le grant kalendrier et compost des Bergiers*, Troyes, 1496)

seven bishops of seven churches
In the New Testament Book of REVELATION, instructions and warnings were issued to the seven bishops of the seven churches in Asia Minor (Ephesus, Smyrna, Pergamum, Thyatira, Sardis, Philadelphia, and Laodicea), with practical suggestions preceding the more mystical revelations.

Seven Cardinal Virtues
Faith, Hope, Charity (the THREE THEOLOGICAL VIRTUES) and Prudence, Temperance, Fortitude, and Justice (the FOUR CARDINAL VIRTUES). These oppose the SEVEN DEADLY SINS.

seven churches
Saint John's letter in Revelation 1–3 was addressed to seven churches in Asia Minor: Ephesus, Smyrna, Pergamum, Thyatira, Sardis, Philadelphia, and Laodicea.

Pharaoh dreams of the seven fat and seven lean years. (From a German edition of the Old Testament, Cologne, 1479)

Seven Deadly Sins
Pride, Envy, Anger, Sloth (or Moroseness), Avarice, Gluttony, and Lust. Popular ALLEGORIES in literature, art, architecture, furniture decoration, sermons (PARABLES, exempla), jewelry (MEMENTO MORI pins and beads), and medical books.

seven fat cows and seven lean cows
In Joseph's interpretation of Pharoah's premonitory dream (Genesis 41), the seven handsome and fat cows represented seven years of abundance and wealth; the seven lean and gaunt cows that followed represented the seven years of famine that would then occur in Egypt. Joseph therefore warned Pharoah of the necessity of storing foodstuffs against possible disaster. The prognostication served to release Joseph from his imprisonment after being accused of attacking POTIPHAR'S WIFE (Genesis 39).

seven-fold flame
Seven tongues of fire symbolic of the power of the HOLY SPIRIT (Acts 2), associated with the SEVEN GIFTS OF THE HOLY SPIRIT.

seven gifts of the Holy Spirit
Sapientia, wisdom; *Intellectus,* understanding; *Concilium,* good council; *Fortitudo* (spiritual) strength; *Scientia,* (rational) knowledge; *Pietas,* piety; and *Timor,* fear (of the Lord). These were prefigured in Isaiah 11.

seven heavens
In KABALLAH and Islam, site of blissful afterlife, the seventh, the best, most ecstatic abode.

seven holy founders
The pious Florentine founders of the Order of the Servites, the Servants of Mary. The Servites dedicated

their lives to prayer and contemplation of her sorrows, led by the physician-saint Philip Benozzi in 1233.

Seven Joys of the Virgin

Seven events in the life of the Virgin, and the devotions associated with those events: the ANNUNCIATION; the VISITATION; the ADORATION of the MAGI; the PRESENTATION OF CHRIST IN THE TEMPLE; Christ among the Doctors; the ASSUMPTION; and the CORONATION OF OUR LADY. These contrast with the SEVEN SORROWS OF THE VIRGIN.

seven lamps

The lights illuminating the way to Truth are the SEVEN GIFTS OF THE HOLY SPIRIT: wisdom, comprehension, direction, spiritual strength, knowledge, piety, and fear of God.

seven liberal arts

The TRIVIUM—Grammar, Rhetoric, and Logic; plus the QUADRIVIUM—Astronomy, Music, Geometry, and Arithmetic—comprised the seven liberal arts. Forming the basic university curriculum, they preceded specialized study in theology, medicine, or law, and were thought "liberal" because they liberated the mind to think and to act. The seven liberal arts were elegantly depicted in the fifth-century ALLEGORY, *The Marriage of Philology and Mercury,* by Martianus Capella.

seven lights of the menorah

The MENORAH's oil vessels or candles signifying the seven days of creation, seven planets, seven eyes of the Almighty, and seven continents of the world.

seven O-antiphons

Seven expostulatory prayers beginning with the letter O. They are sung during the seven days preceding CHRISTMAS to herald the miraculous birth: *O sapientia* (O Wisdom!), *O adonai* (O Adonai!), *O radix jesse* (O Jesse the root!), *O clavis David* (O David the key!), *O oriens* (O rising one!), *O rex gentium* (O King of nations!), and *O Emmanuel* (O Emmanuel!).

seven priest trumpeters

According to the story of Joshua, seven priests blew SHOFARS outside the walls of Jericho to weaken, then destroy them.

seven sacraments

The seven acts conferring Christian GRACE: BAPTISM, COMMUNION, CONFIRMATION, PENANCE (confession), EXTREME UNCTION, HOLY ORDERS, and MATRIMONY.

seven senses

Taste, sight, hearing, smell, touch, speech, and understanding (Ecclesiastes 17:5).

seven sets of seven years

The 49 precursors to the jubilant 50th year, the JUBILEE.

Seven Sisters

The PLEIADES.

Seven Sleepers

Seven youths from Ephesus in the third century either hid or were inadvertently walled in a cave during Roman persecution of Christians. Having slept peacefully for 200 years, they were awakened in the fifth century in the realm of Theodosius II.

Seven Sorrows of the Virgin

Seven agonies piercing the heart of the Virgin Mary: the rejection of her child Jesus; the flight into Egypt; the disappearance of Jesus while disputing with the doctors; His bearing the cross; the CRUCIFIXION; the descent from the cross; and Mary's final parting in her ASCENSION (Luke 2). The Sorrows, focus of a church festival established in 1423 by the Synod of Cologne, oppose the SEVEN JOYS OF THE VIRGIN.

seven stages of life

Ptolemy's chronology of existence ruled by CHRONOCRATERS, comparable to the SEVEN AGES OF MAN.

seven stars of Bishop Hugh

In a dream, Bishop Hugh of Grenoble saw seven stars that were symbolic of Saint Bruno and his six disciples, who would later found the CARTHUSIAN monastic community at GRANDE CHARTREUSE.

seventh seal

According to the Book of REVELATION, at the APOCALYPSE, the LAMB OF GOD will open the final latch of the Great Book of Life, and seven angels sounding seven trumpets will stand before God. The first will cause hail, fire, and blood to consume the earth; the second will quench a great burning mountain thrown into the sea; subsequent angels will release scourges and PLAGUES. The seventh angel will sound a trumpet voicing to the prophets the mystery of God.

seven veils
The erotic dance with veils that Princess Salome performed for her stepfather King Herod, for which he granted her the severed head of Saint John the Baptist, decollated at her request.

several
Private, separate, and individual, as opposed to joint interest in a property or a legal action.

sewer
An arranger of banquet hall dishes before and after their reaching the table.

Sexagesima
(Latin, sixtieth) The 60 days prior to EASTER, commencing with the second Sunday before LENT.

sgraffito
A design scratched with a stiff brush or pointed tool onto STAINED GLASS, MAJOLICA, and DELFT ware.

shaatnez
The Old Testament law (Deuteronomy 22:11) prohibiting mixture of wool and linen in clothing. Such a combination was believed to be unnatural, violating the distinction of each species.

Shaddai
A name of the omnipresent, omnipotent, and omniscient Almighty in Jewish tradition. The word embellished a MEZZUZAH, PHYLACTERIES, and AMULETS.

shagreen
Untanned leather with a rough surface made from the skin of a horse, donkey, shark, or seal, and frequently dyed green.

shambles
A butchery, the FLESH SHAMBLES; also a street or district for butchers.

Shammaites
Strict interpreters of Jewish law, HALAKHAH, in opposition to HILLELITES.

shamos
The starter light or servant candle of the Jewish MENORAH.

shamrock
The three-leaved grass plant whose trifoliate leaves Saint Patrick reputedly used to illustrate the TRINITY; a national EMBLEM of Ireland.

Shavuot
The Jewish feast of WEEKS.

shawm
A double-reeded wind instrument with a slightly conical, narrow bore, producing a nasal and strident sound. The shawm was played at ceremonial events, and particularly to signal the conclusion of a feast.

Sheer Thursday
(Anglo-Saxon *skere* or *sheer,* clean or free from guilt) MAUNDY THURSDAY, during which ABSOLUTION is received and church ALTARs are ceremonially washed clean.

sherte
An undergarment derived from the CHAINSE and CHEMISE, usually made of fine white linen and often ornamented with EMBROIDERY at the neckband and at the sleeve wrists.

shibboleth
(Hebrew, a flooding stream) An identifier used by Jephthah (Judges 12:4–6) to distinguish by accent fugitive Ephraimites from his own Gileadites. Sons of Ephraim did not pronounce "sh," but rather "s." Likewise, a word or phrase meaningless to everyone except adherents or followers of a particular party or sect may be retained as a password or ritual greeting long after its original necessity as identifier.

shipwreck
Ships and seafaring vessels dismantled and destroyed at sea. Abandoned, lost, or sunken ships automatically belonged to the king, not the finder or salvager;

on dry land, however, although a TREASURE TROVE belonged to the king, lost or abandoned property belonged to the finder.

shit
(Anglo-Saxon *sceat,* dirt, soil) Dirt. Chaucer disapproved of a shitty shepherd guarding clean sheep, his analogy for hypocritical clerics protecting good Christians' souls. By PEJORATION, shit meant excrement.

shivaree
The arousing music that accompanied a newly married pair to bed, the rhythms and melody composed to stimulate coupling; also, CHIVAREE and *charivari.*

shochet
A Jewish ritual animal slaughterer who prepares KOSHER meat.

shofar
A ram's horn trumpet sounded in the Jewish SYNAGOGUE on JUBILEEs and on the HIGH HOLY DAYS of ROSH HASHONAH and YOM KIPPUR to stir the congregation to repentance and vigilance against future sin.

shower of gold
In classical mythology, the virgin Danae was impregnated by Jupiter by means of a shower of gold light, in TYPOLOGY a PREFIGURATION of the Virgin Mary's miraculous conception of Christ.

shrine
A receptacle for the RELICs of a holy personage. Visited by the pious on PILGRIMAGE, shrines ranged in size and magnificence from a small box or COFFER to exquisitely ornamented rooms, tombs, CHAPELs, or consecrated buildings surmounted by SPIREs and crenelated towers.

shroud
A death cloak or winding sheet (BRANDEUM), counterpart to the first clothing, the infant's SWADDLING BANDS.

Shrovetide
The festive merrymaking of the Sunday, Shrove Monday, and Shrove Tuesday, the days preceding ASH WEDNESDAY, the first day of the Christian fast of LENT.

Shrove Tuesday
The Tuesday preceding ASH WEDNESDAY, celebrated with merriment, games, plays, and the FASTNACHTSSPIEL.

shul
A SYNAGOGUE. One of the oldest is at Prague, Czechoslovakia.

shulklopper
An Eastern European village SYNAGOGUE official charged with awakening parishioners for morning prayer services by rapping on doors or shutters and shouting "Arise for praising the Creator!"

sibyl
A woman prophet. A pagan priestess of Apollo adopted into early Chrsitian literature, each seer was named after her native land: the Agrippine, Cimmerian, Cumaean, Delphic, Hellespontic, Erythraean, Phrygian, and Tiburtine Sibyl.

Sibyl of the Rhine
Saint Hildegard of Bingen, the great physician, mystic, and prognosticator, who was profoundly admired by Saint Bernard of Clairvaux.

Sic et Non
(Latin, Yes and No) Peter Abelard's discourse demonstrating that biblical or exegetical authority can be found for either side of almost any theological or moral argument.

sickle
A small hand-held agricultural implement, a crescent-shaped blade attached to a handle.

siddur
The traditional Jewish prayer book, rarely decorated, unlike the HAGGADAH.

sideboard
A rectangular table set perpendicular to a banquet hall's HIGH TABLE, at which guests eat seated according to social rank.

sidrah
One of the 54 weekly recited biblical portions of the PENTATEUCH, read or chanted in a SYNAGOGUE, the cycle beginning at the festival of SIMCHAT TORAH.

siege engines
Ingenious mechanical military devices. Those designed by fourteenth-century physician-technologist Guido da Vigevano include CATAPULTs with prefabricated, portable, and multi-purpose parts, paddle-wheel boats, towers using structural iron, and armored fighting wagons powered by crank shaft or windmill. Vegetius's popular treatise on war works inspired important military instrument design and strategy.

sigil
A magical or astrological device receiving its potency from the constellation, planet, or star under which it had been made.

signature
External characteristics corresponding to inner qualities, a demonstration that the ORDO MUNDI is definable through PHYSIOGNOMY.

significator
In ASTROLOGY, a planet ruling a celestial sign particular to the QUERENT's interest. A question about money requires reference to the lord of the second HOUSE.

sign man
A depiction of astrological governance of human anatomy. A nude man pictured with ZODIAC symbols ascribed to each bodily part INFLUENCEd: Aries guiding and guarding the head, Sagittarius the thighs, and Pisces the feet; also called ASTROLOGICAL MAN or ZODIAC MAN.

Silenus's ass
A loud raucous sound, an emergency alert to danger. Priapus, a classical fertility god, tried to rape a nymph who was alerted to her danger by a braying ass (Ovid's *Fasti:* 1). In moralized Christian versions of the tale, the strident sound, as in the Jewish SHOFAR, calls sinners awake.

silesian
A fine linen or cotton fabric for costumes, originally imported from Silesia in Germany.

silete
A musical interlude sung or played by instruments, as in Arnoul Greban's fifteenth-century *Mystère de la Passion.*

silken gold
Silk fabric patterned, threaded, and woven with gold thread. An important Arab manufacture in Spain and Sicily, and later in central and northern Italy, providing rich cloth for ceremonial garments both ecclesiastic and secular.

silly
A blessedly foolish, innocent person. In their ENFANCES, both the Arthurian hero Percival and Tristan are DÜMMLINGS.

simarra
A long-sleeved, floor-length outer ROBE, sometimes belted, worn by secular men of importance and high ranking ecclesiastics, such as cardinals.

Simchat Torah
(Hebrew, celebration of the Torah) A Jewish festival rejoicing in the Law, celebrating the annual beginning of a cycle of TORAH readings with the first SIDRAH.

simile
A literary device intensifying meaning and effect by a comparison using the comparative words *like* or *as.* The next levels of ascending literary abstraction are METAPHOR, SYMBOL, and ALLEGORY.

simnell
A fine-grained white bread; a kitchen staple, with MANCHET and PANDEMAYN.

simony
Purchase of ecclesiastical privileges, benefits, and jobs; the name from the magician Simon Magus's attempt to buy Saint Peter's secrets of power (Acts 8–18).

simple
A plant, mineral, or animal substance used as a drug without compounding with other substances; a

GALENICAL; a dance described in ORCHESOGRAPHY and discussed by Antonius de Arena; or a dance step in the PAVAN and BASSE DANCE.

sine baccho
(Latin, wineless) A praise of APHRODISIACs. According to the Roman dramatist Terence: *sine baccho et cerere friget venus,* without wine and beautiful feasts, love grows cold (*The Eunuch,* 732).

sinecure
(Latin *sine cura,* without responsibility) A cleric's or civil servant's payment for a job having no responsibilities, a work-free guaranteed annual wage.

singspiele
(German, song talk) A dramatic music text—part prose, part verse, part spoken part sung, as Adam de la Halle's *Le Jeu de Robin et Marion,* a CHANT-FABLE.

sinister
Left-handed. According to PHYSIOGNOMIES, clumsy, treacherous, or physiologically incapable of doing things right, unlike the propensity of those who are DEXTER, right-handed.

sink-apace
(French, *cinq pas,* five step) A five-step, six-musical beat dance, also called the CINQ PAS.

sinopia
A reddish-brown pigment, originally from the city of Sinopia in Asia Minor. The color was important in the full-scale FRESCO drawings, the UNDERPAINTING or PENTIMENTI, that preceded the final plaster-painted surface.

siren
A fantastic beast with the head of a woman and the body of a bird, whose seductive song could lure mariners to shoals and reefs and thus destroy their ships.

sirventes
Satiric songs of Provençal TROUBADOURs lambasting rivals, enemies, and political events.

situla
A holy water jar, used with the ASPERGILL or ASPERGE in Christian celebrations at the ALTAR or in ecclesiastical processions.

sivlonot
(Hebrew, gifts) An exchange of gifts between a Jewish bride and groom, usually before signing the KETUBAH; also, the required giving of charitable gifts on certain holidays.

sixes and sevens
Signifying confusion and disorder, the phrase derived from a fourteenth-century gambling game, avoiding the malevolent number 13; number words and number symbols pervade GEMATRIA and the mystical theory behind MAGIC SQUARES.

six requisites for a good dancer
Enumerated by fifteenth-century DANCE MASTERS Antonio Cornazano and Guglielmo Ebreo in their treatises on the art of dance: *memoria* (remembering steps and their sequence correctly); *misura* (keeping good rhythm); *aiere* (pleasing grace of movement); *diversita di cose* (intuitive step variety); *compartimento di terreno* (correct estimation of body in space); and *maneria* (poise and posture).

six tinctures
The heraldic COLORS: AZURE (blue), GULES (red), VERT (green), PURPURA (purple), SABLE (black), and TENNE (orange).

size
Practically pure gelatine made from boiling PARCHMENT fragments in water, used for binding pigments for paint.

skaldic verse
(Icelandic and Old Norse *skald,* poet) Poems of heroic deeds and adventures in war by the 250 skalds who were designated as the political entertainers of Scandinavian and English kings and nobles (from the ninth through the thirteenth centuries).

slashings
Small openings cut in a garment's surface to display an elaborate lining or undergarment, as in CLOAKs,

sleeves, shoes, gloves, and gowns. The tiniest cuts were called MOUCHETUREs. Like DAGGING and CASTELLATED COSTUME, decorative slashing carried to excess contravened SUMPTUARY LAWS.

slip
A fluid mixture of clay and water, often incorporating color oxides, used in casting and surface ornamentations of pottery.

slype
A covered passage to a CLOISTER, usually between the TRANSEPT and CHAPTER HOUSE of a CHURCH, MONASTERY, or CATHEDRAL.

small beer
To discuss trivia, or to drink mild, weak beer rather than strong beer or ale.

snood
A net hair-covering usually ornamented with pearls, jewels, and small designs in precious metal. It was similar to the CAUL and TRESSOUR.

socage
A landholder's obligations to a landowner. The TENURE of a SOKE-man, including such feudal INCIDENTs as fealty, RELIEF, ESCHEAT, and court-holding; or payments of labor a VILLEIN was obligated to make to an overlord, as WEEK-WORK and BOON-WORK. Variants of the basic agreement were free socage, common socage, and both free and common socage.

soccus
A SOCQ.

Society of Pui
The brotherhood of French and English traders in London, united in 1299 both for charitable purposes and for the cultivation of music and poetry.

socle
A low simple block or PLINTH pedestal for a sculpture, column, or vase.

socq
A flaring, regal ceremonial cloak fastened at the right shoulder, worn at coronations or at important secular and ecclesiastical ceremonies.

Socratic
Pertaining to the fifth-century B.C. Athenian philosopher Socrates, whose teaching technique by DEBATE led to his ideal tenet: Know thyself. Socrates was the beloved intellectual and spiritual mentor of the philosopher Plato. In INSTRUCTION BOOKs for dying, the ARS MORIENDI, Socrates was praised for his fortitude in facing death by suicide with hemlock.

soggetto cavato
(Italian *cavato delli vocalli,* carving out vowels) A sixteenth-century technique in music composition. Vowels were carved out of a sentence and transformed to melody according to the SOLMIZATION syllables of the GUIDO'S HAND and the HEXACHORD.

soke
Jurisdiction; a right to hold court and receive fines and forfeits from it; a judicial and administrative unit.

solace
(French, satisfaction) Entertainment, delight, stylistic virtuosity, the opposite of substantive meaning, matter, and SENTENCE; the diverting half of the pedagogic antitheses DOCERE ET DELECTARE.

solace stone
A small, semiprecious, oval-cut, finely smoothed and polished stone, designed to fit easily into the palm of the hand for massaging for emotional equilibrium. LAPIDARIES suggested particular minerals with occult powers, making them superior to mere birth stones, for providing spiritual tranquility.

solar
A sunny, quiet private room or study.

solers
Leather or fabric footgear or slippers.

solitudo
(Latin, loneliness, solitariness) A literary technique in works using a PERSONA "I" in which the author includes details of autobiography and, ultimately, a personal voice. It sounds in Langland's *Piers Plowman* and later in Spenser's *Faery Queene.*

solmization
The systems for indicating pitch on a musical scale by syllables, not letters, as in Guido d'Arezzo's names for the tones C through A: *ut, re, mi, fa, so, la*. From a hymn to Saint John: *Ut* queant laxis; *Re*sonare fibris; *Mi*ra gestorum; *Fa*muli tuorum; *Sol*ve polluti; *La*bii reatum; Sancte Joannes. See GUIDO'S HAND.

solstice
One of two times in the year midway between the two equinoxes, the sun having reached the points farthest from the equator and appearing to stand still. The summer solstice is around June 21, the winter solstice around December 22.

sop
A crouton, a small piece of TOAST or dried bread cut from a loaf or TRENCHER to float atop wine, ale, soup, or tea for nutrition, avoiding waste, and, when spiced with herbs such as TANSY, fragrance. It was a crowning constituent of LAMB'S WOOL.

sorquenie
(Or soucaine) A woman's TUNIC tightly fitted at the bust line, flowing down to the hemline.

sortisatio
The musical improvisation of vocal POLYPHONY using already existing melodies.

sottana
A twelfth- and thirteenth-century Italian solid-color or striped undergown for a TUNIC, worn by both men and women.

soucaine
A SORQUENIE.

souterlidekens
Early Netherlandish monophonic PSALM melodies. An important collection of earlier works was first printed in 1540.

souterrain
An underground passage or chamber.

spa
A health resort, imitative of the famous Belgian mineral springs and medical bathing place called Spa, near Lièges, in which music, food, PHLEBOTOMY, hydrotherapy, and other medical ministrations were applied to ameliorate symptoms, prevent disability, and cure disease.

spa glass
A drinking vessel for curative mineral or spring water treatments and medications, often used in a TENTA INFIRMORUM.

spagna
A significant fifteenth-century monophonic BASSE DANSE melody, often the basis for elaborate POLYPHONY.

spagyric science
The study and craft of separating elements into basic principles or components by natural, chemical, or violent means, to attain their purification.

spalling
Splintering and splitting of PIER masonry because of pressure and thrust, a problem GOTHIC CATHEDRAL engineers solved with various types of FLYING BUTTRESSes.

spaltklang
(German, split sound) Fourteenth- and fifteenth-century musical sonority caused by simultaneous, contrasting, intentionally startling sounds, as in the polyphonic compositions of Machaut and Dufay that unexpectedly sounded the human voice, SHAWM, trombone, and organ together.

spandrel
The triangular space either between the curves of two adjacent arches or between the underside of a staircase and floor.

spangenhelm
A ninth- and tenth-century military helmet of CUIR BOUILLI reinforced with iron strips rising up to a point where they join, topped with a wood or colored glass KNOP.

sparrow
This small bird was supposed to be sexually profligate; its eggs were particularly prized as an APHRODISIAC. Chaucer's most lascivious women are as hot and lecherous as sparrows (in *The Canterbury Tales* and

Parliament of Fowls), a reminder that the bird was thought to be a son of Venus.

speculum
(Latin, mirror) A gynecological viewing instrument consisting of a vaginal dilator sometimes possessing a small angled mirror for reflecting the organs above it. It was also a common mirror, a glass or polished metal surface reflecting reality, or a metaphorical mirror inspiring the ideal, as in the *Speculum Principum*, an INSTRUCTION BOOK for noble etiquette, privileges, and responsibilities, a MIRROR OF PRINCES which ought to reflect princely perfection. Real and metaphorical mirrors shone in art and literature: BIRTH TIME MIRRORS, CONCEPTION TIME MIRRORS, hand mirrors held by such figures of ALLEGORY as Vanity and Sight (one of the FIVE SENSES), or by the Virgin Mary, SPECULUM SINE MACULA (mirror without stain), and water mirrors, such as the MIRROR OF NARCISSUS.

Speculum Musicae
(Latin, Mirror of Music) An important early-fourteenth-century encyclopedic work on music by Jacques de Liège.

speculum sine macula
(Latin, the flawless mirror) The spotless, transparent, luminescent purity of the Virgin Mary, one of the many VIRTUES OF THE VIRGIN, inspired by the Song of Songs.

Sphaera Mundi
(Latin, orbs of the world) An astronomical treatise; specifically, a thirteenth-century astronomy book by Sacrobosco incorporating traditional astrological ideas and scientific observations.

sphygmology
The study of PULSE, closely associated with the development of CLOCKWORK technology, the PULSILOGIUM, CHRONOPHYSICA, and ideas of time.

spill
To spill is to die.

spinster
A woman spinner of such raw materials as flax, wool, cotton, linen, or silk into thread using a DISTAFF, for later weaving.

spiral twist
On furniture and jewelry, a curve winding around a fixed point, but never returning to itself.

spire
A slender, pointed bell tower or turret on a CHURCH, CATHEDRAL, or civic building.

splat
A flat piece of wood, usually the central section of a chairback.

spodic
(Polish, saucer) A high FUR-trimmed hat.

spondee
One of the FIVE METRICAL FEET, consisting of two adjacent long beats.

sponsus
(Latin, bridegroom) A dramatic dialogue set to music between the WISE AND FOOLISH VIRGINS waiting for the bridegroom, a symbol of Christ.

spoon, a long
An epithet for keeping a safe distance from danger. The best kitchen or banquet implement for supping with the Devil was a very long-handled spoon.

S.P.Q.R.
Abbreviation of a motto for identifying public works in classical Rome, often depicted in art: *Senatus Populus que Romanus,* the Senate and the People of Rome.

spread eagle
In ALCHEMY, sublimed sal ammoniac. One of the menagerie of early chemical terms including EAGLE, RED LION, and GREEN LION, which sometimes graphically or metaphorically described the chemical reaction, sometimes purposefully hid the true subject of discourse from those who would not, could not, or should not understand.

spruch
(German, saying or proverb) A moralistic, serious, or satiric song of a MINNESINGER (Walther von der Vogelweide wrote excellent ones), similar to the Provençal SIRVENTES.

Spy Wednesday
The Wednesday before GOOD FRIDAY commemorating Judas Iscariot's betrayal of Christ (Matthew 26:14).

Squarcialupi Codex
The important fourteenth-century musical collection, now in Florence, including works of Francesco Landini.

squinch
An architectural support for a DOME or other superstructure; or a narrow slit in an interior or exterior building wall to allow light or sound to pass through, as in the SQUINT in a MONASTERY or castle hall, or the barrier separating the women's GALLERY from the main SYNAGOGUE.

squint
A peephole, a small, sometimes imperceptible opening or covered slit in a wall, a SQUINCH, curtain, or tapestry to allow peeking through into a hall without being observed. Banquet hall servants and SURVEYORS used it to permit perfect timing of food service and culinary ceremony. In the KABALLAH, physical ecstacy on earth was described as a squint of PARADISE, forecasting the ecstatic union of the pious with the Godhead in heavenly radiance.

squire
A knight's attendant, ranking just below him in feudal hierarchy; or a HOUSEHOLD officer providing personal rather than martial services. The squire in Chaucer's *Canterbury Tales* serves his noble father both these ways.

Stabbat Mater Dolorosa
(Latin, The sorrowful mother was standing) A thirteenth-century prayer commemorating the SEVEN SORROWS OF THE VIRGIN, attributed to Jacopone da Todi. The text was later set to music by Josquin, Palestrina, and Pergolesi (and even later by Haydn, Schubert, Rossini, and Dvorak).

stained glass
Flat pieces of glass colored by metallic oxides and juxtaposed to form figures or patterns, the pieces fitted together by leaded, grooved CALMS. Some colors such as CANTERBURY BLUE were exquisitely radiant. Details, decorations, and facial features were painted on clear or colored glass either before or after its firing. GRISAILLE (a mixture of crushed glass with iron or copper oxides, cobalt, and other mineral pigments) created a delicate gray-green or brown-black shading and details for modeling of figures, features, and draperies; and SGRAFFITO (scratched or abraded lines) reaffirmed designs and emphasized features. CATHEDRAL ROSE WINDOWS usually were ornamented with TRACERY.

stall
A CHURCH CHOIR's wooden or stone high-backed seat, usually one of a row, often with a MISERICORD and carved with TRACERY.

stalled cairn
A long burial mound, a CAIRN with interior earthern walls subdivided into sections.

stamped work
A raised decoration on metal objects created by hammering the surface from behind into a depressed die or mold; REPOUSSE.

stanjant
Describing a heraldic beast in profile, its feet on the ground, head bent towards viewer.

staple
A warehouse used by foreign merchants; or a town's right to oblige foreign merchants to store wares for several days for quantity observation, quality grading, and collection of duties or taxes. In England, the market for wool, leather, and animal skins was governed by the Law of the Staple, and like the MERCHANT ADVENTURERS, all mercantile infractions were tried by juries of peers. A staple also was the length of a strand of wool. MERCHANTS OF THE STAPLE sold their wares in a STAPLE HALL equipped with scales, weights, and measures such as the STEELYARD.

staple hall
An enclosed marketplace, usually for wool trading.

starboard
(Anglo-Saxon, *steorbord*, steering rudder) A boat's or ship's right-hand side. The steering oar of ANGLO-SAXON boats was on the right side, therefore the

steerside with the steerboard, or starboard; the left side was the loading or lading side, lade-board or larboard, the portside.

stationarius

A publisher of new MANUSCRIPTs, or a craftsman producing standardized books for sale in the open market. The stationarius usually was an entrepreneur, a coordinator for the market of productions of calligraphers, artists, and illuminators working in a SCRIPTORIUM. The stationarius often worked with a LIBRARIUS, a bookseller.

station days

Eighty-seven particular days on which the Pope says MASS in specific station churches in Rome with elaborate clerical and popular processions from one church to another, a custom probably beginning in the sixth century with Saint Gregory the Great.

Stations of the Cross

The prayers said in a symbolic recreation of Christ's march towards CRUCIFIXION, or the VIA DOLOROSA. Popularized by the FRANCISCANS, there are 14 stations: (1) Christ's condemnation; (2) receiving the cross; (3) first fall; (4) meeting Mary; (5) Simon of Cyrene bears the cross; (6) Veronica uses her VERNICLE; (7) second fall; (8) meeting women of Jerusalem; (9) third fall; (10) stripping; (11) nailing; (12) Christ dying; (13) descent from the cross; (14) burial.

statute of limitations

The legal time limits within which rights can be enforced and suits brought in court, a STATUTE OF REPOSE. In 1275 in England, a law limited time after which a person claiming SEIZIN in land could provide evidence of title. The statute also barred any action to recover land if the plaintiff delayed too long, a peril of LACHES.

statute of repose

A legal bar to a court action after a specified time has passed, providing possessors of property and perpetrators of acts a time after which they are free from lawsuit; a STATUTE OF LIMITATIONS.

Statute of Uses

England's King Henry VIII, eager for money in 1536, forced on an unwilling Parliament the law to convert the equitable right to use land into legal title and right to possess, transforming CESTUI QUE USE to ownership.

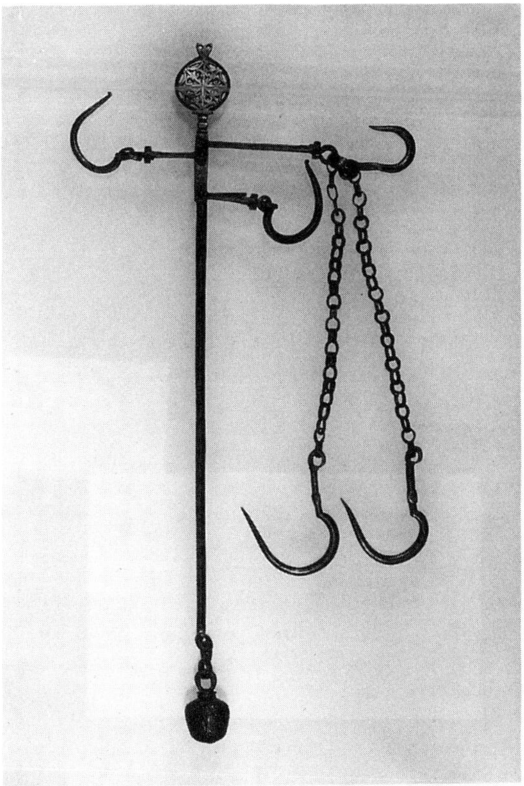

A steelyard scale for weighing produce has hooks for weights on one side and for the item to be weighed on the other. (From Spain, 15th century; courtesy of the Metropolitan Museum of Art)

steelyard

(German *Stalhof,* a pattern [sample or template] courtyard) The Hanseatic merchants' market and warehouse on the north bank of the Thames in fourteenth-century London. Also, the weighing device for dry goods, consisting of an unequal-armed balance on a fulcrum: the object was placed on the shorter arm, and weights were moved on the longer calibrated arm in counterbalance.

steeple

A church bell tower. A CATHEDRAL usually has three steeples. Also, a woman's HENNIN.

stellio
A newt.

stenciling
An artistic duplication of design by cutting out a thin, durable template sheet and dabbing, rubbing, brushing, or pouring a coloring agent through the opening.

stew
A fishpond, bath, SPA, or whorehouse. "The Stews" was a name for fourteenth-century London's red light district, coexisting with the title COCK'S LANE.

sticagron
(Greek *stichos,* verse) BYZANTINE church musical and poetical TROPEs interspersed between the verses of a PSALM; important from the eighth century onward.

stigmata
Wounds on hands, feet, chest, and side, imitative of Christ's at the CRUCIFIXION. Those blessed with stigmata included Saint Catherine of Siena and Saint Francis of Assisi.

stiletto
A short dagger with a thick blade.

stimmtausch
(German, voice swop) A thirteenth-century musical technique in which higher and lower voices exchanged parts in COUNTERPOINT, soprano singing alto, such that several parts moved within the same vocal range.

stimulus amoris
(Latin, a stimulation to love) The title of numerous meditations on Christ's PASSION, written for neophytes to recreate imaginatively the wounds, pain, terrors, and sacrifice of the CRUCIFIXION. An important text profoundly affecting later ICONOGRAPHY was William of Pagula's copy of the thirteenth-century FRANCISCAN James of Milan's description of Christ as a WINE PRESS; the METAPHOR earlier was Saint Augustine's.

stipes
(Latin, an upright log or tree-trunk) An upright, spirally threaded post of a WINE PRESS, an important iconographic representation of Christ's PASSION derived from a STIMULUS AMORIS.

stippling
In painting and ENGRAVING, gradation of shade or color produced by dots or small spots.

stirk
A pasture for young cattle.

stivali
High, soft, close-fitting, light-weight summer boots, usually black or red.

stockfish
Dried codfish, a fish for all seasons and classes. Apparently hated by the poor who needed it as a source of protein (Erasmus thought it nourished no more than a stick), yet it was enjoyed by the nobility in elaborate recipes.

stollen
The two sections of the ABGESANG of the MINNESINGERS' song.

stomacher
In ARMOR, a chest-cover or vest; or a woman's ornamental breast covering that was worn beneath lacings of a bodice.

stone of redness
The final stage of an alchemical process, after the STONE OF WHITENESS, in the transmutation of base metal to gold.

stone of whiteness
The second stage of an alchemical process, changing metals into silver. The STONE OF REDNESS anticipated the final success of AUREFACTION.

strambotto
A fifteenth-century Italian song style with an eight-line stanza rhyming in repetitive line pairs.

strapwork
An ornament of narrow bands folded, crossed, or interlaced in a repeated design, common in wood carving, TALAVERA and other MAJOLICA, decorative metalwork, and stone carving.

stravaganza
(Italian, extravagant) A musical composition with fanciful and extravagant harmonies and dissonances.

streimel
A saucer-shaped hat with a flat fur brim, worn by Jewish men. The rim of a rabbi's streimel consisted of the tails of 13 sable.

stretcher
A brace or rail reinforcing chair legs, tables, and other objects of furniture. Common stretcher designs were flat, carved, scrolled, X-shaped, serpentine, or BARLEY TWIST.

string course
A stone or brick horizontal MOLDING on the face of a wall.

stoup
A stone HOLY WATER FONT or basin near a church's west door.

stucco
Building FACADE of plasterwork imitating stonework.

stumpwork
An elaborate EMBROIDERY technique utilizing knots and APPLIQUE to create the illusion of depth; a BAS RELIEF embroidery.

subinfeudation
The process of granting property interests to smaller and smaller holders of TENURE, each TENANT owing economic and other INCIDENTs to the holder above. The procedure could result in a FEUDAL PYRAMID, and after the thirteenth-century QUIA EMPTORES, was replaced by SUBSTITUTION.

sublimation
Chemical purification of matter by heating, reduction, and volatilization.

substitution
After the statute QUIA EMPTORES, the substitution of land rights and responsibilities from one possessor to another, as opposed to SUBINFEUDATION or continuity of the FEUDAL PYRAMID. This statute marked the beginning of modern property law.

Subtle Doctor
An epithet for the scholastic theologian Duns Scotus, who died in 1308. His analytical pedantry and rigid certitude was memorialized in the word DUNCE.

subtletie
An elaborate, banquet-hall sculpture depicting a scene, personage, or ALLEGORY crafted from pastry, spun sugar, MARZIPAN, or combinations of papier mâché or metal armature with edible coatings and decorations. A subtletie was placed at a site of honor in the banquet hall, or paraded between courses to herald arrival of the next delectable dish. Breaking and eating the subtletie was the final ceremony of a fabulous feast.

succubus
A female demon said to attack men sexually at night and to cause sin; the female counterpart of the INCUBUS.

suckenie
A thirteenth-century German COTELETTE, an unbelted long, sleeveless, side-slit overdress, usually with a drawstring at the neck.

sudarium
A handkerchief or cloth, such as the VERNICLE which Saint Veronica offered to Christ on the road to CALVARY, and upon which his facial features were miraculously inscribed.

sufficit unum lumen in tenebris
(Latin, One light is sufficient in the darkness) But when the flame of a single candle is extinguished, all is lost. So Christ's APOSTLES deserted him at the CRUCIFIXION.

sukenis
The Judaic SARGENES.

sukkah
The ceremonial hut or booth partly open to the sky, decorated with festival fruits and vegetables, in which observant Jews assemble and eat to celebrate SUKKOT.

Sukkot
The Jewish Feast of TABERNACLES or Feast of Booths.

sulphur
The yellow chemical element that can be consumed by fire. In ALCHEMY, sulphur is symbolic of the soul. It is allied with MERCURY, the spirit, and with salt or SAL, the body.

sulphur vive
(Latin, living sulphur) The alchemical sulphur, according to Raymond Lull, the fourteenth-century ALCHEMIST and Christian philosopher from Catalonia, similar to MERCURY, but unlike the common element SULPHUR.

sumptuary laws
Rigorously enforced rules and regulations pronounced by civic or religious authorities to govern food, clothing, entertainment, and articles of ostentatious display. Certain FURS, fabrics, silks, and taffetas could be worn only by particular classes, nationalities, or professions. Fourteenth-century prostitutes could be fined or jailed for wearing FUR-lined hoods, which could be worn only by noble women. Specific COLORS were reserved for special classes, and related legislation required Jews to wear JEWISH BADGES.

superius
In polyphonic music, the voice in the uppermost range.

supertunic
A circular full-sleeved overgarment, often belted at the waist.

supplica stet credula
(Latin, Please do not tear down this advertisement) A warning printed at the bottom of fifteenth-century advertisements such as the one that William Caxton created at Westminster for his edition of the *Sarum Ordinal,* a book prescribing the order of services, rules, and regulations of Salisbury Cathedral.

surcoat
An overgarment, knee-to-floor length, but shorter and with sideslits for horseback riding, sleeveless or half-sleeved, sometimes long with tight sleeves. It was a successor to the BLIAUT.

surplice
(Latin, *super+pellicia,* an over-fur-coat) A loose-fitting overgarment, usually a white ankle-length VESTMENT worn by clerics and choir-singers from the thirteenth century on.

Surroy
The funeral heraldic master CLARENCEUX, with responsibility for services south of the Trent River; opposite of the NORROY.

surtout
(French, over everything) An outer CLOAK, coat, or cape worn over all other garments.

surveying board
Also called a dresser, this banquet hall table was the site for the final food preparation, decoration, dressing, and saucing before service to the HIGH TABLE and to guests at SIDEBOARDS.

surveyor
The master of hospitality in the banquet hall charged with supervising the carving, service of food, musical and dramatic entertainment, parading and placing of SUBTLETIES, seating of guests according to rank, overseeing service at the HIGH TABLE, and general gracious care and feeding of the assemblage.

suspirium
A musical rest equivalent to the MINIMA, equal to a modern half-note.

Su Sung's clock
In 1090 in Hunan Province, China, three centuries before Giovanni da Dondi's ASTRARIUM and CLOCKWORK, Su Sung built a spectacular astronomical clock tower enclosing a water wheel that drove clockwork which rotated an ARMILLARY SPHERE on the top platform and a celestial globe in the upper story, while puppet figures appeared and sounded hours and quarter hours. It was built to forecast the movements of the sun, the moon, and the planets (like twelfth-century Hindu astronomer Bhaskara's perpetual motion mercury wheel), with the time-telling by hours and minutes being secondary to the celestial.

The great gold buckle from the Sutton Hoo burial treasure. (From c. 9th century, London, courtesy of the British Museum)

Sutton Hoo
A magnificent ANGLO-SAXON royal ship burial in an English heathland BARROW at Sutton Hoo in East Anglia, containing gold jewelry, silver bowls, an enamelled ESCUTCHEON, cauldrons, and weaponry. Legally not TREASURE TROVE or crown property, the excavated hoard was a gift to the British Museum.

swaddling bands
Long soft fabric, ribbons, or cloths wrapped around infants from neck to feet for comforting, warming, maintaining good posture and straight limbs, and preventing accidents. This first clothing had its ritual parallel in the corpse's garment, the SHROUD.

swag
An ornamental design created with real fabric or painted or carved imitations of leaf, flower and fruit garlands arranged in hanging loops between anchoring points, festooning a surface or space.

swyve
Sexual intercourse.

syllabic style
The musical setting of a single syllable of text to a single note in GREGORIAN CHANTS and thirteenth-century POLYPHONY; opposite to MELISMA.

symbol
A graphic representation, ATTRIBUTE, or sign, an almost universally accepted pictorial or abstract embodiment of an idea or person, such as a winged lion for Saint Mark, APOCALYPTIC BEASTS for the FOUR EVANGELISTS, and a lily for purity, virginity, or the Virgin Mary.

symphonia
A HURDY-GURDY; or consonance rather than dissonance in music and poetry.

Synagoga-Ecclesia
Allegorical personifications of the Old Testament's SYNAGOGUE depicted as a figure bent forward, shabbily dressed, and blindfolded. Her opposite, the Holy Church, stood tall, beautifully garbed, radiant with the light of knowledge. The pair graphically represented the new order superseding the old, a common TYPOLOGY.

synagogue
(From Greek, to bring together) The Jewish building (Hebrew *beth hamidrash,* house of study) dedicated to the triple purposes of study, prayer, and assembly.

synemmenon
A musical term for the note B-flat and an indicator of chromatic alteration.

syrinx

The PAN PIPE, a row of graduated pipes bound together, each a different pitch; the pipe sometimes was played simultaneously with a TABOR.

syzyges

The astronomical conjunction or opposition of two heavenly bodies, particularly the new and full moon with the sun.

T

tabard

A short-sleeved or sleeveless short coat, open at the sides, worn over a shirt or over ARMOR. As worn by knights, the tabard usually had armorial DEVICES emblazoned on front, back, and sleeves. Special COLORS identified the wearer's social group: for instance, in 1360, all Jews of Rome (except physicians) were required to wear a red tabard.

tabernacle

A miniature chapel, SHRINE, or compartment containing a sacred object (a book, devotional object, consecrated HOST, CROSS, or OSTENSORY). Also, a canopied structure (tomb or shrine) or niche or recess in a wall or pillar.

Tabernacles Feast

The Jewish feast of SUKKOT. An eight-day-long thanksgiving for the harvest, Sukkot was celebrated in outdoor booths or tabernacles to commemorate the Israelites' sojourn in the wilderness (Leviticus 23:42–43).

tablature

An early notational system for music, especially for lute playing. Tones are indicated by letters, figures, and symbols, rather than by NEUMEs. Tablature differs also from MENSURAL NOTATION. The tablature staff represents each lute string to be stopped for a particular pitch; a similar tablature indicates holes on a FLUTE for flute notation.

table dormant

A stationary table. By contrast, TRESTLE TABLES were set up for meals and dismantled when not in use.

table fountain

An elaborately engineered recirculating device for simultaneously serving multiple types of wine. Often made from precious metal and decorated with ENAMEL and jewels, a complex system of piping and spigots allowed the separate vintages to spout in different directions.

A silver gilt table fountain with enamelry courtly scenes, crenelated walls, and, at top, adorsed lions. (From France, late 14th century; courtesy of the Cleveland Museum of Art)

taboo
(Or GEIS) A forbidden word or action. An important concept in literature and folklore (especially MÄRCHEN), a violation of taboo produces dire effects, such as the TRANSFORMATION of a man into a WEREWOLF.

tabor
A drum, especially a light, small drum, played while buckled onto the player's chest or left arm; usually accompanying a PIPE.

tactus
The musical beat which defines the duration of notes and pitches.

tactus eruditus
(Latin, learned touch) In CHRONOPHYSICA, the doctor's fingers' ability to detect information vital for diagnosis, prognosis, and treatment from the patient's PULSE. Its rhythm, strength, and tempo were charted as pulse music.

Tacuinum Sanitatis
(Latin, table of health) The popular health handbook uniting culinary, medical, and practical hygiene lore. It derived from tenth-century Ibn Butlan's *Tables of Health.*

tagelied
(German, day song) A day song or dawn song; the MINNESINGER equivalent of the Provençal ALBA.

take the cake
To win the prize. Breads and cakes were payment for HOUSEHOLD services and common festival prizes. To "take the cake" at the TWELFTH NIGHT festival, one had to find the bean, silver buckle, coin, porcelain doll, or semi-precious jewel baked into a special cake.

talavera
Sixteenth-century Castilian Spanish tin-glazed earthenware. Specializing in tiles decorated with ACANTHUS motifs, STRAPWORK, and GROTESQUERIE in yellow, blue, orange, and olive green on white, the Talavera workshops also produced EWERS, plates, jars, and basins.

taleae
Repeated musical patterns or "cuttings" in ISORHYTHMIC structures of MOTETs.

talisman
A stone or ring engraved with figures or characters believed to possess occult powers deriving from planetary INFLUENCEs at the time of its carving; worn or carried as an amulet to summon good fortune, heal, and avert evil.

tallage
A tax feudal dependents paid to their overlords, variously computed based on the amount of land held. Varieties include Michaelmas tallage (at MICHAELMAS), incoming tallage (at the arrival of a new lord, HERIOT (at a VILLEIN's death), MERCHET (by a villein at his daughter's marriage), RELIEF (when taking over a new landholding), and *wood penny* (for the right to gather dead wood). The church taxed in similar manner, collecting a TITHE (one tenth of the value of crop or CHATTELS) and other taxes such as a mortuary (at the death of a parishioner).

tallit
A fringed prayer shawl worn by Jewish men during worship. The fringes are meant to remind the wearer of his duty to observe all 613 commandments of the TORAH (Numbers 15:37–41).

Talmud
The compilation of Jewish civil and ceremonial law, including the rabbinic codes and commentaries found in the MISHNAH and GEMARRAH.

tambourine
A musical instrument consisting of a membrane or skin stretched over one side of a stiff round frame circled by metal discs that jingle when the tambourine is shaken or struck with the fingers.

tankard
A drinking vessel in the shape of a tall mug or jug. Early tankards were made of wooden staves bound together by hoops. Later versions made of ceramic, glass, or semi-precious metal, usually had one handle and a lid.

tansy
A tall, yellow-flowered plant with pungent taste and fragrance recommended in HERBALS and HEALTH MANUALS for treating an upset stomach and popular for spicing omelets and SOPs in wine.

Tantum Ergo
(Latin, therefore we bend before Him) The last two verses of Saint Thomas Aquinas's hymn PANGUE LINGUA, usually sung while bowing or genuflecting.

tänze
Winter songs (REIEN are summer songs) composed by MINNESINGERs such as Neidhart von Reuenthal in a stately meter similar to that of courtly indoor dances.

tapestry
A hand-woven textile whose design is woven during manufacture and thus forms an integral part of the fabric. Warp threads, usually made of hemp or FLAX, were stretched taut, lengthwise, on a frame or loom. Weft threads, made of variously-colored wool or silk, or gold or silver thread, were worked in, at right angles to the warp, with bobbins and pressed close by a comb, following a laid-out pattern or CARTOON. Types of tapestry produced in Flanders and France include ARRAS, MILLEFLEURS, AUBUSSON, and such masterful individual works and series as the Cluny *Lady with the* UNICORN and the Cloisters' *Unicorn Hunt* and NINE HEROES.

tappit hen
A Scottish pewter CHALICE having a lid with a knob.

tappster
A woman innkeeper or tavern owner. Tappster became a common MATRONYMIC, like brewster, baxter, and other titles held by women in the hostelry profession.

tarot
Playing cards popular in fourteenth-century Europe used as a game and for fortune-telling. Usually 78 cards formed a pack, 56 in four suits and 22 figured trump cards.

tasseaux
Square or circular ornaments worn at shoulder level on the MANTLE or cape, favored by courtly women and men of the twelfth and thirteenth centuries.

tasses
Metal ARMOR hip protectors, usually constructed with four to eight overlapping plates, one side hinged, the other buckled.

tastar
(Italian *tastar de corde,* touching the strings) A free-styled, sixteenth-century Italian LUTE composition.

tawdry
Originally, elaborate lacework named to honor Saint Audrey, patron saint of lace workers. Probably because of the commercial success of lace and trinket fairs on Saint Audrey's Day, by the seventeenth century the term had acquired the modern meaning of cheap and showy.

tayador
A large carving plate or serving dish, also called a tallador.

tazza
A footed wine cup with a wide, shallow bowl, usually covered; or a footed ornamental serving vessel shared between two diners.

tear
A decorative glass pendant in the shape of a tear, a *larme de verre.*

teasle
A stiff brush or comb that raised the nap on the surface of cloth, often used with a NAP BOW.

Te igitur
(Latin, Thee therefore) The first words of the first section of the CANON of the Roman MASS, requesting God's acceptance of the EUCHARIST.

tempera
A painting technique created by emulsifying finely ground pigment in egg white and water (GLAIR), fig sap, or thin glue (*distemper*). Tempera was the favored panel medium of the Middle Ages (oil painting became popular in the fifteenth century) because of its

Temperance and her mechanical clock entertain four women. (From Christine de Pisan's *Othea*, 15th century, Bodleian Library, Oxford)

clear pure colors and water-resistant, durable polished surface. When used on wood panels such as altarpieces, tempera was applied atop GESSO underpainting. When used for painting MURALs, it was known as *fresco secco* (dry fresco) to distinguish it from the *buon fresco* (true fresco) applied on damp walls.

Temperance
With Justice, Prudence, and Fortitude, one of the FOUR CARDINAL VIRTUES. In allegorical depictions, she often appears with a clock or wears a clock headdress demonstrating a measured, well-regulated, rhythmically harmonious order. Other common depictions show her pouring liquid from one pitcher to another (diluting wine with water suggests moderation in drinking), holding a torch and a pitcher (dousing the fire of lust with water suggests sexual restraint), or holding or wearing a bridle.

templet
A small metal ornament for rolling a woman's hair above her ears.

temporal simultaneity
The technique of presenting multiple stages of life of persons or institutions in a single work of art; also called CHRONOSYNCRONISITY. Thus, the same person may be depicted in THREE AGES: youth, prime, and old age; or a couple may be depicted at their wedding, on the nuptial bed, and greeting grandchildren.

tempus
(Latin, time) In thirteenth-century music theory, the smallest unit of musical time, usually represented by the *brevis,* but in the ARS NOVA by the *semi-brevis.*

tenancy
A land INDENTURE in which a feudal landowner parcels out portions of his estate to free or to bound peasants for them to farm. The lord retains ownership of the land and, in return for the opportunity to generate their own livelihood from the land, TENANTs are required to provide goods, services, and rents to the manor LORD.

tenant
In COMMON LAW, a possessor of property under TENURE, not an ALLODIAL owner.

tenant in capiti
(Latin, tenant in chief) In land TENURE, the person holding land directly from the ALLODIAL owner of the property, from whom all others below hold land possession by SUBINFEUDATION.

tenne
In HERALDRY, the COLOR orange.

tennis
The racket sport was already popular among French knights in the early fourteenth century, where balls were made out of cloth from the Egyptian town of Tinnis. As a diplomatic insult, the French dauphin sent England's King Henry V a ton of tennis balls to suggest that he should play with them instead of with armies.

tenor
In thirteenth-century and later POLYPHONY, the voice carrying the CANTUS FIRMUS to which all other parts are added; also called the *vox principalis* or CANTUS.

ten sephirot
As used from the twelfth century in the Jewish mystical tradition of the ZOHAR and the KABALLAH, the

10 emanations through which the Divine is made manifest, or ten levels of mystical insight, as represented by the SEPHIROTIC TREE.

tenson
A Provençal TROUBADOUR's DEBATE or quarrel poem, often an invective full of crude yet incisively witty personal, social, or literary criticism.

tenta infirmorum
An infirmary tent usually attached to a health SPA or medicinal bath.

tenure
(Anglo-Norman, to hold) The land-holding system William the Conqueror established after 1066 to pay off followers for past military service and to obligate them to furnish future duty, goods, and services. He retained absolute ALLODIAL ownership for the crown, granting only rights of possession for grantees. Four basic types of tenure were: KNIGHT'S TENURE, affecting those trading military service for land rights; FRANKALMOIGNE or religious tenure; SERJEANTY, the grand (affecting legal services, court positions) and petit (cooks, firewood gatherers); and SOCAGE or economic tenure. TENANTs owed feudal INCIDENTS such as HOMAGE AND FEALTY, AIDS, FORFEITURE, and death payments such as WARDSHIP, MARRIAGE, RELIEF, and ESCHEAT.

tephillin
Jewish ceremonial PHYLACTERIES.

teratology
Monstrous births, congenital anomalies, Siamese twins, and anatomical defects fascinated physicians, philosophers, and theologians who sought their scientific, spiritual, or physical causes. Drinking water from particular lakes or streams was implicated; gynecological and obstetric treatises such as those by twelfth-century Dr. Trotula of Salerno attributed anomalies to coital positions, ASTROLOGY, and GENETHLIALOGY.

terminus vitae
(Latin, life's end) The astrological termination of life, as determined by planetary courses.

terce
One of the eight CANONICAL HOURS.

terracotta
A hard, reddish-brown, unglazed pottery used in sculpture, vases, tile, and other decorative surface ornamentation.

terrier
A landroll, rent register, or list containing the quantity of acreage, TENANTs' names, and their taxes, obligations, and rights. An ecclesiastical terrier contained details on the possessions of each parish.

terza rima
Dante's three-line rhyming iambic stanzas in the DIVINE COMEDY, intricately linked stanza to stanza: the rhyme scheme proceeded *aba, bcb, cdc, ded,* and so forth. The structure was symbolic of TRINAL TRIPLICITY.

tesselated pavement
A MOSAIC floor, made of TESSERAE.

tesserae
Small blocks of marble, stone, tile, wood, glass or ivory, used to make TESSELATED PAVEMENT and MOSAIC or other INLAY surfaces.

Testamentum Domini
(Latin, God's Will) A short early Christian rule concerning church building, ecclesiastical order, and LITURGY, putatively written by Christ Himself.

tester
A wooden sounding board behind the PULPIT that reflects and amplifies the speaker's voice. Also, a piece of ARMOR worn to protect the head: either a CASQUE, worn by a man, or headgear for a horse with cutouts for eyes and ears.

tester bed
(French *testière,* head covering) A bed with canopy and side hangings either supported by four bedposts or the canopy suspended from the ceiling.

tetrachord
In music, an ascending group of four tones with a specific interval structure.

tetragramamton
The sacred four-letter Hebrew name of God, *JHWH* or *JHVH,* probably *Jahweh,* later rendered *Jehovah.* Since the word was too holy to speak, Jews substituted the word ADONAI (Lord) or *Ha shem* (The Name).

tetramorph
A graphic depiction of unity among the FOUR GOSPELS common in HIBERNO-SAXON art. The tetramorph is a figure with the body of a man (Matthew), eagle's wings (John), calf's legs (Luke), and lion's paws (Mark). It often accompanies CANON TABLES.

tetrastemorium
(Greek *tetarton morion,* the fourth part) A quarter tone, as used by tenth-century musical theorist Regino of Prum.

theophania
EPIPHANY.

Theotokos
(Greek, God-bearer) The title of the Virgin Mary equivalent to DEI GENITRIX or MATER MARIA DEI.

theriac
A medication believed to be a universal PANACEA. Manufactured from vipers' flesh, dill, anancomo, and cardamom, ostensibly it was an antidote to all poisons, especially snakebites. Often theriac was compounded in a public ceremony: in Bologna, pharmacists and physicians argued so vigorously over the ingredients' proportions that the pope had to intervene to restore order.

thewe
A specialized apparatus for the public punishment of women convicted of commercial crimes; used instead of the PILLORY.

thirty-two ways of wisdom
In KEBALLAH, the process of achieving wisdom by uniting the 10 elements of the SEPHIROTIC TREE plus the VIRTUES signified by 22 Hebrew letters.

Thomist
Pertaining to Saint Thomas Aquinas, the ANGELIC DOCTOR. The philosophical doctrines of Thomism were developed by the DOMINICAN Order as a preferred alternative to AUGUSTINIAN tradition.

thorp
A village; an English place-name suffix in the DANELAW.

three ages of man
Infancy, prime, and old age.

three balls of Saint Nicholas
One of the ATTRIBUTES of Saint Nicholas: three golden globes arranged in a modified triangle, later the PAWNBROKER'S BALLS. According to a fourth-century legend, Saint Nicholas of Myra produced a bag of gold as a dowry for each of three deserving girls.

three builders of the City of Ladies
Reason, Righteousness (Rectitude), and Justice. Christine de Pizan's fifteenth-century ALLEGORY *The City of Ladies* described political, social, intellectual, and practical features of a women's utopia.

three churches
According to the APOSTLES' CREED, the Church Triumphant is Heaven, the Church Expectant is Purgatory, the Church Militant is Earth.

three classes of music
The BOETHIAN MUSICA MUNDANA (harmony of the celestial spheres), MUSICA HUMANA (the body's periodic diseases, PULSE, and cyclic fevers), and MUSICA INSTRUMENTIS, (mortal musicianship using instruments and voice). Demonstrating the perfect musical and mathematical order and connectedness of creation, ORDO MUNDI, the three classes of music were precursor to Theodoricus de Campo's FOUR CLASSES OF MUSIC.

three counsels of perfection
The three VOWS of MONASTICISM: chastity, the complete abstention from sexuality; poverty, the complete abjuration of personal property; obedience, the complete submission to a superior's will or to God's will (except for a counsel to sin).

three estates
In France: clergy, nobles, townsmen; in England: clergy, barons and knights, and Commons (later

called Lords Spiritual, Lords Temporal, and Commons); in Scotland: prelates, TENANTS IN CAPITI, townsmen; or three forms of government: monarchy, aristocracy, and democracy.

three estates of the church
Rome, Christendom, and Spiritual Sovereignty, in which the church's ideas and judgment are supreme, each having rights and responsibilities to each. They are represented in the pope's TIARA.

three faces of Prudence
A three-faced figure of Time, often depicted like TEMPERANCE, with a clock upon her head. This allegorical representation incorporated memory of the past, understanding of the present, and foresight for the future. Prudence sometimes is given the NICKNAME or acronym "RAP" because of her three faces: *R*espice sees the past; *A*dspice sees the present; *P*rospice sees the future. Her companion is a THREE-HEADED TIME BEAST.

three Fates
These three spirits determine the destiny and lifespan of each person: Clotho spins life's thread, Lachesis measures it, and Atropos cuts it with her shears. They are derived from Classical Greek and Roman tradition, and are usually depicted as hideous old women.

three-fold interpretation of literature
The third century Alexandrian biblical scholar Origen (influenced by Neoplatonist Philo Judaeus) found three meanings in scripture: somatic, psychic, and pneumatic, corresponding to the three human constituents: body, soul, and spirit. Thus, a given scripture could be read on three levels: literal, moral, and spiritual (or allegorical); an alternative to the AUGUSTINIAN FOUR-FOLD INTERPRETATION.

three Graces
The Classical triumvirate of Aglaia, Euphrosyne, and Thalia, personifying graceful beauty. In ALLEGORY, they represented aspects of generosity (giving, receiving, and returning gifts), the THREE PHASES OF LOVE (Beauty, Desire, and Fulfillment), or Chastity, Beauty, and Love.

three-headed time beast
The fifth-century MACROBIAN vision of time, represented by a monster part wolf (devouring the past), part lion (representing courage in the present), and part dog (remaining a faithful though dangerous companion for the future). This beast often accompanied artistic representations of the THREE FACES OF PRUDENCE.

three holy children
King Nebuchadnezzar cast Shadrach, Meshach, and Abednego, into the fiery furnace (Daniel 1:7); those Babylonian names in hebrew are Azariah, Hananiah, and Mishael. Their prayer or song from the furnace is a dramatic incident of the APOCRAPHA.

three magi
Caspar, Melchior, and Balthasar. These three kings listed in the sixth-century *Excerpta Latina Barbari* are venerated as saints. The MAGI, as described in Matthew 2, who traveled from the East, led by a star, to present gifts to the infant Christ, were probably Persian astrologers. By the third century, they had been redefined as kings, though early Christian art depicts two, four, or six of them. By the later Middle Ages, the magi personified Europe, Asia, and Africa (the three known continents) paying tribute to Christ, hence the tradition of portraying Balthazar with black skin.

three major prophets
Isaiah, Jeremiah, and Ezekial, who complement the TWELVE MINOR PROPHETS.

three Maries
The three holy women who were the first to discover Christ's RESURRECTION from the sepulcher: the Virgin Mary, Mary Magdalene (identifiable by her voluptuously beautiful hair), and one of the other Maries (Mary Cleophas or Mary Salome) of the HOLY KINSHIP. They were collectively known as the MYRRHOPHORES, or bearers of myrrh.

three matters of romance
In thirteenth-century Jean Bodel's description of heroic ROMANCE subjects: the MATTER OF BRITAIN (concerning King Arthur and his knights in ARTHURIAN ROMANCE), the MATTER OF FRANCE (concerning Charlemagne and his DOUZE PERS in the

CHANSON DE GESTES), and the MATTER OF GREECE AND ROME (treating the Trojan War and escapades of Alexander the Great).

three perfect human spaces

The twelfth-century physician and mystic, Hildegard of Bingen, identified three equal spaces in the human body: the distance from top of head to throat, throat to navel, and navel to groin. In her theory uniting the MICROCOSM to the MACROCOSM, these correspond to the equal spaces between the four points of highest firmament, lowest clouds, earth's surface, and earth's center.

three phases of love

Beauty, stimulating Desire, leading to Fulfillment; often personified by the THREE GRACES.

three purposes of madness

The idea that madness, the disease of NEBUCHADNEZZAR'S CHILDREN, was wrought by God to punish the damned, purge sinners, and prove the virtue of saints.

three quick and three dead

A popular MEMENTO MORI SYMBOL, usually depicting three gorgeously apparelled noble figures disporting themselves, unmindful of eternal verities, in opposition to three worm-wrecked skeletons, reminders of the transience of youth and glory.

three stages of Bernardian mysticism

Purgation (pure truth is seen only with a pure heart); ILLUMINATION (surrender to God's will and meditation on the PASSION of Christ are preparations for union with the divine presence); and contemplation (by "imitation" of perfect holiness, the soul becomes one with God). Defined by Saint Bernard, the early thirteenth-century ABBOT of Clairvaux and patron of the BERNARDINES, these stages were important in the CLUNIAC REFORM.

three states of creation

In Plato's *Phaedo,* Socrates names the basic states of all elements of the cosmos: being, doing, and suffering, which indicate respectively the causes of existence, generation, and destruction. Christian interpretors suggested that being may incorporate a duality of doing and suffering, AGERE ET PATI.

three theological virtues

Faith, Hope, and Charity (I Corinthians 13:13). These three theological virtues combine with the FOUR CARDINAL VIRTUES (*Fortitude, Justice, Prudence,* and TEMPERANCE) to make up the SEVEN VIRTUES. Their battles with opposing VICES were popularized in the fourth-century PSYCHOMACHIA by the Spanish poet Prudentius.

three unities

The Aristotelian principles of dramatic writing and decorum; unity of time, of place, and of action.

three virtues of women

The allegorical queens Reason, Righteousness (or Rectitude), and Justice. Noble, exquisite, articulate sisters, they help build Christine De Pizan's utopian *City of Ladies* and appear as wise counsellors in her INSTRUCTION BOOK for women, *The Book of the Three Virtues,* a treasury of practical advice for thinking, active, practical women of affairs exercising responsibility justly for their nations, families, and themselves.

three vows

In MONASTICISM, the MONK or NUN was consecrated to the THREE COUNSELS OF PERFECTION: chastity, poverty, and obedience.

thring

(past tense: throng) To press or push forward in a rough manner: either in battle movements (the Thebens and Greeks battle in Chaucer's *Anelida* "throng now here now there") or in sexual encounters (in the "Merchant's Tale," Damian lifts May's smock "and in he throng").

thrust

The lateral force exerted by an arch or VAULT against an abutment, support, or PIER. The GOTHIC FLYING BUTTRESS was designed to counter the thrust of a CATHEDRAL's NAVE, particularly its vaulted ceiling.

thula

An old Germanic metrical name list, a verse mnemonic used by MINSTRELS in reciting royal pedigrees and qualities.

thule

ULTIMA THULE.

thurible
A CENSER.

thyrsus
A pine-cone-tipped wand, one of the ATTRIBUTEs of Bacchus, the wine god, and his attendants, the satyrs.

tiara
A triple-tiered or triple-crowned headdress worn by, or carried in front of, the pope during important non-liturgical functions. The coronets symbolize the TRINITY or the THREE ESTATES OF THE CHURCH: Rome, Christendom, and Spiritual Sovereignty.

tie-beam
A horizontal wooden beam connecting the feet of principal rafters in a roof or VAULT. Tie-beams extended wall-to-wall and usually were ornamented with carvings, and sometimes GILDED.

tigerware
A sixteenth-century salt-glazed stoneware from RHENISH POTTERIES, speckled with brown and yellow spots resembling tiger skin, used for pitchers and tableware.

tigillum
In early chemistry, either a funnel or a CRUCIBLE.

tincture
In medicine and pharmacy, an alcoholic solution, a type of GALENIC and a cosmetic; in ALCHEMY, a dye or fluid thought to cause TRANSMUTATION; or a spiritual principle whose quality might be infused into a material thing which thus is tinctured. In HERALDRY, the COLORS, METALS, and FURS used in COATS OF ARMS and banners. The SIX TINCTURES specifically refer to the heraldic colors.

tinging
Dyeing. In ALCHEMY, a coloring process often symbolic of the external change that follows spiritual purification.

tippet
Either a hood's long LIRIPIPE or a COTEHARDIE sleeve's pendant streamer.

tiring house
A room in which actors costume themselves and rest between scenes.

tithe
A tax paid to the church in the amount of one-tenth of all income, or one-tenth of the value of all crops or CHATTELS; a kind of TALLAGE.

tithing
A group of 10 village residents or townsmen nominally responsible for one another's good behavior and collectively liable for the misdemeanor of any member.

toad
As represented in BESTIARIES and TRANSI TOMBs, a devourer of human corpses. FOOD FOR WORMS also is food for toads. In ALCHEMY, the toad (sometimes depicted as winged) represented the watery and earthy parts of matter that must be united with the volative to achieve purification.

toadstone
A semi-precious stone, *bufonius lapis.* According to LAPIDARIES, a toadstone set in a gold or silver ring would guard the wearer against kidney disease. Toadstones also protected the health of newborn children.

toast
To drink good cheer. The phrase derives from the practice of floating a toasted morsel of bread, a SOP, in wine or ale. It also may recall the ALLEMAIN, an enormous pudding or wine vat, into which a woman acrobat was submerged in order to leap out to astonish and delight banquet guests. Figuratively the toast in the wine, she became the toast of the occasion.

tocsin
An alarm bell.

todfall
Or HERIOT, a death tax whose abolition was one of the TWELVE ARTICLES of the PEASANTS' REVOLT.

toft
An earthen mound or small hill; an English place-name suffix in the DANELAW.

Toledan Tables
Astrological computations superseded by the ALFONSINE TABLES.

tomb
An indoor or outdoor monument commemorating the dead, usually containing the body, bones, or ashes, unlike an empty CENOTAPH. From the small and simple through grand and gaudy sepulchre, a tomb, especially a TRANSI TOMB, served as MEMENTO MORI for the living.

tombester
A female tumbler, inheritor of the JOCULATORES tradition and accustomed to performing at town fairs.

tonaria
A musical theme book for GREGORIAN CHANTs, which used the CHURCH MODES.

tondo
A circular painting, or HIGH-RELIEF or BAS-RELIEF carving within a circular frame.

tonsure
A distinctive clerical haircut, which involved shaving all or part of the head. Different monastic orders favored shaving the front from ear to ear, or creating a bald circle on the crown.

tonus
A particular musical pitch; or a CHURCH MODE; or the TENOR line of a polyphonic composition; or the RECITING NOTE in PSALMODY.

topaz
In jewelry and LAPIDARIES, a variety of highly esteemed precious stones, variously transparent, opaque, or prismatic in white, yellow, light blue, or light green. Topaz was assumed to have soothing powers and was used as an AMULET, as a pacifier, and, in HERALDRY, as part of a BLAZON of precious stones.

topiary
The ornamental training and clipping of trees and shrubs into fantastic shapes (candelabra, animals, fabulous beasts, heraldic EMBLEMS, and other fanciful forms) in a GARDEN or ARBORETUM.

topos
A formulaic rhetorical or narrative structure with expected, predictable elements and qualities, such as SAPIENTIA ET FORTITUDO, AGERE ET PATI, DOCERE ET DELECTARE, SENEX AMANS, the GREAT CHAIN OF BEING, and the FEAST OF FOOLS.

toque
A small cap worn by men and women, a COIF.

Torah
(Hebrew, teaching or law) The PENTATEUCH (the FIVE BOOKS OF MOSES: Genesis, Exodus, Leviticus, Numbers, and Deuteronomy). *Torah* also refers to the whole body of written and oral Jewish law, together with all the rabbinic commentaries on the law, the TALMUD. In the SYNAGOGUE, the scroll on which the Torah is written (the *sefer torah*) is usually housed in an ARK (the ARON HA-KODESH).

tordion
A fast-tempoed though restrained leaping dance, usually paired with and following the BASSE DANCE. A mild version of the GALLIARD.

torus
A large convex MOLDING, used especially at the base of a column.

touch
A maker's mark or stamp on a metal object, similar to a HALLMARK. Also, the process of testing the quality of gold or silver by rubbing it on a touchstone; or the official mark on the metal indicating that it has been so tested.

touret
A woman's tall headdress, worn with a veil that usually covered the upper part of the face. A mourning hat in the French and Burgundian courts, it became the BARBETTE.

touret de nez
A fabric attachment to a hood, fitting over the upper part of the face, and often including a small transparent pane for visibility, to protect the nose and eyes against the cold.

tout
The buttocks or rump. In the fourteenth-century *Land of Cockaigne,* an ABBOT uses a maiden's white tout as a TABOR to summon MONKs to his CLOISTER.

Tower of Hunger
The prison in which Count Ugolino della Gherardesca, thirteenth-century leader of the Guelph faction in Pisa, died of starvation along with his sons and grandsons, as poignantly described by Dante in the DIVINE COMEDY (Inferno, 32–33) and Chaucer's "Monk's Tale."

trabeated
(Latin *trabs,* a beam) A construction technique utilizing columns and beams, rather than arches (the ARCUATED technique).

tracery
Ornamental interlacing designs in STAINED GLASS windows, on walls, panels, or in arches, carving, or embroidery. Specific forms of stone tracery such as QUATREFOILS and TREFOILS are found in the space between vertical MULLION bars and horizontal TRANSOM bars in GOTHIC STAINED GLASS windows.

tracheotomy
A surgical procedure involving the insertion of a small tube, a CANNULA, into the trachea (windpipe) through a hole in the throat to permit air to enter the lungs. This procedure was recommended by Hippocrates and medieval physicians for patients who were suffocating or undergoing major mouth, throat, head, or neck surgery.

tragedy
A serious narrative telling of a fall from prosperity to misery. FORTUNE may be at fault, though such fall can be fortunate, as in the FELIX CULPA.

transept
The short arms of a cross-shaped church, lying perpendicular to the NAVE.

Transfiguration
As told in the Bible (Matthew 17, Mark 9, and Luke 9), Christ manifested His divinity to His disciples Peter, John, and James during His lifetime, by appearing "shining" to them, accompanied by Moses and Elijah, and with God's voice announcing "This is my Son." Accounts variously place this event on Mount Tabor, Mount Hermon, or the Mount of Olives. Representations of the scene, showing Christ's face as radiant and his clothing brilliant white, were especially common in the art of the eastern Church, where the Transfiguration was celebrated as a feast, beginning in the sixth century. August 6 was not designated as the feast of the Transfiguration in the western Church until the fifteenth century.

transformation
A theme in folk tales, LAIS, FABLIAUX, and popular literature, shape-shifting, from human being to WEREWOLF, or from straw to gold, could be a punishment for violation of a TABOO or a reward for virtue. In chemistry and metallurgy, TRANSMUTATION.

transit
In ASTROLOGY, a planet's passage across a special region of the ZODIAC. In astronomy, the passing of any heavenly body across the disk of another heavenly body or across the meridian of any particular place.

transi tomb
A SARCOPHAGUS topped by a carved portrait of a corpse, in a state ranging from repulsive skeletal decay to peaceful repose. Important as MEMENTO MORI, early transi appealed to the living to pray for the souls of the dead. Later transi became dramatic symbols for the wealthy and powerful, as death resolved all conflict between pride and humility, earthly wealth and holy poverty.

transmutation
The conversion of one element into another. In ALCHEMY, the translation of a baser metal into a more precious one.

transom
A cross-beam or lintel, especially a weight-bearing one, spanning an opening. Also, a horizontal bar, made of wood or stone, separating two vertical parts of a mullioned window, often surmounted by TRACERY.

transplantation
Saints Cosmas and Damian, patron saints of medicine and surgery, miraculously could graft a human leg

or arm onto an amputation stump, as they did by transplanting the leg of a recently dead Moor to the thigh of a bishop whose gangrenous leg had to be amputated.

transubstantiation
In the EUCHARIST, the theological doctrine that during the consecration, the bread and wine are actually converted to Christ's body and blood, with only the appearance and taste remaining ("accidents") of wafer and wine. The Lateran Council in 1215 mandated belief in the doctrine of transubstantiation, with contradiction considered heresy, and Saint Thomas Aquinas gave it full philosophical formulation. Although Protestant theologians later asserted that the body and blood are present only figuratively or symbolically, the literal belief that the confessed supplicant could actually partake of the body and blood of Christ was reaffirmed by the Council of Trent in 1546–63. Graphic representations of the doctrine include the mystic WINE PRESS.

traynour
A fourteenth-century musical technique utilizing conflicting rhythms in different voices of a POLYPHONIC composition.

treasure trove
(French *tresor trove,* found treasure) If money, coin, gold, silver, or other valuable objects are found after being hidden in the earth, they belong to the state or the king, not to the finder. However, abandoned property belongs to the finder. The SUTTON HOO ship burial, the unparalleled discovery of seventh-century royal artifacts, was deemed by coroner's inquest not to be treasure trove.

trebuchet
A relatively simple, mobile military vehicle for launching missiles. A successor to the ONAGER, and a variety of CATAPULT. Also, a CUCKING STOOL used as an instrument of punishment and in such torture methods as the WATER ORDEAL; and an animal trap for catching birds and small mammals.

Trecento
The fourteenth century.

tredding
Trampling. In sexual context, copulation.

Tree of Life
Graphic representation of the structure of all creation, from the infinite to the finite. Similar graphic embodiment of ideas include the JESSE TREE and the SEPHIROTIC TREE.

trefoil
Three-leaved or TRILOBE. In architecture, ornamental stonework or woodwork with an opening divided by CUSPs to suggest a three-lobed leaf, a useful SYMBOL of the TRINITY. Compare QUATREFOIL.

trencher
An edible bread platter, used instead of a plate at table. All foods were placed upon it, and the gravies and sauces absorbed by the fragrant round or square bread slice, which might be colored delicate red with rose petals, green with parsley and rosemary, or gold with saffron. Leftovers were toasted and recycled as breakfast SOPS in wine, or reserved for the dogs or for the poor begging culinary alms (trencher-fee) at the castle gate.

trencher board
A table either in a banquet hall or PANTRY, used for storing bread for cutting ceremonial or daily breads with a prescribed array of knives wielded with ceremonial flourishes.

trencher table
A TRESTLE TABLE.

Trent codices
Seven significant musical manuscripts containing fifteenth-century polyphonic compositions by Dunstable, Dufay, Binchois, Ockeghen, and Isaac.

trepan
A neurosurgical instrument consisting of a skull-boring crown saw for lifting a portion of skull to relieve pressure caused by abscess, tumor, or fracture; a variant is the TREPHINE.

trephine
An elaborated TREPAN with a transverse handle and a skull-boring central pin to anchor the surgical instrument for precise neurosurgical incisions.

trespass
Invading forbidden territory, whether it be geographically (another person's land or house) or sexually:

Chaucer's January in the "Merchant's Tale" warns his young wife, "Alas, I must trespass you, my spouse."

trespass de bonis asportatis
(Latin, trespass for goods carried away) A legal action for injuries to personal property (TRESPASS TO CHATTELS) from which goods or property were carried away.

trespass on the case
A legal action to recover damages for some injury resulting from a breached duty; a precursor of the modern negligence action.

trespass quare clausum fregit
(Latin, trespass because he broke the gate) TRESPASS TO LAND.

trespass to chattels
An unlawful serious interference with another's possessory rights in personal property.

trespass to land
A legal action to recover damages for any unauthorized entry. This action may be asserted by one who has the right of possession, such as a renter; it is not reserved to the titleholder.

tressour
The girding and embellishing of tresses; or, an elaborate jeweled headdress or CAUL.

trestle table
Long boards set athwart trestle supports or saw horses. Also called a horse-and-saddle table, it was set up for meals, and dismantled between them. Compare TABLE DORMANT.

trial by ordeal
The notion, in literature and in life, that questions of truth should be decided in trial by tribulation: the accused is forced to attempt an impossible task, such as walking over hot coals or treading a carpet of sharp blades. Only divine intervention allows successful completion of the ordeal, thus attesting to the ABSOLUTE TRUTH of the accused's testimony. Wives accused of adultery, such as King Arthur's Queen Guinevere and King Mark's Queen Isolt, were so tried.

tricinium
Sixteenth-century three-part vocal music.

trident
A three-tined fork, a standard of authority, usually associated with Poseidon or Neptune.

triduum sacrum
(Latin, the three sacred days), MAUNDY THURSDAY, GOOD FRIDAY, and HOLY SATURDAY. The last three days of HOLY WEEK commemorate the LAST SUPPER, PASSION, and death of Jesus Christ.

triforium
The blind story, or central section of the interior wall of a CHURCH or CATHEDRAL, above the ARCADE and below the CLERESTORY.

trilithon
A stone structure formed by two uprights balancing a horizontal lintel; a term used to describe prehistoric or Druidic ruins such as those at Stonehenge.

trilobe
A three-cusped or TREFOIL ornament.

trinal triplicity
Christian numerological fascination with the perfection of the number 3 led to numerous configurations of threes, three times three, and other numbers multiplied by three in determining architectural, literary, liturgical, and astrological schema. Even the FOUR ELEMENTS and FOUR CONTRARIES were bound by astrological triplicities: the airy (Gemini, Libra, and Aquarius), earthy (Taurus, Virgo, Capricorn), fiery (Aires, Leo, and Sagittarius), and watery (Cancer, Scorpio, and Pisces) ZODIAC signs. This triadic habit of mind is exemplified in the THREE AGES OF MAN, THREE BALLS OF SAINT NICHOLAS, THREE BUILDERS OF THE CITY OF LADIES, THREE CHURCHES, THREE CLASSES OF MUSIC, THREE COUNCILS OF PERFECTION, THREE ESTATES OF THE CHURCH, THREE FACES OF PRUDENCE, THREE FATES, THREE GRACES, THREE-FOLD INTERPRETATION OF LITERATURE, THREE HEADED TIME BEAST, THREE MAGI, THREE MARYS, THREE MATTERS OF ROMANCE, THREE PHASES OF LOVE, THREE PERFECT HUMAN SPACES, THREE PURPOSES OF MADNESS, THREE QUICK AND THREE DEAD, THREE STAGES OF BERNARDIAN MYSTICISM,

THREE STATES OF CREATION, THREE THEOLOGICAL VIRTUES, THREE VIRTUES OF WOMEN.

Trinity
The central Christian mystery of God's unity in Three Persons, that the One God exists in the Father, Son, and Holy Ghost. This central doctrine of Christian theology is taught in Matthew (28:19), developed by Saint Augustine in his *De Trinitate* and by numerous other church fathers and theologians and expressed in the ATHANASIAN CREED. Typical early medieval ICONOGRAPHY shows the trinity as three interlocking circles (the TRIQUETRA); God the Father as an eye or hand emerging from clouds; the Holy Ghost as a dove. Later trinities use figural representation: the Father appears as a bearded patriarch; the Son holding or on the cross, his feet resting on a globe; the dove flying above Christ's head. Compare the TWO TRINITIES.

Trinity Sunday
The first Sunday after PENTECOST or WHITSUNDAY. This feast day honoring the holy TRINITY, was especially popular in England where it was associated with Saint Thomas Becket, who was consecrated in 1162 on that day.

triori
A sixteenth-century BRANSLE-type Breton dance described in Arbeau's ORCHESOGRAPHY.

triple crown
The high, ornate three-crowned TIARA of the pope, insignia of his position and dignity.

triplum
One of the vocal parts above the TENOR in the ORGANUM and CLAUSULA of the NOTRE DAME SCHOOL.

triptych
A series of three hinged panels, arranged and attached so that the two outer wing panels can fold together to cover the central panel. Ranging from pocket-size devotional objects to monumental church altarpieces, triptychs were made of painted wood, carved ivory, or embossed metal. They usually depict Christian holy scenes on up to all six sides of the three panels. The inner sides of the wing panels often include DONOR PORTRAITs or VOTIVE PAINTINGs.

triquetra
An ancient mystical symbol consisting of three interlacing arcs, circles, or pointed ovals. In Christianity, it symbolized the TRINITY and TRINAL TRIPLICITY. Because of the continuous never-beginning and never-ending design, it also represented eternity. The symbol often appeared on Celtic CROSSes and liturgical objects.

triumph
In imitation of Roman warriors' triumphal processions, medieval allegorical figures indulged in triumphal pageants in poems (Petrarch's popular *Triomfi,* Dante's *Purgatorio,* canto 29), and the CASSONE paintings, sculpture, TAPESTRY, and other graphic arts they inspired. In one example, Love rides in a triumphal car only to be overrun by Chastity, then Death, Fame, Time, and, finally, Eternity.

trivallate
Possessing three RAMPARTs.

trivium
Grammar, rhetoric, and logic. These are the rhetorical, intellectual, and literary exercises that form the lower division of the SEVEN LIBERAL ARTS. The QUADRIVIUM (arithmetic, geometry, astronomy, and music) comprises the higher.

trobaritz
Women TROUBADOURs. More than 20 intelligent, literate, and artistically productive women writers flourished in the twelfth and thirteenth centuries in Occitania, Southern France: Countess of Dia, Castelloza, Isabella, Aralais, Garsenda, and many anonymous women poets followed and amended poetic conventions of COURTLY LOVE in speaking directly of love, the ARS AMATORIA, and their own lovers. Strong-minded and strong-willed, insisting on a woman's prerogative to express love, they adhered to contrived VERSE forms of FRONS plus CAUDA, complicated rhyme schemes, formulaic phrases, strict rhythmic patterns, word plays, and the stylistic trappings of the art of mannered passion.

trochaic
One of the FIVE METRICAL FEET, a foot of verse consisting of two syllables, the first stressed, the following unstressed. An example of the rhythm is PANGE LINGUA.

trope
A short dramatic scene interpolated into Christian liturgy from secular sources. The QUEM QUAERITIS TROPE in the EASTER MASS incorporates themes and characters from the JOCULATORES tradition. Tropes influenced the development of MIRACLE and MYSTERY plays. Also, in GREGORIAN CHANT, a short distinctive cadence at the end of a melody; or a phrase, sung by the choir, added as an embellishment to the text of the mass.

troper
A book of liturgical TROPEs, such as the ones created by the SAINT MARTIAL SCHOOL (tenth century) and Winchester School (eleventh century), containing the ORGANUM for over 150 CHANTs. Later, a troper was a book of SEQUENCEs.

tropus
A musical MODE or scale.

troth
A pledge, promise, or word which must be kept, especially by those possessing GENTILESSE and noble spirit.

trotto
A fourteenth-century Italian dance.

troubadour
A Provençal composer-poet-singer flourishing in the twelfth and thirteenth centuries in the south of France. The troubadours were famous for COURTLY LOVE lyrics written in LANGUE D'OC, and such ingenious, mannered, mathematically and metrically complex poetic forms as the ALBA, CANZO, PASTORELLA, SIRVENTES, and TENSON. Troubadours were associated with the courts of Champagne and Aquitaine, and the theories of the ALBIGENSIAN heresy. Notable composers included Count William IX, Bernart de Ventadorn, Marcabru, Jaufre Rudel, Arnaut Daniel, Bertrand de Born, and Peire Vidal. Their female counterparts were the TROBARITZ. Imitators in northern France were called TROUVÈREs; German counterparts were the MINNESINGERs.

trousse
The SCABBARD for a hunting knife, often fitted with compartments for skinning knives and whet steels.

troussoir
A hook for lifting long fourteenth-century skirts, often carried with other necessaries on a CHATELAINE.

trouvère
A northern French poet-composer-singer writing in LANGUE D'OIL, creating heroic CHANSONS DE GESTES as well as COURTLY LOVE lyrics, in imitation of his counterpart in the south of France, the TROUBADOUR.

trover
A legal action to recover the value of stolen goods or CHATTELS. Unlike a REPLEVIN action, where the property itself might be recovered, in trover, recovery was limited to the market value of the stolen property.

True Cross
A geneology of the cross existing in several versions tracks the history of Christ's CROSS from the Garden of Eden through the CRUCIFIXION and on to the seventh century. A continuous chain of events link the Fall, the FELIX CULPA, and the redemption of mankind: Adam takes a branch from the Tree of Knowledge with him when he leaves the Garden of Eden. This wood becomes the pole on which Moses raises the brazen serpent, a common PREFIGURATION of the crucifixion. The Queen of Sheba sees and worships it when she visits King Solomon. The same wood, found floating in the pool of Bethesda, is used to make the Cross. From here, the legend links the wood to political and military successes of Christian emperors when, in the fourth century, Helena, mother of Constantine the Great recovers the ROOD, and later, in the seventh century, Emperor Heraclius rediscovers it and honors it in the EXALTATION OF THE HOLY CROSS.

truffeau
False hair fringes added to natural hair, pads and struts used to create bouffant hairstyles, or jewelry imitations of such hairstyles.

trumba marina
(German *Trumscheit,* drum log) A six-foot-long (or longer) triangular stringed instrument, over which a single string was stretched. Inside the long sound box, at least 20 sympathetic strings were tuned in unison to the outside playing string. A player used one hand to bow the string, and the other to lightly touch it, thus producing harmonic notes. Additionally, the inverted *U*-shaped bridge, with its left foot shorter than the right, freely vibrated against the soundboard, creating a drumming noise.

trumeau
A central pillar in a large doorway supporting the LINTEL, often embellished with sculpture in CHURCH PORTALS.

trumpet
An important military and ceremonial brass horn. Early trumpets did not have the sideholes, crooks, slide, and valves added to later versions. Trumpets were used for FANFAREs, hunting calls, and WAITS' announcements and advertisements.

Trumpets' Feast
New Year's Day or ROSH HASHONAH, the Jewish festival of the first day of the seventh month (Tishri).

trumscheit
A TRUMBA MARINA.

truss
A rigid triangular framework used to strengthen and reinforce.

tuke
A canvas fabric popular in the fifteenth century.

tunic
A shirt-like garment worn by men and women, with a round neck and narrow sleeves. Of knee or ankle length, simple or elaborate according to social class, the tunic was usually worn beneath a SUPERTUNIC.

tunicle
An ecclesiastical VESTMENT, shaped like a small TUNIC and similar to a DALMATIC, often worn over the ALB at celebrations of the EUCHARIST.

turbulent priest
Saint Thomas Becket, Archbishop of Canterbury, who was assassinated in Canterbury CATHEDRAL in 1170. A shrine erected there became a focus of prayers by the sick and a popular destination for PILGRIMAGEs, including that described in Chaucer's *Canterbury Tales.* The phrase is attributed to King Henry II, reported to have said "Will no one rid me of this turbulent priest," and thereby provoking Becket's murder by four knights.

turd
A piece of excrement or FUNDAMENT.

turmkrone
A tower crown, a fifteenth-century Jewish bride's golden headband decorated with small towers.

turret
In architecture, a small cylindrical tower usually placed at the structure's highest point, but sometimes springing from ground level. In costumery, a white, crownless TOQUE, made of linen or soft fabric, and worn with chinband and BARBETTE.

tuwel
A chimney. In sexual or scatological context, the fundamental orifice or anus, which lower chimney might emit odoriferous blasts.

Twelfth Night
The evening of January 5, preceding Twelfth Day or EPIPHANY. The period 12 days after CHRISTMAS was celebrated by merrymaking, BONFIREs, revelry, drama, dance, and mime, and the eating of Twelfth Cake, an ornamental confection containing a coin, bean, or amulet, the finder of which TAKES THE CAKE, thus becoming King or Queen of the festival.

Twelve Apostles
The 12 chief disciples of Christ: Bartholomew, James the Lesser, Andrew, Judas (later replaced by Matthias), Peter, John, Thomas, James the Greater, Philip, Matthew, Jude (or Thaddaeus), and Simon. These original 12 shared Christ's last meal, the LAST SUPPER, usually assumed to be a PASSOVER SEDER. After Judas's suicide, Matthias replaced him in traditional lists of the 12 Apostles. Saint Paul was often classed as an Apostle, as are other saints, including Saint Barnabas. The principal missionary to a given

country was often referred to as its apostle, for example, Saint Augustine as the apostle of England and Saint Patrick the apostle of Ireland.

Twelve Articles

Demands of the PEASANTS' REVOLT in Germany (1525), including abolition of serfdom, TODFALL and similar taxes, and initiation of privileges in fishing, hunting, woodcutting, work rules, rents, and electing pastors.

twelve great feasts

In Christian (particularly Eastern) LITURGY: EPIPHANY, PRESENTATION OF CHRIST IN THE TEMPLE, ANNUNCIATION, PALM SUNDAY, ASCENSION, PENTECOST, TRANSFIGURATION, DORMITION OF THE VIRGIN, NATIVITY OF THE VIRGIN, PRESENTATION OF THE VIRGIN IN THE TEMPLE, CHRISTMAS, and EASTER, the Feast of Feasts.

twelve labors of the months

The months of the year, associated with the TWELVE SIGNS OF THE ZODIAC, are allied with specific tasks of husbandry, as depicted in MINIATURES, BOOKS OF HOURS, and architecture: January (Aquarius the water bearer), a farmer felling trees, or feasting, as the two-faced God Janus watches; February (Pisces the fish), a rustic grafting fruit trees, or peasants at fireside; March (Aries the ram), a farmer digging or pruning vines; April (Taurus the bull), a peasant training or grafting vines, or youth wreathed in flowers; May (Gemini the twins), noble horsemen falconing or a peasant scything grass; June (Cancer the crab), a haymaker scything or haying; July (Leo the lion), a farmer sickling, threshing, or sheaving grain; August (Virgo the virgin), harvesting, flail-threshing, or ox-plowing; September (Libra the balance scale), winemakers gathering, treading, and sorting grapes; October (Scorpio the scorpion), a vintner casking wine in butts or a farmer strewing seed from an apron; November (Sagittarius the centaur archer), farmers gathering wood, picking olives, herding and fattening pigs; December (Capricorn the goat), a husbandman slaughtering pigs, preparing the Christmas feast, or digging barren fields.

In one of the twelve labors of the months, December's bakers prepare Christmas breads and cakes. (From Pierre le Rouge, *Kalendrier des Bergeres,* Bibliothèque Nationale, Paris)

twelve minor prophets

The Old Testament authors of the 12 shorter prophetic books: Hosea, Joel, Amos, Obadiah, Jonah, Micah, Nahum, Habbakuk, Zephaniah, Haggai, Zechariah, and Malachi. Isaiah, Jeremiah and Ezekiel were considered the THREE MAJOR PROPHETS.

twelve patriarchs' testament

The pseudepigraphal deathbed prophetic messages by each of the leaders of the TWELVE TRIBES OF ISRAEL.

twelve signs of the zodiac

Each of the 12 constellations comprising the ZODIAC: Aquarius the water bearer, Pisces the fish, Aries the ram, Taurus the bull, Gemini the twins, Cancer the crab, Leo the lion, Virgo the virgin, Libra with balance, Scorpio the scorpion, Sagittarius the centaur-archer, Capricorn the goat. The signs are equally divided between COMMANDING SIGNS and OBEYING SIGNS.

twelve tribes of Israel

Clans into which the Israelites were divided in the biblical epoch, each descended from a son of Jacob: Reuben, Simeon, Levi, Judah, Issachar, Zebulun, Joseph, Benjamin, Dan, Naphtali, Gad, and Asher.

The twice told Eve was created by divine ostectomy from Adam's rib. (From woodcut Bible, Cologne, Germany, 1479)

When Moses dedicated the tribe of Levi as priests of the Holy Tabernacle, he maintained the number of tribes receiving territory at the symbolic twelve by dividing the tribe of Joseph into the tribes of Ephraim and Manasseh.

twice told Eve

In the Old Testament, Eve is created twice: in Genesis 1:27, male and female, spiritually akin, are created simultaneously and blessed. Then, in Genesis 2:18, Eve is created by divine ostectomy of Adam's spare rib, thus bone of his bones and flesh of his flesh was called woman (Hebrew, *ishshah*) because taken out from man (Hebrew, *ish*). These events begin the EVA-AVE ANTITHESIS.

two horns of Moses

The HORNS OF MOSES.

two sons of Night

ALLEGORY borrowed from ancient Greek ICONOGRAPHY: Night's (Nyx) two sons are Hypnos (Sleep) and Thanatos (Death). MORPHEUS, god of dreams, is the son of Hypnos.

two strings to the bow

A HEDGEd bet, from the archery term referring to the strategy of reserving a second string in case the first snaps.

two trinities

The Virgin Mary, Saint Joseph, and Jesus are the earthly trinity that parallels the heavenly TRINITY of Father, Son, and Holy Ghost.

tympan

A celestial sphere plate, part of an ASTROLABE.

tympanum

The space within an arch or VAULT over a doorway or major window of a GOTHIC CHURCH or CATHEDRAL. It often was decorated with painting, BAS-RELIEF, sculpture, or MOSAIC.

typology

(Or typological symbolism) The interpretation of the Old Testament, themes and characters of both Judaism and Classical Antiquity as PREFIGURATION of the New Testament and prognostication of Christianity's ethics and events. The old order was perceived as incomplete and imperfect, yet necessary precursor to the ABSOLUTE TRUTH of the new order. Examples of this symbolism include extended sequences like the legend of the TRUE CROSS and simpler parallelisms: just as Abraham incompletely sacrifices Isaac in the AKEDAH tale, so God the Father makes the perfect sacrifice of Christ His son; the virgin Danae impregnated by Jupiter foretells the more perfect method of Mary's conception of Christ.

tzitzit

Fringes Jews wear on the TALLIT and ARBA KANFOT.

U

ubi sunt

(Latin, *Ubi sunt quae ante nos fuerunt?* Where are those who went before?) A common refrain in poetry, sadly celebrating mutable FORTUNE, transitory beauty, and short life. ANGLO-SAXON elegists ask Where are the exquisite beauties? the great horse and valiant warrior? the world's powerful leaders? (of Helen of Troy, Alexander, or Caesar). François Villon's *Ballade* asks Where are the snows of yesteryear?

udones

Clerical and secular fabric stockings, ranging in length from above the knee to full leg, comparable to CHAUSSES and HOSE.

Ultima Thule

Ancient Greek and Latin name for the most northerly land of Europe, variously identified as Iceland, Norway, and the Shetland Islands; figuratively, the last place on earth or world's end.

umbrella

(From Latin *umbra,* shade) A portable, foldable round screen held above the head of an ecclesiastic as SYMBOL of dignity and power, or above a secular person as protection against sun or rain, and made of leather, fabric, or lightweight wood.

umbril

In ARMOR, a visor on a helmet to protect the eyes and brow; it is a feature on the BURGONET.

uncial

A style of MANUSCRIPT writing typified by large capital letters, often richly ornamented, utilized for titles and chapter headings and, less frequently, complete works. Originally uncial had the large rounded letter forms typical of early Greek and Latin manuscripts, as distinct from unrounded capital letter form.

undercroft

The CRYPT, underground chamber, VAULT or cellar storage rooms of a MONASTERY, CHURCH, or CATHEDRAL.

underpainting

(Or PENTIMENTI) Preparatory lines and contour designs underlying the final painting. Usually made with warm-brown monochromatic SINOPIA on GESSO or canvas, they reveal artistic method and changes in graphic intention.

ungaresca

(Italian, "Hungarian") Dance tunes from Hungary, found in continental LUTE books and keyboard music anthologies.

unguentarius

(Or unguentary) An ointment maker or seller. A stock character of the JOCULATORES, he appears in MYSTERY plays such as "Noah's Flood"; there the BALSAM maker is badgered by his shrewish wife. Like the MILES GLORIOSUS, the unguentarius provides comic relief in the otherwise serious QUEM QUAERITIS TROPE.

unicorn

In ALLEGORY and art, a white horse-like animal with a single forehead horn. Pure and graceful, the unicorn never could be captured by force, but could be lured to sleep in the lap of a virgin, and there caught. A complex allegory of secular and divine love, the unicorn represented the immaculate INCARNATION of

Christ, the power of virginity, the potency of desire and human sexuality, and the antitheses of mannered passion. Because the unicorn's horn was reputed to have APHRODISIAC power, NARWHALS (also single-horned) were hunted and the horn pulverized to make stimulating ELIXIRS.

unmerciful servant

A PARABLE found in Matthew 18, popular subject of STAINED GLASS and TAPESTRY. A servant forgiven his debt to the king refuses that same COURTESY to a poor fellow-servant, thus causing his colleague's imprisonment. He painfully learns the qualities of mercy, GENTILESSE, and FREEDOM when the king rescinds his debt-forgiveness and has him tortured until he pays in full.

upper crust

At a banquet hall table, the top crust was cut from a round loaf of bread and presented to the most noble or honored at the feast; hence, an adjective meaning high-class. Like the SALT ceremony, the presentation of the upper crust was a political gesture reaffirming a social order or asserting a new one.

upper stocks

HOSE or BREECHES covering the upper leg and lower trunk.

urinalysis

Analysis of a patient's urine sample to compare its color, odor, sedimentation, and taste with urine charts and MATULA DISCS, an important medical diagnostic and prognostic method still used today.

urine flask

A flask used for collecting urine for medical examination (URINALYSIS); an ATTRIBUTE of the physician, as well as one of the insignia of Saints Cosmas and Damian, patron saints of medicine and surgery.

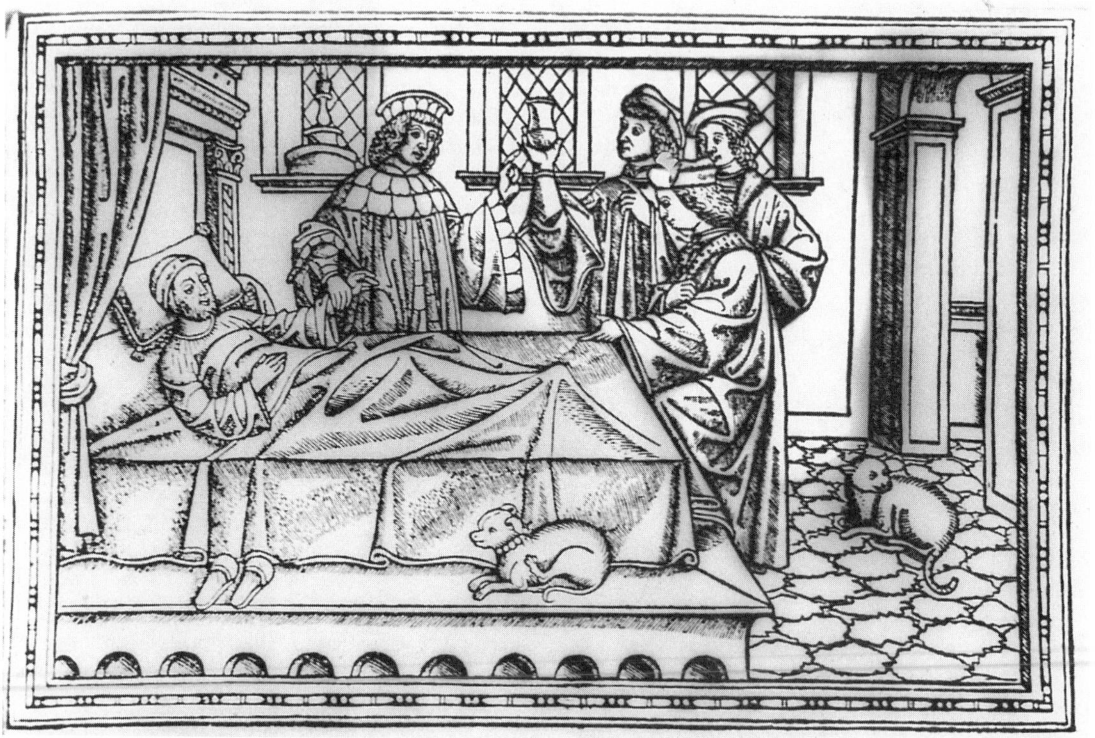

A physician performs urinalysis and demonstrates his *tactus eruditus* while three colleagues consult. (Woodcut, Hugo of Siena, Hippocrates's *Aphorisms*; courtesy of The Bettmann Archive)

urn
A round or OVIFORM vessel for holding water, ashes of the dead, or tears (a *lachrymal).*

uroborus
A snake biting or swallowing its own tail. This ancient ubiquitous image signifies perpetual rejuvenation of nature's cycles. In ALCHEMY, a closed, cyclical process during which liquid is heated, evaporated, cooled, and condensed to help refine or purify substances.

uroscopy
The scientific examination of urine, especially as a means of diagnosing disease, using techniques of URINALYSIS; an integral part of CHRONOPHYSICA.

Ursuline
A member of the women's religious order celebrating the martyrdom of Saint Ursula and the ELEVEN THOUSAND VIRGINS.

V

vade mecum
(Latin, go with me) A useful thing commonly carried about by a person, such as the physician's ASTROLABE used to calculate the most propitious time for administering medicine or performing surgery in CHRONO-PHYSICA; hence, an indispensable object.

vagantendichtung
(German, road song or wanderer's poem) A form of GOLIARDIC LITERATURE.

vaginal dilator
A complex screw-and-rack device used by such gynecologists and obstetricians as twelfth-century Dr. Trotula of Salerno for internal examination, diagnosis, and treatment. Used in conjunction with HERBAL medications and FUMIGATIONs the dilator could open the labia and cause, control, or stop uterine contractions in labor.

vair
The FUR of a north European gray squirrel with a blue-gray back and white belly, highly prized in the thirteenth and fourteenth centuries for trimming or lining robes. Typically, the skins were arranged and sewn together as small alternate colored squares (called *menu vair*). SUMPTUARY LAWS restricted larger squares, *grand* or *gros vair*, for use by the highest social classes. One of the heraldic FURS, it is represented by a series of cup- or bell-shaped spaces of two or more TINCTUREs, usually azure and argent, arranged to alternate in imitation of the way the skins were arranged and sewn together. In heraldic *countervair*, bells of the same tincture are arranged base to base.

valence
A linen helmet cover for ARMOR.

vallum
A defensive earthen wall erected around a fort, especially those constructed by the Romans in northern England and central Scotland.

valor
The time value of a musical note in MENSURAL NOTATION.

vanishing point
The point at which imaginary or drawn lines converge in PERSPECTIVE and in ANAMORPHOSIS experiments.

Vanitas
An ALLEGORY of vanity: futility, worthlessness, conceit, and vacuity.

vanitas omnia vanitas
(Latin, vanity, everything is vanity) From the Old Testament's Ecclesiastes, all human action is reducible to chasing after wind; perfection on earth is unattainable; reputation is mere vainglory; human labor is trivial compared to God's; and pride is the most lethal of the SEVEN DEADLY SINS.

vargueño
(From Vargas, a town near Toledo) A Spanish writing desk or secretary, usually a rectangular cabinet resting on a chest or a trestle stand, with a hinged drop-front, many drawers both obvious and concealed, and often elaborately decorated with INLAY and INTARSIA.

Vanitas is a consort of the Devil. (From Geoffry de Latour Landry's *Ritter von Turn*, Michael Furter, Basle, 1493)

vassal

In FEUDALISM, one holding land from a superior in return for allegiance and homage. A vassal is subordinate to a LORD, and the superior of a VAVASOUR.

vault

A roof of a space with a succession of load-bearing arches in CHURCHes, CATHEDRALS, MONASTERIES, guildhalls, and houses; common types are *barrel vault, Norman vault, early English, decorated,* and *Tudor fan*; the architectural arrangement of timbers, stones, or bricks describing a circle's ARC, including: *annular* (built over space between two concentric walls), *conical* (circular, surmounted by a triangle), *demi-cupola* (a quarter-sphere, as in an APSE), *groined, calotte* (resembling a shallow cap), *pointed* (bound by pointed arches or having transverse RIBS), *rampant* (the two springing points not in the same horizontal plane, as stair steps' unequal PIERS), semi-circular, *skew* (lateral surfaces not right angled to piers, as in viaducts), *spherical* (a hollow hemisphere), *surbased* (the height less than the radius of the curve), and *surmounted* (the height greater than the radius of the curve).

vavasour

(Latin, *vassi vassorum,* vassals of vassals) A feudal TENANT ranking immediately below a baron, holding land in TENURE to a VASSAL.

vein man

In CHRONOPHYSICA, a drawing, painting, ETCHING, or ENGRAVING of a male nude, surrounded by astrological signs indicating the most appropriate time and anatomical location for BLOODLETTING or PHLEBOTOMY.

vellum

A fine grade of PARCHMENT, prepared from the skins of calves, lambs, or kids, and specially soaked, scraped, stretched, cut, and cured for MANUSCRIPT writing. A single copy of a mid-size Bible of 500 leaves required the skins of 250 animals. Later *vellum* applied to any parchment used in the creation of a manuscript.

veneer

A very thin layer of fine wood applied to the surface of furniture made of coarser wood. More elaborate decorative veneers, such as MARQUETRY, parquetry, INLAY, and INTARSIA, use shaped pieces of grained and colored wood, ivory, or other materials to form geometric or figurative patterns.

Veneration of the Cross

A ceremony performed on GOOD FRIDAY, sometimes also called Creeping to the Cross, in which both clergy and congregation kneel and kiss a CRUCIFIX or RELICS at the entrance to the sanctuary. An early description of the ceremony occurs in the tenth-century *Regularis Concordia.*

venetian window

A triple window whose central light is arched, those beside having flat or linteled tops.

Veni Creator

(Latin, Come, Creator) A HYMN to the HOLY GHOST, probably composed during the ninth century by Rabanus Maurus, and used as the VESPERS hymn of WHITSUNTIDE since the tenth century.

Veni Sancte Spiritus

(Latin, Come, Holy Spirit) The beautiful HYMN sung after the second reading on WHITSUNDAY, probably composed in the thirteenth century by Stephen Langton; also called the GOLDEN SEQUENCE.

Venus vulgaris versus Venus coelestis
(Latin, Common Love versus Celestial Love) Two opposing types of love, physical versus spiritual, which under certain conditions might be sequential stages in love's perfection: according to PLATONIC ideas recorded in the *Symposium,* imperfect, temporal Profane Love can lead to perfect, divine and eternal Sacred Love.

verdigris
A green to greenish-blue substance formed by treating the surface of copper with acetic acid, and used as a pigment in green paint for MANUSCRIPT ILLUMINATION, especially favored in the HIBERNO-SAXON style.

verdure
A portrait of a landscape, particularly a TAPESTRY with lush greenery dominating both color and design.

verisimilitude
(Latin, truth-like) Artistic semblance of truth, the illusion of naturalness, reality, and authenticity; MENDILOQUENCE.

verjuice
A semi-fermented sour liquor made from the acid juices of green or unripe apples, oranges, crabapples, grapes, or fennel, used as a condiment, cooking ingredient, and medicine base in the fourteenth and fifteenth centuries.

vermilion
Cinnabar or red crystalline mercuric sulfide. Highly prized for its brilliant scarlet color, vermilion was used as a pigment in MANUSCRIPT ILLUMINATION, dying fabrics, and the manufacture of red sealing wax for legal documents.

vernicle
Saint Veronica's veil or another holy RELIC engraved or painted with the likeness of Christ's face. According to legend, when Veronica wiped the blood and sweat from Jesus's face on the way to CALVARY, one of the STATIONS OF THE CROSS, a perfect likeness of his face remained imprinted on the cloth. Fraudulent relics, such as the one carried by Chaucer's hypocritical Pardoner, duped unwary pilgrims.

verre églomisé
A technique for decorating glass. The back of a piece of glass is painted, gilded, or engraved; then another sheet of glass, a sturdy coat of varnish, or a layer of metal foil is added to sandwich and protect the painting. ZWISCHENGOLDGLAS employed a similar technique.

verse
In poetry, one complete metrical line of a poem. In TROUBADOUR song, a stanza. In GREGORIAN CHANT, the portion of a PSALM or scripture selection sung during the GRADUAL or ALLELUIA. It did not become customary to divide chapters of the Bible into verses until the mid-sixteenth century.

versicle
A short sentence, usually from the Psalms, said or sung antiphonally.

verso
The underside or back of a leaf in a MANUSCRIPT or printed book. A left-hand page in an open book is the verso of one leaf, and faces the RECTO of the next.

vert
Green, one of the SIX TINCTURES or COLORS in HERALDRY.

vervelle
In ARMOR, the decorated connector between the helmet and mail, especially the BASSINET and CAMAIL.

vesica piscis
(Latin, fish's bladder) An ellipse-shaped frame or AUREOLE surrounding a holy figure, the transfigured Christ, or the Virgin Mary after the ASSUMPTION. Also known as the MANDORLA, this variation on the halo or NIMBUS symbolizes the wounds of Christ and the womb of the Virgin Mary.

vespers
(Latin, evening) The solemn evening service of the DIVINE OFFICE, celebrated with HYMNS, VERSES, and CANTICLES; one of the CANONICAL HOURS.

A vervelle band separates bassinet from camail. (From brass rubbing, Sir Thomas Braunstone, Wisbeach Church, Cambridgeshire, England, 1401)

vespertine
Pertaining to the evening, just after sunset.

Vestal Virgin
A priestess of the temple of Vesta, the Roman goddess of hearth and home. The Vestals maintained a perpetual ALTAR fire in the temple and were sworn to absolute chastity; broken vows were punishable by burial alive. Vestals were PREFIGURATIONS of the Virgin Mary.

vestibule
In architecture, a covered space in front of a building entrance, room, or staircase.

vestments
Ecclesiastical garments worn for ceremonial occasions, especially robes, gowns, or outer garments. Tradition and CANON LAW regulated the COLORS and shapes of such vestments as the ALB, CHASUBLE, GLOVES, MANIPLE, MITRE, sandals, SURPLICE, and TIARA.

vestry
A priest's robing room.

Vexilla Regis
(Latin, the King's banners) Seventh-century Venantius Fortunatus' HYMN celebrating Christ triumphant on the CROSS.

via combusta
The COMBUST or fiery way, in astronomy and ASTROLOGY. Astrologers presumed that the period of time from the second half of Libra through the whole sign of Scorpio was always extremely dangerous, as the earth's INFLUENCE was burned up and destroyed at that time of year.

Via Dolorosa
(Latin, the road of anguish) The route to GOLGOTHA, along which Jesus carried His CROSS. Significant events along the way were marked by the 14 STATIONS OF THE CROSS. Devotees (especially FRANCISCANS) commemorate these by visiting each of 14 carved depictions arranged around a church's NAVE or outside it, and reciting specific prayers at each stop: Christ condemned to death; receiving the cross; the three times he staggers under the cross's weight; meeting the Virgin Mary; meeting Simon the Cyrenian; Saint Veronica offering her VERNICLE; meeting the women of Jerusalem; being stripped nearly naked; the nailing to the cross; CRUCIFIXION; PIÈTA; and entombment.

via solis
(Latin, the road of the sun) The sun's orbit, the ECLIPTIC.

vice
(Latin *vitium,* a fault or failing) Depravity or moral corruption. Vices were personified in ALLEGORY, MORALITY plays, art, literature, and popular culture, especially the consortium of SEVEN DEADLY SINS, often in

opposition to VIRTUEs, especially the SEVEN CARDINAL VIRTUES.

Victimae Paschali
(Latin, to the paschal victim) An eleventh-century EASTER HYMN celebrating Christ's triumph over death.

viddui
The formulaic Jewish confession chanted by the dying.

vièlle â roué
A mechanized stringed instrument, also called a wheel fiddle or HURDY-GURDY.

viereckiger schleier
A Jewish woman's cap. Worn to the SYNAGOGUE and during the Sabbath to closely cover the head and hair, it featured two stiffly starched, pointed wings of white linen, and was required by law to have two blue stripes.

vigil
An evening or midnight prayer service preceding feasts such as EASTER and WHITSUNDAY, and often concluding with a celebration of the EUCHARIST. The comparable rite in the Eastern Church, PANNYCHIS, lasts all night long.

vignette
A small decorative design embellishing a blank space. At the beginning or end of a chapter, as vine leaves and tendrils with no definitive boundary or frame; in illuminated MANUSCRIPTs, in BAS-RELIEF, and literature, any ornamental digression from the main subject.

villancico
A fifteenth- and sixteenth-century Spanish poetic and musical form, whose unusual feature is a rhyme scheme disjunct from the music. With amorous and sylvan subjects, many villancicos preserved in CANCIONEIROs have elaborate POLYPHONIC settings.

villanella
A fifteenth-century Italian song, like the FROTTOLA and the CANTI CARNASCIALESCHI.

villein
A feudal serf. The villein was a country laborer or peasant who held land in TENURE by possessing it and working it, paid SOCAGE to a lord, and was required to provide WEEK-WORK and BOON-WORK.

villotta
A lively popular Italian song, incorporating bawdy street songs into its irregular and unpredictable structure.

vinum ardens
(Latin, fiery wine) A volatile liquid distilled in early chemistry to VINUM ARGENS.

vinum argens
(Latin, golden wine) The chemical distillation of VINUM ARDENS, by removing its aqueous part, leaves this golden residue. Hence, in chemistry and metallurgy, the term is used when impurities are removed from a metallic compound. In cookery, it is vegetables steamed in aromatic golden wine.

viol
A musical instrument with 5, 6, or 7 strings, played with a bow.

viola da braccio
(Italian, arm viol) A small stringed instrument with steeply sloping shoulders and crescent-shaped sound holes, played with a convex bow.

viola da gamba
(Italian, knee viol) A large, slender-necked stringed instrument held between the knees and bowed; a prototype of the cello.

virelai
A thirteenth-century French song and dance form with a recurring refrain.

Virgilian
Characteristic of Virgil's subjects and literary style, especially his epic tale of Aeneas's wanderings and the founding of Latium (later Rome) in the *Aeneid*, and his celebration of pastoral life, work, and morality in the *Eclogues* and *Georgics*.

virgo lactans
The Virgin Mary suckling the infant Jesus.

virtu
Eloquent action, stylistic perfection; cultivation of a difficult skill so as to perform with natural ease, inevitable correctness, organic unity, and inherent elegance. Castiglione in *The Courtier* celebrated such virtuosic control.

virtue
(Latin *vir,* man; manliness, valor, or worth) Moral excellence. Virtues were personified in ALLEGORY and in MORALITY PLAYS, and were invoked in exhortations for spiritually correct conduct. The SEVEN CARDINAL VIRTUES, especially the THREE THEOLOGICAL VIRTUES, battled against VICES, particularly the SEVEN DEADLY SINS.

virtue defined by trial
Just as God required proof of obedience and fidelity in the AKEDAH and Book of Job, so true virtue cannot be comprehended until tested. Suffering for love can be salutory, as exemplified in ROMANCES, especially ARTHURIAN ROMANCE, and saints' lives in the GOLDEN LEGEND.

Virtues of the Virgin
The Virgin Mary's epithets in poetry, liturgy, and art, celebrating her purity. Many derive from the Song of Songs: beautiful as the moon, bright as the sun (*pulchra ut luna, electa ut sol,* 6:10); the rose of Sharon (*flos campi,* 2:1); lily among thorns (*lilium inter spinas,* 2:2); David's tower (*turis David,* 4:4); fountain in my gardens (*fons hortorum,* 4:15); a spring of running water (*puteus aquarum viventium,* 4:15); a closed locked garden (*hortus conclusus,* 4:12). In other scripture she was called the flawless mirror (*speculum sine macula,* Book of Wisdom, 7:26) and the closed gate (*porta clausa,* Ezekiel 44:1). Mary is wise (*virgo sapientissima*), the Queen of Heaven (*Regina Coeli*), and God's mother (*Mater dei*).

visio
A MACROBIAN dream which accurately predicts future events.

Visitation of Our Lady
A Christian feast day commemorating the Virgin Mary's visit to her cousin Elizabeth, mother of Saint John the Baptist (Luke 1:39–56), introduced in the thirteenth century, and celebrated on July 2.

The visitation of St. Mary and St. Elizabeth. (Woodcut, Johann Zainer, *Der Geistliche . . . Lebens Jesu Christi,* Ulm, 1485)

visor
The hinged section of an armored helmet, designed to be raised or lowered to protect the forehead and eyes.

vit
In FABLIAUX, the penis.

vita activa
(Latin, active life) The active life. The philosophical opposite is the VITA CONTEMPLATIVA (the contemplative life); their relative merits were weighed in DEBATES, INSTRUCTION BOOKS such as MIRRORS OF PRINCES, and Macrobius's popular commentary on Cicero's *Dream of Scipio.* This TOPOS is comparable to the ideals of FORTITUDO ET SAPIENTIA.

vita contemplativa
(Latin, contemplative life) The ideal contemplative life, opposite of the VITA ACTIVA. These antitheses routinely were paired in literature and ICONOGRAPHY.

vitrified
Referring to stones or other substances that have been converted into glass, fused or glazed by exposure to fire.

vitrine
A display cabinet with glass door and sides.

vitriol
Metallic salt, used in art, medicine, and ALCHEMY. Various naturally occuring or artificially created sulfates of different metals were known by their color: blue vitriol (copper), green vitriol (iron), red vitriol (cobalt), and white vitriol (zinc). The word *vitriol* also applied to oil of vitriol and to concentrated sulphuric acid.

vivaria
Fish ponds providing readily available living food stock, especially on the grounds of a castle, MONASTERY, or manor.

vizard
A VISOR.

void
In architecture and MANUSCRIPT painting, a vacant space or intentionally absent portion of a pattern; in law, an annulment or cancellation making a contract, transaction, or action illegal, invalid, and inoperative; in CHIVALRY, an empty saddle, a riderless horse.

volet
A kerchief or veil worn by women at the back of the head or pendent from a hat or HENNIN. Varieties include the COINTISE, CIMIER, and LAMBREQUIN.

volkslied
A German folk song, thematically and stylistically distinguished from courtly HOFLIED and middle-class GESELLSCHAFTSLIED.

volta
An architectural term for an intersection of two VAULTS. Also, the popular leaping dance, the LAVOLTA.

volute
(From Latin *volvere,* to turn) A spiral scroll on a CAPITAL, or any twist, convolution, or scroll adorning a capital, CROZIER, or article of furniture or jewelry.

volvelle
A device, similar to the ASTROLABE, that doctors used in CHRONOPHYSICA to ascertain astrological convergences and numerical medical data for diagnosis, for treatment planning, and for prognosis. A series of concentric pivoting discs were calibrated with astrological, astronomical, and horarary data. Though some were made of metal, other volvelles are made of PARCHMENT or VELLUM and are integrated into medical books and hygiene texts.

votive painting
A DONOR PORTRAIT depicting the patrons with their saintly namesakes adoring the Virgin and Child, integral to and accompanying a TRIPTYCH, FRESCO, or ALTAR painting (as on the doors or wings of a triptych) donated as gift to a CHURCH, MONASTERY, or civic institution in recompense for some heavenly mercy, as recovery from PLAGUE (especially portraying PLAGUE SAINTS), victory in battle, and business success.

voussoir
A wedge-shaped stone used in constructing an arch; the central one is the KEYSTONE.

vow
A solemn pledge of word, a promise to God, a saint, a lover, or a court in exchange for a favor, an action, a forbearance of action, or another promise. The three vows of a NUN, MONK, or other religious dedicated to poverty, chastity, and obedience, the THREE COUNCILS OF PERFECTION, exchanged abstinence from wealth, sex, and free will on earth for guaranteed salvation after life. An impetuous vow, a RASH BOON or GEIS, was a commonplace in MÄRCHEN, folklore, and ARTHURIAN ROMANCE.

vox
(Latin, voice) Musical sound, tone or color. Also, the two voices of the ORGANUM in MUSICA ENCHIRIADIS, the notes of the scale of GUIDO'S HAND, and the six notes of the HEXACHORD.

vox clamantis in deserto
(Latin, a voice crying out in the wilderness) The description of Saint John the Baptist preaching to the multitude (Luke 3).

vulned
A heraldic description of an animal wounded by another beast or pierced with a weapon.

W

wainscot

Wood panelling covering the lower part of a wall; a DADO.

waits

Civic singers, hired by a town to musically announce important events, entertain at public celebrations, and chant the hours.

wardrobe

A toilet or NECESSARIUM.

wardship

In feudal law, the right of the LORD, as guardian of a minor to possess and use the minor's lands, including all their accrued profits until the "infant" gained majority at age 21; a feudal INCIDENT of land TENURE.

warfare treatises

Military INSTRUCTION BOOKs, which included discussions of martial ideals, practical advice on weaponry from swords to SIEGE ENGINEs, and recommended survival skills. Influenced by Vegetius' classic *De re militaria* were such notable works as Konrad Keyser's *Bellifortis* and Christine de Pizan's treatise on chivalry, later translated as *Book of Feats of Arms and Chivalry.*

wash

A thin, often transparent, coat of watercolor paint spread evenly over a surface.

wassail

(Germanic *wes heil,* be in good health) A salutation and toast when presenting wine: to your good health! *Wassail* also refers to the liquor itself, a spiced ale often topped with crabapples, crutons, SOPs, and heavy cream; and it is the custom of caroling while carrying a wassail bowl or singing traditional songs while sitting or standing around it.

wastelbread

A sweet, flaky bread made with fine flour and butter. A popular delicacy among the nobility and those who aped their habits; Chaucer's Prioress feeds it to her pet dogs.

water marks

Identifying designs impressed into the substance of a sheet of paper, usually only visible when the sheet is held up to the light. Created by raised wires in the manufacturing mold, which cause the paper pulp to spread more thinly, chain lines and water marks first appear in Europe in 1282.

water ordeal

A test to identify a socerer or witch. For a typical cold-water ordeal, a woman would be tied to a CUCKING STOOL and dunked or simply thrown into a pond or river to see if she sank or floated. According to local customary interpretation, which varied widely, she either floated by the grace of God or sank because demons drew her to hell, or she floated because evil spirits buoyed her up unnaturally or sank, purified, thus reaching heaven. In the hot-water ordeal, a suspected witch was forced to immerse her hands or arms in scalding water. Whether blistered or not, she could be burned at the stake for using her WOMEN'S SECRETS.

wattle-and-daub

A technique of building construction consisting of interlaced sticks roughly plastered with clay mixed with straw and reinforced with horsehair.

way bread
(Latin *viaticum,* what accompanies on the road) A nutritious wafer that did not spoil on long journeys. Excellent food for travelers in this world, if consecrated as the HOST, it was necessary for a Christian's passage into the next.

Way of the Cross
Christ's passage on the VIA DOLOROSA, and the prayers (variously between seven and 14) commemorating it.

webster
A professional woman weaver; one of the common MATRONYMICS.

Weeks
The Jewish feast of weeks, *Shavuot* (Hebrew, weeks), celebrates both the grain harvest and the giving of the law on Mount Sinai (Exodus 20). Shavuot, celebrated on the 50th day after PASSOVER, is observed by Christians as the feast of PENTECOST (Greek *pentekoste,* fiftieth day), also known as WHITSUNDAY. In Christian tradition, the HOLY GHOST descended on the APOSTLES on Pentecost (Acts 2:1).

week-work
(Anglo-Saxon *wicweorc*) In feudal TENURE, the labor required of VILLEINs upon the lands of their lord's DEMESNE, the home farm, usually three days out of seven, augmented by BOON-WORK.

weld
(Also woald, wold, would) A common yellow dye, or the plant (*Resceda luteola*) from which it is extracted.

werewolf
A person who was transformed, or could transform himself into a wolf. In Marie de France's LAI, the werewolf sustains itself by drinking human blood. In folklore and FABLIAUX, speaking a forbidden word or violating a TABOO or GEIS could transform the offender into a werewolf.

wergild
(German, man money or person gold) A compensatory fine a killer must pay to his victim's family, in an amount determined by the victim's rank. As implemented according to the *Lex Salica* among the Salian Franks in Germany in the sixth century, a girl's worth was identical to that of a free man throughout his life, but a woman of child-bearing age was worth three times any man, and a slain pregnant woman even more.

Werner's law
The linguistic rule explaining certain sound shifts in cognate words among INDO-EUROPEAN and Germanic languages. Derived from GRIMM'S LAW, Werner's law explains certain exceptions based on accent patterns: if the Indo-European accent is not on the vowel immediately preceding a voiceless spirant, it becomes voiced in Germanic languages (therefore Latin *centum* becomes English *hundred*).

westwork
The multi-storied mass wall including the FACADE and tower found at the western end of a ROMANESQUE CHURCH or CATHEDRAL.

whalebone
Baleen, the elastic horny, thin plates from the upper jaw of a whale. Strips of whalebone were used as struts to stiffen apparel: body corsets, the long-pointed toes of shoes such as POULAINES, tall pointed hats such as HENNINs, and helmet plumes, as well as some banners and flags.

when in Rome
"When in Rome, do as the Romans do." Saint Ambrose's advice to Saint Augustine concerning proper fast days.

white acre
Land planted with grain, unlike the BLACK ACRE's crop of peas and beans; white rent, *blanches firnes,* is paid in silver.

white friar
One of the CARMELITES, one of the FOUR ORDERS OF FRIARS; a FRIAR who wore a white HABIT and SCAPULAR.

white monk
A member of the CISTERCIAN order, so called because their HABIT is made of white or undyed fabric.

Whitsunday

White Sunday, the Christian feast of PENTECOST, or feast of WEEKS, is celebrated on the 50th day after EASTER to honor the descent of the HOLY GHOST upon the APOSTLES. White liturgical VESTMENTS, baptismal garments, and church hangings give the holiday its name.

Whitsuntide

The season of WHITSUNDAY; Whitsunday and the days immediately following.

whores

Prostitutes wore special costumes mandated by SUMPTUARY LAWS. Local laws regulated the oldest profession: prostitutes in fourteenth-century London plied their trade in specific districts, such as the STEWS and COCK'S LANE. Physicians periodically examined them for venereal disease and provided treatment with mercurial inunctions when they were infected. Prostitutes convicted of felonies could not be executed if pregnant.

wicket

A small gate or door in a fence or other enclosure. Also, a small door made in or next to a larger one in a large CHURCH, CATHEDRAL, or castle, allowing a single person to go in or out without opening the large door.

widdershins

In a backwards, unusual, or "perverse" order. The wrong way. Narrative techniques and pictorial and CALLIGRAPHY styles required reading from right to left across a page and from back to front of a book. Christians considered Hebrew books as written widdershins; WITCHes' sabbaths (described in the HAMMER OF WITCHES) prescribed backwards prayers; reverse ROGATION PROCESSIONs signified death.

wild man

(Latin *Homo silvestris,* man of the forest) In literature and art, an unkempt HIRSUTE man, often brandishing a club. The wild man symbolized lust, aggression, and the animality of the human condition; conversely, he represented the simple, sylvan life uncorrupted by courtly civilization. *Homo silvestris* is associated with NEBUCHADNEZZAR'S CHILDREN, a lower link, nearer beasts than angels in the GREAT CHAIN OF BEING, yet also exemplifies the higher link when the madman is a saint. In courtly entertainments, such as the BAL DES ARDENTS, noblemen would dress and act like wild men, at their personal peril.

A wild man warrior with shield precedes two courtiers in the forest. (From *Homo silvestris, Carcel de Amor, Diego de San Pedro,* Burgos, Spain, 1496; courtesy of British Library)

willies

Germanic folk spirits, the wandering wraiths of maidens who die or commit suicide for love.

wimple

A linen or silk headband that framed the face by enveloping the forehead, chin, sides of face, and neck, often augmenting the CAUL.

windlass

A mechanical contrivance for hoisting and hauling, consisting of a roller or beam resting on supports, around which a rope or chain is wound. The windlass was used as a hoist in mines, building construction, and in theaters where players were literally flown in from the wings as DEUS EX MACHINA. Smaller versions functioned as fishing reels, as devices SPINSTERs used to wind yarn, and as a winch for firing a CROSSBOW.

wine press

Saint Augustine's metaphor of Christ as a cluster of grapes from the promised land, crushed under a wine press. His double reference is to Moses's spies returning from Canaan carrying bunches of grapes on a pole (Numbers 13) and God's tramping down the vintage of GRAPES OF WRATH (Isaiah 63). The grapes on the pole prefigure Christ on the CROSS. Christ in the press with his blood/wine flowing, the cross as the screw of a wine press with a spiral thread on its upright (STIPES), illustrates with startling graphic clarity the doctrine of TRANSUBSTANTIATION. The wine press is an important STIMULUS AMORIS.

winnowing basket

An agricultural implement separating SEED from chaff. Like the WINNOWING FAN, the basket when shaken drives off the lighter particles to the wind and the valuable seed remains. In Marguerite de Nevarre's *Heptameron* and other FABLIAUX, the winnowing basket (French, *van a vanner*) is a sexually charged metaphor: the female genitalia are the vessel through which seed penetrates. A covered winnowing basket is as frustrating to a lover as the PORTA CLAUSA.

winnowing fan

A triangular-shaped shallow basket for separating grain into seed and chaff, like the WINNOWING BASKET.

wise and foolish virgins

The PARABLE of the 10 bridesmaids who wait to meet the bridegroom at midnight (Matthew 25:1–13). Five have taken the precaution of filling their lamps with oil, and thus enter the house with the groom when he arrives. The other five dash away to buy oil and return to find the gate locked, their OPPORTUNITY missed. The wise must always be prepared for Christ's SECOND COMING.

witch

(Anglo-Saxon *wicca*, a magician or sorcerer) A woman or man with supernatural powers derived from the devil, described with venomous specificity in the MALLEUS MALEFICARUM; among the people tried, convicted, and burned by the INQUISITION, some putative witches were WOMEN PHYSICIANS AND SURGEONS earlier praised for their magical cures.

Four beautiful witches gather naked with a skull and bone beneath their feet while the Devil watches. (From an engraving by Albrecht Dürer, Germany, 1497)

wizard

(Middle English *wys,* wise) A sage or wise man skilled in occult arts, WITCHcraft, and magic, such as Merlin, the wizzard of ARTHURIAN ROMANCE.

woad

A broad-leaved herb cultivated for its blue dye; also called Dyer's Weed.

women at work

In medicine, literature, art, politics, commerce, crafts, and crime, with rigor, vigor, and men's appreciation.

The professional woman writer Christine de Pizan creates one of her twenty popular books in her study while her faithful dog watches. (From *Christine de Pizan's Collected Works,* Harley manuscript, British Library, London; courtesy of Persea Books and Bard Hall Press, ***A Medieval Woman's Mirror of Honor***)

Professional writers and poets, such as Christine de Pizan, Marguerite de Navarre, and the Countess de Dia, were universally praised and highly paid; medical women practicing surgery, obstetrics, gynecology, ophthalmology, battlefield trauma surgery, pharmacology, epidemiology, and pathology, some directing hospitals, writing medical textbooks, and teaching in medical schools, as Doctors Hildegard of Bingen, Jacqueline Felicia, and Barbara Wissenkirchen; LADY BOSSES, rulers of manors and monasteries, as Eleanor of Aquitaine, Marie of Champagne, and Heloise of Paraclete, hard-laboring administrators both secular and ecclesiastic; women in the mines (especially silver mines), fields, and markets, their family's MATRONYMICS demonstrating potency of their crafts; and women in the illicit and necessary trades: WHORES, smugglers, and murderers demonstrated vigorous ingenuity and professional aplomb in the underworld, town, cottage, and court.

women patronesses of art

Politically powerful women employed artists and poets to praise them and celebrate all women. Notable patronesses of TROUBADOUR songs, ROMANCES, and DEBATES associated with the COURTS OF LOVE include Eleanor of Aquitaine, Marie of Champagne, Margaret of Flanders, and Marguerite of Bavaria, all of whom commissioned durable art important beyond their own courts.

women pharmacists

Laws regulating education, licensing, and practice of pharmacists distinguish between women and men practitioners but not pejoratively. Women apothecaries were required, by a 1322 statute of the City of Paris, to administer medication under jurisdiction of master physicians, swear to follow a corrected copy of a poison antidote text by Nicholas of Salerno, measure medication by accurate weight, use pure medications in prescriptions, and substitute no medicine for that prescribed other than those listed in the QUID PRO QUO. The same strictures applied to men apothecaries.

women physicians and surgeons

Successful female physicians such as Trotula of Salerno, Hildegarde of Bingen, and Jacqueline Felicia of Paris treated men and women patients for most ailments, not simply women with gynecological and obstetric problems. They also wrote theoretical treatises, taught medical students, ministered to male patients, and even treated MONKs in monasteries. So prevalent were women practitioners that in one of Marie de France's LAIS, a philandering wife while her husband is at home sneaks her lover into her bedroom disguised as a lady doctor.

women's secrets

According to Pseudo-Albertus Magnus' text *De Secretis Mulierum* (Women's Secrets), women's bodies and sexuality were naturally polluting and corrupting, thus logically a danger to men. Thirteenth-century natural philosophers advocated avoidance, persecution, and execution of women—a perversion of science to political ends that directly influenced the fifteenth-century treatise on witches, MALLEUS MALEFICARUM, by DOMINICAN inquisitors Heinrich Kramer and Jacob Sprenger.

women writers and poets

Professionally celebrated, and writing for profit as well as praise, women such as the twelfth-century TROBARITZ, Countess of Dia, Castelloza, Isabella, and Aralais, Marie de France, writer of fables and LAIS, and fifteenth-century Christine de Pizan wrote dramas, ROMANCES, satires, courtly etiquette books, imaginary voyages, political panegyrics, histories, biographies, political texts, WARFARE TREATISES, translations, literary diatribes, bitter invectives against immorality, lawlessness, and war. Some staunchly defended womanhood (as Christine de Pizan), some wrote anti-feminist humorous tales, and still others bawdy, hilarious FABLIAUX.

woodcut

A graphic printing technique. A design, inscription, or scene is carved into a block of seasoned hardwood, which is inked and pressed to transfer the design onto paper, producing playing cards, book decorations, or individual prints.

Worchester school

A musical style of fourteenth-century English compositions characterized by elaborate voice exchanges. Probably created at Worchester Cathedral, the texts surviving only in fragments.

word-hoard

An ANGLO-SAXON poet's treasury of words. The word-hoard included formulaic, ALLITERATIVE epithets for loyal warriors and generous leaders, stock phrases for passage of the seasons, martial carnage, exile, and loneliness, and masterful poetic devices as KENNINGS and LITOTES.

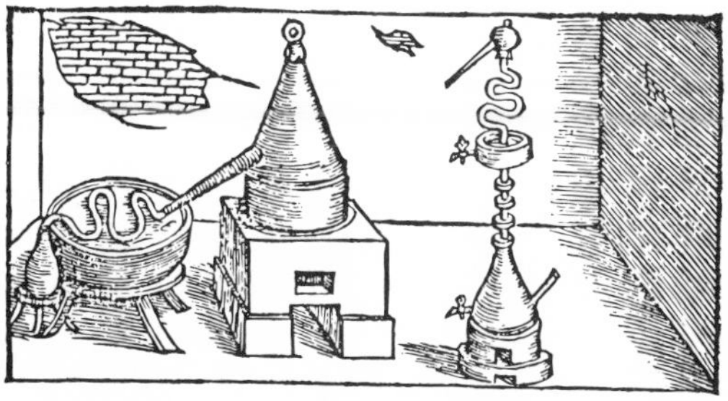

A worm condenser distillation apparatus used in chemistry and alchemy. (From woodcut, Vannoccio Biringuccio, Pirotechnia, 1540)

worm condenser

A serpentine-shaped DISTILLATION vessel used in chemistry and ALCHEMY.

worsted

A strong, long-wearing woollen fabric made of smooth, evenly combed yarn, originally manufactured in Worstead, England, in the thirteenth century.

wound man

An illustration at the beginning of a medical text showing a nude figure displaying common wounds (whether caused by accident, violence, war, or disease) and the weapons or instruments that typically inflict them. This graphic table of contents promises the text's medical and surgical treatments. A wound man often is followed by a ZODIAC MAN.

wrigglework

Sinuous, meandering decorative designs, executed in wood or stone for architectural ornamentation or created by stitching, embroidering, braiding, or cutting fabric, as in DAGGING.

X

xanthareel

An eel whose yellow flesh was an ingredient in medicinal foods for treating eye diseases, especially for aiding healing after removing cataracts by COUCHING.

xenobic

Either pertaining to the fifth-century Florentine Bishop Xenob, famous for restoring the dead to life, or the fourth-century black-skinned Bishop Xenob of Verona, an important exorcist of demons.

XPI

One of Christ's MONOGRAMS, from his NOMEN SACRUM. An extension of the CHI-RHO MONOGRAM, the three Greek letters *XPI* (*chi rho iota*) begin *christos,* literally "the Anointed One."

xyloglyphy

Letter-ENGRAVING on wood, either to ornament the wood itself or for transfer as a WOODCUT.

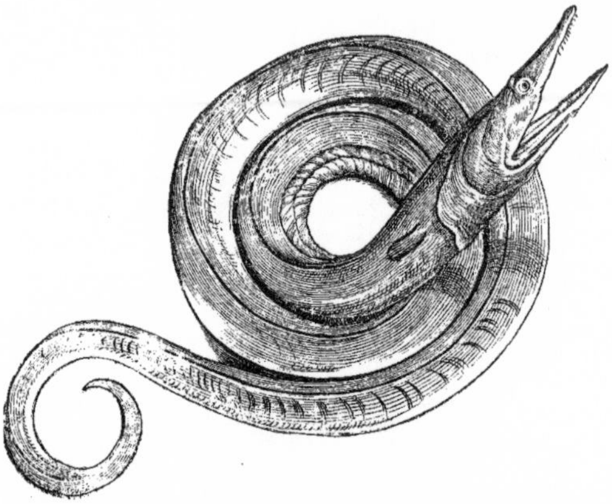

In bestiaries and medical texts, the xanthareel's yellow flesh is helpful against eye diseases. (From Konrad Gessner, *Historia Animalium,* Fischbuch, Zurich, Switzerland, 1563)

Y

yale
A mythic heraldic beast, gracing the COAT OF ARMS of England and many a BESTIARY. An animal the size of a horse with an elephant's tail and a boar's jowls, each of the yale's extravagantly long horns can adjust as battle requires; at need, one horn can point forward, the other behind.

yard
In agricultural or arborial context, an enclosure for planting; in politics, a rod-like symbol of sovereignty or authority; in sexual context, the penis. John Arderne's 1425 treatise on anal fistula recommends a good medication for CANKER of a man's yard; Wycliffe's 1382 translation of Genesis prescribes circumcising the flesh of the furthest part of the yard.

The Yale is an important mammal in heraldry and bestiaries. (From *Bestiary*, 12th century; courtesy of Galeria Medievalia, Tenafly, New Jersey)

yarmulka
A skull cap worn by observant religious Jewish men.

year of great stink
1357 in England; industrial pollution and uncommon summer heat combined to cause eutrophication of the Thames, sludge backwash, and fish-kills.

yeoman
In a royal or noble HOUSEHOLD, an attendant or servant customarily with responsibilities midway between those of a SQUIRE and a PAGE.

yetzer ha ra and yetzer tov
(Hebrew, evil inclination and good inclination) In Jewish tradition, these two opposing natural inclinations struggle within each human being but are subject to the moral controls of the mind and will.

Yew Sunday
PALM SUNDAY. In processions, penitants carried yew branches rather than palm fronds. A classical symbol of immortality, the evergreen yew tree can live for centuries and since ancient times has been planted at cemeteries.

Yizkor
(Hebrew, may He remember) The Jewish mourners' memorial service recited during burial rites at the cemetery and intoned in the synagogue on YOM KIPPUR, SUKKOT, Passover, and SHAVUOT. Yizkor probably originated during the massacres of Jewish communities in the Rhine valley in the CRUSADES.

Yom Kippur

(Hebrew, Day of Awe or Day of Atonement) The most sacred holy day in the Jewish calendar. All-day prayer and fasting begs forgiveness for the year's sins and inscription in God's Book of Life for the coming New Year.

Ypapanti

(transliteration of the Greek, "the Meeting," i.e., of Christ with Simeon) The Eastern Church's name for the feast of CANDLEMAS.

Yule

A Pagan Scandinavian 12-day feast, probably celebrated in December or January, later denoting CHRISTMAS. The yule log was integrated into Christian festivities. Yule of August (probably from *gule,* meaning red or throat) was LAMMAS.

On Yom Kippur, as on Rosh Hashonah, the shofar is sounded and reminiscent of the Akedah. (From German manuscript, early 14th century, Bodleian Library, Oxford)

Z

Zachariah's Feast

A Christian feast day, celebrated on November 5, honoring Saint John the Baptist's father, who in his old age miraculously fathered with his wife Elisabeth a son "filled with the HOLY GHOST" (Luke 1:15) and was later murdered in the Temple pursuant to Herod's command.

zajal

An Arabic song technique wherein stanzas alternate with a refrain. Zajal influenced Western, and particularly twelfth-century, TROUBADOUR poetic style.

Zeuxian perfection

The Greek painter Zeuxis (around 400 B.C.) painted an exquisite portrait of Helen of Troy for the temple of Hera on the Lacinian promontory by selecting the most beautiful anatomical part from each of a multitude of naked maidens. A master of the illusion of realism, his painted grapes looked so natural that birds flew to peck at them (Pliny, *Natural History*).

zink

In music, a wind instrument, the CORNETTO.

zither

A trapezoidal stringed musical instrument.

zodiac

The apparent movements of the sun, moon, and principal planets within an area of the celestial sphere, which extends 8 or 9 degrees on each side of the ECLIPTIC. The zodiac is divided into 12 equal parts, called ZODIAC SIGNS, through one of which the sun passes each month.

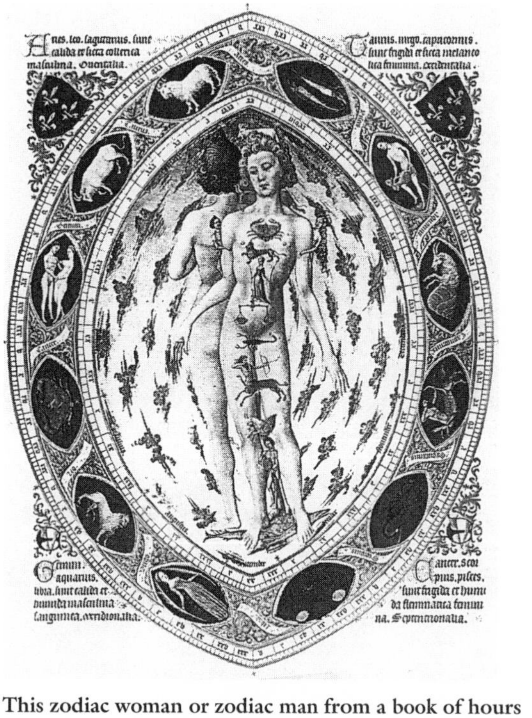

This zodiac woman or zodiac man from a book of hours unites astrology with Christianity. (From the Limbourg Brothers' *Très Riches Heures* of Jean duc de Berry, 15th century, Musée Condé, Chantilly)

zodiac man

Medical treatises depict a naked male body with signs of the ZODIAC ascribed as the guides and governors of each part of the anatomy. In health, disease, or injury, Aries controls the head; Taurus, the neck; Gemini, shoulders; Cancer, heart; Leo, chest; Virgo, stomach; Libra, buttocks; Scorpio, genitals; Sagittarius, thighs; Capricorn, knees; Aquarius, legs; Pisces, feet.

zodiac sign

One of the TWELVE SIGNS OF THE ZODIAC: Aries, Taurus, Gemini, Cancer, Leo, Virgo, Libra, Scorpio, Sagittarius, Capricorn, Aquarius, Pisces. HOROSCOPES would predict the likely astrological effects of being born or conceived under a particular sign. (See BIRTH TIME MIRROR and CONCEPTION TIME MIRROR.) The sign affected character (defined as one of FOUR TEMPERAMENTS), physique, personality, profession, and spiritual condition, discernible by studying GENETHLIALOGY. The constellations are equally divided into COMMANDING SIGNS and OBEYING SIGNS.

zodiac woman

Depicted less frequently than ZODIAC MAN, a nude female figure with astrological signs guarding and guiding each anatomical part. A comparable medical illustration is BLOODLETTING WOMAN.

Zohar

(Hebrew, whiteness or Book of Splendor) A mystical commentary on the TORAH composed by Moses de Leon (1230–1305), emphasizing the SEPHIROTIC TREE. The Zohar is a major text in learned, theosophical KABALLAH.

zond

A CINGULUM.

zoomorphosism

Representation of gods, saints, holy figures, and human beings in animal form or with animal ATTRIBUTEs, as in beast SYMBOLs and the APOCALYPTIC BEASTS.

zoppetto

An Italian limping-hop dance, described in the sixteenth-century dance manuals of Fabritio Caroso.

Zosimus

The frequently cited author of a fourth-century ALCHEMY text, one of the earliest extant.

zwischengoldglas

(German, gold between glass) A gold decoration or painting sandwiched between two pieces of glass; a glass vessel whose exterior is decorated with gold and then encased in a sheath of glass. Comparable in effect to VERRE ÉGLOMISÉ.

SUBJECT INDEX

This index's locators are not only page numbers but lists of terms that direct you to the relevant entries in *Medieval Wordbook*. The lists themselves are cultural markers. We learn much about the art and ceremony of a culture that has hundreds of words for dance and even extends choreography to horse ballets and the dance of death. If you love the anatomy of buildings you will be startled by the magnitude of the architecture entries. If you love anatomy, you will delight in the lists of body parts and their associated ideas in love and sex as well as virginity and chastity. If you love medicine or law, you will be amazed at their medieval intricacies. If you know medieval Christianity (or Judaism) but want to explore medieval Judaism (or Christianity), here is helpful initial vocabulary for its perplexing doctrine, liturgy, mysticism, clothing, food, and philosophy of life.

B

D

N

O

P

U

V

W

X

Y

Z

NAME INDEX

Alphabetization of medieval names follows no rigid formula of "given name" versus "family name." Medieval texts and scholarly custom give priority to one name or the other, sometimes both, or neither. Is Saint Thomas Aquinas better called "Thomas" or "Aquinas"? Both are common in the literature. However, "Dante" is better known than "Alighieri"; Christine de Pizan is usually identified as "Christine"; and Bernart de Ventadorn is called "Bernart." Such inconsistency typical of medieval texts and secondary literature we emulate here for sake of easy retrieval of references.

Jesus Christ and the Virgin Mary are not listed because their names are ubiquitous in this book and best retrieved through the specific doctrinal, symbolic, and other categories under *life of Christ, life of the Virgin Mary,* and other entries under *Christianity* in the **Subject Index.** Adam and Eve similarly are not listed here but in the **Subject Index**. Saints listed in the text only once in the long table titled saints and their attributes are not repeated in this **Name Index**; saints named here are those such as Ambrose, Dominic, John the Baptist, Ursula, and Veronica, who are also mentioned in separate *Medieval Wordbook* entries.

A

B

C

D

E

F

G

H

I

J

K

L

M

N

O

P

R